# Inner-City Poverty in the United States

Laurence E. Lynn, Jr., and
Michael G.H. McGeary, Editors

Committee on National Urban Policy

Commission on Behavioral and
Social Sciences and Education

National Research Council

NATIONAL ACADEMY PRESS

Washington, D.C. 1990

National Academy Press • 2101 Constitution Avenue, N.W. • Washington, D.C. 20418

NOTICE: The project that is the subject of this report was approved by the Governing Board of the National Research Council, whose members are drawn from the councils of the National Academy of Sciences, the National Academy of Engineering, and the Institute of Medicine. The members of the committee responsible for the report were chosen for their special competences and with regard for appropriate balance.

This report has been reviewed by a group other than the authors according to procedures approved by a Report Review Committee consisting of members of the National Academy of Sciences, the National Academy of Engineering, and the Institute of Medicine.

The work that provided the basis for this document was supported by funding under a contract with the U.S. Department of Housing and Urban Development. The substance and findings of that contract work are dedicated to the public. The author and publisher are solely responsible for the accuracy of statements or interpretations in this document. Such interpretations do not necessarily reflect the views of the government.

*Library of Congress Cataloging-in-Publication Data*

Inner-City poverty in the United States / Laurence E. Lynn, Jr., and
    Michael G.H. McGeary, editors.
        p.    cm.
    Includes bibliographical references and index.
    ISBN 0-309-04279-8
    1. Urban poor—United States. 2. Urban poor—Government policy—
    United States. 3. Inner cities—United States. 4. Inner cities—
    Government policy—United States. I. Lynn, Laurence E., 1937–
    II. McGeary, Michael G.H.
    HV4045.I56   1990
    362.5'0973'091732—dc20                                                     90-45776
                                                                                  CIP

Printed in the United States of America

*Cover*: Photograph by Jim Hubbard.

iii

The National Academy of Sciences is a private, nonprofit, self-perpetuating society of distinguished scholars engaged in scientific and engineering research, dedicated to the furtherance of science and technology and to their use for the general welfare. Upon the authority of the charter granted to it by the Congress in 1863, the Academy has a mandate that requires it to advise the federal government on scientific and technical matters. Dr. Frank Press is president of the National Academy of Sciences.

The National Academy of Engineering was established in 1964, under the charter of the National Academy of Sciences, as a parallel organization of outstanding engineers. It is autonomous in its administration and in the selection of its members, sharing with the National Academy of Sciences the responsibility for advising the federal government. The National Academy of Engineering also sponsors engineering programs aimed at meeting national needs, encourages education and research, and recognizes the superior achievements of engineers. Dr. Robert M. White is president of the National Academy of Engineering.

The Institute of Medicine was established in 1970 by the National Academy of Sciences to secure the services of eminent members of appropriate professions in the examination of policy matters pertaining to the health of the public. The Institute acts under the responsibility given to the National Academy of Sciences by its congressional charter to be an advisor to the federal government and, upon its own initiative, to identify issues of medical care, research, and education. Dr. Samuel O. Thier is president of the Institute of Medicine.

The National Research Council was organized by the National Academy of Sciences in 1916 to associate the broad community of science and technology with the Academy's purposes of furthering knowledge and advising the federal government. Functioning in accordance with general policies determined by the Academy, the Council has become the principal operating agency of both the National Academy of Sciences and the National Academy of Engineering in providing services to the government, the public, and the scientific and engineering communities. The Council is administered jointly by both Academies and the Institute of Medicine. Dr. Frank Press and Dr. Robert M. White are chairman and vice chairman, respectively, of the National Research Council.

# Contents

# CONTRIBUTORS

MARY JO BANE, Malcolm Wiener Center for Social Policy, John F.
    Kennedy School of Government, Harvard University
PAUL A. JARGOWSKY, Malcolm Wiener Center for Social Policy, John
    F. Kennedy School of Government, Harvard University
CHRISTOPHER JENCKS, Center for Urban Affairs and Policy
    Research, Northwestern University
SUSAN E. MAYER, Center for Urban Affairs and Policy Research,
    Northwestern University
MICHAEL G.H. McGEARY, National Research Council, Washington,
    D.C.
JOHN C. WEICHER, Office of Policy, Development and Research, U.S.
    Department of Housing and Urban Development

# Preface

The Committee on National Urban Policy was established by the National Research Council at the end of 1985 at the request of the U.S. Department of Housing and Urban Development and the other federal agencies that contribute to the biennial President's Report on National Urban Policy: the U.S. Department of Health and Human Services, the U.S. Department of Labor, the Urban Mass Transportation Administration, and the Economic Development Administration. The committee was asked, over a three-year period, to describe the uncertainties facing cities and their economies and populations; identify the urban policy issues facing state, local, and federal policy makers; and assess possible policy responses at each level of the intergovernmental system.

With the encouragement of its federal sponsors, the committee first undertook to examine closely and carefully the most recent information on the underlying demographic, social, economic, and political trends shaping urban conditions. The results of that examination—eight authored papers and a brief committee report—were published in 1988 by the National Academy Press in a volume entitled *Urban Change and Poverty*.

The present volume represents the committee's efforts to address the main conclusion reported in the earlier volume, namely, that the phenomenon of increasing poverty concentration in inner-city neighborhoods was the most important national urban policy issue meriting the further attention of the committee.

Accordingly, the committee began a series of meetings on concentrated urban poverty during the course of which it was decided to invite a small number of scholars (including two committee members) to address in some depth questions that arose in studying the extent, causes, consequences, and implications for public policy of concentrated urban poverty. After reflecting at length on the resulting papers as well as on other relevant literature, the committee has prepared the present volume, which incorporates the scholarly papers into a report of its deliberations, findings, and conclusions.

Among those who warrant special appreciation for their efforts on behalf of this project are Kenneth J. Beirne, John P. Ross, and George Wright of the U.S. Department of Housing and Urban Development; James Dolson of the U.S. Department of Health and Human Services; Beverly Milkman and David Geddes of the Economic Development Administration; and Fred Williams and Kenneth Bolton of the Urban Mass Transportation Administration; the committee is grateful for the information, support, and encouragement they provided. The committee would also like to thank Michael G.H. McGeary, the committee's study director until September 1988, who organized the committee's activities, prepared extensive literature surveys, oversaw the preparation of the papers, wrote one of them, and prepared much draft material for chapters 1, 2, and 7, and gave the manuscript a final critical review; Christine McShane, editor of the Commission on Behavioral and Social Sciences and Education, who with freelance editors Jean Shirhall and Sherry Snyder edited the volume and prepared it for production; Mary Jo Bane and Paul Jargowsky, who provided valuable advice and assistance during the final stages of manuscript preparation; and the other authors, who submitted patiently to the publication process.

The committee is grateful for the support of the staff of the Commission on Behavioral and Social Sciences and Education, including executive director Suzanne H. Woolsey and associate director for reports Eugenia Grohman.

Finally, I would like to thank the committee members for their invaluable contributions in planning and participating in the activities leading up to the publication of this volume.

> LAURENCE E. LYNN, JR., *Chair*
> Committee on National Urban Policy

# Summary

This study explored the extent and location of ghetto poverty as well as the question of whether poor people living in ghettos are worse off than poor people living elsewhere. By ghettos we mean inner-city neighborhoods with overall poverty rates of 40 percent or more; the ghetto poor, then, are poor people living in a ghetto. The results of our analyses do not necessarily indicate that living in such areas makes poor people worse off than they would be otherwise—but neither do they suggest that living under such conditions does not matter at all.

## FINDINGS

### Extent and Location of Ghetto Poverty

In 1980, there were 2.4 million poor people living in ghettos—8.9 percent of all U.S. poor people. Among these people, there is tremendous racial, regional, and city-to-city variation.

The incidence of ghetto poverty varies sharply by race. In 1980, 2.0 percent of all U.S. non-Hispanic white poor people, 21.1 percent of all U.S. black poor people, and 15.9 percent of all U.S. Hispanic poor people lived in ghettos. Thus, nearly two-thirds of the ghetto poor are black, and most of the rest are Hispanic.

The level of ghetto poverty also varies by region. Within all U.S. metropolitan areas, 28 percent of black poor people lived in ghettos. In the Northeast, however, 34 percent of black poor people lived in ghettos, compared with 30 percent, 26 percent, and 11 percent for the North Central, South, and West regions, respectively. And 37 percent of poor Hispanics lived in ghettos in the Northeast, 21 percent in the South, and many fewer

1

elsewhere. From 1970 to 1980 in the Northeast, the level of ghetto poverty among blacks more than doubled—from 15 to 34 percent. In the South, it dropped from 36 to 26 percent.

As a result of these regional shifts, the distribution of poor people living in ghettos changed substantially between 1970 and 1980. In 1970, two-thirds of the ghetto poor lived in the South; by 1980, the figure was less than 40 percent. The proportion of poor people living in ghettos in the Northeast and the North Central regions, taken together, increased from 27 to 55 percent.

Within regions, there was also city-to-city variation in the growth of ghetto poverty. In the New York metropolitan area, which by 1980 contained nearly one-fifth of all U.S. ghetto poor, the level of ghetto poverty among blacks tripled: from 14.5 to 43.4 percent. In contrast, the Boston metropolitan area had a decrease: from 19.6 to 9.8 percent. Many cities in the South had decreases but remained at high levels; for example, in New Orleans ghetto poverty decreased from 49.7 to 40.7 percent.

What appears to be a national trend of increasing geographic concentration of the poor living in large cities was actually occurring in only a few places. In some large cities, ghetto poverty was small and did not grow during the decade of the 1970s. Other cities began the 1970s with substantial concentrated poverty, which then declined over the next 10 years.

### Effects of Living in Ghettos

Does living in a ghetto in itself exacerbate the problems associated with being poor? Does ghetto poverty feed on itself? The social conditions in such areas—including crime, dilapidated housing, drug use and related violence, problems related to out-of-wedlock births, and chronic unemployment—may simply reflect the large numbers of poor minorities who end up living there and the problems they have regardless of where they live. The increase in ghetto poverty may also be a symptom of other changes—for example, the increasing residential mobility of nonpoor minorities and economic trends that adversely affect minorities with low education and skill levels who were already more likely to live in ghettos.

To assess whether living in a ghetto in itself makes poverty worse, one must compare the people who live there with poor people who live in areas with less severe poverty—say, areas with less than 20 percent poverty. Poor people in the high-poverty census tracts of the 50 largest cities in 1980 experienced higher rates of unemployment than the poor living in areas with less severe poverty; they were also more dependent on welfare and more likely to live in single-parent households. These differences relative to the rates suffered by similar poor people living in areas with less severe poverty were of moderate to substantial size.

Decennial census data cannot rule out systematic unmeasured differences between poor people living in ghettos and those living in areas with less severe poverty. For example, poor people who end up in ghettos may be relatively poorer (that is, further below the poverty line) and may be able to find housing only in the worst areas. Studies of neighborhood effects, (reviewed in Chapter 4), which properly control for the prior differences between those moving in and out of neighborhoods of differing economic and racial composition, have found a significant unexplained residual effect on some types of behavior. Although this effect can be attributed to neighborhood influence, the magnitude of most such effects, where they exist, is usually modest relative to effects of other individual characteristics, especially race, gender, and levels of education and job skills.

The research literature provides some evidence that neighborhood effects are stronger for children, although this evidence is not strong. The effects of living in a poor neighborhood on a number of behaviors of interest have not been extensively examined: Examples are the cognitive development of preschool and grade-school children, sexual and family formation practices, the transition to employment, and school attendance habits of high-school-age youth. Nevertheless, the main point is that children who are minority members, poor, or raised in female-headed families dependent on welfare typically fare poorly in school, marriage, and employment—wherever they live.

The underlying processes associated with trends in poverty concentration also vary by location. Analyses in Chapters 2 and 3 reveal that the performance of the metropolitan economy, rates of in-migration and out-migration of poor and nonpoor people, and changes in racial and household composition played different roles in each city in affecting the concentration or deconcentration of poverty within certain neighborhoods. Larger (exogenous) economic and social forces affecting local economies, population mobility, and social structure were more closely associated with changes in poverty concentration than size or density of place.

Historically, federal policies and programs have had the effect of concentrating poverty in certain areas. First, they have encouraged trends favoring the suburbanization of higher-income people relative to lower-income people, contributing to the residual concentration of the poor, many of them minorities, in large cities. Second, they have encouraged the development of new areas in the South and the West relative to the older, developed metropolitan areas in the Midwest and the Northeast, with the unintended consequence of increasing poverty in the large central cities in those regions. In addition, some federal programs, such as high-rise public housing projects, have had the direct effect of concentrating poverty. After 1968, fair housing laws helped nonpoor minorities to leave ghetto areas, which also contributed to the dramatic increase in concentrated poverty among inner-city minorities during the 1970s. Some federal policies intended to increase the mobility of the poor, such as housing vouchers and mass transit subsidies, have not had the desired effect due to residential or income segregation.

## CONCLUSIONS

On the basis of these findings, the committee reached four major conclusions. First, *recent trends in ghetto poverty are best understood for policy purposes as symptoms of broader economic and social changes.* For example, cross-tabular analysis in Chapter 2 of characteristics associated with different degrees of change in the concentration of poverty in different cities indicates that cities with rapid growth in concentration also experienced increases in the poverty rate, while cities with slow or negative growth in concentration simultaneously experienced reductions in poverty. This association was observed even in cities with very high levels of concentration. The multivariate analysis in Chapter 3 confirms that favorable economic trends in the metropolitan economy—that is, reductions in poverty rates—had a positive impact on the economic fortunes of households in ghettos. Accordingly, the committee believes that developments in the national economy are consequential in determining the extent of ghetto poverty.

Ghetto poverty, like other types of poverty, could be reduced by national demand-side policies that stimulate gains in economic productivity and sustained economic growth. During the first two decades after World War II, poverty rates in the United States were cut nearly in half because of high rates of employment and economic growth. In the decade after 1973, however, slow economic growth increased unemployment and reduced gains in family income. The poverty rate, which is very sensitive to the unemployment rate, also increased during that period and is still relatively high.

In a persistently slack economy, workers with the fewest marketable skills and least education are the least likely to be employed. A lower unemployment rate would reduce the number of people in poverty. At least some of these would be poor people living in ghettos, although the benefits of macroeconomic growth probably would not apply proportionately to central cities and suburbs.

Second, *many ghetto residents would fare poorly in any job market.* The analyses in Chapter 3 indicate that the characteristics of the population were a factor in increasing poverty and unemployment in ghettos. In addition to lacking education, skills, and work experience, many household heads living in ghettos are women with young children who need extensive support services, especially day care. Some ghetto residents would not be prepared to take full advantage of tight labor markets. It would take additional efforts to help this group become productive workers, whom employers will hire at wages high enough to make economic self-sufficiency possible.

The characteristics of poor and unemployed people living in ghettos suggest that policies aimed at enhancing their employability and productivity would effectively complement policies focused on increasing employment opportunities. Such policies need not be specially developed for, or targeted on, ghetto residents; they can instead grow out of broader-based efforts to develop the human capital of poor and disadvantaged people. Such policies include a broad range of investments in education, health (especially preventive programs), and employment and training programs for young people and adults.

Careful analyses and evaluations of such programs indicate that at least some of them (state work-welfare experiments are a good example) are demonstrably effective and deliver benefits that exceed their costs. But these programs will not work miracles. Even in effective programs, benefits are usually modest and at best will achieve small but steady improvements in economic self-sufficiency, not dramatic reductions in poverty or welfare receipt. But effective programs often cost more money than elected officials have been prepared to raise. Governments intending to dent the problem must be prepared to invest current resources in the hope of long-term payoffs. Investments in education, health, and employment and training programs are an important part of a policy that addresses poverty, including ghetto poverty.

Third, *current antipoverty programs and policies meet with special problems in ghettos.* These programs may not be designed to deal with such a high concentration of poverty, and poor people living in ghettos may have less access to them than they would have if they lived in nonpoor neighborhoods. The committee believes that discriminatory barriers preventing mobility to better neighborhoods should be deliberately undermined by federal policies and programs, for example, through full enforcement of fair housing, equal access, and other nondiscrimination laws and regulations, enabling people to leave ghettos if they choose through programs such as housing vouchers and fair-share housing construction throughout metropolitan areas.

A strategy to enhance the mobility of ghetto residents cannot, however, solve the problem of ghetto poverty by itself. It depends on where the poor who move end up. Simply hastening the emptying out of ghettos through residential mobility would not have much impact on the fortunes of poor people who had lived there. They would continue to face problems because of their low levels of education, skills, and work experience; poor health and disabilities; teenage and single parenthood; and racial discrimination.

They would still have problems with access to affordable health care, day care, and transportation.

Increased mobility may also have the unintended effect of spreading ghetto poverty to adjacent areas. Most of the growth in concentrated poverty between 1970 and 1980 occurred through the addition of new ghettos in a few cities, and most of those were contiguous to the ghettos that existed in 1970.

Because of these problems with and limitations to enhanced mobility as a strategy for reducing ghetto poverty, the committee stresses the importance of macroeconomic policies and human capital investment in proposed solutions.

Fourth, *additional research on the causes and effects of ghetto poverty is essential to increasing the government's ability to design and administer policies and programs that are more effective with respect to poverty and its consequences.* The committee was not able to study the effects of federal programs on poverty concentration in great detail, and there are knowledge gaps even in issues that were carefully examined. The knowledge base for policy making needs to be improved.

# 1
# Introduction

In its earlier study, *Urban Change and Poverty*, the Committee on National Urban Policy examined the general state of U.S. cities and urban poverty. The findings were more hopeful than had been expected in certain areas of concern and more disturbing in others. On the hopeful side, cities as a whole were found to be less financially and economically distressed than one might have been led to expect by the rhetoric of urban crisis. A disturbing finding, however, was that poverty appeared to be worse in many large cities than it had been 10 and 20 years before. More significantly, poverty appears to be becoming more spatially concentrated in inner-city neighborhoods.

Some analysts have concluded that an urban underclass consisting of persistently poor people is developing in U.S. cities. Our earlier report suggested that, at the least, poverty is an increasingly serious problem in cities. But we wanted to know more about the extent to which poverty is concentrated in particular neighborhoods and the effects of this concentration on poor people themselves.

With these and related concerns in mind, the committee undertook the current study, which examines the issue of concentrated poverty in U.S. cities. The committee was charged with four main tasks:

- describe the extent to which poverty has become concentrated in particular areas;
- identify causes of this concentration;
- identify the consequences for the poor of living in areas of highly concentrated poverty; and
- analyze implications of the findings for national urban policy.

## TRENDS IN URBAN POVERTY

Since the early 1900s the metropolitan areas of the United States have been the sites of most of the nation's growth in employment and income. American cities attracted those looking for economic opportunity and social advancement from the countryside and abroad (Kasarda, 1988). Within metropolitan areas, however, people and jobs have been migrating to the suburbs and beyond since at least the 1920s (Hawley, 1956; Long, 1981). Inner cities have declined in population, employment, and income relative to fast-growing suburbs. At the regional level, jobs and people have been shifting from the Northeast and the Midwest to the South and the West. The older regions have suffered especially from declines in manufacturing employment, as the growth of the economy has taken the form of increases in the production of information and other services (Garnick, 1988; Noyelle and Stanback, 1984).

In recent decades, middle-income blacks and other minorities have joined better-off whites in moving to the suburbs. These demographic and economic trends have affected the socioeconomic conditions of cities, especially in the Northeast and the Midwest. The exodus from central cities—that is, the largest cities of standard metropolitan statistical areas—has been only partially offset by in-migration, and most of those moving into large cities have been people with low incomes and minorities (Kasarda, 1988:Table 12). Gentrification—that is, the influx of more affluent people—has been limited to a few neighborhoods in particular cities (Berry, 1985; Frey, 1985).

As a result, the proportion of the population living in large central cities has decreased nationally. Average personal income levels have dropped, and the proportions of city residents who are poor, unskilled, poorly educated, unemployed, and members of minority groups have increased relative to those living in the suburbs. For example, the ratio of average city income to average suburban income among families declined from 79.8 percent in 1970 to 76.5 percent in 1980 (Manson and Schnare, 1985:Table II-4). At the same time, the social structure of the city has also been changing: There are fewer employed men and more families headed by women, especially among blacks (Wilson and Neckerman, 1986; McLanahan et al., 1988).[1]

By the early 1980s it was apparent that poverty had shifted from being a mostly rural to a mostly urban phenomenon. That shift did not mean that

---

[1] There are large regional differences in these trends. It is the large central cities (and, in some cases, entire metropolitan areas) in the Midwest and the Northeast that are losing population and where the disparities between central cities and their suburbs are the largest. There is less disparity between central cities and suburbs in the South and the West where the population is increasing in central cities and central cities are able to grow through annexation.

the majority of the poor now lived in central cities, but that the central-city share had grown considerably. More than half of poor people in the United States (56 percent) lived outside metropolitan areas in 1959; less than a third (30 percent) did in 1985. In 1959, about 27 percent of poor people lived in central cities; by 1985, 41 percent did.

The poverty rate, meaning the incidence of poverty in central cities, was 14.2 percent in 1970, reached 19.9 percent in 1982 during the recession, then declined to 18.0 percent in 1986. Central-city poverty rates are now higher than nonmetropolitan poverty rates (18.6 versus 16.9 percent in 1987), and more than double suburban poverty rates (8.5 percent in 1987).

## GHETTO POVERTY

The trends in central-city poverty described in the previous section tell only part of the story. The spatial organization of poverty within metropolitan areas and within cities adds yet another—and we believe significant—dimension. Ghetto poverty, which is the proportion of poor people living in neighborhoods with very high poverty rates, has been increasing rapidly in many large metropolitan areas.

The social conditions in urban ghettos, including crime, dilapidated housing, drug use and drug-related violence, problems related to out-of-wedlock births, and chronic unemployment have been well documented in the popular press. Many observers believe that extreme poverty in a poor person's neighborhood and the social disorganization associated with it exacerbate the problems of poverty and make it all the more difficult for individuals and families to escape poverty. In this section, we review the data on ghetto poverty and consider the possible consequences.

The term *ghetto* has no official definition. As it is typically used in discussions of poverty, the term refers to inner-city neighborhoods with very high levels of poverty. Usually, but not always, these neighborhoods are predominantly black and Hispanic. We follow the convention adopted by Jargowsky and Bane in this volume and use census tracts as a proxy for neighborhoods.[2] They define a ghetto as any neighborhood (i.e., group of census tracts) with an overall poverty rate of 40 percent or more.[3] The ghetto poor, then, are poor people who live in a ghetto. The level of ghetto poverty is the proportion of the poor who live in ghettos. This proportion

---

[2] Census tracts are areas defined by the Census Bureau, typically containing about 2,000 to 8,000 people. In a densely settled neighborhood, a census tract may be the size of four or five city blocks.

[3] Although the phrase "increase in ghetto poverty" is often assumed to mean the same thing as "growing concentration of poverty," the latter term may give a misleading impression. Ghettos in 1980 were typically bigger geographically but less densely populated than in 1970.

can be disaggregated by race, e.g., the level of ghetto poverty among blacks would be the proportion of black poor people living in ghettos.

In 1980, there were 2.4 million poor people living in ghettos—8.9 percent of all U.S. poor people.[4] Thus, it is clearly not true that the typical poor person was a resident of an urban ghetto. Since many politicians, reporters, and members of the public seem to equate poverty with the black residents of urban ghettos, the relatively small size of this percentage deserves emphasis.

The incidence of ghetto poverty varies sharply by race. In 1980, 2.0 percent of all U.S. non-Hispanic white poor people, 21.1 percent of all U.S. black poor people, and 15.9 percent of all U.S. Hispanic poor people lived in ghettos. Thus, nearly two-thirds of the ghetto poor are black, and most of the rest are Hispanic.

The level of ghetto poverty also varies by region. Within all U.S. metropolitan areas, 28 percent of black poor people lived in ghettos. In the Northeast, however, 34 percent of black poor people lived in ghettos, compared with 30 percent, 26 percent, and 11 percent for the North Central, South, and West regions, respectively. And 37 percent of poor Hispanics lived in ghettos in the Northeast, 21 percent in the South, and many fewer elsewhere.

Ghetto poverty, and the social disorganization thought to be associated with it, are often said to be "exploding." The facts, however, create a different picture. The total number of poor people living in ghettos increased 29.5 percent, from 1.9 million in 1970 to 2.4 million, in 1980. However, the total number of poor people in metropolitan areas grew nearly as fast (23.5 percent). Thus, the increase in the level of ghetto poverty relative to overall poverty was more modest: among blacks, the level of ghetto poverty increased from 26.5 percent to 27.7 percent; among Hispanics, it actually decreased from 23.7 to 18.6 percent.

This picture of a modest increase in ghetto poverty among blacks and a decrease among Hispanics seems at odds with common perceptions of a rapidly growing problem. The discrepancy can be resolved, however, by noting the tremendous racial, regional, and city-to-city variation in ghetto poverty. In the Northeast, the level of ghetto poverty among blacks more than doubled—from 15 to 34 percent. In the South, it dropped from 36 to 26 percent.

As a result of these regional shifts, the distribution of poor people living in ghettos changed substantially between 1970 and 1980. Two-thirds of the ghetto poor lived in the South in 1970. By 1980, the figure was less

---

[4] Since census tract data are only available from decennial censuses, the most recent data available on ghetto poverty are for 1980. All data on ghetto poverty presented in this section are from Jargowsky and Bane; see their paper in this volume for details on data sources and methods.

than 40 percent. The proportion of poor people living in ghettos in the Northeast and the North Central regions, taken together, increased from 27 to 55 percent. Because the metropolitan areas in the North tend to be larger than metropolitan areas in the South, ghetto poverty also became more of a "big city" phenomenon. The proportion of poor people living in ghettos in metropolitan areas of more than 1 million people increased from 45 to 63 percent.

Within regions, there was also city-to-city variation in the growth of ghetto poverty. In the New York standard metropolitan statistical area, which by 1980 contained nearly one-fifth of all U.S. ghetto poor, the level of ghetto poverty among blacks tripled: from 14.5 to 43.4 percent. In contrast, the Boston metropolitan area had a decrease: from 19.6 to 9.8 percent. Many cities in the South had decreases but remained at high levels; for example, in New Orleans ghetto poverty decreased from 49.7 to 40.7 percent.

The increases in ghetto poverty did not occur because more poor people moved into fixed areas of cities. Rather, the geographical size of ghettos increased rapidly in many metropolitan areas. In some, even cities with decreases in ghetto poverty had an expansion of the ghetto area as measured by the number of census tracts with poverty rates greater than 40 percent; the expansion of the ghetto area was associated with general exodus from downtown areas. Both poor and nonpoor people moved out of ghettos and mixed income areas, perhaps trying to escape crime and a deteriorating quality of life. The nonpoor moved out faster than the poor, however, so the group left behind was poorer. As a result, many census tracts saw poverty rates rise to 40 percent and higher. Most often, then-new ghetto tracts were adjacent to the old ghetto tracts, so that the ghetto area seemed to expand outward from a central core.

## THE UNDERCLASS HYPOTHESIS

According to numerous journalistic accounts, social pathologies have increased among urban and (usually) young and minority poor residents. The problems highlighted in these accounts include involvement with illegal drugs, violent crime, dropping out of school, unemployment, welfare dependence, pregnancy among the teenage children of welfare recipients, and a disproportionate number of families headed by single women. (Chapter 2 deals with this issue in more detail.)

Some scholars argue that these problems indicate the existence of a growing, largely black, underclass in inner-city ghettos. For example, Wilson (1987:49) argues:

> Inner-city neighborhoods have undergone a profound social transformation in the last several years as reflected not only in their increasing rates of social

dislocation (including crime, joblessness, out-of-wedlock births, female-headed families, and welfare dependency) but also in the changing economic class structure of ghetto neighborhoods. . . . The movement of middle-class black professionals from the inner city, followed in increasing numbers by working-class blacks, has left behind a much higher concentration of the most disadvantaged segments of the black urban population, the population to which I refer when I speak of the ghetto underclass.

Wilson (1987:60) hypothesizes that this "higher concentration of the most disadvantaged segments of the urban black population" has resulted in "concentration effects," which exacerbate unemployment and other conditions associated with poverty. He cites as examples isolation from informal job networks, lack of exposure to norms and behavior patterns of the steadily employed, lack of access to effective schools, and lack of opportunity for women to marry men with stable jobs.

While these observations are certainly provocative, the question of whether ghetto poverty actually *causes* the development of an underclass deserves more careful scrutiny.

This volume directly addresses this issue. Does ghetto poverty in central cities cause or reinforce behaviors deemed socially unacceptable that, in turn, lead to long-term or persistent poverty among affected residents, especially among children? In other words, what are the relationships among several distinct dimensions of urban poverty: ghetto poverty, persistent poverty, and socially unacceptable behavior? Only some poor people remain poor for long periods of time; are they more or less likely than those who are poor for brief periods to live in very poor neighborhoods? Are people engaging in socially unacceptable behavior more or less likely to be persistently poor or residents of very poor neighborhoods? This report examines these questions in terms of currently available data and assesses their implications for policy.

## POLICY ISSUES

This volume addresses three questions, the answers to which have significant policy implications:

1.  To what extent is poverty increasing in urban areas, especially in central cities? Is ghetto poverty increasing as well? Who is affected? Is it a general phenomenon or rather confined to certain cities or regions?

2.  Are there concentration effects—i.e., is it worse to be poor in a very poor neighborhood than in another neighborhood? Is ghetto poverty fostering the growth of a new underclass that is not only poor and disadvantaged but also distinct and deviant in its values and behavior?

3.  If ghetto poverty is increasing in some areas, what is causing it to do so? Are there alternative explanations? Do government policies inadvertently encourage ghettos to form, or do they result from broad economic

changes or from urban-level forces? Are there multiple causes, working in different ways in different cities? What are the policy implications of the increasing ghetto poverty in large cities? Does it require policies specially designed or targeted for certain cities, or is it amenable to a general antipoverty strategy?

In the next chapter Paul Jargowsky and Mary Jo Bane answer basic questions about the geographic location of ghetto poverty, the characteristics of poor people who live there compared with those in nonpoor areas, and trends in ghetto poverty during the 1970s.

In Chapter 3 John Weicher provides a different view of ghetto poverty by following the fortunes of a set of persistently poor inner-city neighborhoods from 1970 to 1980 (and, for a more limited set of neighborhoods, from 1960 to 1980). He analyzes population changes, compares the characteristics of the residents and housing at each census, and tests the association of changes in these characteristics with changes in metropolitan-level population, unemployment, income, and job location (i.e., "suburbanization" of employment).

In Chapter 4 Christopher Jencks and Susan Mayer evaluate the leading quantitative research studies of the effects of living or growing up in a poor rather than a nonpoor neighborhood in terms of several outcomes, including crime, teenage sexual behavior, school achievement, and labor market success. These studies, although plagued with data limitations and methodological shortcomings, provide some insight into the potential importance of the contextual effects of poverty on ghetto residents. Jencks and Mayer conclude with suggestions for research that would better answer questions about the significance and extent of concentration effects for policy makers.

In Chapter 5 Jencks and Mayer evaluate the hypothesis that a growing number of urban jobs have relocated to the suburbs, while exclusionary housing practices have prevented blacks from moving out of inner-city neighborhoods. They also consider the related question of whether black workers who live in the suburbs find better jobs than those who live in inner-city neighborhoods. Finally, they compare the earnings of inner-city blacks who commute to the suburbs with the earnings of similar blacks who work in ghettos.

In Chapter 6 Michael McGeary reviews the research on federal policies and programs, including policies against housing discrimination, transportation programs, economic development, and educational welfare programs, examining them for evidence of their effects on ghetto poverty.

In the last chapter the committee reviews the findings concerning the extent and nature of urban poverty, the relationship of ghetto poverty to the existence of an underclass, and the impact of ghettos per se on the individuals involved. It ends by discussing the possible implications of these findings for federal policy and makes recommendations for both policy and research.

## REFERENCES

Berry, Brian J.L.
    1985    Islands of renewal in seas of decay. Pp. 69-96 in Paul E. Peterson, ed., *The New Urban Reality*. Washington, D.C.: Brookings Institution.
Clark, Kenneth B., and Richard Nathan
    1982    The urban underclass. In *Critical Issues for National Urban Policy: A Reconnaissance and Agenda for Further Study*. Committee on National Urban Policy, National Research Council. Washington, D.C.: National Academy Press.
Frey, William H.
    1985    Mover destination selectivity and the changing suburbanization of metropolitan whites and blacks. *Demography* 22(May):223-243.
Garnick, Daniel H.
    1988    Local area economic growth patterns: A comparison of the 1980s and previous decades. Pp. 199-254 in Michael G.H. McGeary and Laurence E. Lynn, Jr., eds., *Urban Change and Poverty*. Washington, D.C.: National Academy Press.
Hawley, Amos H.
    1956    *The Changing Shape of Metropolitan America: Deconcentration Since 1920*. Glencoe, Ill.: Free Press.
Kasarda, John D.
    1988    Jobs, migration, and emerging urban mismatches. Pp. 148-198 in Michael G.H. McGeary and Laurence E. Lynn, Jr., eds., *Urban Change and Poverty*. Washington, D.C.: National Academy Press.
Long, John F.
    1981    *Population Deconcentration in the United States*. Special Demographic Analyses, CDS-81-5. Bureau of the Census. Washington, D.C.: U.S. Department of Commerce.
McLanahan, Sara S., Irwin Garfinkel, and Dorothy Watson
    1988    Family structure, poverty, and the underclass. Pp. 102-147 in Michael G.H. McGeary and Laurence E. Lynn, Jr., eds., *Urban Change and Poverty*. Washington, D.C.: National Academy Press.
Manson, Donald B., and Ann B. Schnare
    1985    *Change in the City/Suburb Income Gap, 1970-1980*. November. Report for Urban Institute Project 3376. Washington, D.C.: Urban Institute.
Nathan, Richard R.
    1986    The Underclass—Will It Always Be with Us? Paper presented at the New School for Social Research, New York.
National Research Council
    1982    *Critical Issues for National Urban Policy: A Reconnaissance and Agenda for Further Study*. Committee on National Urban Policy. Washington, D.C.: National Academy Press.
Noyelle, Thierry J., and Thomas M. Stanback, Jr.
    1984    *The Economic Transformation of American Cities*. Totowa, N.J.: Rowman & Allanheld.

Wilson, William Julius
    1987    *The Truly Disadvantaged: The Inner City, the Underclass, and Public Policy.* Chicago: University of Chicago Press.
Wilson, William Julius, and Kathryn M. Neckerman
    1986    Poverty and family structure: The widening gap between evidence and public policy issues. Pp. 232-259 in Sheldon H. Danziger and Daniel H. Weinberg, eds., *Fighting Poverty: What Works and What Doesn't.* Cambridge, Mass.: Harvard University Press.

# 2
# Ghetto Poverty: Basic Questions

PAUL A. JARGOWSKY AND MARY JO BANE

## INTRODUCTION

### Dimensions of Urban Poverty

After years of neglect, a series of events in the 1980s rekindled public interest in the problems of urban poverty. The first event was the growing visibility of homeless people in urban areas in the early 1980s. Second, the popular media began to pay attention to what it dubbed the "underclass," a group of persons, mostly black and urban, who were said to be outside the American class system. Prominent examples of this coverage are Ken Auletta's (1982) book on *The Underclass*, Bill Moyer's 1986 television documentary on "The Vanishing Black Family," and a series of articles in *The Atlantic Monthly* by Nicholas Lehmann (1986). Third, academic interest in social problems among urban blacks was rekindled by circulation of papers by University of Chicago sociologist William Julius Wilson. The papers, eventually published as *The Truly Disadvantaged* (1987), represented a return to the study of the urban ghetto that had been choked off by the furor over the Moynihan (1965) report on the black family in the 1960s.

Despite intense interest in the topic, no consensus has emerged on such questions as how to define and measure ghettos, whether ghetto poverty has gotten worse, whether ghettos harm their residents, and what if anything public policy can do about the problem. One of the key reasons for this ongoing confusion is that several different concepts are being discussed simultaneously:

- *Persistent poverty*—individuals and families that remain poor for long periods of time and, perhaps, pass poverty on to their descendants.

- *Neighborhood poverty*—spatially defined areas of high poverty, usually characterized by dilapidated housing stock or public housing and high levels of unemployment.
- *Underclass poverty*—defined in terms of attitudes and behavior, especially behavior that indicates deviance from social norms, such as low attachment to the labor force, drug use and habitual criminal behavior, bearing children out of wedlock, and receiving public assistance.

The first concept is defined in terms of time, the second in terms of space, and the third in terms of behavior.[1] Sometimes, the concepts are combined, for example, in journalistic depictions of third-generation welfare families living in bad neighborhoods and using drugs. Nevertheless, it is important to keep the separate dimensions of the problem clear.

In this chapter, we focus on the spatial dimension—the poverty of neighborhoods. We set up a criterion for defining some neighborhoods as ghettos based on their level of poverty. We then identify ghetto neighborhoods in metropolitan areas and develop a summary measure for standard metropolitan statistical areas (SMSAs) describing the proportion in ghetto neighborhoods. Finally, we review the cross-sectional data and the trends between 1970 and 1980.

We do not attempt to define or measure an underclass. The term is used by many different people in many different ways. In a formal interpretation of the term, it refers to a "heterogeneous grouping of families and individuals who are outside the American occupational system . . . a reality not captured in the more standard designation *lower class*" (Wilson, 1987:8). Thus, the claim that the underclass is growing implies that the lowest income or social class is now more isolated from the mainstream in terms of the opportunity for upward mobility. The census data with which we work cannot answer questions about economic mobility, at least not directly, because they are not longitudinal.

In a less formal use of the term underclass, saying that an underclass has developed amounts to little more than a shorthand way of saying that, on a variety of measures, the poor do worse today than in the past. There is plenty of evidence for this. For example, the rate of labor force participation among the poor has declined, the proportion of children in single-parent families is up, and so on. On some measures, however, the poor do better today than in the past; for example, high school graduation

---

[1] The persistent poverty concept is used by Adams et al. (1988), among others. The underclass concept, defined on the basis of behavior measured at the neighborhood level, is developed by Ricketts and Sawhill (1988). A neighborhood concept is also used by Hughes (1989) in identifying what he calls "impacted ghettos."

is up (Jencks, 1989). We are troubled by the vagueness of the term when it is used this way.

To reiterate, we are not defining or measuring the underclass. Instead, we are defining ghettos and counting the ghetto poor in all metropolitan areas in the United States.[2] We ask several basic questions about ghetto poverty:

- How can the concept be operationalized so that it can be measured over time and across cities?
- How extensive is the problem nationally?
- What are the characteristics of ghetto areas?
- How serious is the problem of ghetto poverty within specific urban areas?
- How does it vary by region and race?
- Has the problem been growing?
- What are the typical patterns associated with the growth of ghetto poverty?

We do not attempt to explain why ghetto poverty has been increasing in some areas and decreasing in others. We do, however, discuss a framework for thinking about these issues.

### Defining and Measuring Ghetto Poverty

The *Random House Dictionary* defines a ghetto as "a section of a city, especially a thickly populated slum area, inhabited predominantly by members of a minority group, often as the result of social or economic restrictions" (Flexner, 1987). Historically, the term referred to segregated Jewish areas of European cities, and in the United States the term was often used to refer to any racial or ethnic enclave, without the emphasis on its economic status. Current usage, however, almost always implies impoverishment of ghetto residents and a run-down housing stock. Thus, a completely black but middle-class neighborhood, an increasingly common occurrence in the United States, is not typically referred to as a ghetto.

People have an idea in their heads of what and where ghetto neighborhoods are. Most city officials in large urban areas could point out on a map which neighborhoods they consider ghettos. But not everyone would agree on what the boundaries were. One person's ghetto might be another's up-and-coming neighborhood ripe for gentrification. In order to

---

[2] Since most definitions of the underclass assume, implicity or explicity, that they live in ghetto neighborhoods, our work could be seen as a starting point from which a national study on the underclass could be done. Van Haitsma (1989), for example, argues that the underclass is defined by (a) poor attachment to the labor force and (b) a social context that supports and encourages poor attachment to the labor force.

study ghetto neighborhoods on a national scale, thus, the concept must be operationalized in a manner that can be consistently applied to the available national data.

There are two basic strategies for operationalizing a measure of ghetto poverty. One is an approach that calculates a summary measure for a metropolitan area.[3] Massey and Eggers (1989), for example, define a measure of poverty concentration as the exposure of the black poor to poverty. This is the probability that a black poor person has poor neighbors. This measure allows characterization of SMSAs according to their overall level of ghetto poverty. It does not, however, identify specific neighborhoods that are ghettos and others that are not.

The second strategy attempts to classify specific neighborhoods as ghettos based on a set of criteria. Wilson (1987) defines an underclass area as a neighborhood (using Chicago's well-known "community areas") with a poverty rate greater than 30 percent. Ricketts and Sawhill (1988) define underclass areas as neighborhoods that are one standard deviation worse than the national norm on four measures: high school graduation, labor force participation of men, welfare receipt, and single-parent families.

For the reasons described above, we do not use the term underclass area and we do not attempt to define or measure underclass neighborhoods. However, we take an approach similar to Wilson's by using census tracts as our proxy for neighborhoods.[4] We then create a summary measure for an SMSA based on the population in ghetto tracts.[5]

We define a ghetto as an area in which the overall census tract poverty rate is greater than 40 percent. We define the ghetto poor as those poor,

---

[3] Massey and Denton (1988a) define five summary measures in the context of racial segregation: evenness, exposure, concentration, centralization, and clustering. These measures and techniques can also be applied in the context of residential segregation of the poor from the nonpoor. The two dimensions, race and poverty, are both involved in creating ghetto neighborhoods. See Massey and Eggers (1989) and Massey et al. (1989) for examples of applying aggregate-level measures of ghetto poverty.

[4] Census tracts are areas defined by the Census Bureau, typically containing about 2,000 to 8,000 people. In a densely settled neighborhood, a census tract may be the size of four or five city blocks.

[5] Massey and Eggers (1989) argue against "ad hoc and arbitrary definitions" of poverty neighborhoods. Further, they argue that standard measures of segregation "use complete information on the spatial distribution of income" (1989:4). This is not entirely true, however. Standard measures of segregation, such as the dissimilarity index and the exposure measure, treat each census tract as if it is an isolated entity. An area's segregation score would not change if all the tracts were scrambled like the pieces of a jigsaw puzzle. Our strategy enables us to identify and map census tracts, which becomes important to understanding the pattern of population movements that led to the observed changes between 1970 and 1980. It is reassuring, however, that Massey and Eggers's main measure of poverty concentration (the exposure of the black poor to poor persons) is highly correlated with the level of ghetto poverty for blacks as we define it. Both measures appear to reflect the same underlying reality.

of any race or ethnic group, who live in such high-poverty census tracts. We define the level of ghetto poverty in an SMSA as the percentage of the SMSA's poor that lives in ghetto census tracts. However, for reasons described below, we usually report levels of ghetto poverty separately for blacks and Hispanics, that is, the percentage of the black poor living in ghetto census tracts and the percentage of the Hispanic poor living in ghetto census tracts. We describe our rationale for these definitions in the sections that follow.

### The 40 Percent Poverty Criterion

In earlier work (Bane and Jargowsky, 1988), we were limited to the poverty rate cutoffs that were used in data published by the Census Bureau, that is, either 20, 30, or 40 percent (Bureau of the Census, 1973b, 1985). Based on visits to several cities,[6] we found that the 40 percent criterion came very close to identifying areas that looked like ghettos in terms of their housing conditions. Moreover, the areas selected on the basis of the 40 percent criterion corresponded rather closely with the judgments of city officials and local Census Bureau officials about which neighborhoods were ghettos. Even though we are now working with data tapes and have the flexibility to choose any poverty rate as the ghetto criterion, we continue to use 40 percent as the dividing line between ghettos and mixed-income neighborhoods. With somewhat less justification, we use 20 percent poverty as the dividing line between mixed-income and nonpoor neighborhoods.

Any fixed cutoff is inherently arbitrary. A census tract with a 39.9 percent poverty rate is not that different from a census tract with a 40.1 percent poverty rate. Moreover, the poverty rate in a census tract is an estimate based on a sample, even in the census. This problem does not affect aggregate numbers because errors will occur in both directions. However, individual census tracts, especially near the boundaries of ghettos, may be misclassified (Coulton et al., 1990). Nonetheless, we are convinced that the 40 percent poverty criterion appropriately identifies most ghetto neighborhoods. To illustrate this, we have mapped the ghetto census tracts in Philadelphia and Memphis. Shown are nonpoor tracts (0 to 20 percent poverty), mixed-income tracts (20 to 40 percent poverty), and ghetto tracts (greater than 40 percent poverty). In Figure 2-1, the large North Philadelphia ghetto is clearly visible. (The island in the middle is

---

[6] The cities we visited include Baltimore, Boston, Detroit, Little Rock, Memphis, Omaha, Philadelphia, San Antonio, and a number of smaller cities. The correspondence of tract poverty rates with the conditions we observed was especially striking because we were using 1980 census tract data as our guide to cities in 1987 to 1989.

FIGURE 2-1    Philadelphia SMSA by Neighborhood Poverty Type, 1980.

Temple University.)[7] This area consists of densely packed 3- to 5-story row houses, many boarded up and vacant. In addition, there are several high- and low-rise housing projects scattered throughout the region. The signs of urban decay are overwhelming in this neighborhood: broken glass, litter, stripped and abandoned automobiles, and young men hanging out on street corners.[8]

The other major ghetto areas in Figure 2-1 are West Philadelphia and Camden, New Jersey, on the other side of the Delaware River. A smaller ghetto area is visible in South Philadelphia. The 20 to 40 percent poverty areas are basically working class and lower middle income. In our visit to Philadelphia, the 40 percent census tracts looked and felt quite different, especially in North Philadelphia.

It is important to distinguish our definition of ghetto tracts, based on a poverty criterion, from a definition of ghettos based on racial composition. Not all majority black tracts are ghettos under our definition, nor are all ghettos black. In general, ghetto tracts are a subset of a city's majority black or Hispanic tracts. Figure 2-2 shows this relationship for Philadelphia. Census tracts are divided into three groups by race: less than one-third minority (white), one-third to two-thirds minority (mixed), and more than

---

[7] Because the majority of tracts were not poor in 1970 and did not become ghettos by 1980, the maps "zoom in" on the downtown areas, where most ghetto and mixed-income tracts are located.

[8] We observed these conditions in a visit to Philadelphia in spring 1988. We were guided to the various areas of the city by an extremely helpful professional employed by the regional office of the Census Bureau.

FIGURE 2-2   Philadelphia SMSA, 1980 Neighborhoods by Race and Poverty Status.

two-thirds minority (minority).[9] Each of these groups is divided into ghetto and nonghetto tracts on the basis of their poverty rates. Given that the overall proportion minority in the city is about 20 percent, the existence of many census tracts that are more than two-thirds minority indicates a high degree of racial segregation.

Most of the ghetto tracts are more than two-thirds minority. Only a few are mixed race, and even fewer non-Hispanic white. There are, however, many segregated minority areas in Philadelphia that are not ghettos by our criterion, as there are in all the cities with substantial black populations we visited.

Figure 2-3 shows the ghetto areas of Memphis. The ghetto area of North Memphis, which is clearly visible, consists of predominantly single-family houses, many in dilapidated condition, although there are a few low-rise housing projects, such as Hurt Village.[10] North of Chelsea Avenue, one of the main corridors in this region, the housing stock is mostly run-down shacks. The high-poverty area continues south, to the east of downtown Memphis, on the Mississippi River. The South Memphis ghetto is mostly two- and three-story housing projects. The one large ghetto tract on the Arkansas side of the river is largely swampland. The other Arkansas ghetto

---

[9] Minority here includes blacks, Hispanics, and "other races."

[10] We visited Memphis in June 1988 and again in May 1989. Many people helped us understand the city, including State Representative Karen Williams and various officials associated with the county's Free the Children project.

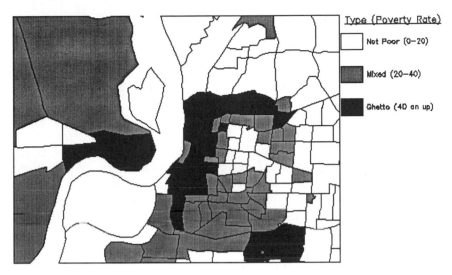

FIGURE 2-3 Memphis SMSA by Neighborhood Poverty Type, 1980.

tracts are in West Memphis City. Here the housing stock is a mixture of single-family homes and rusting trailers.

In both cities, tracts in the 20 to 40 percent range had a very different look and feel. The housing stock is in better condition, and street-corner markets and other businesses are more numerous. Such areas appeared to us to be working-class or lower middle class neighborhoods, not ghettos. Although outside appearances can be deceiving, city and Census Bureau officials and other knowledgeable individuals generally confirmed our assessments.

### The Level of Ghetto Poverty

Having set up a criterion for identifying neighborhoods (census tracts) as either ghettos or not, we now need a way to assess how serious a problem ghetto poverty is within a given metropolitan area. One potential measure could be the percentage of census tracts that are ghettos. Since census tracts vary in population, however, this criterion would be misleading. Other possibilities include the proportion of the population in ghetto areas, the proportion of the poor in ghetto areas, and the proportion of the black and/or Hispanic poor in ghetto areas. All three of these measures are interesting in certain ways. The percentage of the population in ghetto areas is, however, affected by both the overall poverty rate in the SMSA and the proportion of the poor in ghetto areas. Using it as the summary measure for SMSA-level ghetto poverty makes it hard to distinguish the two phenomena.

The percentage of the poor who live in ghetto areas is also a potentially misleading measure.[11] As will be shown below, the white poor almost never live in ghettos, the Hispanic poor sometimes do, and the black poor frequently do. As a result, the percentage of all poor living in ghettos can vary dramatically with the racial composition of the SMSA and is partly a proxy for percent minority. We solve this problem by defining levels of ghetto poverty separately by race. In most of our analyses, we look at the percentage of the black poor and the percentage of the Hispanic poor living in ghettos. The level of ghetto poverty among whites is extremely low and varies very little among regions and cities; consequently, we generally omit whites from our discussion of levels of ghetto poverty.[12]

A potential pitfall of this measure is that it fails to take spatial proximity into account. It seems reasonable to assume that a city with 25 contiguous high-poverty tracts has a worse ghetto problem than one with 25 tracts scattered throughout the metropolitan area.[13] However, in our experience, most of the ghetto tracts in an area tend to be in one or two main clusters. Since this pattern is relatively constant across cities, the lack of a spatial dimension in our measure of ghetto poverty is not much of a problem. Moreover, because our measure identifies specific tracts, we are able to map ghetto tracts and visually inspect their spatial relationships. The value of this approach will be evident below, especially in the section on "The Geography of Ghetto Poverty."

### Data Sources

We have compiled data for all metropolitan census tracts (approximately 40,000) in 1970 and 1980. The data for 1980 are from the Census of Population and Housing, 1980, Summary Tape File 4A. Outside metropolitan areas, county data are included from Summary Tape File 4C, so that the 1980 data set is national in scope. The 1970 data are from the 1970 Census of Population, Fourth Count, File A, and include all metropolitan tracts. Appendix A discusses several issues related to processing the tapes

---

[11] The data reported in our earlier work used this definition of the level of ghetto poverty (Bane and Jargowsky, 1988).

[12] The only places where the level of ghetto poverty among whites is greater than 20 percent are college towns, like Madison, Wisconsin, and Texas towns, where one assumes many of the whites are Hispanic.

[13] Those in the scattered tracts will have partial access to the amenities of their better-off nearby neighbors, more role models, and so on. Readers who find this unconvincing might consider whether they would rather live in one of the scattered tracts or in the center of the 25 census tract ghetto area.

and compiling the data set, such as complementary suppression in 1980 and changes in SMSA boundaries between 1970 and 1980.

The data reported here improve on the data presented in our earlier work (Bane and Jargowsky, 1988) in several ways. First, they cover entire metropolitan areas, not merely central cities. Ghettos such as East St. Louis, Illinois, and Camden, New Jersey, were excluded from our earlier data simply because they were outside the political boundaries of the central cities of their metropolitan areas. Second, all metropolitan areas are included, not just the 100 largest.

It is dangerous to judge a trend from only two data points (1970 and 1980), the most recent of which is almost a decade ago. Nevertheless, there is simply no source of data other than the decennial census that has a large enough sample to allow analysis at the neighborhood level. The Census Bureau's Current Population Survey (CPS) does report "poverty area data" annually, but we do not think these data are useful. First, the criterion used is a poverty rate of 20 percent for the census tract. We argued above that this criterion does not identify ghetto poverty very well. Second, the CPS uses the tract poverty rate from a previous decennial census until the next one becomes available. As a result, the tract poverty rates are attached to data that are as many as 10 or more years out of sync. With the rapid changes and movements common in ghetto areas (see "The Geography of Ghetto Poverty"), this procedure is simply too flawed to make the data it generates useful.

We rely, therefore, on 1970 and 1980 census data. In the next section, as above, we report tract-level data on the characteristics of ghetto neighborhoods in Memphis and Philadelphia. We then present our aggregate analyses of tract-level data for all metropolitan areas in the United States. Next, we return to Memphis and Philadelphia and add Cleveland and Milwaukee in an analysis of the changing geography of ghetto poverty. In the final section, we present our conclusions as well as implications for public policy.

## CHARACTERISTICS OF GHETTO NEIGHBORHOODS

What are the ghetto neighborhoods defined by the 40 percent poverty criterion like? What is known about the quality of life for people who live in ghettos, especially poor people? These questions are addressed in this section.

A separate and quite different question is whether living in a ghetto makes poverty worse. Does living in a ghetto have an independent effect on poor persons? One could attempt to answer this question by comparing poor people who live in ghettos with poor people who do not on a variety of characteristics. Unfortunately, this strategy ignores the possibility of

unobserved differences between the two groups that are directly related to
their residential status. For example, it could be that employed adults move
out of ghettos, leaving the unemployed behind. The resulting difference in
employment rates would reflect selection effects, not neighborhood effects.
Controlled experiments and/or longitudinal data are needed to sort this out.
In Chapter 4, Jencks and Mayer review the data on what is known about
neighborhood effects. In this section we do not deal with neighborhood
effects; we simply describe differences in neighborhood characteristics. As
above, we use data for Philadelphia and Memphis as examples.

### Race/Ethnicity

Table 2-1 shows the distribution by race and Hispanic origin for residents of Memphis and Philadelphia by the level of poverty in their neighborhoods. The poorer the neighborhood, the greater the proportion of
residents who are minority group members. In Memphis, where there are
very few Hispanics, ghettos are nearly 90 percent black; in Philadelphia,
blacks and Hispanics account for nearly 85 percent of ghetto residents.
Nonpoor neighborhoods, those with poverty rates of less than 20 percent,
have just the opposite race/ethnicity composition. Non-Hispanic whites
make up the vast majority of persons in nonpoor neighborhoods and only
a small proportion of those in ghettos.[14]

### Family Structure and Demographics

Family structure is also quite different in ghetto neighborhoods, as
seen in Table 2-2. Three in four families in the Memphis and Philadelphia
SMSAs are married-couple families. Only about 10 percent of all families
are single-parent families with children. In ghetto neighborhoods, however,
the pattern is quite different. Less than half of all families are headed by a
married couple, and less than a quarter are married couples with children.
The modal family type is a single parent with children. Sixty to seventy
percent of all families with children are headed by single parents, compared
with 20 to 30 percent in the SMSAs overall. Looking only at blacks reduces
the differences in family type, but by no means eliminates them.

---

[14]Our estimate of the number of non-Hispanic whites is not completely accurate because the
tract-level data are not categorized simultaneously by race, Hispanic origin, and poverty status.
Although Hispanics can be either white or black, the majority of Hispanics identified themselves
on the 1980 census as either white or "other race." Only 2.6 percent identified themselves as black
(Bureau of the Census, 1983a). Therefore, a pretty good approximation can be achieved with
aggregate data by subtracting black and Hispanic data from the total, which yields non-Hispanic
whites and other races.

TABLE 2-1  Race/Ethnicity Composition of Memphis and Philadelphia, by Neighborhood Poverty Level, 1980

| | | Neighborhood Poverty Level | | |
| | SMSA Total | Not Poor (0-20%) | Mixed (20-40%) | Ghetto (>40%) |
| --- | --- | --- | --- | --- |
| Memphis SMSA | | | | |
| Total persons | 913,468 | 570,331 | 234,890 | 108,247 |
| | | | | |
| Black | 39.8% | 15.8% | 75.6% | 88.9% |
| Hispanic | 0.8 | 0.7 | 1.0 | 0.9 |
| Non-Hispanic white and other races* | 59.4 | 83.6 | 23.5 | 10.2 |
| | | | | |
| Philadelphia SMSA | | | | |
| Total persons | 4,713,242 | 3,825,962 | 620,769 | 266,511 |
| | | | | |
| Black | 18.6% | 7.9% | 62.3% | 69.1% |
| Hispanic | 2.3 | 1.0 | 4.8 | 14.5 |
| Non-Hispanic white and other races* | 79.2 | 91.0 | 32.9 | 16.4 |

*See footnote 14.

TABLE 2-2  Families by Type and Presence of Children: Memphis and Philadelphia SMSA Averages and Ghetto Neighborhoods, 1980

| | Memphis SMSA | | Philadelphia SMSA | |
| | SMSA | Ghetto | SMSA | Ghetto |
| --- | --- | --- | --- | --- |
| Total families | 232,787 | 23,387 | 1,209,923 | 57,508 |
| Married-couple families | | | | |
| With children | 39.1% | 21.1% | 38.7% | 20.1% |
| Without children | 36.4 | 24.7 | 39.9 | 20.4 |
| Single-parent families | | | | |
| With children | 14.7 | 35.0 | 11.0 | 39.6 |
| Without children | 9.8 | 19.1 | 10.5 | 20.0 |
| | | | | |
| Black families | 81,834 | 20,849 | 204,878 | 41,245 |
| Married-couple families | | | | |
| With children | 31.8% | 19.5% | 27.2% | 15.9% |
| Without children | 23.1 | 22.1 | 24.2 | 17.7 |
| Single-parent families | | | | |
| With children | 29.2 | 38.1 | 30.1 | 44.3 |
| Without children | 15.9 | 20.3 | 18.6 | 22.1 |

As a result of this difference in family structure, a much greater proportion of the children in ghetto areas have only one parent. On average, children of single parents are poorer in terms of income and other resources. In addition, one parent often cannot provide the same level of guidance and discipline as two. Children of single-parent families do significantly worse, on average, than other children in terms of educational attainment, earnings, and family formation, and they are somewhat more likely to be arrested (Dembo, 1988; Dornbusch et al., 1985; Garfinkel and McLanahan, 1986).[15]

## Economic Characteristics

Table 2-3 compares the economic characteristics of ghettos in Philadelphia and Memphis with those of their SMSAs. Given that the stratifying variable is the neighborhood poverty rate, one would expect differences on economic measures. Nevertheless, it is interesting to note how large the differences are. Although nearly 90 percent of the males aged 25 to 44 in the SMSA are employed, in ghettos only two-thirds in Memphis and just over half in Philadelphia are employed. A far greater proportion of ghetto males are not in the labor force at all. Those who are in the labor force are three times more likely to be unemployed. Once again, this is partly an effect of the racial composition of the neighborhoods, but after controlling for race, substantial differences remain.

Table 2-3 also shows the median earnings of males who worked full-year, full-time—in effect, the wage rate for full-time male workers multiplied by 2,000 (40 hours times 50 weeks). Consider what these numbers mean. The average wage rate in Memphis for full-year, full-time male workers was about $8.00 per hour ($16,000/2,000) in 1979 dollars. For blacks, the rates were $5.60 for the SMSA and $4.62 for ghettos. In Philadelphia, wage rates were generally higher, although the pattern of differences is the same. Although considerably higher than the minimum wage in 1979 ($2.90), these wage rates suggest that the kinds of jobs ghetto residents are working at, even when they work full-time, year-round, are low paid and probably low skilled. Wage rates for part-year and/or part-time work are undoubtedly lower.

These wage and employment numbers tell a story about three separate factors that contribute to the low average earnings of blacks in ghetto neighborhoods. First, just by virtue of the area's being mostly black, the employment and wage rates for ghetto residents are lower than the SMSA averages. Second, controlling for race, ghetto residents are more often out of the labor force or unemployed. Third, even when black ghetto residents work, they earn lower wages than nonghetto blacks.

The numbers also tell a story about the sources of support for families. The average income of all prime-age men in the Memphis and Philadelphia

---

[15] We have focused on families in this section mainly because we did not find important differences between ghetto areas and the rest of the SMSA in the proportion of nonfamily households. Only about 10 percent of residents live in nonfamily households or group quarters.

TABLE 2-3 Economic Characteristics of Memphis and Philadelphia SMSA Averages and Ghetto Neighborhoods, 1980

| | Memphis SMSA | | Philadelphia SMSA | |
|---|---|---|---|---|
| | SMSA | Ghetto | SMSA | Ghetto |
| **All Races** | | | | |
| Males, aged 25-44 | | | | |
|   Employed | 86.7% | 63.6% | 86.3% | 51.8% |
|   Unemployed | 5.2 | 11.9 | 5.8 | 14.4 |
|   Not in labor force | 8.1 | 24.5 | 7.9 | 33.8 |
|   Unemployment rate | 5.7 | 15.8 | 6.3 | 21.8 |
| Median earnings of full-year, full-time adult male workers | $16,067 | $9,701 | $18,933 | $12,019 |
| Proportion of households with income from | | | | |
|   Earnings | 82.1% | 60.3% | 79.3% | 52.6% |
|   Public assistance | 11.1 | 33.1 | 10.0 | 42.8 |
| **Blacks** | | | | |
| Males, aged 25-44 | | | | |
|   Employed | 75.5 | 62.1 | 69.2 | 49.7 |
|   Unemployed | 10.1 | 13.9 | 12.0 | 17.0 |
|   Not in labor force | 14.3 | 24.1 | 18.8 | 33.3 |
|   Unemployment rate | 11.8 | 18.3 | 14.8 | 25.5 |
| Median earnings of full-year, full-time adult male workers | $11,195 | $9,241 | $13,916 | $11,653 |
| Proportion of households with income from | | | | |
|   Earnings | 74.4% | 59.0% | 71.0% | 50.5% |
|   Public assistance | 24.4 | 36.5 | 28.4 | 47.5 |

ghettos was about $5,700 per year.[16] This was well below the $7,421 that was needed in 1979 to support a family of four at the poverty line. It is perhaps not surprising, therefore, that so many ghetto families are headed by women and that so many rely on income from public assistance.

## Social Characteristics

One common thread of the literature on ghettos, both academic and popular, is that the harshness of living in a ghetto is only partly economic.

---

[16]This is an estimate obtained by multiplying the earnings of full-year, full-time workers by the percent employed. It implicitly assumes that all the employed are working full-year, full-time, and it is thus an overestimate of average earnings.

TABLE 2-4   Social Indicators in Memphis and Philadelphia, by Poverty Level of Neighborhood, 1980

|  | Memphis SMSA | | Philadelphia SMSA | |
|---|---|---|---|---|
|  | SMSA | Ghetto | SMSA | Ghetto |
| Blacks of specified ages | | | | |
| Median years of school completed, age 25 and up | 10.8 | 9.5 | 11.7 | 10.8 |
| Hangout rate, 16-21* | 25.7 | 31.1 | 29.5 | 40.3 |
| MMPI, 25-44* | 60.3 | 44.5 | 53.2 | 32.7 |

*See accompanying text for explanation.

For example, it is highly likely that ghetto residents are more often the victims of crime than nonghetto residents, as well as perpetrators of crime. Ghetto residents probably are more likely to have problems with substance abuse. They are probably more likely to have been victims of racial discrimination, police brutality, and environmental health hazards. Recently, a number of sociologists and ethnographers have painted vivid pictures of ghetto life for specific neighborhoods (Anderson, 1989; Coulton et al., 1990; O'Regan and Wiseman, 1990; Wilson, 1987). The census does not give us such details. There are, however, a few useful measures available at the census-tract level. Differences in attachment to the labor force and in welfare recipiency were noted earlier. Several other differences are shown in Table 2-4. All figures in the table are for blacks only, so none of the differences between neighborhoods is due to racial composition.

The table shows a large difference in years of school completed. This difference may reflect the socioeconomic level of ghetto residents, lower educational aspirations in ghetto neighborhoods, or the quality of education in ghetto schools. Whatever the reason, however, it clearly indicates the low levels of education among ghetto residents. The median adult in a Memphis ghetto, for example, has not finished his or her sophomore year in high school.[17] The other two indicators in the table require some explanation. The "hangout rate" is an attempt to measure "idleness" or exclusion from the mainstream economy among young people. The measure is the proportion of civilian 16- to 21-year-olds who are not in

---

[17]In comparison, the median level for all adults in the SMSA is 12.1 years, indicating a small amount of postsecondary education.

school and not working (either unemployed or not in the labor force).[18] This measure should almost certainly be interpreted differently for men and women, who unfortunately are grouped together in the census-tract data.[19] Among young men, those "hanging out" may be thought of as the pool available for criminal enterprises, although by no means should one assume that all of these individuals turn to crime. Among young women, a significant proportion are likely to be poorly educated and unemployed young mothers, many (at least in the ghetto) unmarried.

In the Philadelphia ghetto, 40 percent of the young adults are "hanging out." Some are almost certainly raising children. Some may be engaged in crime or other aspects of the underground economy. Some may simply be doing nothing at all, which in some ways is equally worrisome. However, the rate for blacks in the SMSA as a whole is just under 30 percent, so the difference is not as great as one might have thought.

The "MMPI" is the Male Marriageable Pool Index, defined by Wilson and Neckerman (1986). As used here, the MMPI is the ratio of employed men aged 25 to 44 to women of the same age. Wilson and Neckerman argue that women are not inclined to marry men who are not in a position to support them and that the low level of the MMPI in ghetto communities helps to explain the high level of female-headed families. The data for Memphis and Philadelphia certainly confirm that the MMPI is dramatically lower in ghettos. In Philadelphia ghettos, there is 1 employed male for every 3 females in the 25 to 44 age group; in Memphis, 9 for every 20. In part, this reflects the census undercount of urban black males. No one, however, alleges an undercount large enough to explain this difference. The second factor contributing to such low MMPI is males who have died, joined the army, or gone to prison. The third factor is the low employment level of the remaining males, as discussed above.

### Public Policy and Ghettos

In short, ghettos contain a concentration of economic and social problems. Census data reveal only the tip of the iceberg; those who live and work in ghetto communities could doubtless paint a much more vivid picture. Although we have not attempted to argue that ghettos have effects on their residents, in some ways it does not matter. It is clear that a great many people with economic hardships, educational deficits, and social problems are clustered in the ghetto. Moreover, the quality of life in ghettos is

---

[18]See Mare and Winship (1984) for a discussion of the importance of considering the employment of black youths in the context of their school enrollment and military enlistment.

[19]The data are from Table PB49, "Age by School Enrollment, Years of School Completed and Labor Force Status," Summary Tape File 4A.

unfortunate enough that a compassionate society should worry about it. If, in addition, later research shows that ghetto poverty makes it even harder for the poor to escape poverty, that will only provide one more incentive to tackle the problem.

## GHETTO POVERTY, 1970–1980:
## THE NATIONAL PICTURE

Having defined ghettos and described their characteristics in two cities, we now step back to examine the national pattern. In this section we estimate the number of ghetto poor in 1980, look at changes between 1970 and 1980, and document regional and city-to-city variations.

### The Number of Ghetto Poor

In 1980, there were 27 million poor persons in the United States—12.4 percent of the population.[20] Of these, 18.8 million (68.7 percent) lived in the 318 SMSAs defined at the time of the census.[21] It would be a mistake, however, to assume that all persons who were poor and lived in metropolitan areas lived in ghettos. The total number of poor persons who lived in a metropolitan census tract in which the poverty rate was greater than 40 percent was 2.4 million. The number of poor, metropolitan poor, and ghetto poor, by race, is shown in Table 2-5.

Several interesting facts emerge from the table. First, less than 9 percent of all poor in the United States lived in ghettos in 1979.[22] Even within metropolitan areas, only 13 percent of the poor lived in ghettos. The rest lived in mixed-income and nonpoor neighborhoods. Thus, ghetto

---

[20] Although the census uses income figures from the previous year, in this case 1979, it reports the residence in the current year, in this case 1980. Moreover, the census somewhat overstates poverty. The CPS poverty rate in 1979 was somewhat lower—11.7 percent. In general, the CPS seems to do a better job of measuring income than the census, which results in a lower measured poverty rate. Underreporting of income in the census may be particularly serious for public assistance and other unearned income. The general direction of bias should be toward some overstatement of poverty rates and perhaps poverty concentrations as well.

[21] Several more SMSAs were defined after the census, and major changes were made in metropolitan area boundaries in 1983. In addition, the terminology was changed somewhat. The term SMSA was eliminated, replaced by consolidated metropolitan statistical areas (CMSAs), primary metropolitan statistical areas (PMSAs), and metropolitan statistical areas (MSAs). CSMAs contain more than one PMSA. PMSAs and MSAs, taken together, are roughly comparable to the pre-1983 SMSAs (Bureau of the Census, 1989:Appendix II). We continue to use the term SMSA to indicate that our data are based on the pre-1983 concepts and boundaries.

[22] Bane and Jargowsky (1988) reported that 6.7 percent of the poor lived in ghettos in the 100 largest central cities. The increase to 8.9 percent reflects the addition of smaller SMSAs and suburbs, i.e., non-central-city portions of SMSAs.

TABLE 2-5  Distribution of Poor Persons, 1980 (thousands)

| | U.S. | Metropolitan Areas | | Ghetto Areas (Poverty > 40%) | |
|---|---|---|---|---|---|
| All | 27,388 (100.0%) | 18,820 | (68.7%) | 2,449 | (8.9%) |
| Black | 7,548 (100.0) | 5,734 | (76.0) | 1,590 | (21.1) |
| Hispanic | 3,348 (100.0) | 2,869 | (85.7) | 534 | (15.9) |
| Non-Hispanic white* | 16,492 (100.0) | 10,217 | (62.0) | 325 | (2.0) |

*See footnote 14.

poverty is a relatively small part of the overall problem of poverty in the United States. This is not to say that the problem is not important—far from it. It may be far more degrading and harmful to be poor in an urban ghetto than elsewhere. Nevertheless, it must be emphasized that the poverty problem in the United States is far broader than just urban ghettos. Policy makers should not assume that the ghetto problem and the poverty problem are synonymous.

Table 2-5 also indicates that the proportion of the poor in ghettos varies dramatically by race. Only 2 percent of the non-Hispanic white poor lived in ghettos, compared with 21 percent of black poor and 16 percent of Hispanic poor. Within metropolitan areas, almost 3 in 10 poor blacks lived in a ghetto. As a result, the 2.4 million ghetto poor in the United States were distributed as follows: black—64.9 percent; Hispanic—21.8 percent; non-Hispanic white and other races—13.3 percent. Thus, ghettos were predominantly populated by blacks and Hispanics, and black and Hispanic poor were much more likely to live in a ghetto than white poor.

### An Aside: Rural High-Poverty Areas

This is a study of urban ghettos. Nevertheless, it is clear that a substantial minority of the poor (31 percent from Table 2-5) live in nonmetropolitan areas and that there are many pockets of poverty in rural areas, particularly among blacks in the South and Hispanics in Texas and Florida. Such areas are not usually divided into census tracts, so poverty rates cannot be calculated for them. Using the county poverty rates as an approximation, however, indicates that of 1.8 million poor blacks in rural areas, 107,716 (5.9 percent) lived in counties with poverty rates over 40 percent. Because a county is so much bigger than a tract, however, these figures are not really comparable with tract-based figures. Almost all rural blacks live in the South, and such counties tend to be highly segregated. Therefore, the black poverty rate for the county may be a better approximation of the neighborhood poverty rate for blacks than the overall poverty rate in the county. Using this criterion for high-poverty areas, a vastly different picture emerges: more than 1 million poor blacks (56.2 percent of non-metropolitan blacks) lived in rural counties in which the black poverty rate was above 40 percent.

Similarly, only 4.2 percent of the country's 479,000 Hispanic rural poor lived in counties in which the overall poverty rate was greater than 40 percent. Twenty-eight percent, however, lived in rural counties in which the Hispanic poverty rate is that high. In Texas, which contains by far the largest number of Hispanic rural poor, 46 percent lived in counties in which the Hispanic poverty rate was greater than 40 percent.

Rural poverty areas often have dreadful conditions. Tunica, Mississippi, is an example.[23] The houses are little more than run-down shacks, without plumbing or sewage fixtures in many cases. The streets are unpaved and social problems are rampant. Clearly, these conditions are in some ways the equal of, if not worse than, conditions in urban ghettos. We know very little about rural pockets of poverty, and the subject deserves much greater attention. Nevertheless, Tunica, Mississippi, and Harlem, New York, are very different places. In the remainder of this chapter, we talk about ghetto poverty in metropolitan areas only.

### The Growth of Ghetto Poverty, 1970–1980

Much of the concern about ghetto poverty stems from a sense that ghettos, and the social problems they contain, have been getting worse. To evaluate these claims, we present data on the changes in ghetto poverty between 1970 and 1980.[24]

Between 1970 and 1980, the number of poor living in ghettos in metropolitan areas increased by 29.5 percent, from 1,890,925 in 1970 to 2,449,324 in 1980. This is a much smaller growth rate than the 66 percent reported previously (Bane and Jargowsky, 1988; Nathan and Lego, 1986). That estimate was based on published data for the 50 largest central cities. The difference comes mainly from our inclusion in these analyses of smaller SMSAs, many of them southern, many of which—as we discuss below—had substantial decreases in ghetto poverty. Thus, the focus on large central cities left out an important part of the story.

---

[23] We visited Tunica in May 1989 as part of a trip that took us from Memphis down through the Mississippi delta area to Jackson and then up through the Arkansas side of the delta to Little Rock.

[24] Not all metropolitan areas that existed in 1980 were defined in 1970, and there were numerous boundary changes. We tried to adjust for significant boundary changes by recoding the 1970 data to be consistent with 1980 boundaries. For more information, see Appendix A.

TABLE 2-6  Change in Number of Ghetto Poor, 1970-1980

| | Number of SMSAs | Ghetto Poor (thousands) | | | Percent Change |
|---|---|---|---|---|---|
| | | 1970 | 1980 | Change | |
| All races | 318 | 1,891 | 2,449 | 558 | +29.5 |
| Increases | 107 | 785 | 1,712 | 927 | +118.0 |
| No change | 44 | 0 | 0 | 0 | -- |
| Decreases | 88 | 1,106 | 668 | −437 | −39.6 |
| New in 1980 | 79 | -- | 67 | 67 | -- |
| Black | 318 | 1,247 | 1,590 | 343 | +27.5 |
| Increases | 96 | 558 | 1,121 | 563 | +100.9 |
| No change | 62 | 0 | 0 | 0 | -- |
| Decreases | 81 | 689 | 426 | −263 | 38.1 |
| New in 1980 | 79 | -- | 42 | 42 | -- |
| Hispanic | 318 | 385 | 534 | 149 | +38.7 |
| Increases | 116 | 96 | 361 | 265 | +277.6 |
| No change | 86 | 0 | 0 | 0 | -- |
| Decreases | 37 | 289 | 170 | −119 | −41.6 |
| New in 1980 | 79 | -- | 3 | 3 | -- |

The number of black ghetto poor grew by 27 percent over the 10-year period and the number of Hispanic poor by 39 percent.[25] The aggregate figures, however, are extremely misleading because they conceal a substantial amount of variation among metropolitan areas. The aggregate increase of more than 500,000 ghetto poor obscures the fact that some metropolitan areas had large increases and some large decreases.

Table 2-6 shows the number of SMSAs with increases and decreases in all ghetto poor, black ghetto poor, and Hispanic ghetto poor. There were more SMSAs with decreases or no change than SMSAs with increases. The number of ghetto poor in those SMSAs in which there were increases more than doubled. For Hispanics, it more than tripled. The metropolitan areas with decreases in ghetto poverty had more than one-third fewer ghetto poor in 1980 as 1970. Also important to note is that the addition of new SMSAs between 1970 and 1980 does not account for much of the growth in ghetto poverty—only about 12 percent of the growth came from new SMSAs, overall.[26]

---

[25] However, the aggregate level of concentration–the percentage of the metropolitan poor living in ghettos—increased only modestly among blacks (from 26.4 to 27.7 percent) and actually decreased among Hispanics (from 23.7 to 18.6 percent). See the following section.

[26] Looking only at the 239 SMSAs that were defined in both years, there was a net increase of just under 500,000, and a growth rate of 25.9 percent.

TABLE 2-7   Metropolitan Areas With the Most Ghetto Poor, 1980

| SMSA | Number of Ghetto Poor | Cumulative Percent |
|------|-----------------------|--------------------|
| New York, N.Y.-N.J. | 477,621 | 19.5 |
| Chicago, Ill. | 194,338 | 27.4 |
| Philadelphia, Pa.-N.J. | 127,134 | 32.6 |
| Baltimore, Md. | 60,983 | 35.1 |
| McAllen-Pharr-Edinburg, Tex. | 58,222 | 37.5 |
| Memphis, Tenn.-Ark.-Miss. | 56,915 | 39.8 |
| New Orleans, La. | 56,504 | 42.1 |
| Newark, N.J. | 54,720 | 44.4 |
| Detroit, Mich. | 54,572 | 46.6 |
| Los Angeles-Long Beach, Calif. | 51,306 | 48.7 |
| Remaining 308 metropolitan areas | 1,257,009 | 100.0 |

Thus, there is a great deal of variation among metropolitan areas. It is important to look more closely at specific SMSAs in order to understand the variations in the level of ghetto poverty and changes over time. As we discuss, the often-cited aggregate figures mask considerable regional variation and, to a lesser degree, city-to-city variation within regions.

### Where Are the Ghetto Poor?

The most visible ghetto poor are those who live in the largest urban areas. These very large cities, in fact, contain a large proportion of the ghetto poor. Slightly more than one-fourth of the ghetto poor in 1980 lived in just two metropolitan areas: New York and Chicago. The 10 metropolitan areas with the largest numbers of ghetto poor in 1980 are shown in Table 2-7. Together, they account for almost half of the ghetto poor.

Every region of the United States is represented on the top 10 list. The South contributes four of the metropolitan areas with the largest numbers of ghetto poor, the Northeast, three, the North Central, two, and the West one. Most of the 10 cities have large black populations, which account for most of the ghetto poor. The exception is McAllen-Pharr-Edinburg, Texas, on the southern tip of the state on the border with Mexico, which has a large Hispanic population that accounts for almost all of its ghetto poor.

The top 10 list in 1970 is similar (Table 2-8), but there are some important differences. For example, the top 10 accounted for only about one-third of the ghetto poor in 1970, rather than one-half. In addition, there was also a greater representation of southern cities (6 of 10), both deep South cities (where the ghetto poor are predominantly black) and Texas cities (where they are predominantly Hispanic).

TABLE 2-8  Metropolitan Areas With the Most Ghetto Poor, 1970

| SMSA | Number of Ghetto Poor | Cumulative Percent |
|------|----------------------|--------------------|
| New York, N.Y.-N.J. | 134,139 | 7.1 |
| McAllen-Pharr-Edinburg, Tex. | 80,477 | 11.3 |
| Memphis, Tenn.-Ark.-Miss. | 77,589 | 15.5 |
| Chicago, Ill. | 74,370 | 19.4 |
| New Orleans, La. | 71,932 | 23.2 |
| San Antonio, Tex. | 54,749 | 26.1 |
| Brownsville-Harlingen-San Benito, Tex. | 53,632 | 28.9 |
| Philadelphia, Pa.-N.J. | 49,657 | 31.5 |
| Baltimore, Md. | 45,732 | 34.0 |
| Los Angeles-Long Beach, Calif. | 41,885 | 36.2 |
| Remaining 229 metropolitan areas | 1,206,763 | 100.0 |

Shifts in the location of ghetto poverty between 1970 and 1980 are well illustrated by charting the cities with the largest increases and decreases in ghetto poverty. Figures 2-4 and 2-5 show the increases and decreases, respectively, for the 10 cities with the largest increases and decreases.

The 10 cities with the largest increases in ghetto poverty accounted for three-fourths (74 percent) of the total increase (Figure 2-4). New York alone accounted for more than one-third, and New York and Chicago together accounted for half. Adding Philadelphia, Newark, and Detroit brings the total to two-thirds. Atlanta and Baltimore, unlike many other cities in the South, also had large increases. The eight northern cities on the list exhibit doubling and tripling of their ghetto poor populations. The increases were largely among blacks, although there was a significant Hispanic increase in New York.

The cities with large decreases (Figure 2-5) are of two types. The first are Texas cities with large decreases in ghetto poverty among Hispanics. The second are southern cities, with large decreases among blacks. The decreases were not nearly as localized in a few cities as were the increases. The 10 cities in the figure account for less than half (46 percent) of the total decrease.

These facts begin to explain the widespread impression of rapidly increasing ghetto poverty. In certain cities, the area of the ghetto and the number of people affected are both increasing rapidly. These cities include some of the nation's largest population centers and the location of many large foundations, universities, and news organizations. What receives less notice are the decreases in ghetto poverty in the deep South and Texas. Many of the largest decreases in ghetto poverty occurred in small- to medium-sized metropolitan areas.

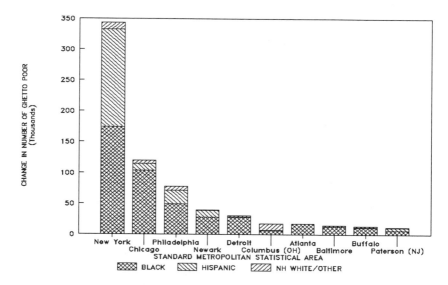

FIGURE 2-4   Increases in Number of Ghetto Poor, 1970-1980, by Race.

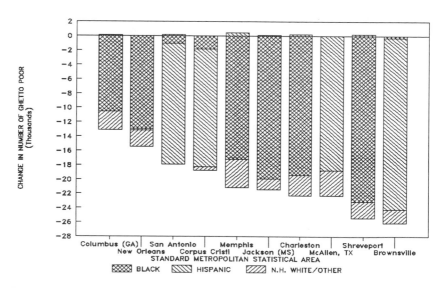

FIGURE 2-5   Decreases in Number of Ghetto Poor, 1970-1980, by Race.

TABLE 2-9  Distribution of Metropolitan Poor, 1970 and 1980, by Neighborhood Type, Region, and City Size

|  | Metropolitan Areas | | Ghetto Areas | |
| --- | --- | --- | --- | --- |
|  | 1970 | 1980 | 1970 | 1980 |
| Poor (thousands) | 15,240 | 18,820 | 1,891 | 2,449 |
|  | 100.0% | 100.0% | 100.0% | 100.0% |
| Region |  |  |  |  |
| Northeast | 25.0 | 24.2 | 13.0 | 32.7 |
| North Central | 22.1 | 21.3 | 14.2 | 21.8 |
| South | 34.4 | 34.5 | 65.0 | 39.4 |
| West | 18.5 | 19.9 | 7.7 | 6.1 |
| Urban area type |  |  |  |  |
| Central city | -- | 51.2 | -- | 86.6 |
| "Suburbs" | -- | 48.4 | -- | 13.4 |
| SMSA size |  |  |  |  |
| Less than 500,000 | 26.7 | 30.2 | 38.5 | 24.0 |
| 500,000-1,000,000 | 16.6 | 16.0 | 16.2 | 13.1 |
| More than 1,000,000 | 56.6 | 53.8 | 45.4 | 62.9 |

The regional pattern is shown in Table 2-9, which also gives distributions by city size. Relative to all metropolitan poor, the ghetto poor in 1980 were more likely to live in the Northeast or North Central region and to live in large cities.[27] A substantial majority were in central cities. Moreover, most of those in "suburbs" were probably in places like East St. Louis, Illinois, and Camden, New Jersey, which are suburbs only in a technical sense. In 1970, in contrast, almost two-thirds of the ghetto poor were in the South, and more than half were in cities of less than a million population.

## The Level of Ghetto Poverty

Table 2-9 shows that the distribution of the total metropolitan poor by region and city size did not change substantially between 1970 and 1980. Thus, changes in the regional and city-size distribution of the ghetto poor must have been brought about because of changes in the percentage of the poor living in ghettos, which we call the level of ghetto poverty.[28]

Looking first at the national data, Table 2-10 shows that the level of ghetto poverty increased only modestly among blacks (+1.2 percentage

---

[27] A few tracts are split across central-city boundaries; we have included these in suburbs. A comparable variable is not available on the 1970 census data tapes.

[28] Both the number of poor living in ghettos and the total number of poor in an area can change. Thus, the change in the number of ghetto poor (described above) and the change in the level of ghetto poverty (described in this section) can be quite different.

TABLE 2-10   Change in the Level of Ghetto Poverty, 1970-1980

|  | No. of SMSAs | Level of Ghetto Poverty | | |
|---|---|---|---|---|
|  |  | 1970 | 1980 | Change |
| Black | 176 | 26.5% | 27.7% | +1.2 |
| Increases | 89 | 19.1 | 31.8 | +12.8 |
| Decreases | 87 | 37.7 | 23.9 | −13.8 |
| Hispanic | 151 | 23.7 | 18.6 | −5.1 |
| Increases | 99 | 14.2 | 28.1 | +14.0 |
| Decreases | 52 | 32.4 | 14.4 | −18.0 |

points) and decreased among Hispanics (−5.1 percentage points). As with the changes in the number of ghetto poor, however, the aggregate levels conceal substantial variation. Some cities experienced large increases in the level of ghetto poverty and other cities experienced large decreases, changes that average out to a very modest national increase in ghetto poverty among blacks. Among Hispanics, the level of ghetto poverty doubled in the 99 cities where it increased, and it fell by more than half in the 52 cities where it decreased.[29]

The suggestion of strong regional shifts mentioned in the preceding section is borne out by the changes in the level of ghetto poverty in the metropolitan areas aggregated by region. The Northeast, dominated by New York, had an increase of nearly 20 percentage points in the level of ghetto poverty among blacks, as shown in Table 2-11. The North Central region also had a substantial increase. The South and West moved in the opposite direction. Again, it is clear that the appearance of a modest aggregate increase in ghetto poverty of 1.2 percentage points is quite misleading.

Table 2-11 also shows the level of ghetto poverty by size of the metropolitan area. The SMSAs are divided into three groups by total population: less than 500,000; 500,000 to 1 million; and more than 1 million. The data for blacks show a remarkable reversal. In 1970, the highest level of concentration was in the smallest metropolitan areas; by 1980, the opposite was true. Disaggregating by region shows that the reversal is due to the fact that most of the smaller SMSAs are in the South. The general decline in the level of ghetto poverty in the South is most evident in smaller SMSAs. The West also had larger decreases in the smaller SMSAs. In the Northeast and North Central regions, however, even smaller

---

[29]The aggregate level of ghetto poverty as reported in the table is the weighted average of SMSAs in the group; some SMSAs were not included because (a) they did not exist in 1970 or (b) they existed but had zero blacks (or Hispanics) in 1970 or 1980 and, therefore, did not have a level of ghetto poverty (division by zero).

TABLE 2-11  Level of Ghetto Poverty by Region and Metropolitan Area Size, Black and Hispanic, 1970 and 1980 (percentage)

| | 1970 SMSA Population | | | | 1980 SMSA Population | | | |
| --- | --- | --- | --- | --- | --- | --- | --- | --- |
| | S | M | L | All SMSAs | S | M | L | All SMSAs |
| Black poor in ghettos | | | | | | | | |
| U.S. metro | 37 | 29 | 22 | 27 | 22 | 25 | 31 | 28 |
| Northeast | 4 | 7 | 17 | 15 | 17 | 17 | 38 | 34 |
| North Central | 7 | 8 | 23 | 20 | 20 | 21 | 33 | 30 |
| South | 45 | 35 | 29 | 36 | 24 | 28 | 28 | 26 |
| West | 21 | 47 | 14 | 16 | 6 | 23 | 11 | 11 |
| Hispanic poor in ghettos | | | | | | | | |
| U.S. metro | 48 | 12 | 14 | 24 | 22 | 10 | 19 | 19 |
| Northeast | 4 | 7 | 21 | 19 | 22 | 18 | 42 | 37 |
| North Central | 4 | 0 | 4 | 3 | 5 | 4 | 10 | 9 |
| South | 64 | 17 | 23 | 45 | 32 | 11 | 11 | 21 |
| West | 11 | 13 | 6 | 8 | 2 | 3 | 5 | 4 |

Note:  S = < 500,000; M = 500,000–999,999; L = > 1 million.  Table contains data for 239 SMSAs in 1970 and 318 SMSAs in 1980.  See Appendix A.

SMSAs showed increases, although not as rapidly as larger SMSAs. Hispanics followed similar patterns.

The regional pattern is quite consistent in the North, less so in the South. In the North, all large cities except Boston had increases in their levels of ghetto poverty among blacks.[30] The size of the increase varied considerably, however. In the South, the picture was more mixed. Most cities had decreases in ghetto poverty levels among blacks, some of them quite large. But Baltimore, Atlanta, and Miami had modest increases in ghetto poverty among blacks, and Fort Lauderdale had a large increase. There were also increases in a few smaller cities.

## Ghetto Poverty and the SMSA Poverty Rate

What accounts for this strong regional pattern?  Many factors are potentially involved, including regional differences in racial and economic segregation, changes in the economic structure of metropolitan areas, and

---

[30] Appendix A provides data for individual cities, organized by region and size of the metropolitan area.

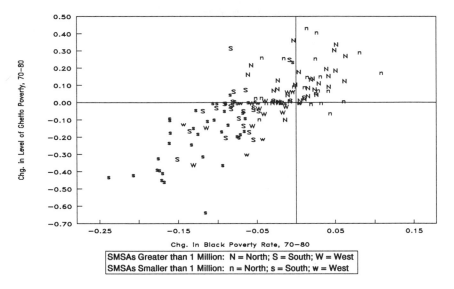

FIGURE 2-6   Ghetto poverty among blacks and the black poverty rate (changes 1970-1980, by region and size).

interregional migration.[31] One set of factors, however, that is clearly important is the SMSA poverty rate among blacks and Hispanics. Figure 2-6 shows the change in the level of ghetto poverty among blacks plotted against the change in the black poverty rate between 1970 and 1980. Each point represents an SMSA, and the symbols indicate the region and size of the metropolitan area.[32]

Clearly, there is a strong relationship between the change in the black poverty rate and the change in the level of ghetto poverty.[33] Moreover, most of the cities with decreases in poverty are southern cities, especially smaller southern cities. Large northern cities are more often in the quadrant

---

[31] To cite just a few examples of research concerning the importance of these different factors, Wilson (1987) argues that changes in economic segregation among blacks play a key role; Massey and Eggers (1989) argue that interactions between black poverty and racial segregation are more important than economic segregation among blacks; others (Hughes, 1989; Kasarda, 1988) examine the role of changes in the location of jobs within the metropolitan area.

[32] Figure 2-6 includes only SMSAs that were defined in both decades and that had at least 10,000 blacks in 1970. Of 318 SMSAs, 148 satisfy both conditions. We excluded the smaller SMSAs because the level of ghetto poverty in such cities depends on the poverty rate of just one or two tracts and is therefore highly subject to random noise.

[33] The relationship is similar among Hispanics. Plotting the levels of poverty against the level of ghetto poverty, rather than against changes in levels, also shows a relationship, but a less strong one.

with increases in black poverty and increases in ghetto poverty among blacks. The strength and consistency of the relationship might lead one to conclude, erroneously as it turns out, that the increases and decreases in ghetto poverty described above arose mechanically from changes in the poverty rate. In other words, as the poverty rate rises, more tracts are above 40 percent poverty and, thus, more of the poor live in ghettos. This is part of what happened, but the full picture is quite a bit more complex. In the section that follows, we look very carefully at the geography of the ghetto. We examine in detail the population movements and changes in poverty that actually occurred in several metropolitan areas. Any theory that attempts to explain what causes ghettos must not only explain the aggregate numbers presented in this section, but also the movements and changes observed at the tract level. As will be abundantly clear, the hypothesis that changes in poverty rate alone explain changes in ghetto poverty falls far short of this standard.

## THE GEOGRAPHY OF GHETTO POVERTY

In the preceding section, we described changes in the number of persons living in ghettos and also in the level of ghetto poverty. We did not say much about the size of the ghetto, the location of the ghetto, nor the typical patterns of economic changes and population movements. This set of topics, which we refer to as the geography of ghetto poverty, is the subject of this section. We look at four specific cities—two with large increases in the level of ghetto poverty, one with a modest increase, and one with a large decrease—and describe what actually happened to the geography of the ghetto. We also describe the population changes that took place in different areas of the city, as a way of beginning to understand the complicated process by which groups of census tracts remain, become, or stop being ghettos. Finally, we look across SMSAs at the relationship between the black poverty rate and ghetto poverty.[34]

### Understanding Increases in Ghetto Poverty

The level of ghetto poverty that we discuss here is the percentage of the black poor living in ghetto areas.[35] This level could have risen between 1970 and 1980 in several different ways:

---

[34] We do not look at interregional migration, despite suggestive evidence of its importance in the previous section. We are exploring this topic in our continuing work, along with other aspects of change in ghetto poverty.

[35] None of the four cities had substantial Hispanic populations.

- More of the black poor could have moved from other areas of the city into the ghetto.
- Without anyone's moving, the poverty rate could have gone up, causing some additional census tracts to go over the 40 percent cutoff. The poor in those tracts were then added to the count of the ghetto poor.
- With no change in the poverty rate, and no movements by poor people, nonpoor people could have move out of mixed-income census tracts. This would cause the group left behind to be poorer, and some additional census tracts would go over the 40 percent cutoff.
- Several of the above could happen simultaneously, with differential fertility and mortality and changes in family structure also playing a role.

Each of these explanations can be identified in the data for specific census tracts. If poor people moving into the ghetto were the cause of the increase in ghetto poverty, there would be no new ghetto poverty tracts, and the number of people in the ghetto tracts would be increasing. If new ghetto tracts were being added mechanically by changes in the poverty rate, then the number of ghetto tracts should increase. The total number of people in both the 1970 ghetto tracts and the new ghetto tracts also should not change very much. The number of poor would go up, but by about the same amount as the decrease in the number of nonpoor—people would simply be reclassified from nonpoor to poor. The data would look quite different, however, if the increase was caused by movement of the nonpoor out of mixed-income tracts. Again, there should be more ghetto tracts. But now, the new ghetto tracts should have fewer people in 1980 than in 1970.

To examine these mechanics, we present data and ghetto maps for four cities: Cleveland, Memphis, Milwaukee, and Philadelphia. We examine the location of the 1970 and 1980 ghetto census tracts and the movement of people into and out of different areas. Identifying who was moving where does not tell us anything about why they moved. The root causes of the increases in ghetto poverty lie beyond these mere descriptions. Understanding these dynamics, however, is an important first step and can help to frame the right questions to ask about the deeper causes.

The four cities show different patterns of change.

- Cleveland is a large north-central city with a high level of poverty concentration in 1970 (32.8 percent) and a modest growth in concentration (3.8 percentage points) from 1970 to 1980 (Figure 2-7).
- Memphis is a large southern city with a large black population. It had an extremely high level of poverty concentration in 1970 (56.2

FIGURE 2-7  Cleveland SMSA change in tract poverty, 1970-1980.

percent) and a large decrease in concentration (-16.9 percentage
points) between 1970 and 1980 (Figure 2-8).

- Milwaukee is a large north-central city with a small but growing
  black population. It had a low level of poverty concentration in 1970
  (8.6 percent) but experienced very rapid growth (15.5 percentage
  points) (Figure 2-9).
- Philadelphia is a large northeastern city with a moderate level
  of poverty concentration in 1970 (21.3 percent) and rapid growth
  in concentration (15.6 percentage points) between 1970 and 1980
  (Figure 2-10).

The maps of the four cities show categories of census tracts, as follows:

- Tracts that were ghettos in 1970, divided into those that remained
  ghettos in 1980 and those that improved;
- Tracts that were mixed income (20 to 40 percent poor) in 1970
  divided into those that had become ghettos by 1980 and those that
  had not;
- Tracts that were not poor (less than 20 percent) in 1970, again
  divided into those that had become ghettos by 1970 and those that
  had not; and

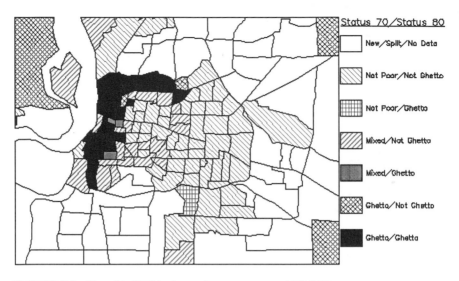

FIGURE 2-8   Memphis SMSA change in tract poverty, 1970-1980.

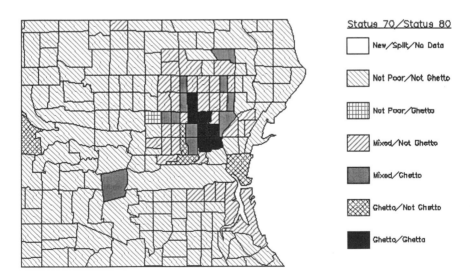

FIGURE 2-9   Milwaukee SMSA change in tract poverty, 1970-1980.

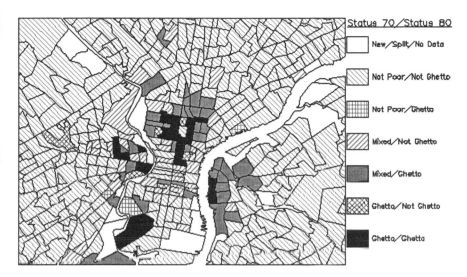

Status 70/Status 80

- New/Split/No Data
- Not Poor/Not Ghetto
- Not Poor/Ghetto
- Mixed/Not Ghetto
- Mixed/Ghetto
- Ghetto/Not Ghetto
- Ghetto/Ghetto

FIGURE 2-10   Philadelphia SMSA change in tract poverty, 1970-1980.

- Tracts that were added to the SMSA between 1970 and 1980, some of which resulted from splitting existing tracts, virtually none of which was poor in 1980.

Table 2-12 shows the number of tracts that fell into the various categories. The table and the maps illustrate some important aspects of how changes in poverty concentration actually took place.

### The Geographic Spread of the Ghetto

The maps of the four cities and Table 2-12 show that the ghetto areas in three of the four cities expanded geographically. Even in Memphis, where the proportion of the poor living in high-poverty areas declined substantially, the number of ghetto tracts decreased by only two. In Philadelphia, Milwaukee, and Cleveland, the geographical areas included in the ghetto expanded dramatically. In general, the areas that became ghettos between 1970 and 1980 were mixed-income tracts in 1970 that were contiguous to the 1970 ghetto areas. The maps illustrate that the process was not completely orderly. Some 1970 ghetto tracts were no longer ghettos in 1980, even in the cities where ghetto poverty increased. Some 1980 ghetto tracts were not contiguous to the 1970 ghetto; a few were not poor—less than 20 percent—in 1970. Nonetheless, the basic pattern was one of expansion of the ghetto into adjacent, mixed-income tracts.

TABLE 2-12  Geographic Expansion of the Ghetto, 1970-1980

| 1970 Neighborhood Type | SMSA | | | |
|---|---|---|---|---|
| | Cleveland | Memphis | Milwaukee | Philadelphia |
| Ghetto tracts 1970 | 19 | 37 | 11 | 26 |
|    Stayed ghetto in 1980 | 18 | 30 | 7 | 19 |
|    Improved by 1980 | 1 | 7 | 4 | 7 |
| Mixed income 1970 | 51 | 31 | 43 | 99 |
|    Became ghetto by 1980 | 21 | 4 | 11 | 43 |
|    Did not become ghetto | 30 | 27 | 32 | 56 |
| Not poor 1970 | 340 | 57 | 303 | 1,047 |
|    Became ghetto by 1980 | 3 | 1 | 1 | 4 |
|    Did not become ghetto | 337 | 56 | 302 | 1,043 |
| Total ghetto tracts, 1980 | 42 | 35 | 19 | 59 |

The expansion of the ghetto rules out the hypothesis that the increases in ghetto poverty (in the three cities with increases) were caused by poor people moving into the ghetto. To distinguish between the other two hypotheses—that tracts became ghettos simply because of poverty rate changes or because the nonpoor moved out—we look next at population movements.

### Movements from Ghetto and Mixed-Income Tracts

Table 2-13 summarizes population changes between 1970 and 1980 in the 1970 ghetto and mixed-income areas. It shows population losses in both areas. This lends support to the idea that the nonpoor were moving out of mixed-income areas, causing them to "tip" and become ghettos. The patterns are complicated, however, and it is useful to lay them out in some detail.

Table 2-13 shows what may appear to be a paradox: The 1970 ghetto area contained a smaller proportion of the black poor in 1980 than in 1970, even in cities in which the level of ghetto poverty increased substantially. The level of ghetto poverty, therefore, would have declined in these cities had not additional tracts been classified as ghettos. Mixed-income areas in all four cities—what can be thought of as potential ghettos—also saw substantial population losses, even in Memphis, where the SMSA population was growing rapidly. In all four cities, the proportion of the black poor living in these areas declined substantially between 1970 and 1980. This is most consistent with the hypothesis that the increase in ghetto poverty was caused by the movement of nonpoor people out of the 1970 mixed-income areas. The poor were leaving as well, but the nonpoor left faster, leaving

TABLE 2-13  Population Loss in Ghetto and Mixed-Income Tracts, 1970-1980

| | SMSA | | | |
| --- | --- | --- | --- | --- |
| | Cleveland | Memphis | Milwaukee | Philadelphia |
| **1970 ghetto areas** | | | | |
| 1970 population | 62,233 | 143,951 | 17,319 | 111,622 |
| Change, population (%) | −36.2 | −21.6 | −31.5 | −24.2 |
| Change, black poor (%) | −26.3 | −23.5 | −30.4 | −14.2 |
| % of black poor 1970 | 32.8 | 54.2 | 15.5 | 21.3 |
| % of black poor 1980 | 21.9 | 38.2 | 7.1 | 14.8 |
| **1970 mixed-income areas** | | | | |
| 1970 population | 151,638 | 134,609 | 119,090 | 491,169 |
| Change, population (%) | −36.8 | −7.0 | −20.9 | −23.8 |
| Change, black poor (%) | −12.8 | −6.1 | +18.5 | −1.6 |
| % of black poor 1970 | 38.0 | 27.4 | 66.4 | 46.4 |
| % of black poor 1980 | 30.0 | 23.7 | 52.0 | 37.0 |

behind a group of people in 1980 that were poorer than in 1970. As a result, some of the 1970 mixed-income tracts became ghettos by 1980. In three of the cities, the addition of the black poor in these new ghetto tracts to the shrinking proportion of the poor in the old ghetto was enough to result in an increase in the proportion of the poor living in ghettos. In other words, the level of ghetto poverty went up only because new areas were classified as ghettos.[36]

Perhaps it is not surprising that ghettos lost population over the decade. The data are consistent with the emptying out of downtown areas that has been observed in many cities. Given the harsh conditions of life in ghetto neighborhoods, anyone who could leave probably did. However, the fact that mixed-income areas also lost a large segment of their residents is somewhat surprising. One might have predicted increases in the number of black poor in these areas, at least in the cities in which ghetto poverty increased, since these are the areas from which new ghetto tracts formed. And one might have expected the people leaving the ghetto to settle there. Some may have, but on balance the population—poor and nonpoor—declined substantially. The population, poor and nonpoor, black and white, was spreading out from poor and mixed-income tracts into other areas. The next "ring," areas that were not poor and mostly white, became mixed-income and often mixed race, that is, they became home to a larger proportion of the black and poor population. The white nonpoor left these areas, which also lost population overall. Population growth took place

---

[36]This is a general pattern. Appendix A shows the number of ghetto census tracts in 1970 and 1980. In almost all of the areas in which the level of ghetto poverty increased, and even in many areas in which it decreased, the ghetto area was spreading out geographically.

TABLE 2-14   Differential Movements in 1970 Mixed-Income Tracts, by Pattern of Change, 1970-1980

|  | SMSA | | |
|  | Cleveland | Milwaukee | Philadelphia |
|---|---|---|---|
| Mixed-Income Tracts | | | |
| That Became Ghettos | | | |
| 1970 population | 53,382 | 27,113 | 246,623 |
| Change, black poor | +1,085 | +1,231 | +4,164 |
| Change, black not poor | −10,556 | −3,149 | −39,604 |
| Change, white | −11,124 | −3,886 | −26,034 |
| Mixed-Income Tracts That | | | |
| Did Not Become Ghettos | | | |
| 1970 population | 98,256 | 91,977 | 244,546 |
| Change, black poor | −5,075 | +2,269 | −5,686 |
| Change, black not poor | −16,323 | −4,220 | −26,619 |
| Change, white | −12,751 | −18,228 | −20,883 |

by and large in tracts at the outskirts of the SMSAs, some of which were added to the metropolitan areas after 1970.

### Tracts Becoming Ghettos

In the three cities in which ghetto poverty increased (Cleveland, Milwaukee, and Philadelphia), a part of what had been the mixed-income area became a ghetto. The number of mixed-income tracts that "tipped" into ghetto status varied by city, but was substantial in all three cities. A comparison of mixed-income tracts that became ghettos with those that did not reveals some interesting commonalities as well as contrasts. Table 2-14 shows population changes by race and poverty status in the 1970 mixed-income tracts that did and did not become ghettos in 1980.

The 1970 mixed-income tracts that became ghettos lost population in all three cities. The number of black poor in these tracts generally went up, but the number of black nonpoor decreased by a much greater number. Since each of these three cities had an increase in the black poverty rate, the increase in the number of black poor came from a change of poverty status among some blacks. Declines in the white population occurred among both poor and nonpoor.

Interestingly, the mixed-income areas that did not become ghettos showed, in all three cities, a pattern of population change that was basically similar to what occurred in the mixed-income tracts that became ghettos—although with somewhat different proportions of black and white, poor and nonpoor, among the movers and stayers. The mixed-income areas that did not become ghettos also lost population, both black and white. The difference between tracts that became ghettos and tracts that did not seems to be more one of degree than of kind.

These data suggest that, at least in these four cities, the process by which geographical areas stayed, became, or stopped being ghettos was quite complicated. In none of the four cities was the process a simple matter of the poor moving into ghetto areas or the nonpoor moving out. Nor can the situation in any city be described as one in which people basically stayed put but changes in the poverty rate caused more areas to be pushed over the 40 percent line. Instead, we see a general pattern of dispersion—probably part of a longer historical trend—interacting with changes in the poverty rate and continuing high levels of racial segregation.

## CONCLUSIONS

The purpose of this analysis was to investigate the problem of ghetto poverty. We have attempted to determine the size and extent of the ghetto problem in the United States and to learn if the problem was getting worse. We began with a belief in the conventional wisdom that urban ghettos were large and growing and deserved focused policy attention.

Our tentative answers to our empirical questions about urban poverty reveal a much more diverse picture than we had anticipated. Our reading of the data for 1980 leads us to the following conclusions:

- There were 2.4 million ghetto poor in the United States, about 9 percent of all poor persons, living predominantly in the central cities of large metropolitan areas.
- About half the ghetto poor lived in the Northeast or North Central regions, and another 40 percent lived in the South.
- The level of ghetto poverty varied greatly from city to city.

The impression that ghetto poverty is growing rapidly turns out to be only partly true. Our reading of the data on the growth of ghetto poverty over the period 1970 to 1980 indicates the following:

- Between 1970 and 1980 the number of ghetto poor increased by 29.5 percent, but the level of ghetto poverty (i.e., the percentage of the poor living in ghettos) increased only modestly among blacks and decreased among Hispanics.
- The aggregate numbers conceal substantial regional variation. Ghetto poverty increased dramatically in large northern cities and decreased equally dramatically in many southern cities, especially small- and medium-sized southern cities.
- Changes in the regional distribution of the ghetto poor were driven by changes in levels of ghetto poverty, which were very different

among regions and to some extent varied from city to city within regions.

- Within four cities that we studied in detail, there was a pattern of emptying out of downtown neighborhoods. Ghettos and mixed-income neighborhoods generally had substantial decreases in population.
- In cities in which ghetto poverty increased, many new census tracts became ghettos. The process was driven by a combination of increases in the poverty rate and differential out-migration of the poor and nonpoor.

There are large and growing ghetto poverty populations in perhaps a dozen large northern SMSAs. But the phenomenon of large and growing ghetto poverty populations characterizes only a *minority* of SMSAs. Previous work on this subject, including but not limited to our own (Bane and Jargowsky, 1988), usually was limited to the 50 or 100 largest metropolitan areas or central cities. The focus on large cities missed an important part of the picture. When we looked at the data for all SMSAs, we found that many had small increases in ghetto poverty and that in the South most SMSAs had substantial decreases.

The implications of these findings for public policy are not entirely clear. For one thing, SMSAs differ dramatically in the scope and nature of their urban poverty problems. Much more needs to be learned, both in the aggregate and at the level of individual SMSAs, before we can draw firm conclusions about the growth of poverty areas and their effects on their residents. However, our reading of the data would lead us to support the following guidelines for public policies concerning ghetto poverty:

- It probably makes sense to have policies that focus specifically on those SMSAs with large and growing problems, rather than a national policy based on an assumption that all cities are alike.
- The policies and programs for those SMSAs with large and growing problems should recognize the strong relationship between the general economic vitality of SMSAs and regions and the problems of particular neighborhoods and population groups.
- Policies that affect the geographic mobility of the poor and nonpoor may play an important role in ghetto formation. Thus, housing and development policies may have an important role to play in many cities.

We offer these as preliminary suggestions, drawn from the data we have examined. More detailed recommendations would need to be based on a better understanding of the causes of the changes and variations documented here. We are investigating the causes of these changes in our ongoing research, and we hope that the basic data presented here encourage others to do the same.

## ACKNOWLEDGMENTS

We would like to acknowledge the support of the Ford and Russell Sage Foundations. We received helpful comments on this paper from David Ellwood, Naomi Goldstein, and Julie Wilson.

## REFERENCES

Adams, Terry, Greg Duncan, and Willard Rodgers
    1988    The persistence of poverty. Pp. 78-79 in *Quiet Riots: Race and Poverty in the United States*, Fred R. Harris and Roger Wilkins, eds. New York: Pantheon Books.
Anderson, Elijah
    1989    Sex codes and family life among inner-city youth. *Annals of the American Academy of Political and Social Science* 501 (January):59-78.
Auletta, Ken
    1982    *The Underclass.* New York: Random House.
Bane, Mary Jo, and Paul A. Jargowsky
    1988    Urban Poverty Areas: Basic Questions Concerning Prevalence, Growth and Dynamics. Center for Health and Human Resources Policy Discussion Paper Series, John F. Kennedy School of Government, Harvard University.
Bean, Frank D., and Marta Tienda
    1987    *The Hispanic Population of the United States.* New York: Russell Sage Foundation.
Bureau of the Census
    1970    *1970 Census User's Guide.* Washington, D.C.: U.S. Government Printing Office.
    1973a   *1970 Census of Population. Detailed Characteristics. United States Summary.* PC(1)-D1. Washington, D.C.: U.S. Government Printing Office.
    1973b   *1970 Census of Population, Subject Reports, Low-Income Areas in Large Cities.* PC(2)-9B. Washington, D.C.: U.S. Government Printing Office.
    1982a   *Census of Population and Housing, 1980: Summary Tape File 3 Technical Documentation.* Washington, D.C.: Bureau of the Census.
    1982b   *User's Guide.* PHC80-R1. Washington, D.C.: U.S. Government Printing Office.
    1983a   *Census of Population, 1980.* Vol. 1, Ch. C: General Social and Economic Characteristics. Part 1: U.S. Summary. PC80-1-C1. Washington, D.C.: U.S. Government Printing Office.
    1983b   *Census of Population and Housing, 1980: Geographic Identification Code Scheme.* PHC80-R5. Washington, D.C.: U.S. Government Printing Office.
    1983c   *Census of Population and Housing, 1980: Census Tracts.* PHC80-2. Washington, D.C.: U.S. Government Printing Office.
    1983d   *Census of Population and Housing, 1980: Summary Tape File 4 Technical Documentation.* Washington, D.C.: Bureau of the Census.
    1985    *Census of Population and Housing, 1980.* Vol. 2: Subject Reports. Poverty Areas in Large Cities. PC80-2-8D. Washington, D.C.: U.S. Government Printing Office.

1989    *Statistical Abstract of the United States*, 109th ed. Washington, D.C.: U.S. Government Printing Office.

Coulton, Claudia J., Julian Chow, and Shanta Pandey
1990    *An Analysis of Poverty and Related Conditions in Cleveland Area Neighborhoods.* Center for Urban Poverty and Social Change. Cleveland, Ohio: Case Western Reserve University.

Danziger, Sheldon H., and Daniel H. Weinberg, eds.
1986    *Fighting Poverty: What Works and What Doesn't.* Cambridge, Mass.: Harvard University Press.

Dembo, Richard
1988    Delinquency among black male youth. In *Young, Black, and Male in America: An Endangered Species*, Jewelle Taylor Gibbs, ed. Dover, Mass.: Auburn House.

Dornbusch, Stanford M., J. Merrill Carlsmith, Steven J. Bushwall, Philip L. Ritter, Herbert Leiderman, Albert H. Hastorf, and Ruth T. Gross
1985    Single parents, extended households, and the control of adolescents. *Child Development* 56:326-341.

Ellwood, David T.
1986    The spatial mismatch hypothesis: Are there jobs missing in the ghetto? Pp. 147-190 in Richard B. Freeman and Harry J. Holzer, eds., *The Black Youth Employment Crisis.* Chicago: University of Chicago Press.

Farley, Reynolds
1984    *Blacks and Whites: Narrowing the Gap?* Cambridge, Mass.: Harvard University Press.
1989    Trends in the Residential Segregation of Social and Economic Groups Among Blacks: 1970 to 1980. Unpublished paper prepared for Conference on the Truly Disadvantaged, October 19-21, 1989, Evanston, Ill.

Flexner, Stuart, ed.
1987    *The Random House Dictionary of the English Language.* 2nd ed. New York: Random House.

Garfinkel, Irwin, and Sara S. McLanahan
1986    *Single Mothers and Their Children.* Washington, D.C.: The Urban Institute Press.

Gibbs, Jewelle Taylor, ed.
1988    *Young, Black, and Male in America: An Endangered Species.* Dover, Mass.: Auburn House.

Hughes, Mark Alan
1989    Misspeaking truth to power: A geographical perspective on the "underclass" fallacy. *Economic Geography* 65(3):187-207.

Jencks, Christopher
1989    What is the underclass—and is it growing? *Focus* 12(1):14-26.

Kasarda, John D.
1988    Jobs, migration, and emerging urban mismatches. Pp. 148-198 in Michael G. H. McGeary and Laurence E. Lynn, Jr., eds., *Urban Change and Poverty.* Washington, D.C.: National Academy Press.

Lehmann, Nicholas
1986    The origins of the underclass. *Atlantic Monthly* June:31-55 (part 1) and July:54-68 (part 2).

Mare, Robert D., and Christopher Winship
   1984    The paradox of lessening racial inequality and joblessness among black youth: Enrollment, enlistment, and employment, 1964-1981. *American Sociological Review* 49:39-55.
Massey, Douglas S., and Nancy A. Denton
   1987    Trends in the residential segregation of blacks, Hispanics, and Asians: 1970-1980. *American Sociological Review* 52:802-825.
   1988a   The dimensions of racial segregation. *Social Forces* 67(2):281-315.
   1988b   Suburbanization and segregation in U.S. metropolitan areas. *American Journal of Sociology* 94(3):592-626.
   1989    Hypersegregation in U.S. metropolitan areas: Black and Hispanic segregation along five dimensions. *Demography* 26(3):373-391.
Massey, Douglas S., and Mitchell L. Eggers
   1990    The ecology of inequality: Minorities and the concentration of poverty, 1970-1980. *American Journal of Sociology* 95(5):1153-1188.
Massey, Douglas S., Mitchell L. Eggers, and Nancy A. Denton
   1989    Disentangling the Causes of Concentrated Poverty. Unpublished paper, Population Research Center, University of Chicago.
McGeary, Michael G. H., and Laurence E. Lynn, Jr., eds.
   1988    *Urban Change and Poverty*. Washington, D.C.: National Academy Press.
Moynihan, Daniel P.
   1965    *The Negro Family: The Case for National Action*. Washington, D.C.: Office for Family Planning and Research, U.S. Department of Labor.
Nathan, Richard
   1986    The Underclass—Will It Always Be with Us? Paper presented at the New School for Social Research, New York City.
Nathan, Richard, and John Lago
   1986    The Changing Size and Concentration of the Poverty Population of Large Cities, 1970-1980. Unpublished memorandum, Princeton University, Princeton, N.J.
O'Regan, Katherine, and Michael Wiseman
   1990    Birth weights and the geography of poverty. *Focus* 12(2):16-22.
Ricketts, Erol R., and Ronald Mincy
   In press The Growth of the Underclass, 1970-1980. *Journal of Human Resources*.
Ricketts, Erol R., and Isabel V. Sawhill
   1988    Defining and measuring the underclass. *Journal of Policy Analysis and Management* 7(2):316-325.
Van Haitsma, Martha
   1989    A contextual definition of the underclass. *Focus* 12(1):27-31.
Wilson, William Julius
   1987    *The Truly Disadvantaged: The Inner City, The Underclass, and Public Policy*. Chicago: University of Chicago Press.
   1988    The American Underclass: Inner City Ghettos and the Norms of Citizenship. The Godkin Lecture, delivered at the John F. Kennedy School of Government, April 26, Harvard University, Cambridge, Mass.
Wilson, William Julius, and Kathryn M. Neckerman
   1986    Poverty and family structure: The widening gap between evidence and public policy issues. Pp. 232-259 in *Fighting Poverty: What Works and What Doesn't*, Sheldon H. Danziger and Daniel H. Weinberg, eds. Cambridge, Mass.: Harvard University Press.

APPENDIX A

## Issues Related to the Processing of Census Tract Tapes

### PRIMARY AND COMPLEMENTARY SUPPRESSION

In order to protect confidentiality, the Census Bureau suppresses some data at the census-tract level (Bureau of the Census, 1983d). If a census tract has fewer than 30 persons, data on persons other than the raw count are suppressed. Similarly, if a tract has fewer than 10 households, data on households other than the count and all data on families are suppressed. The criteria on persons and households are applied independently. Suppression of this type is known as primary suppression. On Summary Tape File 4A, our primary data source for 1980, each census tract may have up to seven separate records, including a total record, a black record, a white record, a Hispanic record, and so on. Primary suppression criteria are applied independently to each record.

A second and more worrisome type of suppression is known as complementary suppression. This refers to the practice of suppressing records for a racial group with more than 30 persons or 10 households. This is done whenever a race-specific record or records could be subtracted from the total record to obtain data on a remaining group of fewer than 30 persons or 10 households. For example, imagine a census tract with 1,000 total persons, 980 whites and 20 blacks. The black data are suppressed (primary suppression) and the white data are also suppressed (complementary suppression). It can also be more complicated. Imagine a census tract with 1,000 total persons, 500 whites, 480 blacks, and 20 Asians. The Asian data are suppressed (primary) and the black data are suppressed (complementary). The white data are not suppressed because complementary suppression is always applied to the smallest possible racial group. As with primary suppression, person-level suppression and household-level complementary suppression are done independently.

The effect of primary suppression is minimal and can easily be ignored. However, complementary suppression is a problem because very large numbers of people (or households) can be affected. Moreover, tracts affected are not selected randomly but occur more frequently in integrated neighborhoods. This could create systematic biases in the data.

We have corrected for complementary suppression in the following way. When the largest racial group was suppressed, the data for all races were substituted if the suppressed group was at least 90 percent of the total. This is the easier case. When the second largest group is suppressed, data for the largest group are subtracted from data for all races, again only if the suppressed group was at least 90 percent of the group derived by subtraction. (The second method works only for counts, not medians.)

After either correction has been applied, the data for a given racial group may contain some data for persons of other races, but no more than 10 percent. In our judgment, this is preferable to systematically missing the other 90 percent. How much difference does this make? Suppose that we wanted to calculate the percentage of children in female-headed families. Suppose that the true rate for blacks is 50 percent, but after fixing complementary suppression the data include 10 percent whites with a 20 percent rate. We would then calculate a 47 percent rate for blacks in the census tract; not correcting for suppression would result in no data for blacks for the tract.

Primary suppression was also used in 1970, but not complementary suppression (Bureau of the Census, 1970). For further information, contact the authors.

## CHANGES IN SMSA BOUNDARIES, 1970–1980

SMSAs are areas defined by the Census Bureau to reflect "a large population nucleus and nearby communities which have a high degree of economic and social integration with that nucleus" (Bureau of the Census, 1982b:Glossary, p. 45). After each decennial census (and at other times based on projections), adjustments are made to the boundaries of SMSAs. The most common adjustment is to add a peripheral county as the SMSA expands. However, more major adjustments are also made. For example, between 1970 and 1980, the Dallas and Ft. Worth, Texas, SMSAs were merged; Nassau and Suffolk counties in New York State were removed from the New York City SMSA and became an entirely new SMSA.

The changes in boundaries must be taken into account when comparing 1970 and 1980 SMSA data. For this chapter we have handled SMSA changes in the following way:

- *Additions of peripheral counties.* Almost half of the SMSAs defined in 1970 had counties added to them between 1970 and 1980 (Bureau of the Census, 1983b:11–17). Many of these counties were sparsely populated in 1970 and suburbanized over the decade. Therefore, we did not make any adjustments. In such cases, the geographic areas being compared are not the same, but the comparison is conceptually consistent. In some cases, however, ignoring these additions may mean that the 1970 and 1980 data are not strictly comparable.
- *Merger of two 1970 SMSAs into one 1980 SMSA.* There are four such cases: Durham and Raleigh, North Carolina; Ft. Worth and Dallas, Texas; Ogden and Salt Lake City, Utah; and Scranton and

Wilkes-Barre, Pennsylvania (Bureau of the Census, 1983b:11-17).
In these cases, we merged the 1970 data to conform to the 1980
boundaries.

- *Transfers of territory between SMSAs.* There are five such cases that
  we have been able to identify.* In each case we adjusted the 1970
  data to conform to the 1980 boundaries, as follows:

  1. Nassau and Suffolk counties, New York, were removed from
     the New York SMSA and became a new SMSA.
  2. Bergen County, New Jersey, was shifted from the Paterson-
     Clifton-Passaic SMSA to the New York SMSA.
  3. Bellingham, Franklin, and Wrentham, Massachusetts, were
     shifted from the Providence-Pawtucket-Warwick, Rhode Island-
     Massachusetts SMSA to the Boston SMSA.
  4. Abington, Hanson, and Stoughton, Massachusetts, were shifted
     from the Brockton SMSA to the Boston SMSA.
  5. LaPeer County, Michigan, was shifted from the Flint SMSA
     to the Detroit SMSA.

- *Creation of new SMSAs.* Sixty-nine completely new SMSAs were
  defined between 1970 and 1980. We included these SMSAs in the
  1980 data. These SMSAs were typically small and had few ghetto
  poor. Thus, the effect on the comparison of the 1970 and 1980
  data is small and is noted in footnotes in the appropriate places.

## BASIC DATA ON GHETTO POVERTY, 1970–1980

As a result of these changes and corrections, we have data on 239 SMSAs
in 1970 and 318 SMSAs in 1980. The table that follows includes data on
the 239 SMSAs that were defined in both 1970 and 1980, ordered by region
and size of metropolitan area in 1980. Within groups, the SMSAs are listed
alphabetically.

---

*We would like to thank James Fitzsimmons of the Population Division, Bureau of the Census,
for helping us to identify these changes.

# GHETTO POVERTY, 1970 AND 1980

| STANDARD METROPOLITAN STATISTICAL AREA — By Region and Metro Area Size, 1980 | NUMBER OF GHETTO TRACTS 1970 | 1980 | NUMBER OF GHETTO POOR — TOTAL 1970 | 1980 | BLACK 1970 | 1980 | HISPANIC 1970 | 1980 | LEVEL OF GHETTO POVERTY — BLACK 1970 | 1980 | HISPANIC 1970 | 1980 |
|---|---|---|---|---|---|---|---|---|---|---|---|---|
| **NORTHEAST** | | | | | | | | | | | | |
| **MORE THAN 1 MILLION** | | | | | | | | | | | | |
| BOSTON, MASS. | 10 | 12 | 14087 | 9046 | 6329 | 3889 | 1964 | 2315 | 19.6% | 9.8% | 26.1% | 10.6% |
| BUFFALO, N.Y. | 3 | 15 | 1501 | 14790 | 999 | 11674 | 128 | 1262 | 3.4% | 30.6% | ** | ** |
| NASSAU–SUFFOLK, N.Y. | 0 | 2 | 0 | 51 | 0 | 0 | 0 | 0 | 0.0% | 0.0% | 0.0% | 0.0% |
| NEW YORK, N.Y.–N.J. | 74 | 314 | 134139 | 477621 | 60444 | 234920 | 62838 | 221173 | 14.5% | 43.3% | 22.1% | 43.4% |
| NEWARK, N.J. | 9 | 39 | 14997 | 54720 | 14199 | 41672 | 472 | 11725 | 18.2% | 37.8% | 4.4% | 33.3% |
| PHILADELPHIA, PA.–N.J. | 28 | 69 | 49657 | 127134 | 43517 | 92867 | 1910 | 23807 | 21.3% | 36.9% | 13.9% | 54.8% |
| PITTSBURGH, PA. | 14 | 19 | 14307 | 17237 | 11812 | 14460 | 0 | 139 | 23.7% | 30.8% | ** | ** |
| **500,000 TO 1 MILLION** | | | | | | | | | | | | |
| ALBANY–SCHENECTADY–TROY, N.Y. | 0 | 3 | 0 | 1102 | 0 | 343 | 0 | 14 | 0.0% | 4.6% | ** | ** |
| ALLENTOWN–BETHLEHEM–EASTON, PA.–N. | 0 | 0 | 0 | 0 | 0 | 0 | 0 | 0 | * | * | ** | ** |
| HARTFORD, CONN. | 4 | 12 | 6620 | 13868 | 4139 | 5746 | 1504 | 7202 | 35.7% | 43.6% | 29.3% | 51.9% |
| JERSEY CITY, N.J. | 0 | 3 | 0 | 4065 | 0 | 2723 | 0 | 1194 | 0.0% | 12.6% | 0.0% | 3.1% |
| NORTHEAST PENNSYLVANIA | 2 | 0 | 969 | 0 | 132 | 0 | 0 | 0 | * | * | ** | ** |
| PROVIDENCE–WARWICK–PAWTUCKET, R.I.– | 1 | 3 | 80 | 3094 | 0 | 1582 | 0 | 465 | 0.0% | 21.9% | ** | ** |
| ROCHESTER, N.Y. | 4 | 8 | 863 | 4339 | 0 | 2942 | 0 | 551 | 0.0% | 14.1% | ** | ** |
| SPRINGFIELD–CHICOPEE–HOLYOKE, MASS. | 1 | 6 | 60 | 9792 | 0 | 756 | 0 | 6842 | 0.0% | 10.5% | 0.0% | 55.0% |
| SYRACUSE, N.Y. | 2 | 7 | 2300 | 7822 | 234 | 3543 | 0 | 248 | 3.7% | 40.0% | ** | ** |
| **LESS THAN 500,000** | | | | | | | | | | | | |
| ALTOONA, PA. | 0 | 0 | 0 | 0 | 0 | 0 | 0 | 0 | * | * | ** | ** |
| ATLANTIC CITY, N.J. | 1 | 4 | 557 | 2653 | 93 | 638 | 89 | 881 | 1.2% | 7.5% | ** | ** |
| BINGHAMTON, N.Y.–PA. | 0 | 0 | 0 | 0 | 0 | 0 | 0 | 0 | * | * | ** | ** |
| BRIDGEPORT, CONN. | 1 | 7 | 2005 | 9784 | 1215 | 4247 | 675 | 4960 | 21.7% | 39.1% | 23.2% | 47.3% |
| BRISTOL, CONN. | 0 | 0 | 0 | 0 | 0 | 0 | 0 | 0 | * | * | ** | ** |
| BROCKTON, MASS. | 1 | 0 | 232 | 0 | 31 | 0 | 0 | 0 | * | * | ** | ** |
| DANBURY, CONN. | 0 | 0 | 0 | 0 | 0 | 0 | 0 | 0 | * | * | ** | ** |
| ERIE, PA. | 0 | 3 | 0 | 1889 | 0 | 864 | 0 | 49 | * | * | ** | ** |
| FALL RIVER, MASS.–R.I. | 0 | 0 | 0 | 0 | 0 | 0 | 0 | 0 | * | * | ** | ** |

| STANDARD METROPOLITAN STATISTICAL AREA By Region and Metro Area Size, 1980 | NUMBER OF GHETTO TRACTS | | NUMBER OF GHETTO POOR | | | | | | LEVEL OF GHETTO POVERTY | | | |
|---|---|---|---|---|---|---|---|---|---|---|---|---|
| | | | TOTAL | | BLACK | | HISPANIC | | BLACK | | HISPANIC | |
| | 1970 | 1980 | 1970 | 1980 | 1970 | 1980 | 1970 | 1980 | 1970 | 1980 | 1970 | 1980 |
| NORTHEAST (CONTINUED) | | | | | | | | | | | | |
| LESS THAN 500,000 (CONTINUED) | | | | | | | | | | | | |
| FITCHBURG–LEOMINSTER, MASS. | 1 | 0 | 48 | 0 | 0 | 0 | 0 | 0 | * | * | ** | ** |
| HARRISBURG, PA. | 0 | 2 | 0 | 2856 | 0 | 2110 | 0 | 233 | 0.0% | 26.5% | ** | ** |
| JOHNSTOWN, PA. | 0 | 0 | 0 | 0 | 0 | 0 | 0 | 0 | * | * | ** | ** |
| LANCASTER, PA. | 0 | 1 | 0 | 1428 | 0 | 707 | 0 | 664 | * | * | ** | ** |
| LAWRENCE–HAVERHILL, MASS.–N.H. | 0 | 1 | 0 | 1338 | 0 | 0 | 0 | 884 | * | * | ** | ** |
| LEWISTON–AUBURN, MAINE | 0 | 0 | 0 | 0 | 0 | 0 | 0 | 0 | * | * | ** | ** |
| LOWELL, MASS.–N.H. | 0 | 1 | 0 | 490 | 0 | 0 | 0 | 235 | * | * | ** | ** |
| MANCHESTER, N.H. | 1 | 0 | 356 | 0 | 0 | 0 | 0 | 0 | * | * | ** | ** |
| MERIDEN, CONN. | 0 | 1 | 0 | 113 | 0 | 0 | 0 | 96 | * | * | ** | ** |
| NASHUA, N.H. | 0 | 0 | 0 | 0 | 0 | 0 | 0 | 0 | * | * | ** | ** |
| NEW BEDFORD, MASS. | 0 | 0 | 0 | 0 | 0 | 0 | 0 | 0 | * | * | ** | ** |
| NEW BRITAIN, CONN. | 0 | 1 | 0 | 562 | 0 | 72 | 0 | 204 | * | * | ** | ** |
| NEW HAVEN–WEST HAVEN, CONN. | 0 | 3 | 0 | 3158 | 0 | 2076 | 0 | 662 | 0.0% | 15.2% | ** | ** |
| NEW LONDON–NORWICH, CONN.–R.I. | 2 | 1 | 180 | 262 | 0 | 27 | 0 | 0 | * | * | ** | ** |
| NORWALK, CONN. | 0 | 0 | 0 | 0 | 0 | 0 | 0 | 0 | * | * | ** | ** |
| PATERSON–CLIFTON–PASSAIC, N.J. | 1 | 11 | 978 | 12917 | 940 | 7105 | 0 | 5107 | 7.8% | 37.1% | 0.0% | 26.5% |
| PITTSFIELD, MASS. | 0 | 0 | 0 | 0 | 0 | 0 | 0 | 0 | * | * | ** | ** |
| PORTLAND, MAINE | 1 | 0 | 146 | 0 | 0 | 0 | 0 | 0 | * | * | ** | ** |
| READING, PA. | 0 | 2 | 0 | 1755 | 0 | 331 | 0 | 1039 | * | * | ** | ** |
| STAMFORD, CONN. | 0 | 0 | 0 | 0 | 0 | 0 | 0 | 0 | 0.0% | 0.0% | ** | ** |
| TRENTON, N.J. | 0 | 1 | 0 | 1327 | 0 | 770 | 0 | 380 | 0.0% | 5.8% | ** | ** |
| UTICA–ROME, N.Y. | 1 | 2 | 660 | 1049 | 573 | 682 | 0 | 0 | 0.7% | 0.0% | ** | ** |
| VINELAND–MILLVILLE–BRIDGETON, N.J. | 1 | 0 | 306 | 0 | 28 | 0 | 152 | 0 | 0.0% | 0.9% | ** | ** |
| WATERBURY, CONN. | 0 | 1 | 0 | 1376 | 0 | 35 | 0 | 1121 | * | * | ** | ** |
| WORCESTER, MASS. | 0 | 1 | 0 | 2535 | 0 | 414 | 0 | 1629 | * | * | ** | ** |
| YORK, PA. | 1 | 0 | 858 | 0 | 649 | 0 | 5 | 0 | * | * | ** | ** |

| STANDARD METROPOLITAN STATISTICAL AREA | NUMBER OF GHETTO TRACTS | | NUMBER OF GHETTO POOR | | | | | | LEVEL OF GHETTO POVERTY | | | |
|---|---|---|---|---|---|---|---|---|---|---|---|---|
| | | | TOTAL | | BLACK | | HISPANIC | | BLACK | | HISPANIC | |
| By Region and Metro Area Size, 1980 | 1970 | 1980 | 1970 | 1980 | 1970 | 1980 | 1970 | 1980 | 1970 | 1980 | 1970 | 1980 |
| **NORTH CENTRAL** | | | | | | | | | | | | |
| **MORE THAN 1 MILLION** | | | | | | | | | | | | |
| CHICAGO, ILL. | 48 | 136 | 74370 | 194338 | 69955 | 173264 | 1377 | 12536 | 23.8% | 42.4% | 2.9% | 10.7% |
| CLEVELAND, OHIO | 20 | 42 | 30312 | 36792 | 26961 | 33275 | 551 | 416 | 32.8% | 36.6% | 15.0% | 7.1% |
| COLUMBUS, OHIO | 6 | 22 | 4980 | 22724 | 2118 | 8766 | 46 | 234 | 8.2% | 26.2% | ** | ** |
| DETROIT, MICH. | 24 | 51 | 24303 | 54572 | 18430 | 46424 | 113 | 842 | 11.5% | 20.6% | 2.5% | 8.4% |
| INDIANAPOLIS, IND. | 4 | 5 | 4885 | 6483 | 3899 | 5107 | 139 | 79 | 12.8% | 14.2% | ** | ** |
| KANSAS CITY, MO.–KANS. | 9 | 12 | 7223 | 8061 | 5764 | 6335 | 40 | 395 | 14.5% | 15.2% | 1.5% | 10.0% |
| MILWAUKEE, WIS. | 11 | 19 | 6724 | 12996 | 4405 | 10361 | 24 | 408 | 15.5% | 24.0% | 1.0% | 6.6% |
| MINNEAPOLIS–ST. PAUL, MINN.–WIS. | 7 | 11 | 5634 | 8896 | 1547 | 2651 | 95 | 337 | 21.2% | 22.1% | 6.4% | 10.5% |
| ST. LOUIS, MO.–ILL. | 18 | 26 | 41373 | 41472 | 37916 | 38982 | 42 | 424 | 32.3% | 32.9% | 3.7% | 15.0% |
| **500,000 TO 1 MILLION** | | | | | | | | | | | | |
| AKRON, OHIO | 3 | 6 | 2257 | 3464 | 1548 | 2106 | 0 | 0 | 11.3% | 13.4% | ** | ** |
| DAYTON, OHIO | 4 | 13 | 2506 | 13361 | 836 | 10038 | 0 | 64 | 4.5% | 38.3% | ** | ** |
| FLINT, MICH. | 0 | 2 | 0 | 1536 | 0 | 1349 | 0 | 113 | 0.0% | 7.8% | ** | ** |
| GARY–HAMMOND–EAST CHICAGO, IND. | 1 | 6 | 736 | 5418 | 699 | 4861 | 0 | 139 | 2.9% | 16.4% | 0.0% | 2.3% |
| GRAND RAPIDS, MICH. | 0 | 3 | 0 | 2081 | 0 | 1389 | 0 | 134 | 0.0% | 16.5% | ** | ** |
| OMAHA, NEBR.–IOWA | 3 | 7 | 2207 | 4838 | 2071 | 3994 | 0 | 13 | 19.2% | 32.3% | ** | ** |
| TOLEDO, OHIO–MICH. | 4 | 12 | 3647 | 7791 | 3070 | 4912 | 0 | 215 | 20.3% | 25.1% | 0.0% | 5.6% |
| YOUNGSTOWN–WARREN, OHIO | 2 | 5 | 1311 | 3145 | 770 | 2697 | 6 | 63 | 6.1% | 17.4% | ** | ** |
| **LESS THAN 500,000** | | | | | | | | | | | | |
| ANDERSON, IND. | 0 | 0 | 0 | 0 | 0 | 0 | 0 | 0 | * | * | ** | ** |
| ANN ARBOR, MICH. | 2 | 4 | 4963 | 6217 | 188 | 799 | 13 | 131 | 6.4% | 15.5% | ** | ** |
| APPLETON–OSHKOSH, WIS. | 0 | 0 | 0 | 0 | 0 | 0 | 0 | 0 | * | * | ** | ** |
| BAY CITY, MICH. | 0 | 0 | 0 | 0 | 0 | 0 | 0 | 0 | * | * | ** | ** |
| BLOOMINGTON–NORMAL, ILL. | 0 | 1 | 0 | 291 | 0 | 16 | 0 | 0 | * | * | ** | ** |
| CANTON, OHIO | 0 | 2 | 0 | 1454 | 0 | 981 | 0 | 0 | 0.0% | 15.4% | ** | ** |
| CEDAR RAPIDS, IOWA | 0 | 0 | 0 | 0 | 0 | 0 | 0 | 0 | * | * | ** | ** |
| CHAMPAIGN–URBANA–RANTOUL, ILL. | 3 | 4 | 3065 | 5435 | 251 | 394 | 7 | 94 | 8.4% | 11.2% | ** | ** |
| COLUMBIA, MO. | 2 | 3 | 1202 | 2321 | 139 | 206 | 19 | 8 | * | * | ** | ** |
| DAVENPORT–ROCK ISLAND–MOLINE, IOWA– | 0 | 1 | 0 | 222 | 0 | 16 | 0 | 0 | 0.0% | 0.3% | ** | ** |
| DECATUR, ILL. | 1 | 1 | 1695 | 1784 | 1019 | 1390 | 126 | 0 | * | * | ** | ** |

| STANDARD METROPOLITAN STATISTICAL AREA | NUMBER OF GHETTO TRACTS | | NUMBER OF GHETTO POOR | | | | | | LEVEL OF GHETTO POVERTY | | | |
|---|---|---|---|---|---|---|---|---|---|---|---|---|
| | | | TOTAL | | BLACK | | HISPANIC | | BLACK | | HISPANIC | |
| By Region and Metro Area Size, 1980 | 1970 | 1980 | 1970 | 1980 | 1970 | 1980 | 1970 | 1980 | 1970 | 1980 | 1970 | 1980 |
| **NORTH CENTRAL (CONTINUED)** | | | | | | | | | | | | |
| **LESS THAN 500,000 (CONTINUED)** | | | | | | | | | | | | |
| DES MOINES, IOWA | 2 | 1 | 295 | 269 | 52 | 93 | 0 | 0 | 1.8% | 3.1% | .. | .. |
| DUBUQUE, IOWA | 1 | 0 | 203 | 0 | 0 | 0 | 0 | 0 | * | * | .. | .. |
| DULUTH-SUPERIOR, MINN.-WIS. | 1 | 1 | 660 | 23 | 0 | 0 | 0 | 0 | * | . | .. | .. |
| FARGO-MOORHEAD, N. DAK.-MINN. | 0 | 0 | 0 | 0 | 0 | 0 | 0 | 0 | * | * | .. | .. |
| FORT WAYNE, IND. | 0 | 1 | 0 | 1684 | 0 | 1617 | 0 | 0 | 0.0% | 25.9% | .. | .. |
| GREEN BAY, WIS. | 0 | 0 | 0 | 0 | 0 | 0 | 0 | 0 | * | . | .. | .. |
| HAMILTON-MIDDLETOWN, OHIO | 0 | 3 | 0 | 4420 | 0 | 1374 | 0 | 21 | 0.0% | 41.0% | .. | .. |
| JACKSON, MICH. | 1 | 0 | 23 | 0 | 0 | 0 | 0 | 0 | * | . | .. | .. |
| KALAMAZOO-PORTAGE, MICH. | 1 | 5 | 727 | 3173 | 33 | 907 | 0 | 106 | * | . | .. | .. |
| KENOSHA, WIS. | 0 | 0 | 0 | 0 | 0 | 0 | 0 | 0 | * | . | .. | .. |
| LA CROSSE, WIS. | 0 | 0 | 0 | 0 | 0 | 0 | 0 | 0 | * | . | .. | .. |
| LAFAYETTE-WEST LAFAYETTE, IND. | 1 | 2 | 173 | 2171 | 7 | 18 | 0 | 36 | * | . | .. | .. |
| LANSING-EAST LANSING, MICH. | 2 | 3 | 364 | 4207 | 9 | 147 | 6 | 37 | 0.3% | 3.3% | .. | .. |
| LIMA, OHIO | 0 | 2 | 0 | 1960 | 0 | 1386 | 0 | 17 | * | . | .. | .. |
| LINCOLN, NEBR. | 1 | 2 | 140 | 808 | 0 | 144 | 20 | 41 | * | . | .. | .. |
| LORAIN-ELYRIA, OHIO | 1 | 0 | 504 | 0 | 208 | 0 | 76 | 0 | 6.0% | 0.0% | 5.7% | 0.0% |
| MADISON, WIS. | 3 | 3 | 4969 | 6392 | 72 | 225 | 24 | 93 | * | . | .. | .. |
| MANSFIELD, OHIO | 0 | 2 | 0 | 551 | 0 | 28 | 0 | 0 | * | . | .. | .. |
| MUNCIE, IND. | 0 | 0 | 0 | 0 | 0 | 0 | 0 | 0 | * | . | .. | .. |
| MUSKEGON-NORTON SHORES-MUSKEGON | 0 | 0 | 0 | 0 | 0 | 0 | 0 | 0 | 0.0% | 0.0% | .. | .. |
| PEORIA, ILL. | 0 | 4 | 0 | 4107 | 0 | 2797 | 0 | 86 | 0.0% | 43.6% | .. | .. |
| RACINE, WIS. | 0 | 0 | 0 | 0 | 0 | 0 | 0 | 0 | 0.0% | 0.0% | .. | .. |
| ROCHESTER, MINN. | 2 | 1 | 396 | 21 | 0 | 0 | 0 | 0 | * | . | .. | .. |
| ROCKFORD, ILL. | 0 | 1 | 0 | 1856 | 0 | 1338 | 0 | 60 | 0.0% | 26.1% | .. | .. |
| SAGINAW, MICH. | 1 | 3 | 1545 | 3785 | 1497 | 2960 | 6 | 560 | 21.5% | 28.7% | .. | .. |
| ST. JOSEPH, MO. | 1 | 0 | 501 | 0 | 91 | 0 | 18 | 0 | * | . | .. | .. |
| SIOUX CITY, IOWA-NEBR. | 0 | 1 | 0 | 723 | 0 | 88 | 0 | 0 | * | . | .. | .. |
| SIOUX FALLS, S. DAK. | 0 | 0 | 0 | 0 | 0 | 0 | 0 | 0 | * | . | .. | .. |
| SOUTH BEND, IND. | 2 | 2 | 2818 | 1843 | 914 | 1662 | 148 | 0 | 19.0% | 28.6% | .. | .. |
| SPRINGFIELD, ILL. | 1 | 0 | 979 | 0 | 778 | 0 | 0 | 0 | * | . | .. | .. |

| STANDARD METROPOLITAN STATISTICAL AREA | NUMBER OF GHETTO TRACTS | | NUMBER OF GHETTO POOR | | | | | | LEVEL OF GHETTO POVERTY | | | |
|---|---|---|---|---|---|---|---|---|---|---|---|---|
| | | | TOTAL | | BLACK | | HISPANIC | | BLACK | | HISPANIC | |
| By Region and Metro Area Size, 1980 | 1970 | 1980 | 1970 | 1980 | 1970 | 1980 | 1970 | 1980 | 1970 | 1980 | 1970 | 1980 |
| **NORTH CENTRAL (CONTINUED)** | | | | | | | | | | | | |
| **LESS THAN 500,000 (CONTINUED)** | | | | | | | | | | | | |
| SPRINGFIELD, MO. | 1 | 1 | 702 | 602 | 0 | 0 | 0 | 0 | * | * | ** | ** |
| SPRINGFIELD, OHIO | 0 | 1 | 0 | 1287 | 0 | 242 | 0 | 0 | 0.0% | 7.0% | ** | ** |
| TERRE HAUTE, IND. | 2 | 0 | 431 | 0 | 28 | 0 | 0 | 0 | * | * | ** | ** |
| TOPEKA, KANS. | 0 | 0 | 0 | 0 | 0 | 0 | 0 | 0 | 0.0% | 0.0% | ** | ** |
| WATERLOO-CEDAR FALLS, IOWA | 0 | 0 | 0 | 0 | 0 | 0 | 0 | 0 | * | * | ** | ** |
| WICHITA, KANS. | 1 | 1 | 1609 | 809 | 1601 | 775 | 0 | 25 | 18.4% | 9.0% | ** | ** |
| **SMSAS THAT OVERLAP MORE THAN ONE REGION — ALL SIZES** | | | | | | | | | | | | |
| CINCINNATI, OHIO-KY.-IND. | 17 | 23 | 26939 | 29491 | 18853 | 23748 | 97 | 299 | 42.9% | 49.5% | ** | ** |
| EVANSVILLE, IND.-KY. | 1 | 1 | 322 | 779 | 17 | 732 | 0 | 0 | 0.4% | 15.4% | ** | ** |
| HUNTINGTON-ASHLAND, W. VA.-KY.-OHIO | 6 | 1 | 6279 | 1610 | 82 | 0 | 0 | 0 | * | * | ** | ** |
| LOUISVILLE, KY.-IND. | 15 | 17 | 17713 | 18738 | 12718 | 13844 | 42 | 50 | 40.2% | 40.5% | ** | ** |
| STEUBENVILLE-WEIRTON, OHIO-W. VA. | 0 | 2 | 0 | 1365 | 0 | 809 | 0 | 0 | * | * | ** | ** |
| WHEELING, W. VA.-OHIO | 0 | 0 | 0 | 0 | 0 | 0 | 0 | 0 | * | * | ** | ** |
| WILMINGTON, DEL.-N.J.-MD. | 4 | 3 | 5204 | 6927 | 4768 | 6261 | 86 | 315 | 28.1% | 32.4% | ** | ** |
| **SOUTH** | | | | | | | | | | | | |
| **MORE THAN 1 MILLION** | | | | | | | | | | | | |
| ATLANTA, GA. | 19 | 36 | 30915 | 48178 | 27491 | 44545 | 0 | 534 | 31.3% | 32.6% | 0.0% | 14.3% |
| BALTIMORE, MD. | 24 | 37 | 45732 | 60983 | 42629 | 55365 | 166 | 637 | 34.6% | 37.6% | 9.1% | 23.0% |
| DALLAS-FORT WORTH, TEX. | 20 | 24 | 33880 | 27190 | 30736 | 23928 | 1548 | 1336 | 30.5% | 23.8% | 6.7% | 2.9% |
| FORT LAUDERDALE-HOLLYWOOD, FLA. | 1 | 4 | 1060 | 9947 | 1012 | 9731 | 78 | 169 | 4.4% | 29.3% | 5.2% | 3.6% |
| HOUSTON, TEX. | 12 | 13 | 19585 | 21158 | 17528 | 16536 | 1716 | 3124 | 15.0% | 14.6% | 4.5% | 4.4% |
| MIAMI, FLA. | 7 | 14 | 18305 | 29262 | 16828 | 24094 | 917 | 3332 | 28.1% | 29.5% | 2.1% | 3.4% |
| NEW ORLEANS, LA. | 30 | 30 | 71932 | 56504 | 67792 | 54836 | 914 | 692 | 49.7% | 40.7% | 11.2% | 9.4% |
| SAN ANTONIO, TEX. | 19 | 18 | 54749 | 37050 | 5547 | 4483 | 47722 | 30893 | 27.7% | 24.7% | 43.2% | 23.8% |
| TAMPA-ST. PETERSBURG, FLA. | 16 | 15 | 22775 | 22448 | 18957 | 19655 | 1211 | 1184 | 45.3% | 40.7% | 15.8% | 10.3% |
| WASHINGTON, D.C.-MD.-VA. | 10 | 10 | 11581 | 12324 | 10787 | 12021 | 50 | 52 | 8.6% | 8.6% | 1.0% | 0.5% |

| STANDARD METROPOLITAN STATISTICAL AREA By Region and Metro Area Size, 1980 | NUMBER OF GHETTO TRACTS | | NUMBER OF GHETTO POOR | | | | | | LEVEL OF GHETTO POVERTY | | | |
|---|---|---|---|---|---|---|---|---|---|---|---|---|
| | | | TOTAL | | BLACK | | HISPANIC | | BLACK | | HISPANIC | |
| | 1970 | 1980 | 1970 | 1980 | 1970 | 1980 | 1970 | 1980 | 1970 | 1980 | 1970 | 1980 |
| **SOUTH (CONTINUED)** | | | | | | | | | | | | |
| **500,000 TO 1 MILLION** | | | | | | | | | | | | |
| AUSTIN, TEX. | 2 | 9 | 5010 | 11011 | 91 | 4001 | 2057 | 1649 | 0.9% | 32.6% | 18.4% | 8.0% |
| BIRMINGHAM, ALA. | 18 | 16 | 27901 | 21518 | 22634 | 20265 | 0 | 391 | 26.8% | 27.5% | ** | ** |
| CHARLOTTE-GASTONIA, N.C. | 7 | 8 | 10120 | 10254 | 9463 | 9761 | 0 | 229 | 30.5% | 28.4% | ** | ** |
| GREENSBORO-WINSTON-SALEM-HIGH POI | 5 | 5 | 8161 | 3949 | 7603 | 3081 | 0 | 105 | 21.7% | 8.4% | ** | ** |
| GREENVILLE-SPARTANBURG, S.C. | 1 | 5 | 1744 | 4667 | 1543 | 4322 | 0 | 59 | 9.7% | 16.3% | ** | ** |
| JACKSONVILLE, FLA. | 7 | 12 | 16703 | 18395 | 14167 | 14249 | 80 | 403 | 30.4% | 26.5% | ** | ** |
| MEMPHIS, TENN.-ARK.-MISS. | 38 | 37 | 77589 | 56915 | 71092 | 53922 | 283 | 734 | 56.2% | 39.3% | ** | ** |
| NASHVILLE-DAVIDSON, TENN. | 5 | 11 | 10471 | 15115 | 8321 | 12228 | 0 | 233 | 27.4% | 34.9% | ** | ** |
| NORFOLK-VIRGINIA BEACH-PORTSMOUTH, | 21 | 17 | 29493 | 19252 | 28577 | 18153 | 112 | 198 | 49.1% | 27.8% | ** | ** |
| OKLAHOMA CITY, OKLA. | 11 | 10 | 8655 | 5423 | 6552 | 2957 | 150 | 202 | 36.7% | 16.5% | 10.1% | 7.4% |
| ORLANDO, FLA. | 5 | 5 | 8494 | 7538 | 7808 | 6988 | 93 | 52 | 28.4% | 23.6% | ** | ** |
| RALEIGH-DURHAM, N.C. | 8 | 3 | 8982 | 1645 | 8256 | 1638 | 0 | 83 | 22.7% | 5.6% | ** | ** |
| RICHMOND, VA. | 7 | 6 | 9226 | 8675 | 8739 | 8374 | 0 | 270 | 24.5% | 21.8% | ** | ** |
| TULSA, OKLA. | 6 | 1 | 7339 | 1301 | 6424 | 1027 | 0 | 0 | 40.3% | 7.8% | ** | ** |
| WEST PALM BEACH-BOCA RATON, FLA. | 4 | 4 | 7086 | 6278 | 6253 | 5595 | 502 | 568 | 27.0% | 23.5% | 22.5% | 12.2% |
| **LESS THAN 500,000** | | | | | | | | | | | | |
| ABILENE, TEX. | 0 | 0 | | 0 | | 0 | | 0 | * | * | 0.0% | 0.0% |
| ALBANY, GA. | 3 | 5 | 9079 | 8471 | 8069 | 7711 | 0 | 97 | 56.9% | 44.4% | ** | ** |
| AMARILLO, TEX. | 0 | 1 | 0 | 859 | 0 | 436 | 0 | 52 | * | * | ** | ** |
| ASHEVILLE, N.C. | 1 | 1 | 1446 | 864 | 1163 | 694 | 0 | 0 | 24.7% | 16.0% | ** | ** |
| AUGUSTA, GA.-S.C. | 6 | 5 | 12697 | 6745 | 11222 | 6188 | 0 | 87 | 40.6% | 22.8% | ** | ** |
| BATON ROUGE, LA. | 6 | 7 | 14273 | 9309 | 11198 | 7610 | 175 | 258 | 34.6% | 18.2% | ** | ** |
| BEAUMONT-PORT ARTHUR-ORANGE, TEX. | 4 | 5 | 3112 | 3589 | 3019 | 3140 | 22 | 173 | 11.9% | 12.9% | 1.2% | 9.5% |
| BILOXI-GULFPORT, MISS. | 2 | 1 | 3272 | 1477 | 2737 | 1390 | 0 | 0 | 26.2% | 11.9% | ** | ** |
| BROWNSVILLE-HARLINGEN-SAN BENITO, T | 24 | 16 | 53632 | 27530 | 301 | 20 | 50378 | 26421 | * | * | 86.7% | 43.3% |
| BRYAN-COLLEGE STATION, TEX. | 4 | 2 | 5689 | 3341 | 4097 | 117 | 863 | 277 | * | * | ** | ** |
| CHARLESTON-NORTH CHARLESTON, S.C. | 19 | 8 | 34676 | 12650 | 31618 | 12202 | 0 | 231 | 65.8% | 27.4% | ** | ** |
| CHARLESTON, W. VA. | 3 | 2 | 3760 | 926 | 1510 | 621 | 0 | 0 | 37.7% | 17.8% | ** | ** |
| CHATTANOOGA, TENN.-GA. | 7 | 6 | 11327 | 9378 | 9413 | 8913 | 0 | 160 | 49.9% | 49.0% | ** | ** |
| COLUMBIA, S.C. | 10 | 4 | 13690 | 4514 | 11887 | 4383 | 0 | 91 | 39.5% | 15.6% | ** | ** |

| STANDARD METROPOLITAN STATISTICAL AREA — By Region and Metro Area Size, 1980 | NUMBER OF GHETTO TRACTS | | NUMBER OF GHETTO POOR — TOTAL | | BLACK | | HISPANIC | | LEVEL OF GHETTO POVERTY — BLACK | | HISPANIC | |
|---|---|---|---|---|---|---|---|---|---|---|---|---|
| | 1970 | 1980 | 1970 | 1980 | 1970 | 1980 | 1970 | 1980 | 1970 | 1980 | 1970 | 1980 |
| **SOUTH (CONTINUED)** | | | | | | | | | | | | |
| **LESS THAN 500,000 (CONTINUED)** | | | | | | | | | | | | |
| COLUMBUS, GA.–ALA. | 17 | 10 | 26602 | 13604 | 21367 | 10821 | 65 | 170 | 71.5% | 40.7% | ** | ** |
| CORPUS CHRISTI, TEX. | 14 | 6 | 28660 | 9930 | 3170 | 1323 | 24432 | 8060 | 72.1% | 36.2% | 50.6% | 20.3% |
| EL PASO, TEX. | 11 | 8 | 26717 | 16705 | 474 | 124 | 25672 | 16207 | ** | * | 44.1% | 18.8% |
| FAYETTEVILLE, N.C. | 6 | 4 | 8983 | 5605 | 7116 | 5071 | 0 | 0 | 41.9% | 24.0% | * | ** |
| FORT SMITH, ARK.–OKLA. | 2 | 0 | 2863 | 0 | 808 | 0 | 0 | 0 | ** | ** | ** | ** |
| GADSDEN, ALA. | 0 | 0 | 0 | 0 | 0 | 0 | 0 | 0 | 0.0% | 0.0% | ** | ** |
| GAINESVILLE, FLA. | 2 | 4 | 4508 | 11057 | 1480 | 1543 | 193 | 832 | 15.8% | 15.8% | 11.2% | 6.2% |
| GALVESTON–TEXAS CITY, TEX. | 3 | 3 | 4367 | 2877 | 3835 | 2683 | 385 | 201 | 34.3% | 29.8% | 11.2% | 6.2% |
| HUNTSVILLE, ALA. | 4 | 3 | 6991 | 4202 | 5493 | 3599 | 0 | 135 | 35.5% | 26.7% | ** | ** |
| JACKSON, MISS. | 16 | 8 | 30024 | 10683 | 30354 | 10445 | 0 | 95 | 64.5% | 25.8% | ** | ** |
| KNOXVILLE, TENN. | 10 | 9 | 13985 | 16780 | 6135 | 4398 | 0 | 183 | 58.6% | 42.5% | ** | ** |
| LAFAYETTE, LA. | 3 | 0 | 6548 | 0 | 5412 | 0 | 0 | 0 | 42.7% | 0.0% | ** | ** |
| LAKE CHARLES, LA. | 4 | 1 | 8230 | 864 | 7479 | 847 | 0 | 0 | 50.5% | 8.8% | ** | ** |
| LAREDO, TEX. | 12 | 8 | 26238 | 15624 | 0 | 0 | 25769 | 15325 | * | * | 84.2% | 48.8% |
| LAWTON, OKLA. | 1 | 1 | 1983 | 400 | 1762 | 36 | 0 | 0 | 46.5% | 1.0% | ** | ** |
| LEXINGTON–FAYETTE, KY. | 1 | 2 | 2456 | 3854 | 1813 | 2532 | 0 | 107 | 23.6% | 24.0% | ** | ** |
| LITTLE ROCK–NORTH LITTLE ROCK, ARK. | 6 | 1 | 12183 | 1993 | 10705 | 1946 | 0 | 26 | 40.1% | 8.3% | ** | ** |
| LUBBOCK, TEX. | 5 | 1 | 5985 | 674 | 3503 | 68 | 2275 | 600 | 64.8% | 1.5% | 17.5% | 5.5% |
| LYNCHBURG, VA. | 0 | 1 | 0 | 82 | 0 | 0 | 0 | 0 | 0.0% | 0.0% | ** | ** |
| MACON, GA. | 8 | 8 | 12439 | 9606 | 10723 | 8361 | 0 | 24 | 40.1% | 29.8% | ** | ** |
| MCALLEN–PHARR–EDINBURG, TEX. | 31 | 21 | 80477 | 58222 | 40 | 17 | 75259 | 56534 | * | * | 92.1% | 60.4% |
| MIDLAND, TEX. | 0 | 0 | 0 | 0 | 0 | 0 | 0 | 0 | ** | ** | ** | ** |
| MOBILE, ALA. | 19 | 16 | 30408 | 22040 | 27507 | 19979 | 81 | 310 | 51.0% | 41.4% | ** | ** |
| MONROE, LA. | 7 | 9 | 14267 | 13305 | 13642 | 12854 | 61 | 141 | 74.6% | 70.6% | ** | ** |
| MONTGOMERY, ALA. | 10 | 6 | 23138 | 14306 | 20732 | 13485 | 94 | 154 | 54.5% | 37.4% | ** | ** |
| NEWPORT NEWS–HAMPTON, VA. | 2 | 2 | 3046 | 3916 | 2904 | 3381 | 0 | 69 | 15.1% | 16.1% | ** | ** |
| ODESSA, TEX. | 0 | 0 | 0 | 0 | 0 | 0 | 0 | 0 | * | * | 0.0% | 0.0% |
| PENSACOLA, FLA. | 5 | 5 | 9792 | 5043 | 8269 | 4366 | 81 | 28 | 42.8% | 23.7% | ** | ** |
| PETERSBURG–COLONIAL HEIGHTS–HOPEW | 0 | 1 | 0 | 129 | 0 | 105 | 0 | 0 | 0.0% | 1.0% | ** | ** |
| PINE BLUFF, ARK. | 7 | 5 | 15294 | 4910 | 13701 | 4468 | 49 | 100 | 71.1% | 30.7% | ** | ** |

| STANDARD METROPOLITAN STATISTICAL AREA By Region and Metro Area Size, 1980 | NUMBER OF GHETTO TRACTS | | NUMBER OF GHETTO POOR TOTAL | | BLACK | | HISPANIC | | LEVEL OF GHETTO POVERTY BLACK | | HISPANIC | |
|---|---|---|---|---|---|---|---|---|---|---|---|---|
| | 1970 | 1980 | 1970 | 1980 | 1970 | 1980 | 1970 | 1980 | 1970 | 1980 | 1970 | 1980 |
| **SOUTH (CONTINUED)** | | | | | | | | | | | | |
| **LESS THAN 500,000 (CONTINUED)** | | | | | | | | | | | | |
| ROANOKE, VA. | 0 | 0 | 0 | 0 | 0 | 0 | 0 | 0 | 0.0% | 0.0% | ** | ** |
| SAN ANGELO, TEX. | 2 | 0 | 2815 | 0 | 803 | 0 | 1894 | 0 | * | * | 39.1% | 0.0% |
| SAVANNAH, GA. | 12 | 13 | 14744 | 13886 | 13845 | 13505 | 0 | 66 | 52.6% | 47.1% | ** | ** |
| SHERMAN-DENISON, TEX. | 0 | 0 | 0 | 0 | 0 | 0 | 0 | 0 | * | * | ** | ** |
| SHREVEPORT, LA. | 16 | 8 | 34540 | 9419 | 32347 | 9275 | 0 | 253 | 66.4% | 22.1% | ** | ** |
| TALLAHASSEE, FLA. | 5 | 6 | 4738 | 8441 | 3131 | 4420 | 109 | 242 | 29.5% | 34.4% | ** | ** |
| TEXARKANA, TEX.-TEXARKANA, ARK. | 1 | 2 | 295 | 2752 | 9 | 2554 | 0 | 30 | 0.1% | 24.0% | ** | ** |
| TUSCALOOSA, ALA. | 3 | 4 | 7392 | 4089 | 6341 | 2870 | 0 | 0 | 43.8% | 20.8% | ** | ** |
| TYLER, TEX. | 0 | 0 | 0 | 0 | 0 | 0 | 0 | 0 | 0.0% | 0.0% | ** | ** |
| WACO, TEX. | 4 | 5 | 6781 | 8012 | 3195 | 2920 | 1282 | 1126 | 30.9% | 31.2% | 34.7% | 29.5% |
| WICHITA FALLS, TEX. | 3 | 2 | 2952 | 2073 | 2545 | 1775 | 256 | 181 | * | * | ** | ** |
| WILMINGTON, N.C. | 3 | 3 | 5612 | 3215 | 4764 | 2784 | 0 | 43 | 38.1% | 28.3% | ** | ** |
| **WEST** | | | | | | | | | | | | |
| **MORE THAN 1 MILLION** | | | | | | | | | | | | |
| ANAHEIM-SANTA ANA-GARDEN GROVE, CA | 0 | 1 | 0 | 20 | 0 | 0 | 0 | 0 | * | * | 0.0% | 0.0% |
| DENVER-BOULDER, COLO. | 10 | 8 | 11147 | 7968 | 3325 | 2141 | 5797 | 4538 | 27.1% | 13.7% | 21.8% | 15.2% |
| LOS ANGELES-LONG BEACH, CALIF. | 33 | 40 | 41885 | 51306 | 28753 | 29325 | 8609 | 17012 | 16.1% | 13.8% | 4.6% | 4.1% |
| PHOENIX, ARIZ. | 13 | 14 | 17451 | 19508 | 4805 | 3498 | 8126 | 10648 | 42.2% | 27.8% | 23.9% | 24.8% |
| PORTLAND, OREG.-WASH. | 3 | 3 | 1910 | 2359 | 291 | 957 | 91 | 48 | 4.9% | 11.0% | 4.6% | 1.3% |
| RIVERSIDE-SAN BERNARDINO-ONTARIO, C | 1 | 1 | 67 | 15 | 27 | 7 | 0 | 8 | 0.2% | 0.0% | 0.0% | 0.0% |
| SACRAMENTO, CALIF. | 1 | 3 | 488 | 1477 | 30 | 211 | 228 | 505 | 0.3% | 1.5% | 1.7% | 2.9% |
| SAN DIEGO, CALIF. | 4 | 2 | 1628 | 1478 | 993 | 255 | 359 | 1158 | 7.9% | 1.4% | 1.5% | 2.1% |
| SAN FRANCISCO-OAKLAND, CALIF. | 13 | 12 | 10821 | 11795 | 6761 | 7599 | 828 | 916 | 9.0% | 9.0% | 2.1% | 2.0% |
| SAN JOSE, CALIF. | 1 | 1 | 1685 | 52 | 90 | 26 | 100 | 14 | 3.7% | 0.5% | 0.4% | 0.0% |
| SEATTLE-EVERETT, WASH. | 3 | 4 | 4564 | 2272 | 747 | 404 | 356 | 77 | 9.1% | 3.6% | 19.1% | 1.8% |

| STANDARD METROPOLITAN STATISTICAL AREA | NUMBER OF GHETTO TRACTS | | NUMBER OF GHETTO POOR | | | | | | LEVEL OF GHETTO POVERTY | | | |
|---|---|---|---|---|---|---|---|---|---|---|---|---|
| | | | TOTAL | | BLACK | | HISPANIC | | BLACK | | HISPANIC | |
| By Region and Metro Area Size, 1980 | 1970 | 1980 | 1970 | 1980 | 1970 | 1980 | 1970 | 1980 | 1970 | 1980 | 1970 | 1980 |
| **WEST (CONTINUED)** | | | | | | | | | | | | |
| **500,000 TO 1 MILLION** | | | | | | | | | | | | |
| FRESNO, CALIF. | 8 | 3 | 11521 | 3793 | 5760 | 2679 | 4873 | 1089 | 71.8% | 35.8% | 13.7% | 2.9% |
| HONOLULU, HAWAII | 3 | 3 | 2217 | 3599 | 9 | 0 | 44 | 363 | * | * | 1.5% | 4.2% |
| OXNARD–SIMI VALLEY–VENTURA, CALIF. | 0 | 0 | 0 | 0 | 0 | 0 | 0 | 0 | * | * | 0.0% | 0.0% |
| SALT LAKE CITY–OGDEN, UTAH | 4 | 4 | 2666 | 2188 | 1057 | 830 | 288 | 374 | * | * | 4.7% | 4.6% |
| TUCSON, ARIZ. | 4 | 3 | 6494 | 6246 | 436 | 177 | 4445 | 1130 | * | * | 24.2% | 5.2% |
| **LESS THAN 500,000** | | | | | | | | | | | | |
| ALBUQUERQUE, N. MEX. | 8 | 3 | 9243 | 3676 | 857 | 0 | 7613 | 953 | * | * | 23.9% | 3.1% |
| BAKERSFIELD, CALIF. | 3 | 2 | 5173 | 2384 | 2846 | 1480 | 1879 | 672 | 38.5% | 26.2% | 12.2% | 3.4% |
| BILLINGS, MONT. | 0 | 0 | 0 | 0 | 0 | 0 | 0 | 0 | * | * | ** | ** |
| BOISE CITY, IDAHO | 0 | 0 | 0 | 0 | 0 | 0 | 0 | 0 | * | * | ** | ** |
| COLORADO SPRINGS, COLO. | 0 | 1 | 0 | 276 | 0 | 0 | 0 | 55 | 0.0% | 0.0% | 0.0% | 1.3% |
| EUGENE–SPRINGFIELD, OREG. | 1 | 1 | 1805 | 2078 | 41 | 19 | 33 | 27 | * | * | ** | ** |
| GREAT FALLS, MONT. | 0 | 0 | 0 | 0 | 0 | 0 | 0 | 0 | * | * | ** | ** |
| LAS VEGAS, NEV. | 1 | 0 | 1243 | 0 | 1175 | 0 | 0 | 0 | 20.8% | 0.0% | 0.0% | 0.0% |
| MODESTO, CALIF. | 0 | 0 | 0 | 0 | 0 | 0 | 0 | 0 | * | * | 0.0% | 0.0% |
| PROVO–OREM, UTAH | 1 | 3 | 1174 | 10472 | 0 | 20 | 0 | 417 | * | * | ** | ** |
| PUEBLO, COLO. | 1 | 1 | 23 | 32 | 0 | 0 | 8 | 7 | * | * | 0.1% | 0.1% |
| RENO, NEV. | 0 | 0 | 0 | 0 | 0 | 0 | 0 | 0 | * | * | ** | ** |
| SALEM, OREG. | 0 | 1 | 0 | 55 | 0 | 0 | 0 | 0 | * | * | ** | ** |
| SALINAS–SEASIDE–MONTEREY, CALIF. | 0 | 0 | 0 | 0 | 0 | 0 | 0 | 0 | 0.0% | 0.0% | 0.0% | 0.0% |
| SANTA BARBARA–SANTA MARIA–LOMPOC, | 3 | 2 | 5364 | 4786 | 126 | 89 | 215 | 426 | * | * | 3.4% | 5.3% |
| SANTA ROSA, CALIF. | 0 | 0 | 0 | 0 | 0 | 0 | 0 | 0 | * | * | 0.0% | 0.0% |
| SPOKANE, WASH. | 4 | 4 | 1996 | 1493 | 46 | 0 | 0 | 89 | * | * | ** | ** |
| STOCKTON, CALIF. | 2 | 4 | 4247 | 2682 | 1985 | 486 | 1484 | 859 | 38.9% | 9.1% | 12.2% | 5.8% |
| TACOMA, WASH. | 1 | 3 | 1554 | 3280 | 206 | 718 | 33 | 151 | 7.2% | 14.1% | ** | ** |
| VALLEJO–FAIRFIELD–NAPA, CALIF. | 0 | 0 | 0 | 0 | 0 | 0 | 0 | 0 | 0.0% | 0.0% | 0.0% | 0.0% |

Note: Includes all SMSAs that were defined in both 1970 and 1980 (using 1980 Boundaries).

* (**) — Fewer than 10,000 blacks (Hispanics) in 1970 — Level Omitted.

# 3
# How Poverty Neighborhoods
# Are Changing

JOHN C. WEICHER

Public concern about urban problems has tended to focus on the notion of an "underclass" during the 1980s. The concept has not been precisely defined, at least to the point where analysts have general agreement on its meaning and composition, but it is perhaps fair to say that the underclass includes people who are persistently poor, especially those who also grew up in poor families, and who live in neighborhoods where much of the population is persistently poor. These neighborhoods might be termed "persistent slums."

This chapter provides a microanalytic perspective on the phenomenon of persistent slums as a contribution to better understanding of the problem. It describes the changes that have occurred in selected urban poverty neighborhoods during the 1970s. The focus of the analysis is on the private characteristics of the slums: the people and the housing—what they are like, and how they are changing.

The chapter also looks at how federal policies have affected poverty neighborhoods. The nature of the available information precludes a systematic evaluation of the impact of particular federal antipoverty policies in particular neighborhoods, but some inferences can be drawn about the ways in which the most important federal policies have affected poverty neighborhoods in general, and some guesses can be made about the likely effectiveness of recent proposals.

The basic methodology of the chapter is a statistical analysis of the neighborhoods. Changes in individual neighborhoods are discussed, but detailed case studies are not presented. The primary sources of information about these neighborhoods are the decennial censuses of population and housing for 1970 and 1980. (Specifically, data have been taken from the Fourth Count Summary Tape for the 1970 census, and from Summary

Tape File 4 for the 1980 census.) The data for census tracts in slum neighborhoods have been aggregated to provide information on persistent slum areas in big cities. The data were produced as a special tabulation for this study by the Princeton University Computer Center, under a contract with the American Enterprise Institute. Changes in the 1960s are also analyzed, using data for a smaller set of poverty neighborhoods that had been compiled from the decennial censuses of 1960 and 1970, as part of a previous study.[1] That data set is used to supplement the basic analysis of the 1970s. It permits a somewhat longer perspective on slum neighborhoods, but the information for the 1960s is more limited, in several ways, and it was originally compiled for a different purpose.

## THE CONCEPT OF A "POVERTY NEIGHBORHOOD"

The poverty neighborhoods included in this study consist of contiguous census tracts, each having 20 percent of its population below the poverty line in both 1970 and 1980. The neighborhoods are delineated with consistent boundaries in both censuses. The 20 percent figure was established after the 1970 census as the cutoff for categorizing a census tract as a *low-income area*. The same criterion was used in 1980, but the term was changed to *poverty area*. A different and more complicated concept was used in the 1960s. As part of the War on Poverty, the Census Bureau and the Office of Economic Opportunity developed an index of poverty, which gave equal weight to five factors: family income (unadjusted for family size), children not living with both parents, adults with less than an eighth-grade education, unskilled male workers, and substandard housing. The lowest ranking 25 percent of all census tracts were then classified as poor (Bureau of the Census, 1966). The 20 percent figure was chosen after the 1970 census as the best approximation to the 1960 method, in terms of classifying tracts as poverty areas (see Bureau of the Census, 1973; Putnam, 1973).

There is a distinction between being poor and living in a poverty neighborhood. Poverty status for individuals depends only on their own income (adjusted for age and family size); poverty status for neighborhoods depends on the incidence of poor individuals within a geographic area. In 1980, for example, 47.5 million people were living in the 100 largest central cities, of whom 8.1 million were poor, 15.5 million lived in poverty areas, and 5.2 million were poor and lived in poverty areas. These figures imply that 2.9 million poor people did not live in poverty areas and that 10.3

---

[1] The data set was assembled for the National Housing Policy Review in 1973. The changes in housing conditions during the 1960s are summarized in the report of the National Housing Policy Review (1974), Ch. 6.

million living in poverty areas were not poor. Most poor people lived in poverty areas, but most people in poverty areas were not poor.

Poverty neighborhoods were delineated by the Office of Economic Opportunity after 1970 as groups of contiguous low-income census tracts with 20,000 or more residents in the aggregate. The smallest of these neighborhoods contained at least three census tracts. The 1970 neighborhoods are the basis for the poverty neighborhoods in this study, with some adjustments and qualifications.

## Poverty Neighborhoods as Neighborhoods

Local planners and other experts were consulted in establishing the boundaries of the poverty neighborhoods so that they conformed as closely as possible to the local sense of neighborhood. A large group of contiguous poor tracts was often broken into several neighborhoods on the basis of racial, ethnic, or other differences between the smaller areas. Nonetheless, poverty areas often overlap neighborhoods defined on other criteria, and they sometimes include only part of a single neighborhood. Only 1 of the 12 poverty neighborhoods in Chicago, and 1 of the 8 in Los Angeles, are coterminous with neighborhoods as formally defined by local planners and analysts (e.g., the Chicago Community Inventory).

## Consistent Neighborhood Boundaries

Individual census tracts can be classified as poor in one decennial census and nonpoor in the next, or vice versa. In fact, the actual number of poverty census tracts has increased, and the territorial extent of poverty areas in cities has grown substantially between 1960 and 1980, especially in the 1970s.

The geographic spread of poverty between 1970 and 1980 occurred partly because of a measurement problem. The Consumer Price Index (CPI), which is used to adjust the poverty line from year to year, overstated the increase in the cost of homeownership during the inflation of the 1970s.[2] Even if the error is corrected, however, it seems clear that both the size and the population of poverty neighborhoods in large cities increased markedly. In Chicago, for example, some 227 census tracts, with a total

---

[2] Compared with either the Gross National Product Deflator or the current CPI, the CPI used during the 1970s overstated change in the price level (and therefore the poverty line) by about 6.5 percent, and also overstated the poverty rate in the United States by about 11.5 percent, or 1.5 percent of the total population, in 1980. The error was corrected, beginning in 1983, but not retroactively. See Weicher (1987) for a fuller discussion of the measurement problem. Corrected data have been published by the Bureau of the Census (1989, Table C and Appendix F) for years beginning in 1974.

population of 818,000, were considered to be poverty areas in 1970. By 1980, the number of tracts increased to 306, with a total population of 1,171,000. The published census reports do not permit the error in the poverty threshold incomes to be corrected on any geographic basis, but it is possible to make a crude adjustment. I estimate that 28 tracts, with a total population of 106,000, would not have been classified as poverty areas in 1980 had the current version of the CPI been in use through the 1970s. (This assumes a rectangular distribution of the population between 75 and 100 percent of the poverty line and uses 92 percent of the official poverty line as the true one.) Even with the correction, there are still 278 tracts and 1,065,000 people in poverty areas in 1980, a larger area and population than in 1970.

Some tracts, and even some neighborhoods, have moved out of poverty status. In Washington, D.C., for example, the southern part of the Capitol Hill neighborhood, between the Capitol and Anacostia, was a sizable poverty area (comprising eight tracts) in 1960. It has since largely been gentrified. By 1970, one tract was no longer counted as part of the poverty area; by 1980, four more tracts had been upgraded, and the remaining poverty area consisted of the three southernmost tracts. It seems likely that by 1990 the entire area will disappear from maps of poverty.

The neighborhood focus of this study and the growth in the size of poverty areas, taken together, mean that it is not particularly useful to describe changes in poverty areas in the aggregate within a city. Instead, the study focuses on changes in individual poverty areas, *keeping the boundaries unchanged.* All tracts in each neighborhood were defined as being poor in each of the past three censuses—the maximum criterion for "persistence," because the available data only go back to 1960. This maximum criterion was established in order to focus on identifiable neighborhoods that have indeed been persistently poor, persistently slums—Watts in Los Angeles, Washington Park in Chicago, the South Bronx in New York.

### Study Neighborhoods

For this study, 79 persistently poor neighborhoods were identified in 12 central cities of standard metropolitan statistical areas (SMSAs). The project has a midwestern and northeastern focus, because these regions have the metropolitan areas with the most persistent slums. There are more midwestern metropolitan areas, but more northeastern neighborhoods in the study. This is because New York City is included. Of the 40 Northeastern poverty neighborhoods, 29 are in New York City; in addition, 5 are in Philadelphia, 4 in Washington, D.C., and 2 in Pittsburgh. Six midwestern metropolitan areas are included, with a total of 29 poverty neighborhoods: 12 in Chicago, 5 in Cleveland, 4 in St. Louis, 4 in Kansas

City, 3 in Milwaukee, and 1 in Gary. The remaining 10 poverty neighborhoods are in the Los Angeles SMSA, 8 from the city of Los Angeles and 2 from Long Beach. The California neighborhoods provide a limited basis for an overview of some regional differences. The sample is obviously dominated by the three supercities of New York, Los Angeles, and Chicago. The differences among these cities constitute an important part of the analysis.

Because of the change in the definition of poverty area from 1960 to 1970, and because of occasional redrawing of census tract boundaries, poverty neighborhoods as defined for this analysis need not correspond to the boundaries of poverty neighborhoods as defined in any of the decennial censuses. Few tracts, however, have moved out of poverty between one census and the next. As it happens, 27 of the 79 neighborhoods have the same boundaries in this study as they officially had in 1970. The other 52 have the same boundaries as they officially had in 1960. Their official boundaries in 1980 were larger (often by only one or two tracts) than in 1970; they are examples of the general pattern, previously noted, of increases in the size and population of poverty areas during the decade. The poverty areas defined in this study can be considered the cores of poverty areas as measured by the 1980 census.

Redrawing of census tract boundaries limited the number of neighborhoods and even eliminated a few large central cities. Boundaries were completely redrawn for the city of Detroit between 1970 and 1980, which makes it impossible to define any poverty neighborhoods consistently. Cincinnati had five poverty neighborhoods in 1960, but only one could have been used in this analysis. The boundaries for so many low-income tracts in Cincinnati were changed that there were only one or two tracts in each of the other neighborhoods that were poor and had consistent boundaries across the three censuses. The Twin Cities had only three poverty neighborhoods in 1960, and only two were consistently comparable. Boston had only two poverty neighborhoods in 1960; re-tracting left only one with consistent boundaries by 1980. Buffalo had no neighborhoods with more than two census tracts.

The only eastern cities that met the study criteria but were excluded were Baltimore (four poverty neighborhoods), and Newark (three). If the study had been given a national scope, a number of southern and western cities could have been included, but only the San Francisco-Oakland area has as many as five eligible neighborhoods. Houston might also have five or more, but it was completely re-tracted between 1960 and 1970. Most of the larger SMSAs in these regions did not have many poverty neighborhoods in 1960; they developed sizable identifiable concentrations of the poor only as they subsequently grew rapidly. But even with a full set of poverty neighborhoods for all large central cities—the 100 largest, for example—

TABLE 3-1 Poverty Neighborhoods in Study and City

| City | Number of Neighborhoods, 1970 | | Population in Poverty Neighborhoods (000), 1970 | | | Population in Poverty Neighborhoods (000), 1980 | | |
|---|---|---|---|---|---|---|---|---|
| | In Study | In City | In Study | In City | % | In Study | In City | % |
| Chicago | 12 | 15 | 547 | 818 | 67 | 394 | 1,171 | 34 |
| Cleveland | 5 | 6 | 166 | 207 | 80 | 103 | 273 | 38 |
| Gary | 1 | 1 | 27 | 33 | 81 | 15 | 64 | 23 |
| Kansas City | 4 | 4 | 94 | 107 | 88 | 63 | 123 | 51 |
| Long Beach | 2 | 2 | 28 | 57 | 49 | 33 | 85 | 39 |
| Los Angeles | 8 | 10 | 367 | 561 | 65 | 408 | 964 | 42 |
| Milwaukee | 3 | 4 | 76 | 132 | 58 | 56 | 161 | 35 |
| New York | 29 | 35 | 1,440 | 2,089 | 69 | 938 | 2,742 | 34 |
| Philadelphia | 5 | 9 | 276 | 494 | 56 | 197 | 712 | 28 |
| Pittsburgh | 2 | 3 | 55 | 113 | 49 | 41 | 121 | 34 |
| St. Louis | 4 | 7 | 143 | 284 | 50 | 88 | 233 | 38 |
| Washington, D.C. | 4 | 5 | 106 | 239 | 44 | 82 | 251 | 33 |
| Total | 79 | 101 | 3,325 | 5,134 | 65 | 2,418 | 6,900 | 35 |

the universe would still be dominated by the largest cities, particularly New York. Limiting the number of metropolitan areas did not greatly reduce the number of neighborhoods.

Table 3-1 presents some basic information about the poverty neighborhoods in this study. Most of the neighborhoods officially delineated in 1970 in the cities involved are included, though not all with the same boundaries. The neighborhoods contained well over half of all people living in poverty neighborhoods in these cities in 1970, except for Long Beach, Pittsburgh (both at 49 percent), and Washington, D.C. By 1980, the neighborhoods' total share was down substantially; they had nearly all lost population, and more tracts in the cities were classified as poverty areas. But they still accounted for over 30 percent of the people living in poverty areas, except in Gary and Philadelphia. (A list of the tracts contained within each poverty neighborhood, for each of the three decennial censuses, is available from the author.)

## NEIGHBORHOOD CHANGES IN THE 1970s

Poverty neighborhoods differ from city to city, but the neighborhoods in eastern and midwestern cities changed in similar ways in the course of the 1970s. These changes are more important in understanding the problems of persistent slums than are the surface differences. It is possible, therefore, to summarize the changes in eastern and midwestern neighborhoods in terms of averages for all 69 neighborhoods from the two regions in the sample (Table 3-2). This is not to say that all of these neighborhoods fit the pattern shown in the table. There were some differences, by region and by size of city, particularly in housing conditions. But the table is a reasonable representation of what happened in most neighborhoods. The few major differences between cities are discussed in a subsequent section.

### Eastern and Midwestern Poverty Neighborhoods: A Study in Decline

The most important similarity among the neighborhoods in the East and Midwest is also the most important and most obvious regional difference between them and the neighborhoods in Los Angeles. In the East and Midwest, nearly all poverty neighborhoods lost population during the 1970s. In Los Angeles, nearly all of them gained population. Moreover, they gained a very different population; typically, Hispanics replaced blacks. The only eastern neighborhoods with population increases were two in New York City, one in Manhattan and one in Brooklyn. Both also experienced the same racial/ethnic turnover.

The typical neighborhood lost about one-third of its total population in the decade, over half its white population, almost one-third of its black population, and almost one-fifth of its Hispanic population. It gained a small number of persons of other races. The averages in 1970 and 1980 mask substantial differences between cities; the white population was concentrated in the smaller midwestern cities, and the Hispanic population in New York. Most of the trends are nonetheless universal. Not many neighborhoods had a large white population in 1970, but nearly all lost most of whatever they had by 1980. There were small numerical gains from a small base in the number of persons of other races, in most neighborhoods. There was substantial growth in the Hispanic population, however, in a number of New York neighborhoods; in the Midwest, no neighborhoods were predominantly Hispanic in either year, and about half lost Hispanic residents over the decade.

The number of households also declined, but by less than the population. The size of the typical household therefore also declined, from about 3.1 to 2.8 persons. The "feminization of poverty" is apparent in these poverty neighborhoods. The number of married couples declined by half, but the number of female-headed households remained about the same. About half the households in the typical neighborhood in 1970 consisted of married couples; about half in 1980 were headed by a single woman. At the same time, the population became older, on average; the number and incidence of children under 18 declined, and the incidence of the elderly increased slightly.

Economic changes were similarly pronounced. Real median household income (in 1980 dollars) fell by about $1,700. In 1970, close to half the

TABLE 3-2 Neighborhood Changes in Midwestern and Eastern Cities

| | 1970 Mean | 1980 Mean | 1970 % | 1980 % | % Change |
|---|---|---|---|---|---|
| People | | | | | |
| Population | 43,300 | 29,200 | | | −30.7 |
| White[a] | 7,100 | 3,100 | 19.9 | 12.2 | |
| Black[a] | 28,600 | 19,500 | 64.1 | 66.1 | |
| Hispanic | 6,900 | 5,700 | 14.6 | 19.4 | |
| Other races[a] | 800 | 900 | 1.7 | 2.4 | |
| Over 65 years | 3,700 | 3,200 | 9.1 | 11.1 | |
| Under 18 years | 16,900 | 9,600 | 38.5 | 33.0 | |
| Households | 13,800 | 10,400 | | | −23.8 |
| Married couples | 6,500 | 3,200 | 47.2 | 31.1 | |
| Female head | 5,400 | 5,200 | 38.6 | 50.6 | |
| Male head, no spouse | 2,000 | 2,000 | 14.2 | 18.3 | |
| | | | | | |
| Income and Economy | | | | | |
| Median household income[b] | $9,100 | $7,400 | | | −18.2 |
| Labor force (16+ years) | | | | | |
| Percent unemployed | 3.7 | 7.2 | | | |
| Percent not in labor force | 49.4 | 53.9 | | | |
| Percent employed | 46.7 | 38.9 | | | |
| Percent with earnings[c] | 81.1 | 58.8 | | | |
| Percent with income transfers[c] | 46.4 | 61.5 | | | |
| Median years of schooling | 9.2 | 10.3 | | | |
| | | | | | |
| Housing | | | | | |
| Housing units | 14,900 | 12,000 | | | −18.8 |
| Occupied housing units | 13,700 | 10,400 | | | −23.1 |
| Vacancy rate (%) | 8.4 | 13.3 | | | |
| Percent renter-occupied | 83.9 | 82.4 | | | |
| Space | | | | | |
| Persons per unit | 3.15 | 2.85 | | | |
| Median rooms per unit | 4.06 | 4.15 | | | |
| Percent crowded | 17.2 | 12.1 | | | |
| Quality | | | | | |
| Percent without complete plumbing | 5.2 | 6.5 | | | |
| Percent without central heat | 13.6 | 14.1 | | | |
| Percent without heat | 0.2 | 0.5 | | | |
| Age | | | | | |
| Percent 30+ years old | 73.0 | 71.0 | | | |
| Percent built pre-1940 | 73.0 | 55.4 | | | |
| Percent <10 years old | 7.5 | 7.9 | | | |
| Percent in 1-unit structures | 14.6 | 16.2 | | | |
| Percent in 5+ unit structures | 59.0 | 59.8 | | | |
| Median home value[b] | $34,000 | $24,200 | | | −29.6 |
| Median rent[b] | $131 | $134 | | | +2.5 |

[a]Non-Hispanic population.
[b]In 1980 dollars.
[c]For families and unrelated individuals in 1970, households in 1980.

individuals over 16 were employed; in 1980, only about 40 percent were. The unemployment rate nearly doubled. Transfer payments apparently became a more important source of income, and earnings from work less important. This inference, however, must be tempered by the fact that the information is reported on a different basis in the two years. In 1970, the Census Bureau published data for "families and unrelated individuals," in 1980 for "households," which can consist of two or more unrelated individuals. Despite the problems with comparability, there probably was a real change in the relative importance of transfer payments and earnings from work.

The one positive feature in this picture is the increase in years of schooling among the adult population. The improvement was only from the ninth-grade to the tenth-grade level, however, which means the typical adult in these neighborhoods was well behind the rest of the population. Schooling seems to run counter to the other trends; the improvement does not translate into better economic circumstances.

The general impression from these changes is that the black middle class, or perhaps more precisely the lower middle class, was moving out of these neighborhoods. People who could afford to leave were doing so. The number of housing units declined, but less rapidly than the number of people or households. This implies that the vacancy rate increased. Vacant units, however, fall into several categories, and the meaning of "vacancy rate" varies among these neighborhoods. Some vacant units are "available for sale or for rent." Others fall into an "other vacant" category, of which the most prominent subcategory is "in boarded-up buildings." These units may be about to drop out of the housing stock altogether. They may be almost indistinguishable from structures that are no longer counted as part of the housing inventory. Boarded-up buildings account for most of the vacant stock in New York and Philadelphia, but a minor fraction of it in the other cities.

The age distribution of the housing stock did not change much, but this fact can be misleading. A substantial share of the prewar housing stock—over 4,000 units in the average neighborhood—was razed or otherwise removed from the inventory. The remaining housing aged 10 years, and a small number of new units were built. It is reasonable to conjecture that some if not all of the new units were built under government housing programs for the poor, but this is only a conjecture; unfortunately, the census tract data do not identify public housing or other subsidized housing. Evidence from the 1960s, to be discussed later, suggests that about half the new units added to poverty neighborhoods in that decade were subsidized.

There was little change in tenure or structure type. Real home values declined in the course of the decade, but real rents rose slightly. The rent figure is obviously the more relevant, because few units were owner-occupied.

One basic measure of housing conditions improved noticeably over the decade. Households enjoyed more space in 1980. The number of persons per unit declined and the number of rooms per unit increased; fewer units were crowded.

The most surprising feature is the increase in the percentage of housing units with fundamental deficiencies. This does not necessarily mean that individual units deteriorated. Because the number of units declined, the increased percentages actually represent stable or declining numbers of units. The average number of units without complete plumbing was almost unchanged, at about 775, and the number without central heat declined from about 2,000 to about 1,700. The change in units without any heat could well reflect sampling error; on average fewer than 100 units per neighborhood reported this problem in each year, and the question was asked only on the census "long form," which was sent to 20 percent of housing units.

The change in housing units without complete plumbing facilities is especially noteworthy. The presence of plumbing is the one measure of housing quality reported in every decennial census of housing since the first one in 1940, and the one attribute included in every definition of adequate or standard quality housing since World War II. There has been dramatic improvement in each decade, both for the population as a whole and for the poor and minorities, insofar as data are available. There was dramatic improvement in poverty neighborhoods in the 1960s. After all the progress, the data for these neighborhoods in the 1970s strike a sour note.

The increase turns out to be the result of a little-noticed change in definition, combined with a much-noticed change in the housing stock. In 1970, a unit was deemed to have complete plumbing if the facilities were located within the structure; in 1980, it was necessary that they be located within the unit. This changes the classification of rooming houses, but that is not the most important effect, statistically. More important is the afore-mentioned increase in vacant, boarded-up buildings, particularly in New York and Philadelphia. The poverty neighborhoods in these two cities were almost the only ones reporting an increase in the incidence of units without plumbing. In the Philadelphia neighborhoods, more than 60 percent of the units lacking complete plumbing in 1980 were in such buildings, compared with less than 20 percent in the Chicago neighborhoods.

### Intraregional Changes

Tables 3-3 through 3-6 show the same information separately for Chicago, New York, and the smaller cities in each region. (Table 3-6

TABLE 3-3  Neighborhood Changes, Chicago

|  | 1970 Mean | 1980 Mean | 1970 % | 1980 % | % Change |
|---|---|---|---|---|---|
| **People** | | | | | |
| Population | 45,600 | 32,900 | | | −25.9 |
| White[a] | 5,100 | 2,600 | 14.6 | 8.8 | |
| Black[a] | 37,400 | 26,700 | 76.2 | 77.5 | |
| Hispanic | 2,600 | 3,000 | 8.1 | 11.8 | |
| Other races[a] | 500 | 600 | 1.1 | 1.9 | |
| Over 65 years | 3,800 | 3,400 | 8.1 | 9.7 | |
| Under 18 years | 19,200 | 12,100 | 42.3 | 37.6 | |
| Households | 14,200 | 11,200 | | | −20.2 |
| Married couples | 6,100 | 3,000 | 43.7 | 28.0 | |
| Female head | 5,500 | 5,900 | 38.6 | 52.6 | |
| Male head, no spouse | 2,500 | 2,300 | 17.7 | 19.4 | |
| **Income and Economy** | | | | | |
| Median household income[b] | $9,300 | $6,900 | | | −26.8 |
| Labor force | | | | | |
| Percent unemployed | 4.1 | 8.3 | | | |
| Percent not in labor force | 49.2 | 55.7 | | | |
| Percent employed | 46.6 | 36.0 | | | |
| Percent with earnings[c] | 79.0 | 54.5 | | | |
| Percent with income transfers[c] | 46.1 | 65.1 | | | |
| Median years of schooling | 9.3 | 10.2 | | | |
| **Housing** | | | | | |
| Housing units | 15,700 | 12,500 | | | −19.8 |
| Occupied housing units | 14,100 | 11,200 | | | −19.4 |
| Vacancy rate (%) | 11.0 | 10.6 | | | |
| Percent renter-occupied | 89.8 | 89.1 | | | |
| Space | | | | | |
| Persons per unit | 3.26 | 3.01 | | | |
| Median rooms per unit | 3.97 | 4.09 | | | |
| Percent crowded | 19.9 | 15.8 | | | |
| Quality | | | | | |
| Percent without complete plumbing | 8.5 | 6.5 | | | |
| Percent without central heat | 19.4 | 23.3 | | | |
| Percent without heat | 0.3 | 0.3 | | | |
| Age | | | | | |
| Percent 30+ years old | 65.2 | 65.9 | | | |
| Percent built pre-1940 | 65.2 | 49.7 | | | |
| Percent <10 years old | 11.3 | 7.9 | | | |
| Percent in 1-unit structures | 6.4 | 6.2 | | | |
| Percent in 5+ unit structures | 67.5 | 68.0 | | | |
| Median home value[b] | $37,800 | $28,900 | | | −29.4 |
| Median rent[b] | $155 | $134 | | | −13.4 |

[a]Non-Hispanic population.
[b]In 1980 dollars.
[c]For families and unrelated individuals in 1970, households in 1980.

TABLE 3-4  Neighborhood Changes, Other Midwestern Cities

|  | 1970 Mean | 1980 Mean | 1970 % | 1980 % | % Change |
|---|---|---|---|---|---|
| **People** | | | | | |
| Population | 29,700 | 19,000 | | | −34.8 |
| White[a] | 7,600 | 3,900 | 29.0 | 21.7 | |
| Black[a] | 21,600 | 14,300 | 68.7 | 73.4 | |
| Hispanic | 700 | 600 | 2.9 | 3.6 | |
| Other races[a] | 200 | 200 | 0.7 | 1.6 | |
| Over 65 years | 3,400 | 2,700 | 11.6 | 14.2 | |
| Under 18 years | 10,900 | 5,700 | 36.2 | 30.2 | |
| Households | 9,900 | 7,100 | | | −27.9 |
| Married couples | 4,400 | 2,100 | 44.7 | 29.7 | |
| Female head | 3,900 | 3,500 | 38.8 | 49.2 | |
| Male head, no spouse | 1,600 | 1,500 | 16.5 | 21.2 | |
| **Income and Economy** | | | | | |
| Median household income[b] | $9,000 | $7,900 | | | −11.5 |
| Labor force | | | | | |
| Percent unemployed | 4.2 | 7.3 | | | |
| Percent not in labor force | 46.2 | 51.1 | | | |
| Percent employed | 49.5 | 41.5 | | | |
| Percent with earnings[c] | 86.5 | 63.5 | | | |
| Percent with income transfers[c] | 46.2 | 61.4 | | | |
| Median years of schooling | 9.4 | 10.6 | | | |
| **Housing** | | | | | |
| Housing units | 11,200 | 8,400 | | | −24.1 |
| Occupied housing units | 9,800 | 7,100 | | | −27.7 |
| Vacancy rate (%) | 11.7 | 15.8 | | | |
| Percent renter-occupied | 72.8 | 69.1 | | | |
| Space | | | | | |
| Persons per unit | 3.02 | 2.70 | | | |
| Median rooms per unit | 4.22 | 4.42 | | | |
| Percent crowded | 12.2 | 7.5 | | | |
| Quality | | | | | |
| Percent without complete plumbing | 6.6 | 4.7 | | | |
| Percent without central heat | 21.6 | 17.4 | | | |
| Percent without heat | 0.2 | 0.3 | | | |
| Age | | | | | |
| Percent 30+ years old | 77.8 | 76.0 | | | |
| Percent built pre-1940 | 77.8 | 60.0 | | | |
| Percent <10 years old | 5.5 | 6.1 | | | |
| Percent in 1-unit structures | 23.9 | 30.1 | | | |
| Percent in 5+ unit structures | 36.4 | 35.8 | | | |
| Median home value[b] | $26,000 | $16,800 | | | −34.4 |
| Median rent[b] | $116 | $105 | | | −9.6 |

[a]Non-Hispanic population.
[b]In 1980 dollars.
[c]For families and unrelated individuals in 1970, households in 1980.

TABLE 3-5  Neighborhood Changes, New York

|  | 1970 Mean | 1980 Mean | 1970 % | 1980 % | % Change |
|---|---|---|---|---|---|
| **People** | | | | | |
| Population | 49,700 | 32,400 | | | −31.7 |
| White[a] | 7,900 | 2,500 | 18.7 | 7.9 | |
| Black[a] | 26,300 | 17,300 | 50.5 | 52.5 | |
| Hispanic | 14,000 | 11,000 | 27.8 | 36.0 | |
| Other races[a] | 1,500 | 1,600 | 3.0 | 3.6 | |
| Over 65 years | 3,600 | 3,000 | 7.3 | 8.8 | |
| Under 18 years | 19,800 | 10,800 | 39.9 | 34.5 | |
| Households | 15,700 | 11,600 | | | −23.6 |
| Married couples | 7,900 | 3,900 | 52.0 | 34.4 | |
| Female head | 5,900 | 5,700 | 37.4 | 50.2 | |
| Male head, no spouse | 1,800 | 2,000 | 10.6 | 15.4 | |
| **Income and Economy** | | | | | |
| Median household income[b] | $9,400 | $7,300 | | | −22.8 |
| Labor force | | | | | |
| Percent unemployed | 3.1 | 6.4 | | | |
| Percent not in labor force | 51.6 | 54.2 | | | |
| Percent employed | 45.0 | 39.3 | | | |
| Percent with earnings[c] | 77.1 | 58.2 | | | |
| Percent with income transfers[c] | 45.0 | 58.4 | | | |
| Median years of schooling | 9.1 | 10.0 | | | |
| **Housing** | | | | | |
| Housing units | 16,200 | 13,100 | | | −16.9 |
| Occupied housing units | 15,500 | 11,600 | | | −22.7 |
| Vacancy rate (%) | 4.7 | 11.6 | | | |
| Percent renter-occupied | 91.7 | 91.7 | | | |
| Space | | | | | |
| Persons per unit | 3.24 | 2.87 | | | |
| Median rooms per unit | 3.94 | 3.90 | | | |
| Percent crowded | 20.6 | 14.2 | | | |
| Quality | | | | | |
| Percent without complete plumbing | 3.3 | 7.2 | | | |
| Percent without central heat | 4.6 | 6.7 | | | |
| Percent without heat | 0.2 | 0.5 | | | |
| Age | | | | | |
| Percent 30+ years old | 71.3 | 67.7 | | | |
| Percent built pre-1940 | 71.3 | 52.5 | | | |
| Percent <10 years old | 7.3 | 9.5 | | | |
| Percent in 1-unit structures | 3.3 | 2.7 | | | |
| Percent in 5+ unit structures | 77.5 | 78.8 | | | |
| Median home value[b] | $44,500 | $30,200 | | | −31.2 |
| Median rent[b] | $133 | $155 | | | +17.4 |

[a]Non-Hispanic population.
[b]In 1980 dollars.
[c]For families and unrelated individuals in 1970, households in 1980.

TABLE 3-6 Neighborhood Changes, Other Eastern Cities

| | 1970 Mean | 1980 Mean | 1970 % | 1980 % | % Change |
|---|---|---|---|---|---|
| People | | | | | |
| Population | 45,300 | 33,300 | | | −26.3 |
| White[a] | 6,200 | 4,000 | 13.6 | 12.2 | |
| Black[a] | 37,300 | 26,700 | 82.8 | 81.0 | |
| Hispanic | 1,500 | 2,100 | 2.7 | 5.6 | |
| Other races[a] | 400 | 400 | 0.9 | 1.3 | |
| Over 65 years | 4,800 | 4,400 | 11.3 | 13.9 | |
| Under 18 years | 16,000 | 9,400 | 33.7 | 27.1 | |
| Households | 14,900 | 11,800 | | | −21.0 |
| Married couples | 6,100 | 3,200 | 40.8 | 27.4 | |
| Female head | 6,300 | 6,100 | 42.2 | 51.8 | |
| Male head, no spouse | 2,500 | 2,500 | 17.0 | 20.8 | |
| Income and Economy | | | | | |
| Median household income[b] | $8,800 | $8,400 | | | −2.3 |
| Labor force | | | | | |
| Percent unemployed | 4.1 | 7.7 | | | |
| Percent not in labor force | 48.6 | 55.6 | | | |
| Percent employed | 47.1 | 36.5 | | | |
| Percent with earnings[c] | 86.7 | 57.8 | | | |
| Percent with income transfers[c] | 51.6 | 67.2 | | | |
| Median years of schooling | 9.4 | 10.6 | | | |
| Housing | | | | | |
| Housing units | 16,700 | 14,500 | | | −13.7 |
| Occupied housing units | 14,800 | 11,800 | | | −20.8 |
| Vacancy rate (%) | 10.9 | 17.9 | | | |
| Percent rented | 71.7 | 67.5 | | | |
| Space | | | | | |
| Persons per unit | 2.99 | 2.80 | | | |
| Median rooms per unit | 4.23 | 4.53 | | | |
| Percent crowded | 12.4 | 8.9 | | | |
| Quality | | | | | |
| Percent without complete plumbing | 3.9 | 6.5 | | | |
| Percent without central heat | 19.5 | 19.8 | | | |
| Percent without heat | 0.3 | 1.2 | | | |
| Age | | | | | |
| Percent 30+ years old | 79.7 | 78.8 | | | |
| Percent built pre-1940 | 79.7 | 63.8 | | | |
| Percent < 10 years old | 6.9 | 6.1 | | | |
| Percent in 1-unit structures | 44.5 | 47.0 | | | |
| Percent in 5+ unit structures | 31.2 | 32.9 | | | |
| Median home value[b] | $27,300 | $30,300 | | | +6.1 |
| Median rent[b] | $128 | $124 | | | −2.6 |

[a]Non-Hispanic population.
[b]In 1980 dollars.
[c]For families and unrelated individuals in 1970, households in 1980.

is included mainly for the sake of completeness; it presents averages for Philadelphia, Washington, and Pittsburgh, three quite different cities with different experiences during the 1970s.) Some of the differences in population and housing characteristics in 1970 and 1980 are very noticeable in these tables, but they are less important than the similarities in trends. The housing stock in New York neighborhoods, to take an obvious example, consisted much more of large apartment buildings in both 1970 and 1980, and surely does today, than in neighborhoods in any other city. In New York and Chicago, rental housing was much more predominant than in the smaller cities; the typical housing unit was smaller; and crowding (defined as having more than one person per room) was much more common. Rents and values were higher. There were also some demographic differences. New York had a much higher Hispanic population, and midwestern cities (except Chicago) had many more white persons living in poverty neighborhoods.

Most of the demographic and economic *trends,* by contrast, are similar. The most noticeable demographic difference is the growth in the Hispanic population in New York neighborhoods. This was concentrated in a few neighborhoods, but 25 of 29 neighborhoods experienced a percentage increase in the Hispanic share of the population. In addition, real income trends differed. Household income declined more in the two big cities, and hardly at all in smaller eastern cities. This latter result occurs because income increases in poverty neighborhoods in Washington offset declines in Philadelphia and Pittsburgh. Some other differences in the changes are statistically significant, but do not matter qualitatively.

Housing trends were more diffuse. The vacancy rate went down in Chicago but rose elsewhere. The average for Chicago was driven by substantial declines in the Cabrini-Green public housing complex and the Woodlawn neighborhood; most other neighborhoods experienced small increases. The overall increase in median rents, shown in Table 3-2, is the net effect of regional divergences: an increase in New York and Washington, a decrease elsewhere. The data for home values in the other eastern cities similarly hide a diversity within the region: values went up by at least 35 percent in each of the four Washington neighborhoods, and down by at least 30 percent in each of the seven Philadelphia and Pittsburgh areas.

The apparent inconsistency in the data on mean home value for the smaller eastern cities occurs because the percentage change is calculated as the mean of the percentage changes for the individual areas, rather than as the percentage change of the means from 1970 to 1980. If the range of decennial mean values is large, the percentage change of the mean is likely to differ from the mean of the percentage changes. A similar phenomenon occurs in some other tables.

The overall increase in the percentage of units without central heat results partly from the phenomenon of boarded-up buildings in New York and Philadelphia, and partly because many of the high-rise public housing projects built in Chicago apparently do not have central heating systems. The highest incidence of units without central heat—over two-thirds— occurs in the neighborhood containing the Cabrini-Green project. Over 75 percent of the residents in the tracts containing the project reported that they did not have central heating. Census tracts in other areas with a significant concentration of public housing also reported a substantial incidence of units without central heating. As the older private housing stock was removed from the inventory during the 1970s, public housing constituted a larger share of the inventory, and the proportion of units without central heat increased. Thus, the reported rise in the Chicago neighborhoods— certainly unexpected at first sight, considering the climate—does not by itself indicate a deterioration in housing quality.

### Los Angeles

Los Angeles is fundamentally different from the midwestern and eastern cities. All but two of its poverty neighborhoods gained population, in every case because the growth in the Hispanic population more than offset declines in whites and blacks (Table 3-7). The incidence of the elderly declined, and the incidence of children increased. The number of households remained about the same, and the average number of people in each household increased. There was no shift away from married couples to female-headed households; both increased slightly, and the share of households headed by a single man declined.

Changes in the labor force were also minor, compared with those in the East and Midwest. There was a small increase rather than a large decrease in labor force participation, and the unemployment rate went up much less. There may also have been a smaller shift away from earnings from work, and toward transfers, as sources of income, though the change in the data makes this uncertain. It is clear, however, that in 1980 more households relied on earnings from work, rather than transfers, for their income, again unlike the East and Midwest. Real household income went up slightly, rather than down; and years of schooling remained about the same, rather than rising.

Housing conditions were consistent with the growth in population. The housing stock was utilized more intensively. There was a small decline in the total number of units but no change in the number of occupied units. The vacancy rate fell. The average number of people per unit increased while the number of rooms per unit declined, resulting in a sharp increase in crowding. Quality changes were ambiguous: Increases in the proportions

TABLE 3-7　Neighborhood Changes, Los Angeles and Long Beach

| | 1970 Mean | 1980 Mean | 1970 % | 1980 % | % Change |
|---|---|---|---|---|---|
| **People** | | | | | |
| Population | 39,500 | 44,100 | | | +13.5 |
| White[a] | 6,500 | 4,900 | 22.7 | 13.6 | |
| Black[a] | 20,500 | 16,300 | 44.6 | 35.8 | |
| Hispanic | 10,500 | 20,300 | 27.3 | 44.6 | |
| Other races[a] | 2,000 | 2,600 | 5.3 | 6.1 | |
| Over 65 years | 4,300 | 4,200 | 12.0 | 9.8 | |
| Under 18 years | 13,600 | 14,400 | 33.9 | 33.8 | |
| Households | 14,300 | 14,100 | | | −0.1 |
| Married couples | 5,800 | 6,300 | 42.8 | 43.6 | |
| Female head | 5,100 | 5,400 | 36.0 | 38.9 | |
| Male head, no spouse | 3,300 | 2,400 | 21.4 | 17.5 | |
| **Income and Economy** | | | | | |
| Median household income[b] | $8,200 | $8,500 | | | +4.2 |
| Labor force | | | | | |
| Percent unemployed | 5.3 | 6.3 | | | |
| Percent not in labor force | 50.3 | 48.3 | | | |
| Percent employed | 43.6 | 45.3 | | | |
| Percent with earnings[c] | 79.7 | 66.2 | | | |
| Percent with income transfers[c] | 52.2 | 53.2 | | | |
| Median years of schooling | 10.0 | 10.0 | | | |
| **Housing** | | | | | |
| Housing units | 15,400 | 15,100 | | | −0.6 |
| Occupied housing units | 14,200 | 14,100 | | | +0.6 |
| Vacancy rate (%) | 7.5 | 6.3 | | | |
| Percent renter-occupied | 78.0 | 79.1 | | | |
| Space | | | | | |
| Person per unit | 2.85 | 3.17 | | | |
| Median room per unit | 3.40 | 3.24 | | | |
| Percent crowded | 17.7 | 26.2 | | | |
| Quality | | | | | |
| Percent without complete plumbing | 5.4 | 6.5 | | | |
| Percent without central heat | 75.6 | 62.3 | | | |
| Percent without heat | 4.8 | 7.5 | | | |
| Age | | | | | |
| Percent 30+ years old | 54.0 | 60.6 | | | |
| Percent built pre-1940 | 54.0 | 38.8 | | | |
| Percent <10 years old | 11.0 | 8.2 | | | |
| Percent in 1-unit structures | 41.7 | 39.5 | | | |
| Percent in 5+ unit structures | 39.4 | 43.6 | | | |
| Median home value[b] | $43,700 | $48,400 | | | +9.5 |
| Median rent[b] | $128 | $152 | | | +18.6 |

[a]Non-Hispanic population.
[b]In 1980 dollars.
[c]For families and unrelated individuals in 1970, households in 1980.

of units without complete plumbing and units with no heat were offset by a larger decrease in units without central heating. Heating equipment is not a basic indicator of housing quality in Los Angeles, so perhaps only the change in units without complete plumbing merits attention. The housing stock was newer in Los Angeles, and it aged a bit more in the course of the decade, although there was a decline of about one-third in the number of prewar units. Both rents and values increased, reflecting the greater demand for housing in these areas and the population growth in Los Angeles as a whole.

The decline in black population in these neighborhoods deserves special attention. It mainly indicates a geographic dispersal of the black population from these poverty neighborhoods, rather than any dramatic improvement in the status of blacks. There was virtually no change in the various measures of poverty and location from 1970 to 1980. The total number of blacks in the city, the number who were poor, the number living in poverty areas, and the number of poor blacks in poverty areas—all changed by less than 5,000 in 10 years. The number of census tracts classified as poverty areas, however, increased from 162 to 234. Most of the Los Angeles poverty neighborhoods in this study are close to the Civic Center. The poor black population in these neighborhoods apparently moved to nearby census tracts, causing many of them to be classified as poverty areas in 1980 and causing a spread of poverty to a wider area around the Civic Center, particularly to the southwest and south.

## NEIGHBORHOOD CHANGES IN A LONGER PERSPECTIVE

Although comparable data for the same set of neighborhoods could not be obtained from the 1960 census, as noted, data were available for a different set. These areas were chosen on the same principles: They were poverty areas, or the cores of poverty areas, in both 1960 and 1970. They were chosen for a different purpose, however, namely to analyze changes in housing conditions as part of a national housing policy study. The information about these neighborhoods is therefore more limited; it includes most of the housing data, but otherwise only population and income. Household composition and economic status were omitted. The neighborhoods were also selected on a different basis. The data set includes just a few neighborhoods, typically one or two, from each of 29 cities, and all parts of the country are represented. The total number of neighborhoods is only 50 (Table 3-8).

Seven neighborhoods turned up in both samples, which makes it possible to look at the changes in these neighborhoods on a consistent basis over both decades. (Another 12 neighborhoods differed by only one or two census tracts, but a longitudinal analysis of these areas was not attempted.

TABLE 3-8  Location of Poverty Neighborhoods in 1960–1970 Data Set

| Region | City | Number of Neighborhoods |
|--------|------|-------------------------|
| East |  | 14 |
|  | New York | 4 |
|  | Baltimore | 2 |
|  | Boston | 2 |
|  | Philadelphia | 2 |
|  | Washington, D.C. | 2 |
|  | Newark | 1 |
|  | Pittsburgh | 1 |
| Midwest |  | 18 |
|  | Chicago | 5 |
|  | St. Louis | 3 |
|  | Cincinnati | 2 |
|  | Cleveland | 2 |
|  | Detroit | 2 |
|  | Gary | 1 |
|  | Indianapolis | 1 |
|  | Milwaukee | 1 |
|  | Minneapolis | 1 |
| South |  | 11 |
|  | Atlanta | 2 |
|  | Dallas | 2 |
|  | Houston | 2 |
|  | Birmingham | 1 |
|  | Memphis | 1 |
|  | Miami | 1 |
|  | New Orleans | 1 |
|  | San Antonio | 1 |
| West |  | 7 |
|  | Los Angeles | 3 |
|  | Denver | 1 |
|  | Oakland | 1 |
|  | San Diego | 1 |
|  | San Francisco | 1 |

In every instance, the boundaries were larger in the later data set, and the added tracts were higher income areas, with better housing; a longitudinal analysis would therefore understate the decline in population and overstate the improvement in income and housing conditions.)

### Population and Housing Changes in the 1960s

Table 3-9 summarizes the population and housing conditions in 1960 and 1970 for the sample of 50 neighborhoods. All but one lost population

TABLE 3-9   Neighborhood Changes in the 1960s

|  | 1960 Mean | 1970 Mean | 1960 % | 1970 % | % Change |
|---|---|---|---|---|---|
| **Population and Income** | | | | | |
| Population | 54,200 | 43,200 | | | −20.1 |
| White[a] | 22,800 | 12,900 | 42.0 | 29.9 | |
| Black[b] | 28,000 | 26,000 | 51.7 | 60.1 | |
| Hispanic | 3,400 | 4,300 | 6.3 | 10.0 | |
| Median household income[c] | $4,500 | $4,700 | | | +4.1 |
| **Housing** | | | | | |
| Housing units | 18,800 | 16,100 | | | −14.3 |
| Occupied housing units | 17,200 | 14,500 | | | −15.5 |
| Vacancy rate (%) | 8.6 | 11.5 | | | |
| Percent rented | 81.0 | 85.0 | | | |
| Space | | | | | |
| Persons per unit | 3.16 | 2.68 | | | |
| Median rooms per unit | 3.77 | 3.95 | | | |
| Percent crowded | 18.4 | 15.1 | | | |
| Percent without complete plumbing | 19.7 | 10.2 | | | |
| Percent in 1-unit structures | 36.2 | 41.7 | | | |
| Median home value[c] | $14,500 | $13,300 | | | −9.5 |
| Median rent[c] | $77 | $76 | | | −1.3 |

[a]Excludes Hispanic population, includes persons of other races.
[b]Non-Hispanic population.
[c]In 1970 dollars.

over the decade; the exception was a neighborhood in Miami that received an influx of Cuban refugees. Coincidentally, this data set includes two of the Los Angeles neighborhoods that had a growing Hispanic population in the 1970s; both were much less Hispanic in 1960 and lost population during the decade. They did, however, lose less population than the average during the decade, as was also true of the few other neighborhoods with a substantial Hispanic minority in 1960. The housing changes in the Miami neighborhood in the 1960s were much like the changes in the Hispanic neighborhoods in Los Angeles in the 1970s: a lower vacancy rate, higher rents, more crowding, and an increase in units without complete plumbing. As far as the data go, they suggest that Hispanic poverty neighborhoods were consistently different from white Anglo and black poverty areas.

In general, the data for the 1960s are much like the data for eastern and midwestern neighborhoods in the 1970s. The average decline in population was smaller in the 1960s—about one-fifth versus one-third—but this can be accounted for by the small declines in the southern and western neighborhoods that were excluded from the later data set. As in the 1970s, there was a 50 percent decline in the white population (including other races), and a modest gain on average in the number and incidence of

Hispanics. The black population declined on average, but much less than in the 1970s. It appears that the white middle class may have been moving out during the 1960s, the black middle class in the 1970s.

The economic circumstances of the people in these neighborhoods improved in the 1960s. There was a modest gain in real income, unlike in the 1970s. The difference may be explained by the fact that the earlier decade saw a much greater rate of economic growth for the country as a whole. Housing changes were similar in both decades. There was a decline in the number of units, a larger decline in the number of occupied units, and a rise in the vacancy rate. The typical household had more space: There were fewer persons per unit, more rooms per unit, and a lower incidence of crowding. For the small number of homeowners, values declined in real terms; for the large number of renters, real rents were stable. Data on the age of the housing stock were not collected on a comparable basis in 1960, but it seems likely that the experience was similar—a large loss among the oldest housing units and a small volume of new construction.

The big difference between the decades is the big drop in units without complete plumbing in the 1960s. This is the main reason why the reported increase in the 1970s was so surprising; it was inconsistent with the previous decade.

### From 1960 to 1980

The seven neighborhoods in both data sets confirm the consistency of the long-term trends. Data for these neighborhoods are shown in Table 3-10. Many of the neighborhoods have been nationally known for their housing or other problems: Bedford-Stuyvesant in Brooklyn, Watts in Los Angeles, Hough in Cleveland, Woodlawn and East Garfield Park in Chicago, as well as neighborhoods in Philadelphia and St. Louis. What has happened in them, as their notoriety has faded, may be of interest for its own sake, as well as being potentially indicative of changes elsewhere.

The seven neighborhoods lost about half their population from 1960 to 1980. Nearly all the white population moved out in the 1960s, and half of the small remainder moved out during the next decade. The black population declined slightly in the 1960s and substantially in the 1970s; its share grew in the first decade and was stable in the second. None of these neighborhoods had a large Hispanic or other population at any time; they are perhaps representative of the older slums in the older cities.

The typical family enjoyed a modest increase in real income over the 1960s, followed by a 25 percent decrease in the 1970s; the net effect was a substantial decline. In each decade, households in these areas fared much worse than the typical American household.

TABLE 3–10  Average Neighborhood Changes, 1960–1980

|  | 1960 | 1970 | 1980 |
|---|---|---|---|
| Population | 63,700 | 48,300 | 32,800 |
| White[a] | 15,500 | 4,100 | 2,000 |
| Black[a] | 45,000 | 41,000 | 27,300 |
| Hispanic | 3,100 | 3,000 | 3,300 |
| Other races | 100 | 200 | 200 |
| Median household income[b] | $9,500 | $10,400 | $7,900 |
| Housing units | 19,200 | 16,000 | 12,900 |
| Occupied | 18,100 | 14,500 | 11,000 |
| Vacancy rate (%) | 6.0 | 9.1 | 13.1 |
| Percent single family | 36.0 | 30.1 | 32.2 |
| Percent owner occupied | 17.4 | 26.6 | 29.2 |
| Persons per unit | 3.64 | 3.35 | 3.07 |
| Rooms per unit | 4.11 | 4.44 | 4.56 |
| Percent crowded | 23.0 | 17.3 | 13.0 |
| Percent without complete plumbing | 16.2 | 4.8 | 5.5 |
| Median value[b] | $45,500 | $33,300 | $22,400 |
| Median rent[b] | $151 | $139 | $129 |

[a]Non-Hispanic only.
[b]In 1980 dollars.

SOURCES: Special tabulations of 1960 census tracts by Oak Ridge National Laboratory, and of 1970 and 1980 tracts by Princeton University Computer Center.

The housing stock decreased, the vacancy rate increased, and real rents fell over both decades. All measures of housing space showed steady improvement. The plumbing data for 1980 are affected by the boarded-up buildings in New York and Philadelphia; the other five neighborhoods showed a decline in units without complete plumbing in both decades.

The data on homeownership and home values can be misleading. The neighborhoods in Los Angeles and Philadelphia have predominantly single-family housing; the St. Louis neighborhood was about half single-family in 1960. The Philadelphia neighborhood accounted for more than half the total number of owner-occupied units; the Los Angeles and St. Louis neighborhoods, nearly all the rest. Average changes therefore should be viewed with caution. In the 1960s, only Watts experienced an increase in real home values, of about 10 percent. All the others, including Philadelphia, had a nominal increase of less than 10 percent, or a slight nominal decrease. The 1970s saw a similar regional disparity. The average changes shown in the table slightly understate the declines in the East and Midwest—declines that really matter only for Philadelphia and St. Louis—and completely misrepresent what happened in Watts.

## THE FILTERING PROCESS AND THE CULTURE OF POVERTY

### The Bottom of the Barrel

The changes in the eastern and midwestern poverty neighborhoods suggest that a "filtering process" is at work in the metropolitan areas as a whole, and these neighborhoods are the dregs. The term "filtering" has been used to describe many processes of change in urban areas. In this study, it is used to describe a system of changes in residential location and changes in neighborhood housing costs. The filtering process begins when economic growth makes it possible for high-income families to move into new housing. As they move out, their old housing becomes available and more affordable to middle-income families, who then are able to move to the suburbs that the high-income families are leaving. Their housing in turn becomes available to families with somewhat lower incomes. Eventually, some poor people living in poverty neighborhoods are able to move into housing outside the neighborhood, housing that moderate-income families are leaving. These poor people are likely to be relatively the richest and most stable, economically and socially. They leave behind the poorest of their neighbors. As the poverty neighborhoods empty out, the worst housing within them drops out of the housing stock or stands vacant. The smallest and least desirable units are often but not always the oldest. The decline in population reflects a decline in the desirability of the neighborhood, so rents and values fall even though the housing stock, on average, has improved.

### Mobility Between and Within Neighborhoods

The "filtering" metaphor has some limitations, however. The neighborhoods do not "empty out" so much as they "churn." Mobility data for all poverty neighborhoods in these cities (not limited to the persistent slums) show that the overwhelming majority of residents in 1980 moved into their apartments after 1970. Between 45 and 62 percent had moved in since 1975; between 63 and 78 percent during the full decade.

These mobility rates were typically just a few percentage points higher than those for the remainder of the cities, so not too much should be read into them. Nonetheless, they may have policy implications for community development or neighborhood revitalization efforts. From that perspective, the question of inter- vs. intra-neighborhood mobility may be important. If most residents have moved within the neighborhood, or for a short distance, then the population at the end of the decade includes many people who were there at the beginning, and the stability of the population might give the neighborhood some basis for revitalization. If instead most of the residents come from some other neighborhood, and few stay for more than a few years, then any effort at revitalization is likely to be much more difficult, because the population may have very little sense of neighborhood attachment.

The census data identify previous residence only by municipality, not by neighborhood. Most of the residents of these neighborhoods moved in from elsewhere inside the city, if they did not live in the same house for the full decade. There have been a few studies of neighborhood mobility for the poor, for example as part of the Supply Experiment within the Experimental Housing Allowance Program. They show that most poor people move within the neighborhood, or for a short distance (see for example, Butler et al., 1969; Greenberg and Boswell, 1972; Lowry, 1983). This limited evidence is not fully relevant, however, because poor people, especially renters, move frequently. If they move three or four times in the course of a decade, one of those moves might be to a different neighborhood, even if all the others covered a short distance.

Some of the evidence in this study is consistent with a pattern of predominantly intra-neighborhood moves. The richest households and the worst housing units are simultaneously "leaving the neighborhood," so the remaining poor people may be moving to the better housing. But this argument cannot be pushed too far. It implies that there would be a greater improvement in housing quality in neighborhoods that lost the most people. In fact, there was no correlation between population change and quality improvements, except for crowding. The argument also implies that, for neighborhoods with larger population declines and neighborhoods with more improvement in housing quality, fewer of the residents would be living in the same house at the end of the decade. These correlations also do not appear in the data.

It is possible that the neighborhoods, bad as they are, could be attracting low-income households from other areas because the local housing is a bargain. It appears that real rents for housing of a given quality declined over the decade, although this cannot be demonstrated rigorously. If that did occur, low-income people could have moved in to take advantage of the fall in price.

A more detailed inspection of some Chicago census tracts reveals an interesting pattern. Turnover is much lower in public housing projects than in private low-income housing. In Cabrini-Green, 59 percent of the households had lived in the same unit for five years; in the rest of that poverty neighborhood, the proportion was 40 percent. Similar but less pronounced differences occur in other areas, for instance between Henry Horner Homes and the rest of the Near West Side, and between the high-rise projects stretching south of the Loop along State Street and the nearby older, low-rise private housing.

### The New Immigration

The poverty areas in Los Angeles are more like the traditional slums of the older big cities, at least in a statistical sense, than the old neighborhoods are themselves. They are ports of entry into the United States, or into the urban United States. About 10 percent of the 1980 residents of these areas had moved into the United States since 1975, presumably from Mexico and Latin America. Virtually nobody moved into the Chicago poverty neighborhoods from abroad. Population densities in the Los Angeles neighborhoods are lower than in the neighborhoods in the eastern and midwestern cities, but in the local context they are "teeming slums." Indeed, the housing is much more crowded in Los Angeles than in the East, though the density of dwelling units per acre is clearly lower. They are also vibrant rather than stagnant. People are working and doing better, rather than living on transfer payments and doing worse.

### STATISTICAL ANALYSES OF NEIGHBORHOOD CHANGES

Support for the notion of a filtering process at work comes from more sophisticated statistical analyses of some of the changes in the 79 poverty neighborhoods. The dependent variables include population, income, unemployment, and several measures of housing conditions. In each case, changes in the poverty neighborhoods are related both to changes in the metropolitan areas as a whole and to other changes in the neighborhoods that might be causal factors. Separate regression results are reported in the tables below for all 79 poverty neighborhoods, all neighborhoods except Los Angeles, and all neighborhoods except Los Angeles and New York. Los Angeles is omitted because of the very different changes that occurred there, New York because the large number of poor neighborhoods could dominate the analysis and obscure important relationships in other cities.

The variables in the regressions are generally expressed in percentage terms, either as percentage changes over the decade in population, income, or the stock of housing, or as changes in the percentage of units falling into a given category, such as the change in the percentage of the population that is Hispanic, or the change in the percentage of households that are headed by a woman. The reported regressions usually include only statistically significant variables; some interesting insignificant results—dogs that did not bark—are discussed in the text.

### General Findings

Before turning to the detailed discussion of relationships, it is worthwhile to take a broader perspective. The 79 neighborhoods are clearly integral parts of their metropolitan areas, not isolated islands. Population, income, and unemployment changes in the neighborhoods are all significantly and positively related to the corresponding changes in the SMSA. If the SMSA prospered, the poverty neighborhoods shared in the prosperity. The relationships are not proportionate, however. Neighborhood gains were smaller than metropolitan gains for population and income, but larger for the unemployment rate.

There is also statistical evidence of filtering. The concept is measured as the rate of new housing production relative to net household formation during the 1970s, for the SMSA as a whole. A high ratio—implying a greater possibility for filtering—is associated with better neighborhood housing conditions and perhaps with a greater decline in neighborhood population.

The most consistently important neighborhood factor is the growth in Hispanic population, which tends to put pressure on the local housing stock at the same time that local income and employment rise. Changes in household composition also matter.

### New Housing and Neighborhood Changes

The effects of new housing on the neighborhood deserve special mention. Building low-income housing in slum neighborhoods has been a public policy since the 1930s. Census data do not identify subsidized housing; new housing in the aggregate is the nearest approximation to new subsidized housing, though it is not the same thing. Even in persistent slums, some housing construction is reported in the decennial census. The data for the 50 poverty neighborhoods in the 1960s included new subsidized units from a special tabulation produced for the U.S. Department of Housing and Urban Development (HUD), showing the location of housing projects by census tract.[3] Surprisingly, the HUD programs accounted for only about half of the new units reported in the 1970 census. In several neighborhoods there were no new subsidized units, according to HUD, but 10 to 20 percent of the stock was added during the decade, according to the census.

Public and private construction are likely to arise from different circumstances and to have different effects on a neighborhood. New private construction is a sign of neighborhood strength or revitalization; it probably occurs if income is rising and other economic and social characteristics are improving. Subsidized housing, on the other hand, is often built in deteriorating neighborhoods. New subsidized projects will hold population in

---

[3] The data on subsidized housing in the HUD tabulation give the HUD program, the number of units, the census tract, and the year built, through 1972.

the neighborhood or bring residents in from other areas, but income and employment will not necessarily rise; indeed, they may fall.

The indirect evidence is mixed, but it suggests that most of the new housing in these neighborhoods is subsidized. Housing construction during the 1970s is consistently and positively associated with population change; neighborhoods decline more slowly. It is not related, however, to most of the measures of housing quality. Construction does result in a decline in crowding in the smallest sample, but the effect is small. There is also a weaker and smaller relationship in the largest sample, significant only at the 20 percent level.

In the plumbing and heating regressions, there is no effect at all. This is odd. All new housing units must have complete plumbing, and most will have central heating (perhaps excluding some public housing projects). They must be better, on average, than the units they are replacing, but the improvement does not appear statistically. The explanation may be partly the change in the census definition of "lacking complete plumbing" and partly the fact that not all new housing in these neighborhoods is subsidized by the government. In an earlier analysis of poverty neighborhoods during the 1960s (Weicher, 1973), new subsidized housing had a larger and more significant effect on the decline in units without complete plumbing, than did new private construction. Private construction may be more common in neighborhoods where the rest of the housing stock is relatively good. It is also possible that there are errors in the census data on "year structure built." The information is provided by the resident on the census questionnaire; if the current resident is not the original occupant, he or she may not know the correct year.

### Population

Population changes distinguish improving poverty neighborhoods from deteriorating ones, so an explanation of population change is central to the analysis. It is therefore unfortunate even though understandable that the results vary substantially among the samples (Table 3-11).

The high growth rate in Los Angeles, for both total and Hispanic population, results in a growing population for most of its poverty neighborhoods. The Los Angeles experience is so different from the other cities that the relationships are statistically significant even though Los Angeles accounts for only 10 of the 79 neighborhoods.

When the sample is restricted to the eastern and midwestern neighborhoods, New York accounts for almost half of it. For this half, SMSA population changes, and other changes, were the same. At the same time, population changes among New York neighborhoods were more variable

TABLE 3-11  Regression Analysis of Neighborhood Population Changes

| Variable | Sample | | |
| --- | --- | --- | --- |
| | All 79 Neighborhoods | Excluding Los Angeles | Excluding Los Angeles and New York |
| Constant | −.31 | −.02 | −.33 |
| SMSA population change | +.93 (3.0) | — | — |
| SMSA Hispanic population change | +2.09 (2.4) | — | — |
| SMSA Filtering | — | — | −.59 (1.8) |
| Hispanic population change | +.47 (2.3) | +.52 (2.4) | +.76 (3.8) |
| New housing | +.61 (3.1) | +.55 (2.5) | +.96 (3.9) |
| Crowded housing in 1970 | −.67 (2.5) | −.83 (2.9) | — |
| One-room units in 1970 | +.58 (2.8) | — | — |
| Old housing units in 1970 | — | −.29 (2.2) | −.71 (2.1) |
| $R^2$ | .68 | .26 | .50 |

NOTE:  Figures in parentheses are t-ratios of the regression coefficients.  All variables refer to the neighborhood unless "SMSA" is specified.  All variables are expressed as percentages or percentage changes.

than in the rest of the sample.  New York had the only two neighborhoods with population increases, and also the three neighborhoods with the largest decreases (over 75 percent decline in a decade).  None of this variability can be explained statistically by anything that happened to the New York metropolitan area as a whole; all of it has to be explained by changes within the individual neighborhoods.  Thus, it is not surprising that no SMSA changes are significant in the East/Midwest regression, and the ability of any regression model to explain population changes is relatively weak.

Finally, when New York is excluded, population changes for the remaining 40 neighborhoods (spread across nine cities) are again affected by changes in the SMSA.  The availability of housing in the SMSA—the filtering variable—apparently makes it possible for people to leave the neighborhood.  This relationship is on the margin of statistical significance, but it is reasonable.

Neighborhood-specific factors also affect population change.  Two are significant for all three samples, and also for the New York neighborhoods considered by themselves (not shown in Table 3-11).  One is new housing production; the other is the growth in the neighborhood's Hispanic population. This matters even when the sample is restricted to the cities with small Hispanic populations.

There is also some evidence of a "flight from blight," especially in New York. Population declined more in neighborhoods with a higher percentage of old housing units at the beginning of the decade in the full East/Midwest sample, but not when Los Angeles was included or New York was excluded. For the two larger samples, population declined more in the neighborhoods that were the most crowded in 1970. Finally, and oddly, in the full sample, population growth was greater in neighborhoods with a larger share of single-room units—rooming houses—in 1970. This variable was originally included in the expectation that rooming houses and other small units were becoming increasingly undesirable. The opposite effect appears in the results. This apparently occurs because two Los Angeles neighborhoods with very high concentrations of rooming houses gained population.

## Income

Most of the other changes in these neighborhoods can be explained by the same factors in all of the samples. The decline in real household income, one of the most discouraging trends, is consistently related to both the strength of the metropolitan area economy, and to the change in the incidence of female-headed families (Table 3-12). Poverty neighborhood incomes tended to rise, or at least to fall less, in the most prosperous metropolitan areas. This indicates that the neighborhoods did not function as isolated economic units apart from the larger regions. At the same time, however, these areas lagged behind the rest of the SMSA. If the metropolitan area enjoyed a 10 percent growth in real household income, the typical poverty neighborhood gained only 4 percent; if the area enjoyed a 5 percent growth, the poverty neighborhood lost about 2 percent.

Real income declined the most in the neighborhoods with the greatest percentage increase in the incidence of female-headed households. In the two larger samples, income changes also were positively correlated with changes in the proportion of adults who were employed; the more people who worked, the better off the neighborhood. In addition, income rose more in the neighborhoods where the housing stock increased. These were mainly the Hispanic neighborhoods, but statistically, however, employment and housing stock changes mattered more than the change in the Hispanic population. When New York and Los Angeles were excluded, neither employment nor housing stock changes were significant. Instead, income change was negatively related to the change in the black population; incomes fell more in the neighborhoods where the black population increased.

TABLE 3-12  Regression Analysis of Neighborhood Income Changes

| Variable | Sample All 79 Neighborhoods | Excluding Los Angeles | Excluding Los Angeles and New York |
|---|---|---|---|
| Constant | −.09 | −.06 | −.06 |
| SMSA income change | +1.28 | +1.27 | +1.67 |
|  | (5.5) | (5.1) | (3.1) |
| Black population change | — | — | −.58 |
|  |  |  | (2.0) |
| Female-headed household change | −.39 | −.45 | −.84 |
|  | (5.2) | (5.0) | (5.2) |
| Employment change | +1.03 | +1.16 | +.65 |
|  | (4.9) | (4.7) | (1.3) |
| Occupied housing stock change | +.14 | +.16 | — |
|  | (2.0) | (2.1) |  |
| $R^2$ | .67 | .59 | .66 |

NOTE: Figures in parentheses are t-ratios of the regression coefficients. All variables refer to the neighborhood unless "SMSA" is specified. All variables are expressed as percentages or percentage changes.

## Housing Conditions

Three aspects of neighborhood housing are analyzed: crowding, the absence of complete plumbing, and the absence of central heating. In each case, the neighborhood housing market turns out to be greatly affected by the metropolitan market.

The change in crowding is affected by population pressures both within and outside the neighborhood: the overall growth rate in the two larger samples, and the neighborhood growth in both total and Hispanic population in all three samples (Table 3-13). It also may be related to new housing construction within the neighborhood.

The importance of the change in definition (from "within structure" to "within unit") shows up clearly in the analysis of units lacking complete plumbing. The most significant and important factors are the change in the local vacancy rate, which reflects the increase in the boarded-up buildings in New York and Philadelphia, and the change in one-room units, many of them presumably located in rooming houses (Table 3-14). Conditions in the metropolitan area were also important. A high construction rate allowed units without complete plumbing to drop out of the stock. Outside of New York and Los Angeles, also, more units without plumbing dropped out of the stock as more people left the neighborhood. They were probably the worst units to begin with.

Metropolitan conditions also affected the incidence of units without central heating (Table 3-15). A high rate of SMSA population growth put

TABLE 3-13  Regression Analysis of Neighborhood Changes in Crowding

| | Sample | | |
| Variable | All 79 Neighborhoods | Excluding Los Angeles | Excluding Los Angeles and New York |
|---|---|---|---|
| Constant | −.00 | −.02 | +.01 |
| SMSA income change | +.30 | +.24 | — |
| | (3.6) | (2.3) | |
| Population change | +.14 | +.09 | +.14 |
| | (4.5) | (3.5) | (2.1) |
| Hispanic population change | +.14 | +.10 | +.27 |
| | (2.4) | (2.1) | (2.9) |
| New housing | −.08 | — | −.29 |
| | (1.3) | | (2.0) |
| $R^2$ | .68 | .29 | .48 |

NOTES: Figures in parentheses are t-ratios of the regression coefficients. All variables refer to the neighborhood unless "SMSA" is specified. All variables are expressed as percentages or percentage changes.


TABLE 3-14  Regression Analysis of Change in Housing Units Without Complete Plumbing

| | Sample | | |
| Variable | All 79 Neighborhoods | Excluding Los Angeles | Excluding Los Angeles and New York |
|---|---|---|---|
| Constant | +.02 | +.02 | +.04 |
| SMSA filtering | −.32 | −.31 | −.24 |
| | (3.0) | (2.9) | (1.6) |
| Vacancy rate change | +.27 | +.20 | +.31 |
| | (4.8) | (2.9) | (3.3) |
| Change in one-room housing units | +.63 | +.83 | +.82 |
| | (6.5) | (6.2) | (4.2) |
| Change in occupied housing stock | — | — | +.12 |
| | | | (2.2) |
| $R^2$ | .55 | .58 | .52 |

NOTES: Figures in parentheses are t-ratios of the regression coefficients. All variables refer to the neighborhood unless "SMSA" is specified. All variables are expressed as percentages or percentage changes.


pressure on the neighborhood housing stock and kept those units in use. Conversely, a high rate of economic growth and a high rate of housing construction permitted abandonment or destruction, or alternatively upgrading. Outside of New York, at least, units without central heating were disproportionately the units vacated or removed from the neighborhood stock.

TABLE 3-15 Regression Analysis of Change in Housing Units Without Central Heating

| Variable | Sample | |
|---|---|---|
| | Excluding Los Angeles | Excluding Los Angeles and New York |
| Constant | +.13 | +.20 |
| SMSA population change | +.89 | +.77 |
| | (4.2) | (2.9) |
| SMSA income change | −.54 | −.90 |
| | (3.3) | (3.4) |
| SMSA filtering | −.86 | −.78 |
| | (3.4) | (2.6) |
| Change in occupied housing stock | — | +.18 |
| | | (1.7) |
| $R^2$ | .37 | .49 |

NOTES: Figures in parentheses are t-ratios of the regression coefficients. All variables refer to the neighborhood unless "SMSA" is specified. All variables are expressed as percentages or percentage changes. Los Angeles neighborhoods omitted because of the climate.

## Unemployment and Labor Force Participation

The analysis of unemployment and labor force participation indicates that these neighborhoods should be regarded as local sources of labor for a metropolitan market, rather than as isolated local labor markets. The ability and willingness of the neighborhood's residents to supply labor—to work—depend on their personal characteristics, such as age, skills, and preferences (whether a woman has a small child to care for, for instance). The willingness of employers to hire them depends on the demand for the firm's output—in the aggregate, on the demand for the output of all firms in the metropolitan area. The analysis of neighborhood unemployment and labor force participation (Tables 3-16 and 3-17) is essentially a reduced form of this model; the SMSA unemployment rate is the proxy for the demand for labor, and labor force participation is measured by the fraction of the adult population that is not in the labor force.

Both metropolitan demand and local supply contributed to the labor force changes. A rise in the SMSA unemployment rate raised the neighborhood unemployment rate, in all samples, on about a one-for-one basis. Several attributes of the neighborhood were related to the local unemployment rate, particularly the growth in Hispanic population and changes in household composition, in different samples (Table 3-16). It is encouraging to note that the unemployment rate fell more in neighborhoods where the educational level of the population increased more, but this effect unfortunately disappeared when Los Angeles was excluded.

TABLE 3-16  Regression Analysis of Changes in Neighborhood Unemployment Rate

| Variable | Sample | | |
| | All 79 Neighborhoods | Excluding Los Angeles | Excluding Los Angeles and New York |
| --- | --- | --- | --- |
| Constant | +.02 | +.01 | +.01 |
| SMSA unemployment rate change | +.75 | +.90 | +1.09 |
| | (6.7) | (4.7) | (4.7) |
| Hispanic population change | −.05 | −.05 | — |
| | (3.3) | (2.9) | |
| Change in median years of schooling | −.53 | — | — |
| | (2.4) | | |
| Married couple change | — | −.05 | — |
| | | (2.3) | |
| Female-headed household change | — | — | +.03 |
| | | | (1.9) |
| Change in occupied housing stock | — | — | +.06 |
| | | | (2.2) |
| $R^2$ | .48 | .35 | .53 |

NOTES:  Figures in parentheses are t-ratios of the regression coefficients. All variables refer to the neighborhood unless "SMSA" is specified. All variables are expressed as percentage changes except the change in schooling, which is the change in the median number of years.

Labor force participation was less affected by the SMSA unemployment rate and more by the neighborhood attributes: age and race consistently, schooling and household composition in some cases (Table 3-17).

In most of these neighborhoods, the unemployment rate rose over the decade and labor force participation declined. It is frequently argued that one important factor contributing to unemployment in urban ghettos is suburbanization; increasingly businesses and jobs are moving to the suburbs, leaving the urban poor, particularly minorities, unable to get to them—in effect, unable to supply their labor. Solutions to the problem range from improving public transit systems to building subsidized housing in the suburbs. (For an exposition of this view, see Kasarda, 1986.)

Data on job location within SMSAs, available in the decennial census, permit some investigation of this issue. Individuals report whether they worked the week that the census is taken—the week of April 1—and where they worked: in the central business district, elsewhere in the central city, or in the suburbs. These responses were aggregated for the entire SMSA to obtain a picture of the changes in job location and included in the statistical analysis. Changes in job location for the central business district, the rest of the central city, and the central city as a whole, were included as separate independent variables in the analyses of unemployment and labor force participation. Generally, the findings indicate that job suburbanization has not mattered to the people in these poverty neighborhoods. None of the

TABLE 3-17 Regression Analysis of Neighborhood Changes in Labor Force Participation (measured as percentage of adults not in the labor force)

| Variable | Sample | | |
| --- | --- | --- | --- |
| | All 76 Neighborhoods | Excluding Los Angeles | Excluding Los Angeles and New York |
| Constant | +.05 | +.07 | −.04 |
| Change in city's share of SMSA jobs | −.12 | −.10 | +.12 |
| | (3.5) | (2.7) | (1.4) |
| SMSA unemployment rate change | — | — | +.03 |
| | | | (2.5) |
| Elderly population change | +1.14 | +1.00 | +.67 |
| | (4.7) | (4.2) | (2.7) |
| Youth population change | +.53 | +.63 | +.35 |
| | (2.9) | (3.4) | (1.6) |
| Hispanic population change | −.10 | −.12 | −.17 |
| | (1.6) | (2.1) | (1.5) |
| Change in population of "other races" | −.54 | −.82 | — |
| | (2.6) | (3.9) | |
| Female-headed household change | — | — | +.11 |
| | | | (2.5) |
| Change in median years of schooling | +.01 | — | — |
| | (1.3) | | |
| $R^2$ | .55 | .50 | .52 |

NOTES: Figures in parentheses are t-ratios of the regression coefficients. All variables refer to the neighborhood unless "SMSA" is specified. All variables are expressed as percentage changes except the change in schooling, which is the change in the median number of years. Long Beach and Gary omitted.

locational changes was significant in any of the unemployment regressions. Jobs have become more dispersed in most of these SMSAs, but that has not affected the unemployment rates in the poverty neighborhoods.

The labor force regressions present a somewhat different picture. In the two larger samples, a shift in jobs from the city to the suburbs results in an increase in the proportion of neighborhood residents who choose to drop out of the labor force altogether. The effect is small, however. A decline of 17 percentage points in the city's share of SMSA jobs—the largest for any city in this sample—is associated with a 2 percentage point decline in the labor force participation rate. Moreover, the relationship disappears, and in fact is reversed, when New York and Los Angeles are excluded. The coefficient for the smallest sample is positive, and equally large in absolute value, but it is not conventionally significant.

These results suggest that suburbanization of jobs is a problem for people living in poverty neighborhoods in New York and Los Angeles, but not in the other large eastern and midwestern cities. One might speculate that the problem is more serious in New York, though the regression results do not particularly suggest it. Half the New York neighborhoods are in Brooklyn; the nearest suburbs are in Nassau County, with Queens in between. (There is only one poverty neighborhood in Queens.) Some Manhattan residents are close to New Jersey, but the census data for the borough as a whole show relatively little commuting in that direction. Most of the Los Angeles neighborhoods are close to the Civic Center and have good access to freeways. Several neighborhoods are just inside the city limits; Watts is essentially a peninsula surrounded by suburbs on three sides.

This is about as far as one can go with the current data set. More detailed information on job location would be needed, as well as further tabulations of census tract data on automobile ownership. It would also be desirable to include other cities in the analysis.

## POLICY IMPLICATIONS: WHAT MIGHT HELP?

Poverty neighborhoods clearly have persistent problems and they may be deteriorating. Public policy at best kept them from getting worse during the 1970s; it did not make them better. One purpose of this committee's study is to evaluate alternative policies that might help. In this concluding section, some past and present policies are considered in light of the changes and current conditions in these neighborhoods. It is convenient to categorize policies in terms of their orientation: Do they try to help people or try to help places? Some programs have tried to do both, but most have a primary focus on one or the other.

### Programs for the Poor

Income transfers are increasingly important to the people in poverty neighborhoods, though they are not necessarily urban programs. Transfer payments probably account for a larger share of neighborhood income; certainly more residents have been receiving them. The data tabulated for this chapter do not distinguish between Social Security and welfare programs, but given the changing age distribution and household composition in these neighborhoods, it is likely that both have become more important income sources. These transfers are surely helping the people, but they are probably not doing much to make the neighborhoods more desirable places to live.

The Family Support Act of 1988 may help. This welfare reform legislation has several features intended to deter the formation of single-parent families. The law establishes mandatory child support by absentee fathers, including establishing paternity, automated tracking of support payments, and use of Social Security numbers. In addition, states can deny Aid to Families With Dependent Children to single mothers who are minors, if they have moved out of their parents' home. These changes may reduce the proportion of female-headed families in these poverty neighborhoods. As a by-product, they would also probably reduce the demand for housing units; some married couples would exist in place of two separate households, and some young women would continue to live with their parents. The worst housing in these neighborhoods would drop out of the housing stock more rapidly.

The Family Support Act also includes a "workfare" component that consists of mandatory job training or schooling, as appropriate. Either could help some people in these neighborhoods to participate more effectively in the labor force. One of the few positive factors in these neighborhoods has been the improving educational level of the adult population, which apparently increased labor force participation and reduced neighborhood unemployment; this did not, however, translate into higher incomes in the neighborhoods. Unfortunately, the typical adult still had less than a high school education.

Education and training will not completely reverse the decline in labor force participation, no matter how successful they are. Many residents are out of the labor force simply because they are old. A one percentage point growth in the elderly population translated into a one percentage point decline in labor force participation, and the growth in the elderly population in the average neighborhood accounted for about a quarter of the decline in participation.

Single mothers accounted for another substantial share of the decline in participation, and they might benefit from welfare reform in the long run. Mothers with very young children would not have to participate in workfare, so the short-term effectiveness would depend on whether the full package of reforms successfully deterred single parenthood.

### Housing

Housing programs are in an intermediate category; they attempt to help people and places at the same time. The decade of the 1970s witnessed unprecedented production of both private and subsidized housing. The subsidy programs may have helped improve the quality of life in the poverty neighborhoods. New low-income housing projects seem to have slowed the loss of population, and they may have given the residents more space to live in.

The housing programs of the 1970s had other purposes as well. At the beginning of the decade, Sections 235 and 236 had as one objective opening up the suburbs for the urban poor.[4] They could have contributed

---

[4]Most subsidized housing programs (including Section 235 and 236) are commonly known by the number of the section of the National Housing Act in which they are created, or else (as in

to the emptying of poverty neighborhoods. Apparently, however, they did not. The programs were large but short-lived, and suburban subsidized housing did not affect city housing conditions during the early 1970s (Weicher, 1982). Section 8, in the last half of the decade, was even larger. The Section 8 New Construction program, at least during the 1970s, disproportionately served the white elderly poor, allowing them to live in decent neighborhoods. It might have contributed to the population decline in the poverty neighborhoods, but the program came so late in the decade that any substantial effect by 1980 is not likely. The Section 8 program evaluations to date have not addressed this issue.

Whatever effects housing construction programs had during the 1970s, they will probably prove to have smaller effects during the 1980s. The Section 8 New Construction program was terminated in 1983 and no construction program has been passed to replace it, but even so, a substantial number of new units have been added to the stock during this decade. Moreover, the "pipeline" is long; like other federal low-income construction programs, Section 8 New Construction projects often take several years to complete. Nonetheless, a larger share of the newly subsidized households in the 1980s live in existing housing and receive rental assistance under the Section 8 Existing Housing certificate program or the more recent voucher program. These programs serve many households who already live in decent housing but have a high rent burden, and they stimulate some modest improvements and perhaps some increased maintenance of the existing stock. The programs can also be used to move into better housing in a better neighborhood. The effect on the neighborhood depends basically on the general quality of housing to begin with. If the local private housing stock is generally decent, the programs help poor people afford the housing and promote neighborhood stability. If the stock is substandard, the programs help poor people move out of the neighborhood. The neighborhoods in this study probably fall more in the latter category.

Several of these neighborhoods include traditional public housing projects. Public housing offers special problems and special opportunities. Many urban projects consist of concentrations of the poorest and least skilled members of society. Some projects have been notoriously undermaintained, and many of the largest public housing authorities have been officially designated as "troubled" by the U.S. Department of Housing and Urban Development (HUD), meaning that they fail to manage their projects efficiently. At the same time, much of the public housing stock is

---

the case of Section 8) by their section number in the act adding them to the National Housing Act.

structurally adequate and decent; it is better than the private housing available in many poverty neighborhoods. Moreover, public housing projects have more stable populations than poverty neighborhoods in general.

Resident management and tenant ownership of public housing have been strongly advocated by the Bush administration and by HUD Secretary Jack Kemp. They may be one way to achieve neighborhood improvement. At first sight, this may seem an unlikely strategy; many public housing residents are very poor, and projects in many poverty neighborhoods consist of high-rise apartment buildings. Tenant ownership must perforce take the form of cooperative or condominium ownership, or ownership by a resident management corporation. Nonetheless, there have been some spectacular resident management success stories in urban public housing projects, and a number of projects have been converted to resident ownership since 1985, in a demonstration sponsored by HUD. Some badly deteriorated projects have been turned into attractive communities. The process of managing and owning a project has enabled the residents to acquire skills that they can use in other aspects of their lives. Since resident ownership and tenant management have become important components of housing policy, they have generated significant expressions of interest from public housing residents in many projects across the country.

Tenant ownership typically requires financial support from the federal government. Some projects need to be rehabilitated. In addition, because the tenants are often very poor, they may need subsidies to meet the ongoing operating costs of the projects, at least for a time, just as they did while renting.

### Community Development Strategies

It is hard to assess the potential of programs to help places rather than people in poverty neighborhoods. Since they are persistent slums, they are by definition places where local economic development either has not been tried or has not worked. If it had succeeded, the neighborhood would have moved out of poverty.

There may have been some successful neighborhood development projects in low-income urban areas, but not many. A few census tracts in the cities under study moved out of poverty during the 1970s, but very few were in or near the poverty neighborhoods. The reason for the improvement cannot be ascertained from census data alone. The Washington, D.C., neighborhood mentioned earlier is an example of pure gentrification, rather than a public or private community development effort to help the poor.

The major urban policy proposal of the Reagan and Bush administrations has been the enterprise zone. The current zone proposal offers both capital and labor subsidies, in the form of tax incentives, to businesses located in areas with high unemployment. It is intended to promote entrepreneurship and business formation, as well as job creation. The labor subsidy takes the form of a 5 percent refundable tax credit for the first $10,500 of wages paid to individuals working in the zone and having total wages of less than $20,000. The credit phases out between $20,000 and $25,000.

A related policy is the subminimum training wage included in the minimum wage increase enacted in 1989. This may enable residents of poverty areas to find their first job and get a start on a better life, even if they are not immediately lifted out of poverty. At the same time, the overall minimum wage increase will tend to reduce employment of low-skilled poverty neighborhood residents, if anything.

### National Economic Policy and Poverty Neighborhoods

The differences between the 1960s and 1970s and the connections between the neighborhood and metropolitan area economies illustrate the importance of national economic changes and macroeconomic policies. Real economic growth was substantial in the 1960s, and people in poverty neighborhoods fared better in real terms, though they lost ground relative to people in the rest of the SMSA. Economic performance was weaker in the 1970s; the increase in family income for the nation as a whole was half as great. In most of the poverty neighborhoods in this study, real incomes declined.

Macroeconomic policies had other neighborhood repercussions. Housing production was much greater in the 1970s, in large part because of accelerating inflation. Early in the decade, a stimulative macroeconomic policy held interest rates down and encouraged record housing production. In the late 1970s, double-digit inflation fueled a speculative housing boom as part of a flight from financial assets to real ones. Geographically, the suburbs became more popular, the cities became less desirable, and the poverty neighborhoods emptied out. Inflation promoted filtering.

Despite the strong record of economic growth during the 1980s, it seems clear that the decade will be similar in key respects to the 1970s. The poverty rate for central cities was substantially higher in 1988 (the latest year available) than it was in 1979: 18.3 versus 15.7 percent. (Measured consistently, the rate was 16.5 percent in 1988 and about 14 percent in 1979.) While 1989 was a year of continued economic growth, the poverty rate surely did not decline to the 1979 level. The rate during the 1970s also increased; it was 13.4 percent in 1969. (Poverty neighborhoods are delineated after each decennial census on the basis of annual incomes reported for the preceding year.)

The overall increase in central-city poverty in the 1980s is the net result of a sharp rise during the recession years from 1980 to 1982, and a steady but smaller decrease during each year of the economic recovery that continued through the rest of the decade. The official central-city poverty rate rose from 15.7 percent in 1979—the last full year of the cyclical recovery that began in 1975—to 19.9 percent in 1982. The rate rose substantially during the mild 1980 recession to 17.2 percent for the year. This is of some interest because the 1980 election marked a significant and controversial change in social welfare policy, and because public discussion of poverty trends during the decade often confuses the economic cycle that started at the beginning of 1980 with the political policy shift that started at the beginning of 1981. Although central-city poverty increased in both cycles, the increase during the Reagan administration (1980–1988) will probably be noticeably less than the increase during the decade of the 1980s (1979–1989).

The last two decades have seen a disturbing concentration of poverty in central cities. The overall poverty rate in 1988 was slightly lower than in 1969 (measured consistently), but the central-city rate was markedly higher. The logical inference from these data is that poverty neighborhoods in big cities expanded geographically during the 1980s, repeating the pattern of the 1970s.

## CONCLUSION: PROSPECTS AND POSSIBILITIES

Looking at places rather than people is inherently discouraging. The hypothetical average person living in a poverty neighborhood was worse off in 1980 than 1970, in many ways. But any real individual probably did better than this hypothetical average. There were fewer people in the neighborhoods in 1980, and many of them may not have lived there in 1970. We tend to think in terms of neighborhoods because data exist for neighborhoods. Because "the neighborhoods" are worse off both relatively and absolutely, we think of their residents as an underclass. But this is potentially misleading, because of mobility. The slums have persisted, but many of the people have moved on, and we do not know whether they are better or worse off.

As a society, we are really more interested in the well-being of people than places. In fact, the most important public policies toward poverty neighborhoods have not been place oriented. Explicit public policy has increasingly centered on income maintenance; implicitly, policy has encouraged people to leave poverty areas. That is not a bad combination for the future. It should be abundantly clear by now that poverty neighborhoods are generally unattractive places to live. We should expect people to seek better neighborhoods, if they can. At the same time, we can probably improve current income maintenance programs so that they help beneficiaries find their own way out of poverty, and perhaps out of poverty neighborhoods.

Part of the income maintenance and also part of the inducement to move could be a housing voucher program or an expansion of the Section 8 Existing Housing certificate program. Public housing, Section 8 New Construction, and other low-income construction programs have proven to be much more expensive than using the existing stock to house the poor. Public housing changes the neighborhood as well as the housing stock. It has slowed the rate of population decline in poverty neighborhoods and lowered the turnover. Improvements in neighborhood housing quality, however, have been small at best. Overall, the beneficial effects on the neighborhood, if there are any, are probably far too small to justify the expense. This conclusion is based on the objective neighborhood changes reported in the decennial census. This chapter has not tried to analyze the role of subsidized housing construction in creating an underclass or promoting a culture of poverty, which are more important but more nebulous issues.

A declining but substantial minor fraction of the people in these neighborhoods are children (about one-third in 1980, down from about 40 percent in 1970). The strategy of income maintenance for the current residents may not help the children get out of poverty when they grow up. They need more and better education. A campaign to discourage dropping out of school would help. Public schools in many poverty neighborhoods do not provide an adequate education, however. Improving the schools would make the neighborhoods more desirable places to live, but that is obviously a tall order. Education vouchers would let poor people send their children to better schools outside the neighborhood, which might keep relatively high-income households in the poverty neighborhoods when their children reach school age. That would promote neighborhood stability and perhaps neighborhood development.

Whatever policies are followed, the prognosis is for further population decline. This need not be the fate of every poverty neighborhood; some can probably be turned around. But these neighborhoods seem to be attractive mainly to new immigrants in growing metropolitan areas. Some of the neighborhoods in the eastern and midwestern cities were ports of entry for immigrants from Europe until immigration was restricted after 1924. A few have drawn the new immigrants from Latin America; if the study were extended to include more southern and western cities, there would be more such neighborhoods. The Simpson-Mazzoli Act of 1988, if it is effective, will discourage new immigration in the future. Within a few years, the Los Angeles poverty neighborhoods are likely to start losing population as some of the new immigrants move up on the economic ladder and can afford better places to live. The poverty neighborhoods in the East, which have seen some influx of Hispanics and Asians, will continue to empty out, probably faster.

## ACKNOWLEDGMENTS

The author benefited from discussions with Cicero Wilson and assistance from Carlton Henry and David Hover in the initial stages of the research, and from comments on an earlier draft by John L. Goodman, Jr., Daniel Weinberg, and the members of the Committee on National Urban Policy. Sole responsibility for any errors rests with the author.

This study was supported by a grant from the Joyce Foundation to the American Enterprise Institute, and was completed while the author was in residence at the American Enterprise Institute. The opinions and conclusions are also those of the author, and not necessarily those of the American Enterprise Institute, the Joyce Foundation, or the U.S. Department of Housing and Urban Development.

## REFERENCES

Bureau of the Census
    1966    *Characteristics of Families Residing in "Poverty Areas": March 1966.* Current Population Reports, Series P-23, No. 19. Washington, D.C.: U.S. Department of Commerce.
    1973    *Characteristics of Low-Income Areas.* 1970 Census of Population, Vol. II, No. 9B. Washington, D.C.: U.S. Department of Commerce.
    1989    *Money Income and Poverty Status in the United States: 1988 (Advance Data from the March 1989 Current Population Survey).* Series P-60, No. 166. Washington, D.C.: U.S. Department of Commerce.
Butler, Edgar, et al.
    1969    *Moving Behavior and Residential Choice: A National Survey.* National Cooperative Highway Research Program Report No. 81. Washington, D.C.
Greenberg, Michael R., and Thomas D. Boswell
    1972    Neighborhood deterioration as a factor in intraurban migration: a case study in New York City. *Professional Geographer* 24(February):11-16.
Kasarda, John D.
    1986    The regional and urban redistribution of people and jobs in the U.S. Paper prepared for the Committee on National Urban Policy, National Research Council, Washington, D.C.
Lowry, Ira S., ed.
    1983    *Experimenting with Housing Allowances.* Cambridge, Mass.: Oelgeschlager, Gunn & Hain.
Nathan, Richard
    1986    The Underclass—Will It Always Be With Us? Paper prepared for a symposium at the New School for Social Research, November.
National Housing Policy Review
    1974    *Housing in the Seventies.* Washington, D.C.: U.S. Department of Housing and Urban Development.

Putnam, Israel
    1973     Poverty Neighborhoods in 105 Large Central Cities, A Special Tabulation From the 1970 Census. Photocopy. Available from John C. Weicher, U.S. Department of Housing and Urban Development.
Weicher, John C.
    1973     The Causes of Housing Improvement in Low-Income Neighborhoods. Paper prepared for the National Housing Policy Review. Available from the author.
    1982     *The Relationship Between Subsidized Housing Production and Loss Rates Within Metropolitan Areas.* Contract Report No. 1484-01 to the U.S. Department of Housing and Urban Development. Washington, D.C.: Urban Institute.
    1987     Mismeasuring poverty and progress, *CATO Journal* 7(Winter):715-730.

# 4
# The Social Consequences of Growing Up in a Poor Neighborhood

CHRISTOPHER JENCKS AND SUSAN E. MAYER

## INTRODUCTION

Children from affluent schools know more, stay in school longer, and end up with better jobs than children from schools that enroll mostly poor children. Children who live in affluent neighborhoods also get into less trouble with the law and have fewer illegitimate children than children who live in poor neighborhoods. Similar patterns are found when we compare white neighborhoods to black neighborhoods. These patterns have convinced many social scientists, policy analysts, and ordinary citizens that a neighborhood or school's social composition really influences children's life chances. But this need not be the case. The differences we observe could simply reflect the fact that children from affluent families do better than children from poor families no matter where they live. Similarly, white children may fare better than black children regardless of their neighborhood's racial mix. In order to determine how much a neighborhood or school's mean socioeconomic status (SES) affects a child's life chances, we need to compare children from similar families who grew up in different kinds of neighborhoods. This study examines what social scientists have learned from studies of this kind.

We give considerable attention to the policy implications of the studies we discuss. Many observers (notably W. Wilson, 1987) believe that when poor children have predominantly poor neighbors, their chances of escaping from poverty decline. If this is so, a strong case can be made for governmental efforts to reduce the geographic isolation of poor children. Yet such evidence as we have suggests that the poor—or at least poor blacks—are becoming more geographically isolated rather than less so (Jargowsky and Bane, in this volume; Massey and Eggers, 1990; Weicher, in this volume).

111

At present, the main goal of federal subsidies for low-income housing is to build as many low-income units as possible for as little money as possible. The best way to achieve this goal is usually to build in low-income neighborhoods. As a result, federal subsidies are quite likely to increase economic segregation. If the federal government wanted to reduce economic segregation, it would either have to help poor families move to better neighborhoods or encourage more affluent families to remain in poor neighborhoods (perhaps through mortgage subsidies).

In assessing these policy alternatives, it is important to ask how they will affect both rich and poor children. We cannot answer that question, because social scientists have not yet accumulated the information we would need to answer it. The best we can do is summarize the available evidence and offer some guidelines for interpreting it.

We focus on quantitative studies that try to separate neighborhood or school effects from family effects through statistical analysis of survey data. We ignore qualitative studies, not because we think them incapable of answering the question that concerns us but because we found no qualitative research that tried to answer this question. The ethnographic studies we reviewed never tried to compare children from similar families who lived in different neighborhoods. Nor did they follow families as they moved from one neighborhood to another, describing how the moves affected the children. As a result, they cannot help us disentangle neighborhood or school effects from family effects.

Our definition of a "neighborhood" is very broad. We include elementary school attendance areas, which usually coincide fairly closely with what people mean by a neighborhood (hence the term "neighborhood school"). But we also include high school attendance areas, which are usually larger than what most people mean by a neighborhood. We include research on the effect of living in one kind of census tract rather than another, even though census tracts are much smaller than elementary school attendance areas. And we also include research that uses postal zip codes to define neighborhoods, even though zip code areas are likely to be somewhat larger than a traditional neighborhood.

Although our definition of a neighborhood is broad, it is always geographic rather than social. We have not tried to review the effects of nongeographic communities of various kinds, such as friendship networks. Nor have we tried to review the work of social psychologists on the way "social context" affects behavior. Readers should not interpret these omissions as an implicit judgment that nongeographic communities or social contexts are less important than geographic communities. The available evidence suggests the contrary. When placed in a room with a group of stooges who claim that the longer of two lines is the shorter, for example, most experimental subjects will reject the evidence of their senses and agree with the stooges (Asch, 1951). This demonstrates that individuals seldom defy the unanimous opinion of others, at least in the short run. The relevance of this fact to the study of geographic communities is minimal, however, because geographic communities are never completely homogeneous. The experiment just described shows that homogeneity is crucial, for when even one stooge concedes that the longer line is indeed longer, most subjects give the correct answer. When the opinions of others vary, in other words, individuals do more than just count noses and espouse the views of the majority.

The principal conclusion we draw from work like Asch's is that the way social context influences individual behavior varies with the problem the individual confronts, his or her experience, and the mix of opinions and role models available in a given social context. This variability makes it almost impossible to generalize from laboratory experiments to neighborhood or school settings.

There are currently three schools of thought about how the social composition of a neighborhood or school affects young people's behavior. Most Americans assume that advantaged neighbors or classmates encourage "good" behavior. A few assume that advantaged neighbors or classmates encourage "bad" behavior. And some assume that advantaged neighbors or classmates have no effect one way or the other. Each of these three schools of thought is compatible with a variety of theories about the mechanisms by which neighborhoods and schools influence individuals. We take up the three theories in turn.

### The Advantages of Advantaged Neighbors

Most Americans assume that children who grow up in a "good" neighborhood are more likely than those who grow up in a "bad" neighborhood to work hard in school, stay out of trouble, go to college, and get a good job when they become adults. Social scientists have suggested three mechanisms that could produce this result: peer influences, indigenous adult influences, and outside adult influences. Those who emphasize peer influences usually construct what we call *epidemic* models of how neighborhoods affect individuals. Those who emphasize the role of indigenous adults construct what we call *collective socialization* models. Those who emphasize the role of outside adults usually construct what we call *institutional* models.

Epidemic models focus on the way in which peers influence one another's behavior, and they assume that "like begets like." If children grow up in a community where a lot of their neighbors steal cars, for example, the children will be more likely to steal cars themselves. Conversely, if children grow up in neighborhoods where all their neighbors finish high school, the children will feel obliged to finish school themselves. Because "bad" behavior is more common in poor neighborhoods, epidemic models predict that, if we compare children from similar families, those reared in poor neighborhoods will behave worse than those reared in affluent neighborhoods.[1]

Many writers assume that bad behavior is contagious, but few examine the implications of this idea in detail. Many seem to assume, for example, that each school or neighborhood has a single dominant set of norms, to which every child, or at least every teenager, tries to conform. The dominant norm about any given form of behavior derives, in turn, from observing what others do. If "most" teenage girls in the neighborhood wear short skirts, then "every" teenager wants a short skirt. Similarly, if most teenage girls have babies before they marry, every teenage girl wants one. If this simple notion were correct, however, all neighborhoods would end up internally homogeneous. Either every girl would have a baby before marrying, for example, or none would.

To be convincing, epidemic models must allow for individual differences in susceptibility to neighborhood or school influences. Epidemic models of antisocial or self-destructive behavior usually impute differential susceptibility to differences in upbringing, but the model works in the same way if we impute individual differences to heredity or to chance. The critical feature of the model is that among individuals of any given susceptibility, the likelihood of antisocial or self-destructive behavior increases with exposure to others who engage in similar behavior. If children from low-SES families are more susceptible to such influences, increases in the proportion of low-SES families in a neighborhood will lead to exponential increases in bad behavior.

Whereas epidemic models focus on the way in which peers influence one another, collective socialization models focus on the way the adults in a neighborhood influence young people who are not their children. Those who believe in this model (e.g., W. Wilson, 1987) see affluent adults as role models whose existence proves that success is possible if you work hard and

---

[1] Here and throughout we use the adjectives "affluent," "advantaged," and "high-SES" as synonyms. Thus, when we refer to "affluent" neighborhoods, we mean neighborhoods that have a variety of social and economic advantages besides high family income. We also use the terms "affluent," "advantaged," and "high-SES" in a relative rather than an absolute sense. When we speak of "affluent" neighborhoods, for example, we often mean all neighborhoods that are more affluent than "poor neighborhoods," not neighborhoods that are more affluent than the national average. Likewise, when we speak of "high-SES" students, we often mean all students whose socioeconomic status is higher than that of "low-SES" students. As a result, "high-SES" students may merely be students whose parents hold steady jobs and earn average incomes, not students whose parents are high-level executives or professionals.

behave prudently. They also see affluent adults as potential "enforcers," who keep children from running wild on the streets, call the police when trouble occurs, and generally help maintain public order.

Institutional models also focus on the way adults affect children, but they focus primarily on adults from outside the community who work in the schools, the police force, and other neighborhood institutions. Almost everyone assumes, for example, that elementary schools in affluent neighborhoods get better teachers than those in poor neighborhoods and that this affects how much students learn. Many people also assume that the police treat delinquents differently in rich and poor neighborhoods and that this affects a teenager's chances of acquiring a criminal record. If such assumptions are correct, a neighborhood's mean SES could affect children's life chances even if neighbors per se were irrelevant.

From an empirical viewpoint it is often difficult to choose among these three models. All three predict that students will learn more when their schoolmates come from affluent families, for example. The institutional model attributes this to the fact that affluent schools have better teachers and a more demanding curriculum. The contagion model attributes it to the fact that affluent students serve as role models for the less affluent. The social control model attributes it to the fact that affluent parents force their children's schools to set high standards. When we look at real schools, the three models are hard to distinguish.

Because this issue is difficult to resolve empirically, social scientists often try to resolve it ideologically. Conservatives tend to espouse contagion or social control models that focus on the way the poor affect one another's attitudes, values, or behavior. Liberals prefer institutional models because they shift responsibility for what happens in a poor neighborhood to middle-class outsiders. The work we review throws little light on this controversy. Almost all of it relies on a "black box" model of neighborhood and school effects that makes no assumptions about how social composition influences individual behavior. Models of this kind try to answer the question, How much would an individual's behavior change if he or she moved from a low-SES to a high-SES neighborhood or school? They do not purport to explain *why* moving has an effect.

As a matter of literary convenience, we sometimes attribute hypothetical changes in individual behavior to neighbors or schoolmates rather than neighborhood institutions or school practices. Readers should treat this as verbal shorthand, not as an empirical judgment that the contagion or social control model is superior to the institutional model. What we describe as an effect of having affluent neighbors may be an effect of the neighborhood institutions that the affluent create for themselves and their neighbors.

## The Disadvantages of Advantaged Neighbors

Epidemic models, collective socialization models, and institutional models all assume that growing up in an affluent neighborhood encourages children to do what adults want them to do: learn a lot in school, stay out of trouble, and get good jobs when they grow up. Models that emphasize concepts like relative deprivation, cultural conflict, and competition for scarce resources imply, in contrast, that affluent neighbors often influence children's behavior in ways that most adults regard as undesirable.

Relative deprivation models assume that people judge their success or failure by comparing themselves with others around them. If people want to know how well they are doing economically, for example, they compare their standard of living with that of their friends and neighbors. It follows that if their income remains constant, they feel poorer when they have rich neighbors than when they have poor neighbors. Likewise, a college dropout feels less culturally competent if his or her neighbors all have Ph.D.'s than if they are all high school dropouts.

The same logic also applies to children. Children judge their economic position by comparing their standard of living with that of their schoolmates and neighbors. They judge their academic success by comparing their school performance with that of their classmates. Other things equal, low-SES children do worse in school than high-SES children. Low-SES children will therefore form a more favorable opinion of their abilities if they attend a low-SES school than if they attend a high-SES school. (The same is, of course, also true for a high-SES child.)

Some children who do not compete successfully respond by trying harder; others drop out of the competition. The relative frequency of these two responses depends on a wide range of factors, which are not well understood. But if most young people eventually respond to poor academic performance by refusing to do any more work, moving them from a low-SES school to a high-SES school will not only lower their relative performance but also reduce their academic effort. As a result, moving a child from a low-SES to a high-SES school may also increase the child's chances of quitting school, becoming a teenage mother, or committing violent crimes.

The theory of relative deprivation is a theory about individual psychology that purports to explain when people judge themselves successful and unsuccessful. It interprets deviant behavior as a by-product of these individual judgments. Theories that emphasize cultural conflict are similar in their underlying structure, but they focus on the way groups create a common culture. These theories suggest that when large numbers of individuals are unable to do what society as a whole expects them to do (finish school, get a respectable job, create and support a family), they will try to create a common culture to deal with their common failure. This culture will accept as "normal" and in some cases even praiseworthy what the rest of society regards as aberrant and reprehensible.

If the creation of a deviant subculture is a collective reaction to relative failure, such a subculture is more likely to arise in settings where success is very unequally distributed. Deviant subcultures will therefore be stronger in neighborhoods or schools where the poor rub shoulders with the rich than in places where the poor only rub shoulders with one another.

Competition for scarce resources can also make affluent neighbors a liability. We noted above that schoolchildren compete for grades and that the competition is tougher in high-SES schools. But the same logic applies when teenagers compete for jobs. In both cases a big frog in a small pond is probably better off than a small frog in a big pond.

### The Irrelevance of Advantaged Neighbors

Strong individualists—especially economists—often assume that neighbors have no direct effect on an individual's behavior. They believe that people base their decisions on their own circumstances and long-term interests, not on their neighbors' ideas about what is sensible, desirable, or acceptable. Most anthropologists and sociologists, as well as many psychologists, reject this view, arguing that individual decisions consist largely of choosing among a menu of culturally defined alternatives and that an individual's menu depends in part on the alternatives his friends and neighbors are considering. This "sociological" view need not deny that most people are rational utility maximizers. It merely denies that they are *imaginative* utility maximizers.

Even if individuals restrict themselves to choosing among familiar alternatives, however, a neighborhood's social composition may not have much effect on individual behavior. Most people prefer friends like themselves. So long as neighborhoods and schools are moderately heterogeneous, most young people can indulge this preference. Even in the poorest neighborhoods, a teenager can find friends who stay out of trouble, finish high school, go on to college, and get good jobs. And even the most affluent neighborhood has some teenagers who hate schoolwork, reject adult standards of behavior, and get into the same sorts of trouble as teenagers in poor neighborhoods. Prospective troublemakers can therefore find coconspirators in a rich neighborhood, even though they are scarcer than they would be in the ghetto.

There are, of course, some cases in which a neighborhood's social composition has a big effect on friendship patterns. Rosenbaum et al. (1986) found, for example, that poor black families who had been lured to white Chicago suburbs by Section 8 housing certificates reported that their children had more white friends after moving than before.[2] This is an extreme case, however. In the absence of strong financial incentives such as those that lured these poor black families to the Chicago suburbs, families seldom move to neighborhoods where their children have trouble finding friends like themselves.

Nonetheless, a neighborhood or school's social composition surely has *some* effect on a youngster's choice of friends, even when the neighborhood or school is somewhat heterogeneous. These contextual influences on friendship patterns must, in turn, have some effect on the alternatives that young people consider open to them. These effects may well be weak. Indeed, they may be too weak to deserve serious attention. But they are unlikely to be zero.

There is, however, a plausible scenario in which the social composition of a school or neighborhood will not appear to affect individual behavior. Suppose that both the epidemic model and the relative deprivation model are partially correct. In such a world high-SES neighbors might have two offsetting effects, one positive and the other negative. If these effects were of roughly equal magnitude, a neighborhood or school's mean SES would not appear to matter at all. As we shall see, this is roughly what we found when we tried to disentangle the effects of a high school's mean SES on its graduates' chances of attending college.

The remainder of this chapter proceeds as follows. In the next section we discuss six methodological issues that will recur over and over when we try to interpret the results of studies that assess the long-term effects of neighborhoods or schools on children's life chances. We then review the evidence about how a neighborhood or school's social composition affects children's eventual educational attainment, cognitive skills, crime rates, sexual behavior, and labor market success. In the closing section we summarize our findings and discuss their implications for those who do research and those who finance it.

## PROBLEMS IN MEASURING NEIGHBORHOOD EFFECTS ON CHILDREN

Anyone who wants to make policy inferences from the currently available studies of neighborhood or school effects confronts two difficulties. First, it is hard to be sure whether the causal inferences that social scientists make from survey data are valid. Second, even if those inferences are

---

[2] Pursuant to a finding that the Chicago Housing Authority (CHA) had deliberately segregated its public housing projects during the 1950s and 1960s, the *Gautreaux* decision ordered the CHA to provide some black public housing residents and applicants with Section 8 housing certificates that could only be used in white areas. Rosenbaum et al. (1986) studied families with children who had volunteered to move in order to get those subsidies.

valid, they are seldom sufficiently detailed or precise to predict the effects of specific public policies. Because these general difficulties recur over and over in the studies we review, we discuss them here rather than rehearse them throughout the chapter. We begin with the problems of making causal inferences from survey data.

### Controlling Exogenous Influences

Perhaps the most fundamental problem confronting anyone who wants to estimate neighborhoods' effects on children is distinguishing between neighborhood effects and family effects. Family characteristics exert a major influence on children's life chances no matter where a child lives. A family's characteristics also influence where it lives. This means that children who grow up in rich neighborhoods would differ to some extent from children who grow up in poor neighborhoods even if neighborhoods had no effect whatever.

From a scientific viewpoint, the best way to estimate neighborhood effects would be to conduct controlled experiments in which we assigned families randomly to different neighborhoods, persuaded each family to remain in its assigned neighborhood for a protracted period, and then measured each neighborhood's effects on the children involved. Fortunately, social scientists cannot conduct experiments of this kind. In their absence, social scientists rely on surveys that collect information on both family and neighborhood characteristics. They then compare children from apparently similar families who live in different neighborhoods. This kind of statistical analysis poses several problems, however.

First, we must decide which parental characteristics are exogenous and which are endogenous. (Family characteristics are exogenous if they do not depend on where the family lives. They are endogenous if they change when families move from one neighborhood to another.) There is no simple formula for deciding whether a family characteristic is exogenous. Many people believe, for example, that neighborhoods affect their residents' job opportunities. If this is true, conventional measures of parental SES, such as father's occupation and family income, are partly endogenous. Some part of what we attribute to parental SES may therefore be traceable to the neighborhood in which a family lives. But while neighborhoods may have some effect on adults' job opportunities, no one claims that they explain a large fraction of the total variance in adults' occupational status or income. (We review this literature in Chapter 5 of this volume.) It follows that estimates of a neighborhood's effect on children will be far less biased if parental SES is controlled than if it is not.

Similar arguments apply to family composition. As we show below, the neighborhood in which a teenage girl lives affects her chances of having a child out of wedlock. Neighborhoods may also influence marriage and divorce rates. This means that both the number of children and the number of adults in a family depend in part on where the family lives. But no one has argued that neighborhoods have anything like as much influence on family composition as family composition has on where people live. Thus, if we want to estimate a neighborhood's impact on children, we will get less biased results if we compare children from families of similar size and structure than if we treat family composition as endogenous.

We have restricted this review to studies that control at least one measure of parental SES when estimating neighborhood or school effects on children. But the studies we review seldom include all the standard indicators of parental SES (mother's and father's education, mother's and father's occupation, and family income) or family composition. Omitting or mismeasuring these family characteristics tends to inflate neighborhoods' estimated effects on children, because a neighborhood's mean SES is a partial proxy for unmeasured variation in individual SES.

At present, we have no idea which specific family characteristics we must control in order to get relatively unbiased estimates of neighborhood effects. Such information is crucial for assessing the likely degree of bias in studies that include only one or two measures of parental SES, as most studies do.

### Longitudinal Versus Cross-sectional Models

A second possible way to estimate neighborhood effects would be to study families that moved voluntarily from one neighborhood to another. Studying families that move allows us to control all the stable family characteristics, measured and unmeasured, that influence both where families live and their children's life chances. If we found that moving to a better neighborhood lowered poor black teenagers' arrest rates relative to those of their older siblings, for example, we would have more confidence that this was a true neighborhood effect than if we merely found that poor black teenagers who lived in good neighborhoods committed fewer crimes than those who lived in bad neighborhoods.

Longitudinal data on the characteristics of the neighborhoods through which families have moved were just becoming available for the first time when we finished this review, so none of the studies we discuss uses such data.[3] Even when such data become available, they will have important

---

[3] Rosenbaum et al. (1986) tried to assess the effects of moving from segregated inner-city Chicago neighborhoods to white suburbs, but they relied on retrospective parental reports to describe children's experiences before they moved, and they did not examine any of the outcomes that concern us in this review.

limitations.[4] Families usually move because their circumstances have changed. No survey can identify all the changes in a family's circumstances that lead to a move. As a result, if children's behavior changes after they move, we can never be sure whether these changes reflect the influence of the new neighborhood or the influence of the factors that led to the move. If a father takes to drink, loses his job, and is unable to pay the rent, for example, the family may move to a cheaper neighborhood and the children may start misbehaving. Unless we know about the drinking, we may erroneously impute the change in the children's behavior to the change in neighborhood.

The studies we review ignore the issue of change; they measure neighborhood characteristics at a single moment in time and implicitly assume that these neighborhood characteristics have remained stable throughout the respondent's childhood. If neighborhood effects accumulate slowly—as we might expect in the case of school achievement, for example—measuring neighborhood characteristics at a single point in time can lead to serious measurement errors. Just as failure to measure a family's past income may inflate neighborhoods' apparent effects (because current neighborhood is a proxy for past income), so too failure to measure where children have lived in the past may inflate the apparent importance of individual characteristics (because individual characteristics are proxies for prior neighborhood characteristics).

Even cross-sectional surveys could tell us more than they now do about the effects of changing neighborhoods if they asked respondents how long they had lived in their current neighborhood and whether their current neighbors were richer or poorer than their previous ones. If we had this kind of information, we could determine whether the strength of a neighborhood's apparent effect depended either on how long the respondent had lived there or on having lived in similar neighborhoods before. If neither length of residence nor prior neighborhood characteristics proved important, we would have to abandon many popular theories about how neighborhoods affect children.

## Nonlinear Effects of Socioeconomic Mix

We turn now to a series of problems that arise when we try to predict the likely effects of government policy from the kinds of causal models that social scientists usually estimate. Unlike the problems discussed in the two

---

[4]The Institute for Social Research at the University of Michigan is currently adding neighborhood data to the Panel Study of Income Dynamics. These data should be available in 1990.

previous subsections, which are widely recognized but hard to solve without better data, the problems we discuss in the next four subsections are for the most part easy to solve once we recognize them.

Most of the studies we review assume that a neighborhood's mean SES has linear effects. None of the studies that make this assumption tries to test its validity, however. Social scientists have used linear approximations because their aim has been to determine whether the mean SES of a neighborhood or school has any effect whatever on a particular outcome. Linear approximations are usually satisfactory for this purpose. But if we want to predict the likely effect of housing policies that alter the degree of residential segregation, linear approximations will not tell us what we need to know.

Suppose, for example, that poor neighbors encourage antisocial behavior and that the effect of each additional poor neighbor is the same. In such a world, distributing the poor more evenly across a metropolitan area will redistribute the cost of having poor neighbors from the poor to the more affluent, but it will not reduce the cost to society as a whole. To see why, imagine a town with two neighborhoods of equal size, East Side and West Side. The poverty rate is 30 percent in East Side and 10 percent in West Side, and the annual burglary rate is 15 percent in East Side and 5 percent in West Side. Now imagine that the town provides housing vouchers to the poor in East Side so they can move to West Side and that it subsidizes developers who want to build expensive housing in East Side so as to attract affluent residents from West Side. Five years later the poverty rate is 20 percent in both neighborhoods.

If burglary rates are a linear function of poverty rates, the burglary rate should fall from 15 to 10 percent in East Side and should rise from 5 to 10 percent in West Side. The citywide burglary rate will therefore remain unchanged. Needless to say, if the residents of West Side anticipate this outcome, they will oppose housing vouchers. Since the affluent have more political influence than the poor, and since in this case they have the status quo on their side, they will probably prevail. Dispersing the poor will only command majority support if most people believe that it will improve poor neighborhoods a lot more than it will harm more affluent ones. The effect of poor neighbors must, in other words, be strongly nonlinear.

Only one study (Crane, forthcoming) devotes much attention to the shape of the relationship between individual outcomes and the mean SES of a neighborhood or school. Several other studies do, however, present data that bear on this question. Most of these studies divide neighborhoods into three or more socioeconomic levels and report mean outcomes for individuals in neighborhoods at each level. But since none reports the characteristics of neighborhoods at different levels, we cannot use their findings to estimate the likely effect of redistributing people between neighborhoods.[5]

Recent discussions of the underclass and concentrated poverty have focused on the effects of living in the worst 5 or 10 percent of all neighborhoods. Many believe that such neighborhoods have become breeding grounds for crime, drug abuse, teenage pregnancy, and welfare dependency. Many also believe that we could reduce the incidence of such problems by moving the poor to better neighborhoods.

If we want to know whether very bad neighborhoods have substantial effects on children, we must look at what happens to children who actually grow up in such neighborhoods. Extrapolating from differences among children who grow up in neighborhoods that are a little better or a little worse than average may be quite misleading. The work of Hogan and Kitagawa (1985) on teenage pregnancy in Chicago underlines the potential dangers of such extrapolation. Hogan and Kitagawa studied black teenagers living in the city of Chicago. They divided the black neighborhoods in which the girls lived into three groups (best quarter, middle half, and worst quarter), based on their mean SES. Girls who lived in the worst quarter of black neighborhoods were substantially more likely to become pregnant than girls living in better black neighborhoods, even when their family characteristics were the same. The effect of living in the best quarter rather than the middle half of black neighborhoods was trivial.

Very few Chicago whites live in neighborhoods as bad as the worst quarter of black neighborhoods. (Four-fifths of the families in these neighborhoods lived in public housing.) Thus, if we were to survey a representative sample of all Chicago-area residents, fewer than 1 in 10 would probably live in a neighborhood bad enough to have a detectable effect on the teenage pregnancy rate. If this were the case, using a linear model to estimate neighborhood effects would show that mean SES had very little effect on teenage childbearing. That conclusion would be correct for most neighborhoods, but it would be seriously misleading if we were mainly concerned with the effects of the very worst ghetto neighborhoods.

### Interactions Between Neighborhood SES and Individual SES

Most of the studies we review assume that neighborhoods and schools have the same effect on everyone, regardless of their family background. Yet those who advocate governmental programs for reducing residential

---

[5] In order to estimate the effect of moving people between neighborhoods, we need to know the shape of the relationship between neighborhoods' mean SES and the outcome of interest. We cannot determine the shape of this relationship from grouped data unless we know the mean SES of neighborhoods in each group.

segregation usually argue that such programs would help the poor more than they would hurt the more affluent.[6] There are at least two plausible rationales for this assumption. First, there is some evidence that the social networks of poor families are more geographically restricted than those of affluent families (Bott, 1957). The social composition of a poor child's neighborhood may therefore have more effect on the child's choice of friends than the social composition of a rich child's neighborhood does. Second, poor parents seldom have the skills they need to join the middle class, so poor children must learn such skills at school if they are to learn them at all. Middle-class children, in contrast, can learn the required skills at home if they do not learn them at school. As a result, good schools may be more important for the poor than for the more affluent.[7]

The simplest and most reliable way to test such theories is to conduct separate analyses of high-SES and low-SES respondents. Older studies that used cross-tabulations often did this. More recent studies that use multivariate methods rarely do it (but see Corcoran et al., 1989; Crane, forthcoming).

Several studies present separate analyses of neighborhood effects on blacks and whites. Because most areas with high concentrations of poverty are either black or Hispanic, dispersing the poor more evenly across a metropolitan area means dispersing blacks and Hispanics more evenly. Knowing whether such changes would help blacks or Hispanics more than they would hurt their new white neighbors is therefore quite important.

But even if the average black or Hispanic gained more from residential desegregation than the average white lost, *poor* blacks or Hispanics might not gain more than the average white lost. Suppose schools in affluent white areas ignore the special problems of the poor or track them into "slow" classes. Middle-income blacks might then gain a lot from moving to such neighborhoods while poor blacks gained very little. Recognizing this, some middle-income blacks would probably move to more affluent neighborhoods when the opportunity arose, but most poor blacks would spend their limited resources in other ways. The result would be a decline in racial segregation and an increase in economic segregation. This is precisely what appears to have happened between 1970 and 1980 (Massey and Denton, 1987; Massey and Eggers, 1990).

---

[6] If the effects of individual SES and neighborhood SES are not additive, neighborhood effects will ordinarily appear to be nonlinear. But neighborhood effects can be nonlinear even if the effects of individual SES and neighborhood SES are completely additive.

[7] If low-SES students are more sensitive to school quality than high-SES students, the between-school variance in, say, test performance should be greater for low-SES students. If the within-school variance is the same for both groups, the total variance should also be greater for low-SES students. We found no studies that compared the variability of outcomes for high-SES and low-SES children.

None of the studies we review presents separate estimates of neighborhoods' effects on poor blacks or Hispanics, who would presumably be the primary beneficiaries of housing policies aimed at reducing residential segregation. Filling this gap should be a top priority in future work.

### Choosing Appropriate Measures of Neighborhood Composition

Very few studies offer any strong theoretical or empirical rationale for focusing on one measure of a neighborhood's mean SES rather than another. The studies we review typically include one or more of the following measures: mean or median family income, the mean education of one or both parents, some measure of occupational mix, the percentage of families with female heads, and the percentage on welfare. Many investigators combine several of these measures into a single composite.

We describe all such measures as indicators of a neighborhood's "mean SES," regardless of how they were constructed. Despite this common terminology, however, what we call "mean SES" does not always measure the same thing or rank neighborhoods in the same way. Different measures of mean SES are likely to be quite highly correlated with one another, but even when investigators constructed several measures of mean SES they did not report their intercorrelation. Nor have investigators who experimented with several different measures reported the results of these experiments in enough detail for us to generalize about how the choice of one measure rather than another might affect other studies' findings.

From the viewpoint of a policy analyst, composite measures of mean SES have several drawbacks. First, they make it impossible to determine which particular neighborhood characteristics are important and which are not. It makes a big difference, for example, whether poor black teenagers' pregnancy rates fall when their parents live in affluent black neighborhoods or only when they live in predominantly white neighborhoods.

A second drawback of composite SES measures is that investigators seldom report the weights they gave different neighborhood characteristics, so we cannot use their results to predict how any specific combination of neighborhood characteristics would alter children's life chances. Nor can we be sure whether the characteristics that went into the composite were weighted in such a way as to capture their full effect on the outcome of interest. If racial mix is critical, for example, and other neighborhood characteristics are of marginal importance, an index that includes racial mix as one of four equally weighted components may seriously underestimate neighborhoods' actual importance.

A third problem is that composites seldom tell us the effects of the most politically relevant neighborhood characteristics. To test the hypothesis that poor neighbors affect children's opportunities or behavior, for example, we need to estimate the effect of a neighborhood's poverty rate with nothing else controlled. We found only one study that did this. Likewise, if we want to predict the effect of racial desegregation, we need to estimate the effect of racial mix with nothing else controlled. A few studies present this information, but most do not.

## Estimating Neighborhoods' Overall Effect

This review focuses on estimating the effects on children of neighborhoods' and schools' social composition. For policy purposes this is part of a larger question, namely, whether *any* feature of a neighborhood or school affects children's life chances. To answer this larger question, we need two kinds of information. First, we need to know how much the outcome we are studying varies from one neighborhood or school to the next. Second, we need to know how much of this variation is attributable to exogenous factors like family background.

If we want to know how much influence a high school has on its students' chances of graduating, for example, our first question should be how much the graduation rate varies from school to school. Our second question should be how much the graduation rate varies once we adjust it to eliminate the effects of differences among the students entering different high schools.[8] Studies of schools occasionally do this. Studies of neighborhoods almost never do.

Once we know how much impact each neighborhood or school has on the outcome that interests us, we can ask whether its impact is attributable to its mean SES, its racial composition, or some other measured or unmeasured characteristic. School studies suggest that socioeconomic mix plays a relatively modest role in determining a school's overall impact on its students. Jencks and Brown (1975a) show, for example, that white students learned quite different amounts in different high schools in the early 1960s. Yet a school's socioeconomic mix had no consistent effect on how much its students learned. Other factors, which Jencks and Brown were unable to identify, were far more important.

Analyses of neighborhoods' and schools' total effects are easy to do, but they are quite rare. As a result, we seldom know whether unmeasured neighborhood characteristics have important effects. In the absence of such data, readers should not interpret negative findings about the effects

---

[8] To estimate neighborhoods' explanatory power with the effects of family background controlled, we need an analysis of covariance, a regression equation that includes a separate dummy variable for each school, or some statistically equivalent method. Hauser (1971) and Alwin (1976) discuss the statistical rationale for such methods. Bryk and Raudenbush (1987, 1988) discuss hierarchical linear models for estimating neighborhood or school effects.

of mean SES or racial composition as evidence that neighborhoods or schools "don't matter."

## EDUCATIONAL ATTAINMENT

We use the term "educational attainment" as shorthand for the number of years of school an individual completes. Educational attainment is the cumulative product of a series of decisions about whether to complete high school, enter college, complete college, and so on. These decisions are made at different ages and are subject to different social and economic influences. The factors that shape decisions about whether to finish high school, for example, may not be the same as those that shape decisions about whether to enter college (Mare, 1980), so we discuss them separately whenever we can.

### High School SES and College Attendance

The earliest quantitative studies of "neighborhood" effects were conducted in the late 1950s and early 1960s and dealt with the effects of a high school's mean SES on graduating seniors' college plans. These studies seemed to show that twelfth graders in high-SES schools had higher aspirations than those in low-SES schools, even with their own family's SES controlled (Michael, 1961; Turner, 1964; A. Wilson, 1959). Sewell and Armer (1966) argued that the influence of schools' mean SES had been exaggerated, but even they found that students from similar families with similar eleventh-grade IQ scores were more likely to plan on attending college if they were graduating from a high school that drew its students from a high-SES neighborhood.

The usual explanation of this finding was that high-SES schools developed a schoolwide culture that defined college attendance as both inevitable and desirable. This schoolwide culture supposedly altered even working-class students' attitudes toward college. Conversely, schools with a working-class majority developed a schoolwide culture that defined college attendance as impractical and perhaps even undesirable. In such schools even middle-class students might not attend college.

In 1966 James A. Davis published an article ("The Campus as a Frog Pond") that challenged this line of reasoning. Drawing on Samuel Stouffer's work on relative deprivation among soldiers during World War II, Davis argued that reference groups had both a normative function (as "sources and reinforcers of standards") and a comparison function (a "point against which the person can evaluate himself and others"). Because of this second function, he argued, advantaged classmates were not always as much of an advantage as most people assumed.

Davis showed that the more academically selective a college was, the lower any given student could expect his or her grades to be. As a result, students who attended selective colleges were less likely to choose careers that required graduate training. Davis did not extend his analysis to high schools, but the analogy was obvious. High-SES schools usually have higher academic standards than low-SES schools. For students of any given ability, therefore, attending a high-SES school is almost certain to mean a lower rank in the graduating class, and it is likely to mean lower grades as well. This change is likely to lower students' academic self-confidence and their interest in attending college.

In 1970 John Meyer published a paper that tried to reconcile these two conflicting models of how a high school's social composition might affect seniors' college plans. Meyer showed that attending a high-SES school had a positive effect on students' chances of planning to attend college but that attending school with students who scored high on standardized tests had a negative effect. Because a school's mean SES and mean test scores were highly correlated, the net effect of attending a high-SES school was quite small.

Almost all subsequent studies support Meyer's findings. A school's mean SES tends to have a small positive effect on individual students' college plans, but its mean test score tends to have a small negative effect. Since the two are highly correlated, the net impact of mean SES on college plans is close to zero (see especially, Alexander and Eckland, 1975; and Hauser et al., 1976; but also Alwin and Otto, 1977; Hotchkiss, 1984; McDill and Rigsby, 1973; and Nelson, 1972).

Skeptics may wonder whether studies of college plans really tell us much about college attendance and completion. Innumerable studies have shown that college plans are not a very good predictor of subsequent behavior (e.g., Sewell et al., 1980). If students from high-SES secondary schools were more likely than other students to realize their college plans, a school's mean SES could affect its graduates' eventual educational attainment even though it did not affect their plans at the time they graduated.

When investigators have looked at high school seniors' eventual educational attainment, they have found much the same thing as when they looked at twelfth graders' plans (Table 4-1). Attending a high-SES school has a small positive effect on subsequent educational attainment, and attending a school with high test scores has a small negative effect. The net effect is, therefore, close to zero.

No study explicitly investigates whether low-SES students are especially sensitive to the mean SES of their peers, as advocates of school desegregation often assume. Hauser et al. (1976) do, however, provide data relevant to this point. If low-SES students are especially sensitive to school quality, then the effect of parental SES on whether students attend

TABLE 4-1 Effects of Schools' Mean SES and Mean Ability on Students' Educational Attainment, With Family Background Controlled

| Survey | Measure of School Composition | Standardized Regression Coefficient |
|---|---|---|
| Alexander and Eckland (1975) National sample of 10th graders in 1955 (N = 2,077) Dependent variable: educational attainment in 1970 (5 categories) | Mean SES Mean ability | .09 −.09 |
| Hauser et al. (1976) Sample of Wisconsin 12th graders in 1957 (N = 7,052) Dependent variable: educational attainment in 1964 (in years: S.D. = 1.83) | Mean mother's education Mean father's education Mean father's occupation Mean family income Mean 11th grade IQ score | .05 −.02 .07 −.01 −.05 |
| Jencks and Brown (1975b) Two follow-ups of a national sample of 9th graders in 1960 Dependent variable: educational attainment in 1964 (in years: S.D. = 1.41) | Mean SES Mean college plans Mean test score | .045 .022 −.091 |
| Dependent variable: educational attainment in 1968 (in years: S.D. = 2.05) | Mean SES Mean college plans Mean test score | −.053 .115 −.064 |

NOTES: All estimates control sex, individual SES, and individual ability. Alexander and Eckland measure ability in 10th grade; Hauser et al. measure it in 11th grade; and Jencks and Brown measure it in 9th grade. Jencks and Brown also control 9th-grade college plans, curriculum assignment, and grades. Jencks and Brown's published beta coefficients have been restandardized using the individual-level S.D. of educational attainment.

college should be weaker in high-quality schools than in low-quality schools. Hauser et al. found, however, that the strength of the relationship between family background and a student's eventual educational attainment did not vary significantly from one high school to another in a sample of 20 Milwaukee-area schools. This does not mean that the effect of parental SES is really exactly the same in every school. That is unlikely. But Hauser et al.'s findings do suggest that school-to-school differences in the impact of parental SES are fairly modest. If that is the case, high-quality schools increase high-SES students' chances of attending college about as much as they increase low-SES students' chances.

There are, however, intriguing hints that black students may benefit more from attending a high-SES school than white students do. Meyer (1970) found that mean SES and mean test performance both had positive effects on southern black twelfth graders' college plans. This implies that the reduced-form effect of mean SES was fairly large and positive for southern blacks. The all-black southern schools covered by Meyer's 1955 data are no longer legally segregated, and most have either closed or been desegregated, so his findings may not hold for southern blacks today. But Thornton and Eckland's (1980) analysis of the High School Class of 1972 also suggests that both mean SES and mean test performance have positive effects on black students' college attendance.[9]

Although the effect of a school's mean SES on blacks remains uncertain, the basic findings for whites are so clear and robust as to leave little doubt about their approximate validity. Attending a high-SES secondary school does not appreciably alter a white student's college plans. This conclusion raises a puzzling question, however. How could mean SES have had positive effects on high school seniors' college plans in studies published before 1970 but have no effect in studies published after 1970? The obvious answer is that the world changed, but that explanation turns out to be untenable. Most of the studies conducted after 1970 relied on data collected in the 1950s and 1960s. Indeed, several of the studies conducted after 1970 used the same data as the earlier studies. We cannot, therefore, attribute the dramatic change in social scientists' conclusions to a change in the real world.

The reason for the change appears to have been methodological. Studies published before 1970 used two-way and three-way cross-tabulations to control the effects of exogenous student characteristics. As a result, investigators could only control one measure of parental SES, typically broken down into only two or three categories, when they estimated the effect of a school's mean SES. Studies conducted after 1970 used regression equations to estimate school effects. Regression equations enable investigators both to control all the family characteristics on which they have data and to treat these measures as continuous variables. Better controls for exogenous influences reduced the estimated effect of a school's mean SES almost to zero.

This methodological finding has important implications not just for our understanding of college plans but for our understanding of school and neighborhood effects generally. It warns us that studies which control

---

[9] Thornton and Eckland do not present means, standard deviations, correlations, sampling errors, or reduced-form estimates. We estimated the reduced-form coefficients from their structural equations and used data from other samples to estimate the missing means and standard deviations. With exogenous influences controlled, we calculated that the proportion of black students who entered college fell by about .07 when they attended a high school in the bottom 10 percent of the SES distribution rather than an average high school. The sampling error of the estimate was about .03, so the true effect could have been considerably larger or smaller. The situation may also have changed since 1972, when many blacks in high-SES schools were attending newly desegregated southern schools, whose effect on their subsequent educational attainment was not positive (see below).

only one or two exogenous family characteristics are likely to overestimate school and neighborhood effects.

### High School Racial Composition and College Attendance

Race has a substantial effect on academic achievement, even when we compare blacks to whites whose parents have comparable jobs and incomes (Broman et al., 1975). The same pattern recurs for teenage sexual activity and crime.[10] A school's racial composition could therefore have quite different effects from its socioeconomic composition, even though the two are quite strongly correlated.

St. John (1975) reviewed 25 studies that looked at the effect of desegregated schooling on black students' educational and occupational aspirations. Almost all these studies were conducted in the North. St. John found that desegregation seldom raised black students' aspirations significantly and often lowered them significantly. This is precisely what Davis's "frog pond" model predicts.

Studies that focus on black students' actual attainment tell a rather different story, however. Crain (1971) found that among blacks who had graduated from high school in the 1940s and 1950s, those who had attended racially mixed northern schools were more likely to have attended college than those who had attended all-black northern schools. Crain and Mahard (1978) tell a similar story using the National Longitudinal Survey of the High School Class of 1972 (hereafter NLS-72). They found that northern blacks were more likely to enter college and more likely to stay there continuously for the first three years after they finished high school if they had attended a racially mixed rather than an all-black high school.[11] The

---

[10] Furstenberg et al. (1987) present data on racial differences in the age at which teenagers initiate sexual activity. The odds that black 15- and 16-year-olds have had intercourse are 3.7 times the odds for whites of the same age. Controlling either mother's education or family income reduced the black-white odds ratio to 3.3. Furstenberg et al. do not report the effect of controlling all available measures of parental SES, but if controlling a single measure only reduces the odds ratio from 3.7 to 3.3, multiple measures are unlikely to reduce it to 1.0.

We do not have reliable data on criminal activity by race and parental SES simultaneously, but both victims' reports and arrest data suggest that blacks are three to six times more likely than whites to engage in serious crimes (Bureau of Justice Statistics, 1987). Because parental SES has a very modest effect on criminal activity in most studies (Hindelang et al., 1981), it is hard to see how differences in parental SES could account for the racial difference in serious crimes.

[11] When estimating the effects of Percent White, Crain and Mahard (1978) controlled the mean SES of the blacks in a given school rather than controlling individual SES. If the mean SES of blacks in a school affects individual blacks' postsecondary enrollment, and if blacks' mean SES is positively correlated with Percent White, controlling blacks' mean SES will lower the coefficient of Percent White more than controlling individual SES would. Crain and Mahard conducted quite ingenious tests to determine whether the apparent effect of Percent White was due to selection bias and concluded that it was not.

degree of segregation in a school district did not seem to have much effect on northern whites' chances of entering college or staying there.

These findings suggest that we should be very cautious about studies of black aspirations. Many black high school students report very ambitious plans for the future, but many have taken none of the steps necessary to realize these plans. The available data suggest that this is especially common in all-black northern schools. Blacks in such schools are, it seems, likely to say they plan to attend college but less likely to do so. Thus, while desegregation seems to lower northern black high school graduates' educational aspirations, it seems to enhance their chances of actually entering and completing college. This is surely a worthwhile trade-off.

Turning to the South, however, the picture changes. Crain and Mahard (1978) found that, at least in 1972, attending high school with whites *decreased* both the chances that southern blacks would enter college and the chances that they would remain there continuously for three consecutive years. Once again, the degree of racial segregation in a southern school district did not seem to have much effect on white high school graduates' chances of entering college or remaining there. We do not have more recent data on this point.

### High School Graduation

A high school's social composition is likely to have more influence on whether its entering students graduate than on whether its graduates attend college. In Chicago, to take an extreme example, many students report having quit high school because gangs controlled their school, making it dangerous to go there. Gangs have less influence in high-SES schools. We would therefore expect low-SES students to graduate more often if they attend high-SES Chicago schools than if they attend low-SES Chicago schools. We would not expect a Chicago high school's mean SES to exert an analogous effect on whether its graduates attended college, because gangs are less common on college campuses.

Two studies have estimated the effect of a high school's mean SES on students' chances of graduating using data from the High School and Beyond (HSB) survey.[12] HSB collected information on tenth graders' race, socioeconomic background, and academic background in 1980 and followed

---

[12]Both Alexander and Eckland (1975) and Jencks and Brown (1975b) followed up high school dropouts as well as graduates, so in principle, their results indicate that a high school's mean SES does not have a major impact on high school graduation rates. But neither study was very successful in locating high school dropouts, so almost all the variance in educational attainment in both studies is attributable to variance in whether high school graduates attended and completed college.

up the students in 1982. Bryk and Driscoll (1988) used data from 357 of the HSB schools to investigate the effects of various school characteristics on students' chances of still being in school two years later, when they should have been in the twelfth grade.

Bryk and Driscoll found that high school graduation was subject to the same contradictory influences as college entrance. As a school's mean SES fell, as its student body became more economically diverse, and as its minority enrollment increased, tenth graders of any given race, SES, and academic background were more likely to drop out. But with the school's racial and socioeconomic mix held constant, schools in which students had high scores in tenth grade tended to have high dropout rates. These findings suggest that academic competition increases attrition while high-SES peers reduce attrition. Since these two school characteristics are highly correlated, the net effect of having advantaged rather than disadvantaged classmates is probably small, but we cannot estimate the size of the net effect from Bryk and Driscoll's data.[13]

Mayer (forthcoming) used the full HSB sample (26,425 students from 968 schools) to investigate the impact of a high school's social mix on a tenth grader's chances of still being in school two years later. For students of average SES in average schools, the dropout rate averaged 13 percent for blacks, 14 percent for non-Hispanic whites, and 16 percent for Hispanics. For students one standard deviation below the mean on parental SES in average schools, the dropout rate rose 4 points for blacks, 10 points for whites, and 5 points for Hispanics. The finding that blacks drop out less than whites of comparable SES, and that this is particularly true for low-SES blacks and whites, recurs in other data sets (Jencks, forthcoming).

Since Mayer wanted an "upper bound" estimate for the cumulative impact of schools' social mix, her estimates of school effects control only those student characteristics that schools cannot influence, namely parental SES and ethnicity. She did not control student characteristics that might depend on the social mix of the schools a student attended prior to the tenth grade. Using this approach, she found that when an average non-Hispanic white tenth grader attended high school with classmates whose mean SES was one standard deviation below average, his or her chance of dropping out rose from 14 to 17 percent. For blacks, the increase was from 13 to 15 percent. For Hispanics it was from 16 to 18 percent. The effect of a change in classmates' mean SES was thus between a third and a half as large as the effect of a comparable change in parental SES.[14]

---

[13] For a further analysis of compositional effects on high school graduation rates using the same HSB data, see Bryk and Thum (1988).

[14] In order to make the comparisons in the text, Mayer used the standard deviation for individuals to describe changes in both parental SES and classmates' mean SES. Thirty-four percent

Having black or Hispanic classmates also increased the likelihood that a tenth grader would drop out prior to graduating, even with their mean SES controlled. The absolute effect of a change in classmates' mean SES on dropout rates was somewhat greater among low-SES students than among average students, because their base rate was higher.

If neighborhood effects depend on homogeneity, the block on which a youngster grows up may be more important than the school he or she attends. Crane (forthcoming) studied the effect of a census tract's mean SES on its residents' chances of finishing high school using a unique 1970 census sample that links individual records to aggregate data on roughly 1,500 nearby families.[15] To estimate residents' chances of finishing high school, Crane investigated whether 16- to 18-year-olds who were still living at home had left school without graduating.[16] The neighborhood characteristic that best predicted an individual's chance of quitting school was the percentage of professional and managerial workers living in the neighborhood. Crane interprets this finding not as evidence that professionals and managers are important in their own right, but rather as evidence that professionals and managers are in a good position to flee bad neighborhoods.

Crane compared teenagers from families whose education, occupational status, and income are at the national average but who live in different neighborhoods. Among 16- to 18-year-old whites living in neighborhoods where 30 to 35 percent of all workers have professional or managerial jobs, only 4 percent had left school without graduating. Among whites from similar families living in neighborhoods where only 5 to 10 percent of all workers had professional or managerial jobs, about 6 percent had dropped out. Among teenagers from typical black and Hispanic families in similar neighborhoods, dropout rates were about double the white rate. For blacks from typical families who lived in the very worst neighborhoods (where less

---

of the observed variance in parental SES is between schools, so the standard deviation of mean SES is 58 percent of the standard deviation for individuals. A change of one individual-level standard deviation therefore implies a change of 1.72 school-level standard deviations, which is the difference between a school at the 5th percentile of the school-level distribution and a school at the 50th percentile.

[15] To maintain confidentiality, the Census Bureau did not merge individual records with regular census tract data, but instead created new "pseudotracts" from block-level data. The pseudotracts were about the same size as regular tracts, that is, about 4,000 people. Such tracts should be considerably more homogeneous than a high school attendance area, but we have no empirical estimates of their homogeneity.

[16] Crane focused on 16- to 18-year-olds who lived at home because they were the only teenagers for whom parental characteristics were available and the only ones whose place of residence was exogenous. Crane reports that 84 percent of all 16- to 18-year-olds live at home. Omitting dropouts who no longer lived at home could bias the estimated impact of a neighborhood's median income either upward or downward.

than 5 percent of all workers had professional or managerial jobs), almost 20 percent of 16- to 18-year-olds were dropouts.[17]

### Neighborhoods' Cumulative Effect

We located only two studies that linked young people's eventual educational attainment to the socioeconomic mix of the neighborhood in which they grew up. Both use data drawn from the Panel Study of Income Dynamics (PSID), and both use 1970 census data on the zip code in which teenagers lived to estimate the effect of neighborhood characteristics on educational attainment. There are 10 to 20 census tracts in a typical zip code, so zip codes, like high schools, are likely to be more socially diverse than census tracts or blocks.

Datcher (1982) studied urban males who were between the ages of 13 and 22 and lived with their parents in 1968. Table 4-2 shows the estimated effects of a zip code's mean income and racial mix on the number of years of school Datcher's respondents had completed in 1978, when they were 23 to 32 years old. The estimates control parental income in 1968, the parents' educational attainment, the family head's educational aspirations for his or her children, the number of children in the family, region, community size, and age.[18]

A $1,000 increase in a zip code's mean income appears to raise educational attainment by 0.103 years for whites and 0.087 years for blacks.[19] This black-white difference is too small to be either statistically reliable or

---

[17]The percentages of dropouts would all be higher if Crane had focused exclusively on 18-year-olds and if he had had data on individuals who no longer lived at home. The percentages would be lower today than in 1970, at least for blacks.

[18]Datcher did not control the household head's verbal score or occupational status. Nor did she control income in years other than 1968. The household head's occupation is usually the best single predictor of a son's educational attainment (Sewell et al., 1980), and a parent's verbal score is the best exogenous predictor of children's verbal scores (Jencks et al., 1972). These omissions may have led Datcher to overestimate neighborhood effects. Controlling parents' aspirations could, in principle, lead to some downward bias in a neighborhood's estimated effects, but the effect of parental aspirations in Datcher's model is very small, so the bias is probably trivial.

[19]Table 4-2 shows that the coefficient of neighborhood income is only 1.4 times its standard error for blacks. This may lead some readers to conclude that neighborhood income has an "insignificant" effect on black men's educational attainment. That would be a mistake, for three reasons. First, in the absence of other information our best estimate of a neighborhood's effect is the value in Table 4-2, not zero. Second, since the coefficients for blacks and whites do not differ significantly and are quite close to one another, the hypothesis that the true coefficient is the same for both groups is more plausible than the hypothesis that the true coefficient is zero for blacks. Third, Datcher reports that when she entered neighborhood income but not neighborhood racial mix, the coefficient of neighborhood income was significant for blacks as well as whites. Unfortunately, she does not report these reduced-form estimates for either blacks or whites.

TABLE 4-2    Effects of Neighborhoods' Mean Income and Racial Composition in 1968 on Years of School Completed by 23- to 32-Year-Olds in 1978

|  | Mean Family Income ($1,000s) | | Percent White (0 to 100) | |
|---|---|---|---|---|
|  | Blacks | Whites | Blacks | Whites |
| Regression coefficient | .087 | .103 | .0064 | −.0056 |
| (Standard error) | (.061) | (.035) | (.0043) | (.0082) |
| Mean | 9.18 | 11.97 | 42.18 | 93.67 |
| Mean for poorest 25% | 8.53 | 11.08 | 33.63 | 92.52 |
| N | 196 | 356 | 196 | 356 |

SOURCE:  Datcher (1982).

substantively important. The mean income for an urban zip code averaged about $11,500 in 1970; hence, Table 4-2 implies that a 10 percent increase in neighborhood income increased respondents' eventual educational attainment by about a tenth of a year regardless of their race.

Unlike the effects of income, the effects of a zip code's racial composition differed for blacks and whites. Blacks tended to get more education if they had white neighbors, while whites got more education if they had black neighbors. Cheering as this scenario is, the large sampling errors of both coefficients are also consistent with the hypothesis that a zip code's racial composition has no effect on anyone's educational attainment if the neighborhood's mean income is the same.

A zip code whose economic and racial mix mirrored that of urban America as a whole would have had a mean income of $11,500 and would have been about 86 percent white in 1970. Poor blacks lived in zip codes that were 34 percent white and had mean incomes of $8,500. Datcher's model therefore implies that moving a poor black male to an average zip code would have raised his educational attainment by 0.6 years. Moving rich whites into these same zip codes would have had no effect on their educational attainment, since the costs of having slightly poorer neighbors would have been offset by the benefits of having slightly more black neighbors. These estimates are consistent with two quite different hypotheses:

- Both blacks and whites benefit equally from living in affluent zip codes. Once we take this into account, neither group is affected by the zip code's racial composition. If this hypothesis is correct, reducing racial and economic segregation would help blacks and hurt whites.

- Blacks benefit both from living in affluent zip codes and from living in white zip codes. Whites benefit from living in affluent zip codes but suffer from living in white zip codes. If this hypothesis is correct, reducing racial segregation would benefit both blacks and whites.

Datcher's data do not allow us to choose between these hypotheses.

Corcoran et al. (1987) used more recent PSID data to investigate zip code effects on educational attainment. They used only respondents who were between the ages of 10 and 17 in 1968, so they did not miss as many college students as Datcher did. They also controlled more parental characteristics than Datcher did, and they looked at women as well as men. Their results support Datcher's finding that growing up in a "good" zip code leads to more schooling. Moving from a "typical" black neighborhood to a "typical" white neighborhood increased expected educational attainment by 0.41 years for men and 0.22 years for women.[20] Unfortunately, Corcoran et al. do not present separate estimates for blacks and whites, so we cannot tell whether blacks gain more than whites from living in good neighborhoods.

### Conclusions about Educational Attainment

Taken together, the results of Crane, Datcher, and Corcoran et al. strongly suggest that growing up in a high-SES neighborhood raises a teenager's expected educational attainment, even when the teenager's own family characteristics are the same. A high school's social composition, in contrast, has very little effect on a student's chances of finishing high school or attending college.

The finding that neighborhood mix matters while school mix does not is puzzling for two reasons. First, we would expect neighborhood mix to be quite highly correlated with school mix. Thus, even if neighborhood

---

[20]The calculations in the text are for men and women whose parents received no income from welfare. Contrary to what advocates of residential desegregation usually expect, Corcoran et al. found that good neighborhoods conferred smaller educational benefits on children whose families received a significant fraction of their income from welfare than on children whose families received no such income. If these results are correct, segregating welfare families (e.g., into public housing) would help nonwelfare families more than it would hurt welfare families. Without careful tests of alternative explanations, however, we are not inclined to take this result at face value.

Datcher's data imply that moving from an average black neighborhood to an average white neighborhood would raise male educational attainment by an average of about 0.1 years compared to Corcoran et al.'s 0.4 years. This difference could reflect differences in the two studies' sampling strategies, random error, or the fact that Corcoran et al. used more measures of neighborhood characteristics than Datcher did.

mix is critical and school mix is unimportant, we would expect school mix to appear important when neighborhood mix was not controlled. Indeed, several early studies of school mix used census tract data to characterize high school attendance areas.

Second, even if neighborhood and school mix were not strongly correlated, we would expect them to have somewhat similar effects because most of the same social processes should be at work in both contexts. The main exception to this rule is that neighborhoods, unlike schools, do not assign students grades for their academic performance. As a result, growing up in a high-SES neighborhood may not have an adverse effect on students' academic self-concept unless it leads to attending a high-SES school.

Before anyone invests too much ingenuity in explaining the difference between neighborhood and school effects, however, more effort should be invested in making sure that parallel analyses of the HSB, PSID, and 1970 census data really yield contradictory results. The apparent difference between school and neighborhood effects on educational attainment could derive from differences in analytic method rather than differences in the underlying causal connections.

The racial composition of a school seems to have had different effects on blacks in the North and South, at least in the past. Racially mixed schools appear to have benefited northern blacks who attended them. But at least in 1972, southern blacks did not appear to benefit from attending racially mixed schools. We found no evidence on whether a high school's racial mix affected white students' eventual educational attainment.

## COGNITIVE SKILLS

By "cognitive skill" we mean performance on any standardized test of mental skill or information. Test manufacturers often draw a distinction between "aptitude" and "achievement" tests. But most studies suggest that both family background and school characteristics have about the same influence on aptitude scores (e.g., vocabulary scores) as on achievement scores (e.g., social studies information scores). Thus, we treat aptitude and achievement tests as interchangeable.

We found no studies of whether test performance depended on the social composition of the neighborhood in which a student grew up, as distinct from the composition of the school the student attended. Thus, this section deals exclusively with the effects of a school's social composition on test performance. We look first at the effect of a school's mean SES and then turn to the effect of its racial composition. In assessing the impact of mean SES we look first at high schools, about which we know a fair amount, and then at elementary schools, about which we know far less.

## Effects of High Schools' Mean SES

The "Coleman report" (Coleman et al., 1966) was the first study of how a school's mean SES affected students' cognitive skills. The report was based on the 1965 Equality of Educational Opportunity (EEO) survey, which collected data on first, third, sixth, ninth, and twelfth graders in a more or less representative national sample of public schools. No comparable survey has been conducted since, so the data are still of considerable interest, even though schools have changed in many ways since 1965.

Coleman et al. analyzed the EEO data at a time when regression equations were just becoming a part of sociologists' statistical tool kit, and their presentation emphasized changes in $R^2$ rather than regression coefficients. As several economists immediately pointed out, this made Coleman et al.'s findings hard to interpret correctly. But unlike most economists, Coleman et al. also reported the means, standard deviations, and correlations of the variables they used in their analyses. Thus, we can reanalyze their data in such a way as to address the questions posed in this review without going back to the original data tapes.

Coleman et al.'s matrices include only one measure of a school's mean SES, namely, the percentage of students who said their families owned an encyclopedia.[21] The matrices include seven exogenous family background characteristics: parental education, material possessions in the home, reading materials in the home, family size, family structure, urbanism, and speaking a foreign language at home. The matrices do not include any direct measure of parental income or occupational status. Nor did the survey measure students' test scores when they entered a school.[22]

Table 4-3 shows the effect of mean encyclopedia ownership on test performance in the sixth, ninth, and twelfth grades with all seven background measures controlled.[23] Measures of school quality, such as expenditures or teachers' credentials, are not controlled. The apparent effects of mean SES may, therefore, derive either from the fact that high-SES schools get more money, better teachers, and so forth, or from the fact that high-SES students create a more favorable climate for teaching and learning.

---

[21] Encyclopedias are not an ideal measure of mean SES, but they predict achievement as accurately as the school mean of any other single SES measure collected from these students.

[22] The absence of initial scores would pose no problem if the measures of individual SES captured all school-to-school differences in initial ability, but this requirement is not fully met (Jencks, 1972a,b). Failing to control first-grade scores tends to bias the estimated effect of mean SES upward. Using the percentage of families with encyclopedias as the sole measure of mean SES tends to bias the estimated effect of mean SES downward. The net bias is uncertain.

[23] We cannot make analogous estimates for first or third graders, because family background measures for first and third graders are inadequate and the third-grade tests are flawed (Mosteller and Moynihan, 1972).

TABLE 4-3 Effects of Mean SES on Test Scores With Seven Background Measures Controlled, Northern Whites and Blacks, 1965

| | Black | | White | | | | |
|---|---|---|---|---|---|---|---|
| | Test Score | | Coefficient of Proportion Owning an Encyclopedia | | | Test Score | | Coefficient of Proportion Owning an Encyclopedia | | |
| | Mean | S.D. | B | (S.E.) | Beta | Mean | S.D. | B | (S.E.) | Beta |

| | Mean | S.D. | B | (S.E.) | Beta | Mean | S.D. | B | (S.E.) | Beta |
|---|---|---|---|---|---|---|---|---|---|---|
| **12th grade tests** | | | | | | | | | | |
| Verbal | 52.7 | (14.5) | 30.3 | (5.4) | .182 | 67.6 | (14.1) | 10.8 | (6.3) | .055 |
| Reading | 61.6 | (17.2) | 24.2 | (7.5) | .122 | 76.1 | (16.8) | 3.6 | (7.8) | .015 |
| Math | 32.2 | (19.0) | 17.1 | (7.4) | .078 | 57.6 | (17.1) | -1.1 | (8.0) | -.004 |
| General information | 42.2 | (11.7) | 21.3 | (4.4) | .158 | 56.2 | (12.4) | 4.3 | (5.6) | .025 |
| Mean of four tests | 47.2 | | 23.2 | | .135 | 64.4 | | 4.4 | | .023 |
| **9th grade tests** | | | | | | | | | | |
| Verbal | 40.9 | (12.6) | 13.6 | (3.9)) | .116 | 55.4 | (13.9) | 8.0 | (5.6) | .045 |
| Reading | 47.1 | (16.5) | 6.3 | (5.2) | .041 | 61.7 | (17.2) | 10.8 | (7.2) | .050 |
| Math | 36.0 | (13.8) | 7.9 | (4.4) | .061 | 49.0 | (14.0) | 1.9 | (5.8) | .011 |
| General information | 39.0 | (12.8) | 13.6 | (4.0) | .113 | 55.1 | (14.7) | 8.1 | (5.9) | .044 |
| Mean of four tests | 32.6 | | 10.3 | | .083 | 55.3 | | 7.2 | | .038 |
| **6th grade tests** | | | | | | | | | | |
| Verbal | 24.2 | (9.1) | 7.1 | (2.0) | .114 | 36.1 | (11.4) | 7.2 | (3.2) | .072 |
| Reading | 31.2 | (13.5) | 8.2 | (3.0) | .088 | 43.9 | (15.8) | 7.9 | (4.6) | .056 |
| Math | 22.0 | (9.9) | 5.0 | (2.2) | .074 | 34.1 | (11.5) | 7.4 | (3.4) | .073 |
| Mean of three tests | 25.8 | | 6.7 | | .092 | 38.0 | | 7.5 | | .067 |

Proportion owning an encyclopedia

| | Black | | White | |
|---|---|---|---|---|
| | Mean | S.D. | Mean | S.D. |
| 12th grade | .794 | (.087) | .850 | (.072) |
| 9th grade | .758 | (.107) | .851 | (.079) |
| 6th grade | .642 | (.146) | .807 | (.114) |

SOURCE: Coleman et al. (1966): Supplemental Appendix. We estimated the regression coefficients from Coleman et al.'s matrices.

Table 4-3 includes two notable results for high school students: First, mean SES has almost no effect on northern white high school students' achievement. Averaging across all four tests, the standardized coefficients of encyclopedia ownership among whites are .038 for ninth graders and .023 for twelfth graders. Coefficients of this size are too small to be substantively significant, and none is reliably different from zero.[24] The effect of mean SES on white students' test scores also diminishes between the ninth and twelfth grades. It follows that if we were to control students' ninth-grade test scores when predicting their twelfth-grade scores, the estimated effect of mean SES on white students' twelfth-grade scores would be even smaller than Table 4-3 implies.

Second, mean SES has a sizable effect on northern black high school students' achievement. For blacks, the standardized coefficients of mean encyclopedia ownership average .083 in ninth grade and .135 in twelfth grade. These coefficients are large enough to be substantively important and almost all of them are reliably greater than zero. Note, too, that the apparent effect of mean SES increases between the ninth and twelfth grades. Thus, even if we could control black students' ninth-grade scores, the estimated effect of a high school's mean SES on black high school students' cognitive growth would be substantial.

The results in Table 4-3 are subject to three major sources of potential error. First, the measures of individual SES contain a lot of error. Second, students' initial test scores are not controlled. Third, the measure of mean SES is not very precise. The first two problems tend to inflate the estimated effect of mean SES, while the third deflates it. Jencks and Brown (1975b) tried to deal with these three problems using data collected by Project Talent, which tested ninth graders in 1960 and retested those who were still enrolled in the same school in 1963, when they were in the twelfth grade. Jencks and Brown analyzed changes between ninth and twelfth grade in vocabulary, social studies information, reading comprehension, arithmetic reasoning, arithmetic computation, and abstract reasoning among students enrolled in 91 predominantly white, comprehensive public schools. In addition to SES, sex, and family size, they treated ninth graders' college plans, curriculum assignment, previous grades, and test performance as exogenous. Their conclusions, therefore, apply only to cognitive growth *after* ninth grade.

---

[24] Some readers may suspect that mean encyclopedia ownership has little impact on white ninth and twelfth graders' test scores because it is a poor measure of mean SES. Were that hypothesis correct, however, it should apply with equal force to white sixth graders and to blacks at all grade levels. Since Table 4-3 indicates that mean encyclopedia ownership makes a difference for all these groups, the tiny effect among white ninth and twelfth graders cannot be dismissed as a methodological artifact.

After adjusting for both exogenous factors and measurement error, Jencks and Brown found that differences between high schools accounted for between 1.0 and 3.4 percent of the variation in twelfth-grade test scores. They also found that schools which did a good job raising students' scores on one test were not especially likely to do a good job on other tests. (The correlation between schools' estimated effects on different tests averaged only .17.) They concluded that variation in high school quality would have explained less than 1 percent of the variation in a composite achievement measure based on all six tests.

High-SES schools had a positive effect on vocabulary and arithmetic reasoning scores and a negative effect on social studies and reading comprehension scores, but none of the effects was large enough to rule out the possibility that it was due to chance. Jencks and Brown's analysis is therefore consistent with the EEO data for white ninth and twelfth graders. Both analyses imply that a high school's mean SES has a negligible effect on white students' academic progress.

The High School and Beyond (HSB) survey provides the best current evidence on these issues. In 1980, HSB gave vocabulary, reading, writing, civics, math, and science tests to a national sample of more than 30,000 tenth graders in roughly 1,000 public and private schools. In 1982 HSB retested the same students, most of whom were in twelfth grade.

Myers (1985) analyzed the effect of a school's poverty rate on tenth and twelfth graders' reading and math achievement. He did not exploit the longitudinal feature of the survey by including tenth-grade scores in the equation predicting twelfth-grade scores.[25] His analyses, therefore, measure (or at least try to measure) the cumulative effect of mean SES up to tenth or twelfth grade, not the effect of mean SES on cognitive growth between tenth and twelfth grade.[26] Nonetheless, Myers's results are of some interest, because they focus directly on the effects of concentrated poverty. The poverty rate in Myers's sample of HSB schools averages 21 percent, with a standard deviation of 15 points. A 30-point increase in a high school's poverty rate (e.g., from 20 to 50 percent) lowers reading scores by 0.25 standard deviations in tenth grade and 0.35 standard deviations in twelfth grade. For math scores the difference is 0.33 standard deviations in

---

[25] Myers does present an analysis of what he calls "learning," based on changes between the tenth and twelfth grades in the regression coefficient of the school's poverty rate. For reasons discussed below in our critique of Jencks and Brown (1975a), we do not believe that this comparison measures the effect of the poverty rate on learning

[26] Because high schools draw from a wider area than elementary schools, poverty rates vary less in high schools than in elementary schools. This fact should not bias the coefficient of the poverty rate in Myers's analyses, but it could lead us to underestimate the potential benefits of moving students from poor schools to average schools because the poorest elementary schools are poorer than the poorest high schools.

tenth grade and 0.46 standard deviations in twelfth grade. These are very large effects, but they may be attributable to the fact that Myers did not control a number of important exogenous variables.[27]

Gamoran (1987) presents a technically superior analysis of the HSB data, which focuses on cognitive growth between the tenth and twelfth grades. His measures of both individual SES and mean SES are composites that give equal weight to father's education, father's occupation, mother's education, family income, and possessions in the home. He estimates the effect of a public school's mean SES on each of the six HSB twelfth-grade tests, controlling tenth-grade vocabulary, reading, and math scores plus gender, ethnicity, and individual SES.[28] With these controls, the standardized coefficient of a school's mean SES ranges from a maximum of .026 for the vocabulary test to a minimum of −.011 for the science test. The arithmetic mean of the six standardized coefficients is .009, and none of the six coefficients is reliably different from this mean. Thus, Gamoran's data suggest that moving from an average school to one with an extremely high concentration of poverty in tenth grade would lower a student's twelfth-grade test performance by something like .02 of a standard deviation. An effect of this magnitude would almost never be substantively significant.

Unlike Gamoran, Bryk and Driscoll (1988) concluded that mean SES had a statistically reliable effect on twelfth-grade math scores in their sample of 357 HSB schools that had participated in the 1984 Administrator and Teacher Survey. Bryk and Driscoll control essentially the same exogenous variables as Gamoran, but they include more measures of a school's socioeconomic and ethnic mix, so their results are not strictly comparable to Gamoran's. Nor do they present enough information for us to estimate the effect of mean SES with other school characteristics omitted.

Bryk and Driscoll also found that the gap between the math scores of advantaged and disadvantaged students is greater in high-SES and mixed-SES schools than in low-SES schools. They do not present enough information for us to determine whether low-SES students are actually worse off when they move from low-SES to mixed- or high-SES schools. Low-SES

---

[27] When estimating the effects of a school's poverty rate, Myers controlled a student's gender, ethnicity, family size and structure, mother's education, mother's employment history, and whether the student's family was poor. He did not control father's education, father's occupation, or income differences among families above the poverty line. For reasons he does not explain, his analysis covers only a quarter of the original HSB sample. His tables and text also contain several internal inconsistencies.

[28] Gamoran also controls a school's mean tenth-grade math or reading score and its ethnic composition, but these variables have such small coefficients that their inclusion is unlikely to have an appreciable effect on the coefficient of mean SES. The standardized coefficient of the school's mean score on the relevant tenth-grade test averages .002; the standardized coefficient of the proportion black averages −.0003.

students may just gain less than high-SES students when they move from a low-SES to a high-SES school.

Bryk and Driscoll's findings imply that the weak effect of mean SES on math achievement in Gamoran's analysis of the HSB data may mask gains for some and losses for others. This issue requires more detailed investigation. If Bryk and Driscoll are correct that high-SES students gain more from attending high-SES schools than low-SES students do, reducing economic segregation in high schools would hurt advantaged students more than it would help disadvantaged students. As a result, economic desegregation would lower a school system's mean achievement. Before accepting this finding at face value, however, we should check it using statistical methods that focus explicitly on this issue.

Our reanalyses of Coleman et al.'s EEO matrices, Jencks and Brown's analysis of Project Talent, and Gamoran's analysis of HSB all indicate that a high school's mean SES has a negligible impact on how much the average student learns in high school. Bryk and Driscoll seem to find the opposite, but we are not yet ready to conclude that the earlier consensus on this point was wrong, because their model does not provide a clean test of the hypothesis.

Such evidence as we have also suggests, however, that studying the effect of a high school's mean SES on the "average" student may conceal more than it reveals. A high school's mean SES may well have a substantial impact on some students but very little on others. Coleman et al.'s matrices suggest that mean SES has more impact on blacks than on whites. Bryk and Driscoll's results suggest that mean SES has more effect on high-SES students than on low-SES students. Taken at face value these results support policies aimed at reducing racial segregation while increasing economic segregation, but they should not be taken at face value until they are replicated.[29]

### Effects of Elementary School's Mean SES

Turning from high schools to elementary schools, the evidence regarding determinants of academic achievement is much worse. Table 4-3 suggests that in 1965 mean SES had a moderate impact on the achievement scores of both black and white sixth graders. The standardized coefficient of encyclopedia ownership averages .08 for sixth graders. This coefficient does not vary significantly by race; nor does it vary significantly from one academic subject to another. Thus, the EEO data imply that moving from a school in the bottom 5 percent of the socioeconomic distribution to a

---

[29] Mayer is engaged in an analysis of HSB that focuses on precisely these issues.

school of average SES would raise students' test performance by one-sixth of a standard deviation.

Unfortunately, this estimate is even shakier than those for ninth and twelfth graders. The EEO measures of individual SES are based on students' reports about their parents. Because sixth graders' reports about their parents are not very accurate, an elementary school's mean SES may be a proxy for unmeasured aspects of individual SES. There may also have been differences in initial achievement between sixth graders of apparently similar SES who attended high-SES rather than low-SES elementary schools. These considerations suggest that Table 4-3 may overestimate the impact of mean SES. On the other hand, reports of encyclopedia ownership are hardly an ideal measure of mean SES. A better measure would probably have a larger coefficient.[30]

Partly because the EEO survey had such serious limitations, the federal government initiated a major new study of elementary education in 1976. The Sustaining Effects (SE) study collected background data directly from parents and tested first through sixth graders in both the fall and the spring of three successive academic years. In principle, these data should provide a lot more information about the impact of a school's mean SES on a child's cognitive growth than the EEO survey did.

Unfortunately, the Department of Education has never made the SE data available to outside social scientists in usable form. As a result, only one study (Myers, 1985) uses the SE data to investigate whether a school's mean SES affects students' cognitive skills independent of their family background. Myers used the poverty rate for families in a school as his measure of mean SES and treated children's gender, ethnicity, mother's education, mother's employment status, family size, family structure, and whether their family's income was below the poverty line as exogenous. He did not exploit the longitudinal feature of the SE data, but instead conducted a series of cross-sectional analyses.

When Myers used a school's poverty rate to predict reading scores, its standardized coefficient was .05 at the beginning of first grade, .08 at the end of first grade, .15 at the beginning of second grade, and .11 at the end of second grade. The standardized coefficient fell slightly after the end of second grade and was .09 at the end of sixth grade. These standardized coefficients are quite misleading, however, because they ignore the fact that the dispersion of test performance increases with age. The absolute

---

[30] Jencks (1972a) obtained somewhat larger effects using data derived from the full northern urban EEO sample and a better measure of mean SES. Because the measures of family background in the original EEO survey are inadequate, Jencks's analysis probably overstates the impact of mean SES on test performance.

effect of mean SES increased as children got older, which is what everyday experience would lead us to expect.

The SE survey had better measures than the EEO survey for both individual SES and mean SES. These improvements evidently offset one another, leaving the standardized effect of mean SES in sixth grade almost unchanged. Myers reports a standardized coefficient for mean SES in sixth grade that is almost identical to the standardized coefficient in Table 4-3, which is based on the EEO. Controlling students' initial scores would have lowered the effect of mean SES in both surveys, but we doubt that such controls would have cut the effect by more than a third.[31]

The poverty rate in the SE schools that Myers studied averaged 18 percent (with a standard deviation of 18 points). Thus, the SE data suggest that moving a student from a school with a poverty rate of 54 percent to an average school with a poverty rate of 18 percent would raise his or her sixth-grade reading score by something like one-sixth of a standard deviation.

### Effects of Racial Composition on Blacks

The Coleman report was also the first major study of how a school's racial composition affected its students' achievement. The effects of racial composition are, of course, somewhat confounded with the effects of mean SES, since predominantly white schools usually have more affluent students than predominantly black schools. But the correlation between mean SES and racial mix is far from perfect.[32] Some all-black schools enroll a lot of middle-class students, and some all-white schools enroll very few.

Moreover, in comparisons of black and white students whose parents have the same number of years of school, the same occupational status, and the same income, whites do far better on standardized tests. This is

---

[31] Longitudinal surveys suggest that the standardized coefficient of first-grade scores in an equation predicting sixth-grade scores is unlikely to exceed .60. In the absence of school effects, therefore, an 0.05 standard deviation difference between two students entering first grade would translate into a difference of only 0.03 standard deviations in sixth grade. Since the apparent effect of mean SES in sixth grade is about 0.09 standard deviations, the "school effect" would be at least $0.09 - 0.03 = 0.06$ standard deviations. We should note that this estimate differs from Myers's estimate of the relationship between a school's poverty rate and student "learning." For reasons discussed in our assessment of Jencks and Brown (1975a), we think his analysis of learning is wrong.

[32] The correlations between Proportion White and Proportion Owning Encyclopedias in schools attended by northern whites in the EEO survey were .25 for twelfth graders, .40 for ninth graders, and .43 for sixth graders. The correlations in schools attended by northern blacks were .45 for twelfth graders, .49 for ninth graders, and .51 for sixth graders. The correlations are higher for blacks than for whites because Proportion White has more variance among blacks than among whites. Better measures of mean SES would yield higher correlations.

true even among four-year-olds, almost none of whom had attended school (Broman et al., 1975). A school's racial composition, therefore, is a partial proxy for its students' mean test performance, even after its mean SES is controlled. Thus, it would not be surprising if a school's racial composition affected its curriculum, its teachers' expectations about how much their students could learn, its students' expectations about how much they could learn, or the amount students really did learn.

Coleman et al. reported that attending school with white classmates increased black students' test scores in the North, but they did not estimate the magnitude of the effect. Table 4-4 uses their correlation matrices to estimate the effect of Proportion White on black students' test scores in the sixth, ninth, and twelfth grades. These estimates do not control mean SES. Rather, they try to estimate the effect of moving a student from a predominantly black school to a predominantly white school. Once again, we control the seven exogenous family background characteristics available in the published matrices.

Combining the coefficients in Table 4-4 with the standard deviations in Table 4-3 and averaging over all tests, we estimate that blacks in 90 percent white schools scored 0.30 standard deviation higher than blacks from similar backgrounds in all-black schools. The magnitude of this effect shows no statistically reliable trend between sixth and twelfth grade. Crain and Mahard (1978) obtained essentially identical results for northern black twelfth graders in 1972 using data from the National Longitudinal Survey of the Class of 1972 (NLS-72).[33]

In the South, where desegregation had just begun in 1972, a school's racial composition had virtually no effect on black students' performance. This may be because blacks in desegregated high schools had only been there a few years or because their experiences in newly desegregated southern schools were often unpleasant. There have been no studies using more recent data.

Controlling initial ability might change the picture somewhat. Jencks and Brown (1975a) present EEO test scores for northern urban blacks in schools that were more than 75 percent black and in schools that were less than 10 percent black. This gap averaged 0.39 standard deviations in

---

[33] Crain and Mahard report that the effect of moving from an all-black to a 90 percent white school was half a standard deviation rather than a third of a standard deviation. But the difference is 3.69 points, and their tables leave little doubt that their tests were standardized to a national mean of 50 and standard deviation of 10.

Crain and Mahard controlled the mean SES of all blacks in a school rather than the SES of individual blacks. If blacks in predominantly white schools came from high-SES families, this procedure might lead to some downward bias in the estimated effect of Proportion White, since the coefficient of mean black SES is likely to exceed the coefficient of SES for individual blacks. Fortunately, mean black SES is uncorrelated with Proportion White in both NLS-72 and the 1965 EEO, so this source of bias is not cause for concern.

TABLE 4-4  Effects of Proportion White on Test Scores, With Seven Background Measures Controlled, Northern Blacks and Whites, 1965

| | Blacks | | | Whites | | |
|---|---|---|---|---|---|---|
| | B | (S.E.) | Beta | B | (S.E.) | Beta |
| 12th grade | | | | | | |
| Verbal | 6.1 | (1.3) | .147 | 4.6 | (3.4) | .040 |
| Reading | 3.9 | (1.6) | .079 | 4.7 | (4.2) | .034 |
| Math | 7.0 | (1.7) | .129 | 7.5 | (4.3) | .054 |
| General information | 5.7 | (1.0) | .171 | 5.1 | (3.0) | .051 |
| Mean of four tests | 5.7 | | .132 | 5.5 | | .045 |
| 9th grade | | | | | | |
| Verbal | 2.2 | (1.2) | .057 | 8.9 | (3.0) | .087 |
| Reading | 3.2 | (1.5) | .065 | 11.7 | (3.8) | .093 |
| Math | 4.1 | (1.3) | .098 | 9.9 | (3.1) | .097 |
| General information | 6.0 | (1.2) | .156 | 11.9 | (3.1) | .111 |
| Mean of four tests | 3.9 | | .094 | 10.6 | | .097 |
| 6th grade | | | | | | |
| Verbal | 4.4 | (0.9) | .147 | 8.6 | (2.3) | .108 |
| Reading | 2.0 | (1.3) | .045 | 8.0 | (3.4) | .072 |
| Math | 3.1 | (1.0) | .095 | 7.2 | (2.5) | .090 |
| Mean of three tests | 3.2 | | .096 | 7.9 | | .090 |

| | Mean Proportion White | | S.D. of Proportion White | |
|---|---|---|---|---|
| | Blacks | Whites | Blacks | Whites |
| 12th grade | .413 | .899 | .349 | .122 |
| 9th grade | .311 | .881 | .329 | .157 |
| 6th grade | .243 | .877 | .303 | .143 |

SOURCE:  Coleman et al. (1966:Supplemental Appendix).

twelfth grade, 0.38 standard deviations in sixth grade, and 0.42 standard deviations in first grade. Since the gap is as large in first grade as in twelfth grade, it is tempting to attribute the twelfth-grade gap to the first-grade gap. Indeed, that is precisely what Jencks and Brown did. Such reasoning is misleading, however.

Suppose we were to find that among blacks who attended the same school twelfth-grade scores correlated .60 with their grade scores—a quite plausible estimate. This would indicate that when two blacks in the same school had scores that differed by 0.42 standard deviations in first grade, their scores typically differed by only $(0.60)(0.42) = 0.25$ standard deviations in twelfth grade. Yet when black first graders in all-black and predominantly white schools differ by 0.42 standard deviations, they differ by 0.39 standard deviations in twelfth grade. The gap is thus 0.14 standard deviations larger than it would have been if the children in question had attended the same school.

We do not know the actual correlation between first- and twelfth-grade scores, but we know it is less than 1.00. Thus, if a school's racial composition had no independent effect on black students' scores, the standardized difference between blacks entering all-black schools and those entering 90 percent white schools would decline as the students got older. Since this does not happen, we must conclude that something about the schools themselves helps perpetuate the initial differences among their entering black students.

Unfortunately, while this logic supports our earlier conclusion that racial composition matters, it does not tell us *how much* it matters. We cannot resolve that question without longitudinal data. In principle, the HSB and SE surveys provide such data, but in practice, no one has analyzed either survey with this in mind.[34]

## The First Year of Desegregation

No one has studied the long-term impact of schools' racial mix on their students' achievement since the mid-1970s. Social scientists have concentrated instead on estimating the short-term effect of desegregation plans. Most such studies share three major limitations: (1) They estimate the effect of a single year in a desegregated school, not the cumulative effect of attending desegregated elementary and secondary schools. (2) They focus on the year in which a desegregation plan was first implemented, which is typically quite chaotic. (3) They ignore secondary schools.

The first limitation is especially critical. There is no way of using data on the effect of 1 year in a desegregated school to infer the effect of 12 years in such schools. Yet the cumulative effect of desegregation is what matters.

Studies of what happens during the first year of desegregation are so numerous that we have not tried to review them all. Instead, we have reviewed the reviews. Since the late 1970s such reviews have taken quantitative form and have been called meta-analyses. A meta-analysis records all the apparently relevant attributes of each study (grade level, type of test, use of a pretest, location, and so forth), along with the estimated effect of desegregation on student achievement. The meta-analyst then estimates the mean gain in studies with various attributes.

---

[34]Several analyses of the HSB data look at the effect of racial composition on the achievement of a pooled sample of blacks and whites, but because the bulk of the HSB sample is white, the results do not indicate much about the effect of racial composition on blacks. We discuss these studies below.

Meta-analysts typically report that during the first year of desegregation a desegregated black student's reading score rises about 0.10 standard deviations more than a segregated black student's score (Cook, 1984). Depending on the principles that meta-analysts use to select studies, they can push the estimated effect as high as 0.30 (Crain and Mahard, 1983) or as low as 0.06 (Armor, 1984).[35] The first year of desegregation does not appear to affect black students' math scores (Cook, 1984).

Crain and Mahard (1983) argue that most meta-analysts underestimate desegregation's effect on black reading scores, for two reasons. First, gains are larger in studies using random assignment, which is the preferred method for ensuring that desegregated students are initially similar to segregated students. But as Cook (1984) notes, almost all the evidence using random assignment comes from Hartford, where relatively small numbers of inner-city blacks were bused to suburban schools that had volunteered to accept them. The Hartford experiment was unusual in many respects, so its results are probably not generalizable. Second, Crain and Mahard argue that kindergarteners and first graders gain more from desegregation than older students. They interpret this as evidence that young children are especially influenced by desegregation. But whether desegregation appears to have more effect on young children than on older children depends entirely on how we measure the effect.

Like almost all meta-analysts, Crain and Mahard express gains at different ages as a percentage of the initial standard deviation. They find that one year of desegregation raises black students' reading scores by an average of only 0.09 standard deviations in sixth grade compared with 0.20 standard deviations in first grade. They conclude that desegregation does more good in first grade than in sixth grade.

Unfortunately, comparing standardized test scores at different ages ignores a crucial feature of test performance, namely that performance becomes more unequal as children get older. A 0.09 standard deviation difference between two sixth graders is far larger, in absolute terms, than a 0.20 standard deviation difference between two first graders. One way to make this clear is to express differences not in terms of standard deviations but in terms of time.

Myers's (1985) analysis of the SE data indicates, for example, that children's reading scores typically rise by 1.8 standard deviations between the fall and spring of first grade. If blacks gain 0.20 standard deviations more in desegregated schools than in segregated schools, therefore, they must be learning about $0.20/1.8 = 11$ percent more than they otherwise would. In

---

[35] Cook (1984) notes that the mean gain is larger than the median, because a few small studies show large positive gains and no studies show large losses.

temporal terms, attending a desegregated first grade boosts black achievement as much as an extra month of schooling. Myers reports that children typically gain only 0.42 standard deviations between the fall and spring of sixth grade. Since desegregated schooling increases black children's gains by 0.09 standard deviations in sixth grade, it increases the amount they learn by about 0.09/0.42 = 21 percent, which is roughly equivalent to a two-month gain. Using this approach, therefore, desegregation is more valuable for older students, not younger students.

We do not know for sure that the temporal metric is correct. If we had a true interval scale for measuring reading skills, we might find that students learned more per month at some ages than at others. But the temporal metric surely approximates an interval scale more closely than the standardized metric favored by meta-analysts. In the absence of better evidence we must therefore conclude either that desegregation helps older blacks more than younger blacks or that there is no sensible basis for making such comparisons.

The crucial question, however, is how 12 years of desegregated schooling affects black students' achievement. Krol (1980) estimates the mean effect of two or more years in a desegregated school at about 0.2 standard deviations, compared with 0.1 standard deviations for a single year. But he found so few studies covering more than one year that this difference was not statistically reliable, and none of the studies he found covered more than three years of desegregated schooling. Our best estimates of the cumulative impact of school desegregation are, therefore, still based on the 1965 EEO and NLS-72. These two surveys suggest that black students who attended overwhelmingly white rather than all-black schools in the North in the 1960s scored something like one-third of a standard deviation higher on most tests as a result. Since the overall difference between northern blacks and whites was about one standard deviation, the benefits of desegregation were substantial.

### Nonlinearities

The discussion to this point has assumed that a 1 percentage point change in a school's racial mix has the same effect on individual achievement regardless of whether the school is initially all-white, all-black, or somewhere in between. Yet many advocates of desegregation assume that racial mix has nonlinear effects. Blacks often assume that something like a 50-50 mix of blacks and whites is optimal, at least for blacks. Whites often assume that a small black minority is optimal, at least for whites.

Jencks and Brown (1975a) thought they had found evidence that blacks gained most in elementary schools that were 51 to 75 percent white. Summers and Wolfe (1977) found the same thing in Philadelphia. Both studies have serious limitations for our purposes, but they suggest that nonlinear effects deserve more attention.

### Effects of Racial Composition on Whites

Table 4-4 implies that whites are at least as sensitive as blacks to the effects of a school's racial composition. Indeed, among sixth and ninth graders, white classmates appear to be worth two or three times as much to white students as to black students. Readers with long memories may find this result somewhat surprising, since Coleman et al. (1966) reported that racial composition explained a much larger fraction of the variance in black students' scores than in white students' scores. The reason for this difference, which Coleman et al. evidently overlooked, was that racial composition varied far more among blacks than among whites (see the bottom of Table 4-4). Many other analysts (including Jencks, 1969) also overlooked this fact and used Coleman et al.'s findings to argue that desegregation would help blacks more than it hurt whites.

If Table 4-4 provides a realistic estimate of desegregation's true effect on whites, mixing students from all-black and all-white elementary schools would lower white students' scores far more than it would raise black students' scores. Since there are many more whites than blacks in the nation as a whole, school desegregation on a national scale would increase the proportion of whites in the typical black student's school far more than it would reduce the proportion of whites in the typical white student's school. The costs of desegregation to the typical white would therefore be smaller than the benefits to the typical black. But because there are many more whites than blacks, the aggregate cost to society as a whole would still be substantial.[36]

We have several reasons for doubting the validity of this conclusion, however. First, imprecise measurement of students' family background and initial ability probably inflates the estimated effect of Proportion White more for whites than for blacks. White students' measured SES was quite strongly correlated with their school's racial mix in both the 1965 EEO and the NLS-72, which suggest that high-SES white parents avoided schools with high black enrollments. Controlling measured SES reduces the estimated effect of Proportion White on white achievement by a third. Controlling unmeasured aspects of SES and initial ability would therefore be likely to

---

[36]The expected effect of desegregation on mean test performance for the nation as a whole depends on whether the unstandardized coefficient of Proportion White is larger for blacks or whites. If the coefficient is positive and larger for whites, as it is for the sixth and ninth grades in Table 4-4, desegregation will lower the national average. If the coefficient of Proportion White is larger for blacks than for whites, desegregation will raise the national average.

reduce the estimated effect of Proportion White on white achievement by more than a third.

Among blacks, in contrast, an individual's SES was almost uncorrelated with his or her school's racial mix in the 1965 and 1972 surveys, which suggests that high-SES black parents made little effort to enroll their children in predominantly white schools. If this explanation is correct, controlling a wider array of background measures would not reduce the estimated effect of Proportion White on black students' achievement.

A second reason for skepticism about the estimates in Table 4-4 is that, at least in 1965, very few northern whites attended schools that were more than 25 percent black. Thus, the estimated effect of racial composition on white students in the EEO survey is based largely on differences among schools that are overwhelmingly white. Extrapolating to predominantly black schools could be quite misleading.

Our third reason for doubting that desegregation lowers white students' achievement as much as Table 4-4 implies is that in Gamoran's (1987) HSB sample, which was 90 percent white, a school's racial composition had no consistent impact on cognitive growth between the tenth and twelfth grades. With mean SES, mean tenth-grade scores, and individual attributes in tenth grade held constant, students in all-white schools learned significantly more science but significantly less civics than students in schools with significant black enrollment. Averaging across all six HSB tests, students gained only 0.015 standard deviations more between tenth and twelfth grades if they attended all-white schools than if they attended all-black schools. Even allowing for the fact that all-white schools are also high-SES schools and have above-average tenth-grade scores, students in all-white schools only appear to have gained about 0.03 standard deviations more than initially similar students in all-black schools.[37]

Those who have reviewed studies of the first year of desegregation also claim that those studies show no effect of desegregation on white achievement. St. John (1975), for example, reviewed 23 studies. Two reported statistically reliable increases for whites, 3 reported statistically reliable declines, and 18 reported no statistically reliable change. This evidence is not

---

[37] Using the subsample of HSB schools that participated in the Administrator and Teacher Survey, Bryk and Driscoll (1988) tell a somewhat different story about math scores than Gamoran tells. After controlling the same variables as Gamoran, plus two additional measures of socioeconomic and racial diversity, Bryk and Driscoll found that Proportion Black had a statistically reliable positive effect on twelfth-grade math scores and that Mean SES had a reliable negative effect. Gamoran obtained the same signs in his math equations, but his coefficients were smaller and were not reliably different from zero. This apparent difference could reflect differences in the control variables included in each study, or it could reflect differences in the samples or estimation procedures. Hotchkiss (1984) examined the effect of mandatory busing on achievement in the HSB survey and concluded that the effect was small. He did not look at blacks and whites separately.

as convincing as it sounds, however. Most of the studies cover relatively small samples. Thus, if one year of desegregation typically lowered white students' reading scores by, say, 0.10 standard deviations, most studies would find that the estimated effect was "statistically insignificant." We would need a meta-analysis that pooled all such studies to estimate the true effect. No one has done such an analysis.

### Conclusions About Cognitive Skills

What we currently know about the effects of a school's mean SES on individual achievement can be summarized as follows:

- A high school's mean SES has very little effect on white ninth graders' subsequent cognitive growth. Bryk and Driscoll's (1988) work is the major exception here.
- A high school's mean SES may have an appreciable effect on black ninth graders' subsequent cognitive growth, but we would need a study using longitudinal data to be sure about this.
- An elementary school's mean SES appears to have an appreciable effect on both black and white students' cognitive growth, but again, longitudinal analysis is needed to be sure about this.

We can summarize what we currently know about the effects of racial composition on test performance as follows:

- The first year of school desegregation usually has small positive effects on black elementary school students' reading skills but not on their math skills.
- Twelve years in a predominantly white northern school probably has a substantial positive effect on black students' achievement.
- We do not know anything reliable about the cumulative impact of desegregated schooling in the South.
- The effect of desegregated schooling on white students is uncertain.

This is a rather thin harvest from a quarter century of research. School desegregation has been one of the most controversial political issues of the past generation. Assumptions about its effect on both black and white achievement have influenced the behavior of judges, legislators, educators, and parents. Court-ordered desegregation has profoundly altered the lives of millions of children, especially in the South. Yet there has been no serious effort to assess its cumulative impact since the mid-1970s.

The dearth of work in this area is particularly disturbing in light of the fact that the federal government has already collected data that could significantly advance our knowledge in this area. The High School and Beyond survey could tell us a lot more than we currently know about how a high school's racial and economic mix affects the academic achievement of various kinds of students. If the Sustaining Effects study were readily available to scholars, it would be even more valuable, since it would allow us to estimate the cumulative impact of an elementary school's racial and economic mix on cognitive growth from first through sixth grades.

The fact that neither the federal government nor individual social scientists have used the HSB and SE surveys to address these questions suggests that we need to rethink the way in which we organize social research on politically controversial topics.

## CRIME

Regardless of whether we look at official police statistics or residents' reports about the frequency with which they have been victimized, we find more serious crime in poor neighborhoods than in affluent ones. Indeed, one major reason people move out of poor neighborhoods is to escape crime.

Social scientists have invented a multitude of theories to explain why there is more crime in poor neighborhoods. Many of these theories assume that living in a poor neighborhood increases an individual's chances of committing serious crimes. But very little research has tried to test this assumption.

### School Effects: Nashville in the 1950s

We located only two studies of how a school's social composition affected its students' chances of engaging in serious crime, and only one of these studies is useful for our purposes. Reiss and Rhodes (1961) studied 9,238 white males over the age of 12 who were attending Nashville-area schools in 1958. After excluding traffic offenses, Reiss and Rhodes found that the Davidson County juvenile court had judged 5.9 percent of these boys delinquent at some time between 1950 and 1958. Reiss and Rhodes then cross-tabulated delinquency rates by individual SES and a school's mean SES.[38] Table 4-5 summarizes their results.

Overall, 8.1 percent of low-SES boys had been judged delinquent, compared to 3.0 percent of high-SES boys. The socioeconomic mix of a boy's school also had a substantial effect on his chances of having been judged delinquent, independent of his own SES. Taking Table 4-5 at face

---

[38] Reiss and Rhodes assigned each boy to one of three SES levels based on his father's occupation. They assigned each of their 39 schools to one of seven SES levels, based on the mix of fathers' occupations reported by students. In order to increase cell sizes and reduce sampling error, in Table 4-5 we combined schools in their top two SES groups and in their middle two SES groups, leaving five school SES levels instead of seven.

TABLE 4-5  Percentage of White Males Judged Delinquent in Nashville SMSA, 1950–1958

| School SES | Father's Occupational Status | | | |
|---|---|---|---|---|
|  | High | Middle | Low | All |
| High | 1.8 | 1.4 | 0 | 1.6 |
| (12 schools) | (681) | (419) | (41) | (1,141) |
| Upper-Middle | 3.9 | 3.7 | 4.4 | 3.8 |
| (7 schools) | (567) | (1,039) | (372) | (1,978) |
| Middle | 3.6 | 5.6 | 6.5 | 5.5 |
| (8 schools) | (277) | (892) | (511) | (1,680) |
| Lower-Middle | 3.4 | 7.5 | 8.4 | 7.4 |
| (7 schools) | (237) | (1,026) | (914) | (2,177) |
| Low | 6.0 | 13.5 | 14.5 | 13.4 |
| (5 schools) | (289) | (1,449) | (1,267) | (3,005) |
| Total | 3.0 | 6.0 | 8.1 | 5.9 |
| (N) | (1,814) | (3,799) | (2,191) | (7,804) |

NOTE:  Number of cases in parentheses.

SOURCE:  Reiss and Rhodes (1961): Table 2, with traffic offenses excluded.

value, a school's socioeconomic mix had far more impact on low-SES students than on high-SES students. For low-SES boys, moving from a low-SES school to an average school lowered the probability of being judged delinquent from .145 to .065. For high-SES boys, moving from an average school to a high-SES school only raises the probability of being judged delinquent from .018 to .036. Economic segregation thus increases delinquency among low-SES boys far more (.080) than it reduces delinquency among high-SES boys (.018).[39]

Unfortunately, Table 4-5 is likely to exaggerate the impact of a school's mean SES on individual behavior. Reiss and Rhodes controlled only one measure of parental SES, the father's occupation. Part of what looks like a "school effect" is therefore likely to be an effect of unmeasured socioeconomic differences between boys in high-SES and low-SES schools. This may, in other words, be another instance in which multiple regression equations would tell a different story from cross-tabulations.

---

[39] Reiss and Rhodes view the low delinquency rate of low-SES boys in high-SES schools as evidence that the dominant socioeconomic group in a given school, be it high-SES or low-SES, has the highest delinquency rate. The rest of Table 4-5 does not support this view, however. We therefore assume that the absence of any delinquency among the 41 low-SES boys in high-SES schools is due to sampling error.

If a school's mean SES really had the effect on crime that Table 4-5 implies it had, eliminating economic segregation would have reduced deliquency, but not by much. If all high-SES schools had had a representative socioeconomic mix, and if that had produced individual delinquency rates comparable to those in Nashville's middle-SES schools, the overall delinquency rate would have fallen by less than one-tenth (from 5.9 to 5.4 percent).[40] If Table 4-5 overestimates the impact of a school's mean SES, as seems likely, economic desegregation would have reduced delinquency by even less.

The second study that provides data on schools' social composition and crime (D. Gottfredson et al., 1987) covered students enrolled in 20 junior and senior high schools located in Baltimore, Charleston, Chicago, Christiansted, and Kalamazoo. Unfortunately for our purposes, the schools were selected because they had high crime rates. Because Gottfredson et al. did not adjust their results to take account of the fact that they sampled only high-crime schools, their findings do not tell us much about the effects of mean SES in representative samples of schools.[41]

### Neighborhood Effects: Chicago in 1972

Reiss and Rhodes's work has two major limitations: inadequate controls for individual SES and an exclusively white male sample. Johnstone's (1978) work overcomes both these limitations, but it covers only 1,124 teenagers who were between the ages of 14 and 18 and lived in the Chicago

---

[40] We do not know for sure that the mean SES of what we have called "middle-SES" schools is the same as that for the sample as a whole, because Reiss and Rhodes do not report schools' mean SES. Assuming that moving all students to middle-SES schools left the delinquency rates for high-SES, middle-SES, and low-SES boys the same as those that Reiss and Rhodes found in middle-SES schools, the overall delinquency rate would be $[(.036)(1,814) + (.056)(3,799) + (.065)(2,191)]/7,804 = 0.054$. The expected effect of economic desegregation on crime derives from the fact that a school's mean SES appears to have nonlinear effects on crime, even with individual SES controlled. We cannot test this hypothesis rigorously without knowing the mean SES of schools at each SES level.

[41] D. Gottfredson et al. used factor analysis to construct two orthogonal indices of community characteristics, which they label "Disorganization" and "Affluence and Education." Unfortunately, the Disorganization index does not measure community disorganization in the vernacular sense, because it is constructed so as to be uncorrelated with "Affluence and Education." This is achieved by giving it strong negative loadings on education and family income and strong positive loadings on welfare use, poverty, female-headed households, and the like. In any event, the Affluence and Education measure had an average correlation of $-.001$ with respondents' reports of their involvement in interpersonal aggression, theft and vandalism, and drug involvement. Given the sampling procedure, this result does not prove that mean SES has no effect on crime. D. Gottfredson et al. also estimate standardized coefficients with individual-level variables controlled, but because those equations control endogenous as well as exogenous factors, they are not useful for our purposes.

metropolitan area in 1972. The survey asked them whether they had committed various crimes, how often they had done so, whether they had been arrested, and whether they had been the victim of various crimes.

Johnstone categorized individuals into three SES groups based on parental education, the occupation of the household head, and the interviewer's assessment of the household's material standard of living. He also categorized the 221 census tracts in which the respondents lived into three SES levels, based on the percentage of high school graduates in the tract, the percentage of labor force participants in professional or managerial occupations, and median family income.

Johnstone defined "serious" crimes as those listed in Part I of the Federal Bureau of Investigation's Uniform Crime Reports. Table 4-6 shows the mean number of serious crimes and the mean number of arrests that teenagers reported, broken down by their own SES and their neighborhood's mean SES.[42] As we would expect, low-SES teenagers reported having committed more serious crimes than did high-SES teenagers. Because the ratio of arrests to self-reported serious crimes did not vary consistently with individual SES, we cannot attribute differences in arrest rates to police prejudice against low-SES teenagers.

Teenagers in low-SES neighborhoods also reported committing more serious crimes than those in high-SES neighborhoods. Arrest rates, in contrast, did not vary appreciably by neighborhood SES. In theory, this discrepancy could mean that teenagers in high-SES neighborhoods were less willing to report serious crimes than teenagers in low-SES neighborhoods. In order to accept this explanation, however, we must be willing to claim that either (1) there is no more crime in low-SES than in high-SES neighborhoods or (2) high crime rates in low-SES neighborhoods are attributable to high-SES teenagers who journey to low-SES neighborhoods to commit crimes. Neither of these theories is plausible. We conclude, therefore, that the residents of low-SES Chicago neighborhoods did, in fact, commit more serious crimes than the residents of high-SES neighborhoods. It follows that self-reports are a better guide to neighborhood differences in criminal behavior than arrest rates are, at least in Chicago. The low ratio of arrests to crimes in low-SES neighborhoods could indicate that the police make less effort to solve a given crime if it occurs in a low-SES neighborhood, that the police have greater difficulty identifying culprits in low-SES neighborhoods, or both.[43]

---

[42]The questionnaire did not cover all Part I offenses, so both the means and the differences between neighborhoods are biased downward. Johnstone also gave repeat offenders a maximum score of 2 when calculating means, so if the ratio of repeat offenders to total offenders varies across neighborhoods, his results may be misleading.

[43]Smith's (1986) analysis of police behavior in the Rochester, St. Louis, and Tampa metropolitan areas shows that when the police actually come in contact with someone whose behavior might

TABLE 4-6 Self-Reported Serious Crimes and Arrests Per Person Among 14- to 18-Year-Olds in the Chicago SMSA, 1972

| Census Tract SES | Individual SES | | | |
|---|---|---|---|---|
| | High | Middle | Low | All |
| High | | | | |
| Serious crimes | 0.62 | 0.69 | 1.80 | 0.81 |
| Arrests | 0.40 | 0.34 | 0.98 | 0.46 |
| (N) | (209) | (111) | (52) | (372) |
| Middle | | | | |
| Serious crimes | 0.60 | 0.81 | 1.72 | 1.00 |
| Arrests | 0.14 | 0.38 | 0.72 | 0.41 |
| (N) | (125) | (207) | (124) | (456) |
| Low | | | | |
| Serious crimes | 0.38 | 1.45 | 1.39 | 1.30 |
| Arrests | 0.08 | 0.44 | 0.50 | 0.43 |
| (N) | (42) | (125) | (211) | (378) |
| All | | | | |
| Serious crimes | 0.59 | 0.96 | 1.55 | 1.03 |
| Arrests | 0.28 | 0.39 | 0.63 | 0.43 |
| (N) | (376) | (443) | (387) | (1,206) |

NOTES: Number of weighted cases in parentheses. The total number of unweighted cases is 1,124.

SOURCE: Johnstone (1978).

In Chicago as in Nashville, neighborhood effects appear to be nonlinear. Indeed, with Johnstone's detailed controls for individual SES, living in a high-SES rather than a middle-SES neighborhood does not seem to have any consistent effect on an individual's chances of committing serious crimes.[44] Only low-SES neighborhoods appear to make a difference.

Reiss and Rhodes's work leads us to expect that living in a low-SES neighborhood will raise the amount of serious crime among all sorts of teenagers, but that it will have its largest effect on low-SES teenagers. In Chicago, the story is more complex:

---

lead to an arrest and all other circumstances are the same, they are more likely to make the arrest if they are in a low-SES neighborhood. We infer, therefore, that the low ratio of arrests to self-reported serious crimes in low-SES neighborhoods reflects the fact that the police identify fewer suspects per serious crime in low-SES neighborhoods, not a tendency to treat suspects more leniently.

[44] Johnstone does not report the variances of these measures, so we cannot do formal significance tests, but given his small sample sizes and what he says about how his measures were constructed, we doubt that the differences between high-SES and middle-SES neighborhoods are significant.

- There are not enough high-SES teenagers in low-SES neighborhoods to draw any strong conclusions about how neighborhoods
  affect their crime rate.
- Among middle-SES teenagers, living in a low-SES neighborhood
  appears to increase serious crime, just as it did in Nashville.
- Among low-SES teenagers, living in a low-SES neighborhood appears to *lower* the amount of serious crime by about a fifth. This is
  exactly the opposite of what Reiss and Rhodes found for low-SES
  whites in the Nashville-area schools.

How are we to explain the fact that low-SES teenagers reported committing
fewer serious crimes (and also reported fewer arrests for such crimes) if
they lived in "bad" neighborhoods than if they lived in relatively "good"
neighborhoods? Sampling error is one possibility. Johnstone does not
provide enough information to determine whether the differences are statistically reliable. Relative deprivation is a second possible explanation.
Low-SES teenagers may commit more crimes when they are in constant
contact—and competition—with higher-SES neighbors.

Another question is how Johnstone could have found that low-SES
teenagers committed fewer crimes when they lived in low-SES neighborhoods when Reiss and Rhodes found the opposite. Three possibilities come
to mind. First, Johnstone studied census tracts whereas Reiss and Rhodes
studied secondary school attendance areas. Second, Johnstone's low-SES
sample is likely to have been mainly black, whereas Reiss and Rhodes's
sample was all white. Third, Nashville in the 1950s may have been different
from Chicago in the 1970s.

If living in a high-SES neighborhood really does increase low-SES
teenagers' chances of committing serious crimes, as Johnstone's findings
imply, redistributing low-SES teenagers more evenly across a metropolitan
area would raise the crime rate rather than lower it.

Simcha-Fagan and Schwartz (1986) also studied neighborhood effects
on teenage crime, but their work is not useful for our purposes. They
studied 553 males between the ages of 11 and 18 who were living in 12 New
York City neighborhoods in 1982. Unfortunately, their sample excluded
neighborhoods whose mean SES was more than 0.75 standard deviations
above or below the citywide mean. Their results do not, therefore, say
anything about neighborhoods with high concentrations of poverty. They
also selected their neighborhoods so as to minimize the correlation between
neighborhood SES and other neighborhood characteristics, so even within
the narrow range covered by their sample, their high-SES and low-SES
neighborhoods are atypical. Thus, we cannot draw any conclusions from
their work about the effects of a neighborhood's mean SES on crime.

## Rearrests Among Ex-Offenders: Baltimore in 1978–1980

Although studies of recidivism among ex-offenders deal with adults rather than teenagers, we include them here for three reasons. First, most ex-offenders are quite young. Indeed, some are still teenagers. Second, given the paucity of evidence about how neighborhoods affect teenagers, it seems foolish to ignore potentially relevant evidence on young adults. Third, theories about how a neighborhood's mean SES ought to affect teenage crime appear to make similar predictions about adult ex-offenders. Epidemic models suggest, for example, that both teenagers and ex-offenders should commit more crimes if they live in neighborhoods that already have high crime rates. Furthermore, since the police are more overworked in neighborhoods with high crime rates, crime is less likely to be punished in such neighborhoods, which should lead to still more crime both among teenagers and among ex-offenders. If it is harder to find unskilled jobs in low-SES neighborhoods, as many assume, this should also encourage both teenagers and ex-offenders to turn to crime. Relative deprivation theories, in contrast, suggest that both teenagers and ex-offenders may be more resentful if they live in high-SES neighborhoods. (Ex-offenders are, however, freer to move if they do not like having rich neighbors.) Both teenagers and ex-offenders should also have more lucrative nearby opportunities to commit crimes if they settle in high-SES neighborhoods.

S. Gottfredson and Taylor (1986) tried to predict whether men released from Maryland prisons between 1978 and 1980 would be rearrested before January 1982, and if they were rearrested, how serious the charges would be. Their sample included approximately 500 men who moved into 67 different Baltimore neighborhoods. Once they controlled for a man's personal characteristics and criminal history, neighborhood characteristics had no effect on his chances of being rearrested. Nor did neighborhood characteristics affect the seriousness of the offenses with which the police charged the men they rearrested.[45]

S. Gottfredson and Taylor (1987) extended their earlier analysis by using a somewhat different sample and including three direct measures of a

---

[45] S. Gottfredson and Taylor classified neighborhoods along three dimensions: racial composition, a cluster of locally visible "incivilities" (such as graffiti) that predicted the neighborhood crime rate, and industrial versus residential land use. They did not include a neighborhood's mean SES, but both racial composition and neighborhood "incivilities" are strongly correlated with mean SES. None of their three neighborhood measures had a significant effect on recidivism. They also used the neighborhood's mean recidivism rate to predict individual recidivism. This raised $R^2$ by .055. They describe this increase as highly significant, but their significance test ignores the fact that they used 55 degrees of freedom in computing neighborhood recidivism rates. There were only eight respondents in a typical neighborhood, so roughly one-eighth of the unexplained variance in recidivism should have fallen between neighborhoods by chance. That is roughly what they found, so there is no evidence of neighborhood effects.

neighborhood's economic characteristics: household income, percentage of workers with white-collar jobs, and housing prices. They found no evidence that these three neighborhood characteristics affected either the likelihood that ex-offenders would be rearrested or the seriousness of the offenses with which they were charged.

One important limitation of Gottfredson and Taylor's studies is that the ex-offenders had not spent very long in their new neighborhoods at the time the authors assessed neighborhood effects. A third of the ex-offenders were rearrested within six months of release and half were rearrested within a year. None had been out of prison much more than three years when he was followed up. The sample size is also quite small, so small effects are unlikely to be statistically significant even if they are present.

### Conclusions about Crime

The two best studies of teenage crime appear to show the following:

- Attending an affluent high school in the Nashville area in the 1950s lowered the likelihood that white teenagers would engage in behavior that led the county juvenile courts to judge them delinquent. This was especially true for low-SES whites. These effects are probably overestimated, however, because the authors only controlled one measure of parental SES.
- Living in a poor Chicago-area neighborhood in 1972 increased the likelihood that middle-SES teenagers would report having committed serious crimes, but it reduced the likelihood that low-SES teenagers would report having committed such crimes. We cannot separate the effects of race and SES in this study.
- The Nashville study implies that reducing the geographic isolation of the poor would reduce the overall crime rate. The Chicago study implies that reducing the geographic isolation of the poor would increase the crime rate.
- Studies in Baltimore suggest that the neighborhoods in which ex-offenders settle have no effect on recidivism rates.

We badly need better studies of neighborhoods' impact on teenage crime. We especially need studies that focus on the effects of very poor neighborhoods, including large public housing projects. We also need studies that follow families as they move in and out of very poor neighborhoods and examine how such moves affect teenagers' behavior.

### TEENAGE SEXUAL BEHAVIOR

Our concern in this section is with the factors that influence young people's chances of having children before they are sufficiently mature to make good parents. There is no general agreement about the optimal age for parenthood, but almost everyone agrees that teenagers are "too young." The likelihood that teenagers will become parents depends on a number of distinct factors: the age at which they initiate intercourse, the frequency with which they have intercourse, the care with which they use contraceptives, and the proportion who get abortions when they conceive a child. The well-being of the children also depends on the proportion of teenage parents who get married and stay married. The social composition of a neighborhood or school can, in principle, influence all these factors, but it is likely to have more effect on some than on others.

If we want to understand how growing up in a poor neighborhood influences teenagers' chances of having children, we need to look at the way neighborhoods influence each step along the way. Unfortunately, we cannot do this with currently available data. We located only three studies that dealt with neighborhood effects on teenage sexual behavior and only two that dealt with school effects on such behavior. Each of these studies looks at a different measure of sexual behavior. We begin by looking at the determinants of teenage motherhood, then look at teenage pregnancy, contraception, and age of first intercourse.

### Single Teenage Motherhood

Crane (forthcoming) used the 1970 census sample described above to investigate the effects of a census tract's social composition on whether unmarried 16- to 18-year-olds had had a child. Because Crane wanted to separate neighborhood effects from family background effects, and because the census only provides data on teenagers' family background if they still live with their parents, he looked only at 16- to 18-year-old girls who were still living at home.[46]

Crane found that living in a poor neighborhood substantially increased the probability that 16- to 18-year-old girls had had a child out of wedlock, even after controlling parental education, occupation, and income. This pattern recurred for both blacks and whites. Among black 16- to 18-year-old girls of average SES who were living at home, the proportion who had had a child was 7 percent in the best neighborhoods, 10 percent

---

[46] Crane reports that 85 percent of all 16- to 18-year-old girls lived with their parents in 1970, but only a third of all 16- to 18-year-old mothers were living at home. Among those still living at home, Crane found no relationship between parental income and having had a child out of wedlock. This startling result suggests that girls who have children out of wedlock are more likely to leave home if their parents are poor. This kind of sample selection bias would not affect Crane's estimates of neighborhood effects so long as it was based entirely on family income, not neighborhood characteristics. Crane did not try to determine whether neighborhoods influenced the probability that teenagers would live at home.

in average neighborhoods, and 16 percent in the worst neighborhoods. Among whites, the rate was less than 1 percent in all but the very worst neighborhoods, where it rose to 3 percent. The effect of living in the very worst neighborhoods was especially marked in big cities. Including teenage mothers who no longer lived at home would have raised the proportions of 16- to 18-year-old mothers substantially, but would not necessarily raise the estimated effect of growing up in one neighborhood rather than another.

Abrahamse et al. (1988) have also investigated the effect of social context on teenage girls' chances of becoming unwed mothers, but they looked at the effect of a high school's social mix rather than the effect of a neighborhood's social mix. They studied tenth-grade girls who participated in the HSB survey in 1980. Two years later 4.3 percent of the whites, 9.5 percent of the Hispanics, and 13.0 percent of the blacks had become mothers. Of these mothers, 70 percent of the whites, 53 percent of the Hispanics, and 6 percent of the blacks had married.

The HSB survey asked tenth graders, "Would you consider having a child if you weren't married?" Twenty-two percent of the white, 26 percent of the Hispanic, and 42 percent of the black tenth graders said yes or maybe. Abrahamse et al. defined schools as "accepting" if the proportion of students answering yes or maybe exceeded the national median for respondents of a given race. After controlling girls' own race, family background, and academic ability, attending an "accepting" school raised a typical tenth grader's probability of having a child out of wedlock during the next two years from about 1.1 to 4.5 percent among whites, from 3.4 to 6.1 percent among Hispanics, and from 9.4 to 11.9 percent for blacks.

Abrahamse et al. report a modest relationship between family background and the probability that a teenager would have a child out of wedlock, but they do not report the relationship between a school's mean SES and peer acceptance of having children out of wedlock. Thus, while their findings are broadly consistent with the view that low-SES schools encourage out-of-wedlock childbearing, we cannot estimate the strength of the relationship.

Mayer (forthcoming) used the HSB data to estimate the effect of a high school's social mix on tenth graders' chances of having a baby prior to expected graduation. Among students of any given ethnic background and SES, attending school with either low-SES or minority classmates increased the likelihood of having a baby before graduating. A one standard deviation reduction in parental SES increased the average non-Hispanic white tenth grader's chances of having a baby from 4.2 to 7.4 percent. A comparable change in the mean SES of her classmates increased her chances of having a baby from 4.2 to 6.4 percent. These effects were larger for low-SES students. For blacks, a one standard deviation decline in parental SES raised the probability from 7.9 to 12.3 percent, while a one standard deviation decline in a school's mean SES only raised the probability from 7.9 to 8.6 percent.

## Pregnancy

Hogan and Kitagawa (1985) studied 1,078 unmarried black Chicago women who were between the ages of 13 and 19 in 1979. Hogan and Kitagawa used a census tract's racial composition, median family income, percent poor, male-female ratio, children per ever-married female, and juvenile police contacts to construct an index of neighborhood quality. They then classified the best quarter of all tracts as high-SES, the middle half as middle-SES, and the bottom quarter as low-SES neighborhoods. Their low-SES neighborhoods are the kind that social critics have in mind when they talk about "concentrated poverty" and "the underclass." Four out of five respondents in these neighborhoods lived in public housing.

In this sample of unmarried Chicago blacks, 28 percent had become pregnant by the age of 19. When Hogan and Kitagawa controlled the parents' marital status, fertility, and SES (a trichotomy based on parental education, occupation, income, employment status, and housing characteristics), they found that teenage pregnancy rates in medium- and high-quality neighborhoods did not differ in statistically reliable or substantively significant ways. Living in a low-SES neighborhood did, however, raise black teenagers' chances of becoming pregnant in a given month by a third. This pattern is consistent with Johnstone's findings for teenage crime in Chicago, which also show negligible differences between middle-SES and high-SES neighborhoods.

Hogan and Kitagawa also compared girls living on Chicago's West Side with girls living elsewhere in the city—mostly on the South Side. The West Side was not settled by blacks until after World War II. It has fewer community organizations and churches, more first-generation migrants from the South, and a reputation for being an especially "bad" area. After controlling both family characteristics and the demographic attributes of census tracts, they found that living on the West Side still raised the pregnancy rate in a given month by two-fifths. This may be evidence that institutions matter, that culture matters, or both. It certainly suggests that if we want to understand neighborhood effects on teenagers' sexual behavior we need to look at more than just neighborhoods' demographic attributes.

Hogan and Kitagawa did not investigate whether poor blacks were more sensitive to neighborhood quality than middle-income blacks, but the strong effect of very bad neighborhoods is what we would expect if low-SES black girls were more sensitive than high-SES black girls to their neighborhood's mean SES. Whatever the explanation, their findings imply that distributing poor blacks more evenly across the city would somewhat reduce the black teenage pregnancy rate.

## Contraception

Hogan et al. (1985) used the Chicago survey described above to investigate contraceptive use among black teenagers. They found that with family background controlled black girls in very poor neighborhoods were only half as likely as those in better neighborhoods to use contraception at the time of first intercourse. This seems likely to explain a good part of the neighborhood effect on pregnancy rates. The data do not indicate whether teenagers in better neighborhoods were more likely to use contraception because they had better information about it or for other reasons.

## Age at First Intercourse

Furstenberg et al. (1987) used a national sample of 15- and 16-year-olds to investigate the effect of a school's racial mix on whether its students had had sexual intercourse. Among the 33 black teenagers in classrooms in which at least four-fifths of the other students were black, 67 percent reported having had intercourse. Among the 60 blacks in classrooms in which less than four-fifths of the other students were black, only 40 percent reported having had intercourse. This difference persisted with mother's education controlled.

Because black parents' SES is not strongly correlated with their children's chances of attending school with whites, the fact that Furstenberg et al. control only one measure of parental SES does not seriously threaten the validity of their findings.[47] Sampling error is a more serious problem. The 95 percent confidence interval for the difference in sexual activity between black teenagers in all-black versus racially mixed classrooms runs from 7 to 47 points. The former effect would be trivial, the latter huge. Thus, Furstenberg et al.'s findings suggest that school segregation encourages early sexual activity among black teenagers, but they do not indicate whether the effect is large or small.

Among whites, being in a classroom that was more than one-fifth black raised the likelihood of having had had intercourse from 17 to 24 percent. Because of small sample size, however, the true effect of having

---

[47] Another potential problem is that low-scoring blacks in racially mixed schools are often tracked into overwhelmingly black classes while high-scoring blacks more often end up in racially mixed classes. The racial composition of black students' classrooms may, therefore, be a proxy for their academic aptitude as well as their school's racial composition. Low test scores sharply increase the likelihood that teenage girls will become pregnant (Sum, 1986). Low scores may also be associated with early sexual activity.

black classmates could be to raise the proportion of whites who had had intercourse by as much as 23 points or to lower it by as much as 9 points. This range of uncertainty is too wide to justify any firm conclusions.

Hogan and Kitagawa (1985) also estimated the effect of neighborhood characteristics on the age at which black teenage girls become sexually active. They found that girls in low-SES Chicago neighborhoods became sexually active earlier than those in higher SES neighborhoods. They do not present multivariate results suitable for estimating neighborhood effects with family background controlled, but the evidence they do present suggests that neighborhood effects on age at first intercourse and pregnancy are quite similar.[48]

## Conclusions

The evidence on how neighborhoods and schools influence teenagers' sexual behavior is thin, but it suggests that teenagers' sexual behavior is quite sensitive to their classmates' and neighbors' SES and race. Holding race and family background constant, 16- to 18-year-old girls were substantially more likely to have had children out of wedlock if they lived in poor neighborhoods than if they lived in average neighborhoods. Black girls from very poor neighborhoods were also less likely to use contraception and more likely to become pregnant than black girls from similiar families who lived in better neighborhoods. Black 15- and 16-year-olds in largely black schools were also more likely to have had sexual intercourse than those in predominantly white schools.

Despite its limitations, the available evidence suggests to us that neighbors and classmates probably have a stronger (or at least more consistent) effect on sexual behavior than on cognitive skills, school enrollment decisions, or even criminal activity.

## LABOR MARKET SUCCESS

The literature relating neighborhood and school characteristics to adolescents' eventual labor market success is extremely sparse. We located only five studies that threw light on this question.

---

[48]Hogan and Kitagawa present an equation that controls family background, whether the girl's parents supervised her dating behavior, whether the girl had a sister who had been a teenage mother, and the girl's career aspirations. The last three measures depend partly on a neighborhood's mean SES, so controlling them biases the neighborhood coefficients towards zero. With these three variables controlled, a neighborhood's mean SES does not affect either the age at which girls became sexually active or whether they become pregnant.

TABLE 4-7 Effects of Neighborhoods' Mean Income and Racial Composition in 1968 on Black and White Men's Hourly and Annual Earnings in 1978

| | Neighborhood Characteristic | | | |
| --- | --- | --- | --- | --- |
| | Mean Family Income ($1,000s) | | Percent White (0 to 100) | |
| Dependent Variable | Blacks | Whites | Blacks | Whites |
| In annual earnings | | | | |
| B | .030 | .003 | .0049 | .0071 |
| (S.E.) | (.035) | (.012) | (.0025) | (.0027) |
| In hourly earnings | | | | |
| B | −.005 | .001 | .0024 | .0052 |
| (S.E.) | (.020) | (.007) | (.0014) | (.0018) |
| In hours worked | | | | |
| (B1 - B2) | .035 | .002 | .0025 | .0019 |
| | | | | |
| Sample sizes | | | | |
| Annual earnings | 177 | 348 | | |
| Hourly earnings | 147 | 292 | | |

NOTE: See Table 4-2 for means of neighborhood characteristics.

SOURCE: Datcher (1982).

## Neighborhood Effects

Datcher (1982) used the Panel Study of Income Dynamics to estimate the effect of the neighborhood in which an urban male grew up on his earnings in early adulthood. Her sample covered 525 men who were between the ages of 13 and 22 and living at home in 1968. She used 1970 census data to estimate the percentage of whites and the mean family income of families living in the respondent's postal zip code. When estimating the effect of these two neighborhood characteristics, she controlled region, total family income in 1968, whether the family received government transfer payments in 1968, the number of children in the family, the family head's education, whether the head expected his or her children to attend college, and whether the head liked to do "difficult and challenging things"; she did not control the family head's occupation or the family's income in years other than 1968. She used these variables to predict men's earnings in 1978, when they were between the ages of 23 and 32. Table 4-7 summarizes her findings.

Whereas a neighborhood's mean income appeared to be its most salient characteristic when predicting how much education its residents would get (see Table 4-2), a neighborhood's racial composition has more effect on how much money its residents make when they grow up. Young urban whites typically lived in zip code areas that were 94 percent white in 1970, while poor young urban blacks typically lived in zip code areas that were only 34 percent white. When all else was equal, growing up in an area that was 34 rather than 94 percent white lowered a man's expected 1978 earnings by 35 percent if he was white and by 27 percent if he was black.[49]

Once we control for a neighborhood's racial composition, the effect of its mean family income appears to be quite small. Urban whites typically lived in areas with mean incomes of $12,000 in 1970, whereas poor urban blacks lived in areas with mean incomes of $8,500. A $3,500 drop in the neighbors' mean income lowered a young man's expected 1978 earnings by 1 percent if he was white and 10 percent if he was black. The estimated effect on blacks is large enough to be of substantive interest, but its sampling error is very large, so the true value could either be huge or negligible.

Datcher's results are striking but not definitive. Her sample was small, and it underrepresented those who left home at an early age. She omitted a number of parental characteristics whose inclusion might have altered neighborhoods' apparent effects. Her respondents were very young when she measured their earnings, and we know that the effect of family background on earnings increases with age, both in the PSID and in other samples (Jencks et al., 1979).

Corcoran et al. (1989) use a more recent PSID sample to solve some of the above problems. Their sample covers about 800 men who were between the ages of 10 and 17 in 1968. They control more exogenous family characteristics and fewer potentially endogenous ones than Datcher did. They use a zip code's median family income, unemployment rate, proportion of families receiving Aid to Families with Dependent Children, and proportion of families headed by women to predict respondents' average economic position between the ages of 25 and 32.

Because Corcoran et al. used four neighborhood characteristics that are highly correlated with one another, the estimated effect of each specific characteristic has a large sampling error and none is reliably different from zero. Nonetheless, their cumulative effect is quite large. Table 4-8 summarizes their results.

Just as in Datcher's study, we can summarize Corcoran et al.'s findings by calculating the effect of growing up in a "bad" black area rather than an average white area. In this case we define "bad" black areas as those whose characteristics fall one standard deviation below the mean for all blacks. Table 4-8 shows that these "bad" areas had median family incomes that were only 59 percent of the median in the typical white area. Bad black areas also had unemployment rates twice those in the typical white area, female headship rates almost four times those in the typical white

---

[49]The estimate in the text is calculated as $1 - \exp(-60)(.0071)$ for whites and $1 - \exp(-60)(.0052)$ for blacks.

TABLE 4-8  Effects of Growing Up in Poor Black Neighborhoods on Economic Status at
Ages 25 to 33

|  | Ln Median Family Income | Percent Males Unemployed | Percent Female Heads | Percent Families on Welfare | Total |
|---|---|---|---|---|---|
| White mean[1] | 9.21 | 4 | 9 | 4 | |
| Poor black mean[1] | 8.68 | 8 | 34 | 18 | |
| Difference | −.53 | 4 | 25 | 14 | |
| Effect of one unit change in neighborhood mean if:[2] | | | | | |
| Mother got no welfare | .018 | −.017 | .001 | .010 | |
| Mother got $5,000/yr in welfare | .018 | −.017 | .001 | .0035 | |
| Estimated effect of difference between average white neighborhood and poor black neighborhood if: | | | | | |
| Mother got no welfare[3] | −.010 | −.068 | .025 | −.140 | −.193 |
| Mother got $5,000/yr in welfare[4] | −.010 | −.068 | .025 | .049 | −.004 |

[1]Taken from Corcoran et al. (1987), with proportions converted to percentages. Estimates for poor black neighborhoods are one standard deviation below the overall black mean.
[2]Taken from Corcoran et al. (1989), Table 2. For mothers receiving $5,000 a year from welfare, the estimated effect of a one point increase in the percentage of families receiving welfare in the zip code area is −.010 + (.027) ($5,000/$10,000) = .0035.
[3](Line 3) (Line 4). Total is sum of columns 1 through 4.
[4](Line 3) (Line 5). Total is sum of columns 1 through 4.

area, and welfare recipiency rates more than four times those in the typical white area.

Looking first at men whose parents had no income from welfare, we find that growing up in a "bad" black area rather than a typical white area lowers their expected earnings by 18 percent.[50] Datcher's work, in contrast, implies that growing up in a bad black neighborhood can lower young men's earnings by 27 to 35 percent.[51] Still, even the estimate based on Corcoran et al.'s work is sizable.[52] Among men whose families got a lot

[50]The value in the text is calculated from Table 4-8, row 6. $Exp(-.193) = .82$, so growing up in a bad black neighborhood lowers earnings by $1 - .82 = 18$ percent.

[51]Corcoran et al. do not include racial composition in their model. The difference between their results and Datcher's could derive entirely from this omission, or it could derive from the fact that Corcoran et al. have better background controls and a larger sample.

[52]We cannot calculate sampling errors for our estimates of overall neighborhood effects from the data that Corcoran et al. present, but they are very large.

of income from welfare, in contrast, neighborhoods had almost no effect.[53] Unfortunately, small sample size and large sampling errors mean we cannot have much confidence in either estimate.

## School Effects

### Mean SES

Jencks and Brown (1975b) estimated the effect of a high school's mean SES on students' subsequent occupational status and career plans using data from 91 predominantly white comprehensive public schools surveyed by Project Talent. Their initial sample included all ninth graders in those schools in 1960. The follow-up was conducted in 1968, five years after most of the sample had graduated. An increase of one standard deviation in a high school's mean SES raised men's subsequent scores on the Duncan scale (which runs from 0 to 96) by one point. The effect on women was equally small, as was the effect on career plans.

Altonji (1988) estimated the effect of a school's racial mix and mean SES on male high school graduates' earnings, using data collected between 1972 and 1986 from the High School Class of 1972. His analysis included so many school characteristics that we could not estimate the reduced-form effect of mean SES, but he reestimated the model for us using only parents' education to measure mean SES. Holding men's family background constant, a one-year increase in mean parental education raised a man's expected wage by less than 1 percent.

### Racial Composition

Crain (1970) surveyed 1,624 urban blacks who had attended high school between the late 1930s and the early 1960s. Roughly one in five had attended a racially mixed northern high school. Three results are noteworthy:

- Blacks were more likely to work in predominantly white occupations if they had attended racially mixed northern high schools than if they had attended all-black northern schools.
- Black women entered somewhat higher prestige occupations if they had attended racially mixed rather than all-black northern high schools, but black men's occupational prestige was only trivially higher if they had attended racially mixed schools.

---

[53]The coefficient of the interaction between neighborhood welfare recipiency rate and parental welfare income is only 2.1 times its standard error.

- Black men earned 7 percent more if they had attended racially mixed northern high schools than if they had attended all-black northern schools. Younger northern blacks were more likely to have attended all-black schools.[54] After controlling for this fact, Crain found that attending a racially mixed school raised black men's earnings only 4 percent.[55]

Altonji's (1988) work on the High School Class of 1972 tells much the same story as Crain's study. Attending an all-black rather than an all-white school lowered men's expected earnings by only 1 percent. (Altonji does not present separate analyses for blacks and whites, but he does control the respondent's race.)

In the late 1960s, Project Concern offered a random sample of low-income black elementary schoolchildren from Hartford's inner-city schools an opportunity to enroll in white suburban schools outside Hartford. Crain and Strauss (1985) followed up these students in 1983, along with a sample of students from inner-city schools who had not been offered a chance to move to the suburbs. Most blacks who had been offered a chance to move had done so, but in order to avoid selection bias Crain and Strauss included all students invited to participate in the "treatment" group, regardless of whether they had actually participated. The follow-up covered approximately 700 students.

Crain and Strauss do not document the differences between the suburban and inner-city schools in detail, but it seems fair to assume that blacks who attended suburban schools not only had more white classmates but had more affluent classmates, better teachers, smaller classes, and so forth. Those blacks invited to attend suburban schools were more likely than the control group to be in college at the time of the follow-up. Among respondents who were working, 30 percent of those invited to attend suburban schools held white-collar jobs, compared with 13 percent of those who attended inner-city schools. This was a highly significant difference. Suburban schooling did not affect unemployment rates. Crain and Strauss provide no data on earnings.

---

[54] Younger northern blacks were more likely to have attended all-black schools because the number of all-black schools rose as the absolute number of blacks in the North rose.

[55] The 4 percent earnings advantage of blacks who attended racially mixed schools could be attributable to the fact that they got more schooling (Crain, 1971). Crain does not report sampling errors, but assuming a typical dispersion of earnings, the 95 percent confidence interval for the effect of racially mixed schooling would run from a positive effect of about 21 percent to a negative effect of about 13 percent.

## Conclusions About Labor Market Success

The literature on neighborhoods, schools, and labor market success suggests two tentative conclusions:

- Attending a racially mixed high school increases blacks' chances of working in "white" occupations. Attending racially mixed schools does not seem to have much effect on young men's eventual earnings. Growing up in a black zip code area or in one with high welfare dependency probably reduces both black and white men's eventual earnings.
- A high school's mean SES does not have much effect on its graduates' economic prospects. Nor does a neighborhood's median income have much effect on young men's economic prospects once we control racial composition and welfare dependency.

### SUMMARY AND CONCLUSIONS

In this review we have tried to determine how much effect the social composition of a neighborhood or school has on children's life chances. That is not a simple question. We limited ourselves to five outcomes: educational attainment, cognitive skills, criminal activity, sexual behavior, and economic success. But each of these outcomes has several components, and there is no reason to expect schools or neighborhoods to affect each component in the same way. A neighborhood's social composition may have more effect on teenage childbearing than on teenage sexual activity, for example. Or a school's racial mix may have more effect on sixth-grade test scores than on twelfth-grade scores. In practice, therefore, we ended up looking at more than a dozen outcomes.

We also looked at the effects of four compositional measures: a neighborhood's mean SES, a neighborhood's racial mix, a school's mean SES, and a school's racial mix. With a dozen dependent variables and four independent variables, we would need at least 48 coefficients to summarize our findings. But that is just the beginning. We want to know not only the average strength of the 48 relationships, but also whether their strength varies with the race or SES of the child's family. For that, we need estimates of something like 200 relationships.

If we had accurate estimates of all these relationships, we might be able to summarize them in a few elegant generalizations. But no estimates are available for many of the relationships that concern us, and sample bias, random sampling error, measurement error, and specification error distort the estimates that are available. Thus, even if neighborhood and school effects followed a simple underlying pattern in the real world, our chances of detecting it would be low.

Our first and strongest conclusion is that there is no general pattern of neighborhood or school effects that recurs across all outcomes. Before offering any other generalizations we must therefore review what we have learned about each specific outcome that concerns us.

## Educational Attainment

Studies of schools and studies of neighborhoods yield superficially contradictory conclusions about the determinants of educational attainment. In comparisons of white high school graduates who had the same test scores in ninth or tenth grade and came from families with the same SES, the mean SES of their classmates had almost no effect on their chances of planning to attend college, actually attending college, or graduating from college. There is some evidence that a high school's mean SES may have more impact on college attendance among blacks than among whites, but that evidence is not conclusive. A high school's mean SES does appear to affect entrants' chances of graduating, even after we control family background, but we do not know if this effect persists with entrants' test scores and plans controlled.

Teenagers who grow up in affluent neighborhoods end up with more schooling than teenagers from similar families who grow up in poorer neighborhoods. This is probably partly because teenagers in affluent neighborhoods are more likely to finish high school than teenagers from comparable families in poorer neighborhoods. We do not know whether high school graduates from similar families are more likely to attend college if they grow up in affluent neighborhoods.

The effects of a school's racial composition on students' educational attainment are even less certain than the effects of its socioeconomic composition. Whites who graduated from racially mixed high schools in 1972 were as likely to attend college as those who graduated from all-white schools. Northern blacks who attended all-black high schools during the 1960s and early 1970s were more likely than those who attended racially mixed schools to plan on attending college, but they were less likely to enter college and less likely to remain there. In the South, attending a racially mixed high school reduced a black student's chances of attending college in 1972, when school desegregation was just beginning. No data on this point are available for more recent years.

## Cognitive Skills

Studies of how a school's mean SES affects students' academic achievement yield mixed results, depending on the students' race and grade level.

A high school's mean SES does not seem to affect the amount white students learn between ninth and twelfth grade, but it may have an effect on how much black students learn. An elementary school's mean SES appears to have a substantial effect on how much both black and white students learn, but we cannot be sure of this without longitudinal studies.

A school's racial composition has different effects from its socioeconomic composition, even though the two are highly correlated. Data collected in 1965 and 1972 suggest that northern blacks at all grade levels learned more in predominantly white schools than in predominantly black schools, even with family background controlled. This was not true in the South, at least in 1972. We found no studies of this issue using more recent data. Most experts believe that a school's racial mix does not affect white students' achievement, but the evidence for this view is not conclusive.

The first year of school desegregation usually has a small positive effect on black elementary school students' reading skills but not on their math skills. Unfortunately, the numerous studies covering one year of desegregation provide no useful information on the cumulative impact of attending racially mixed schools from first through twelfth grade.

### Crime

Despite the existence of many complex theories about the ways in which neighborhoods affect teenage crime, the evidence for such effects is thin and contradictory. Regardless of their SES, white Nashville-area teenagers were more likely to have been arrested for serious crimes in the 1950s if they attended school with low-SES classmates than if they attended school with high-SES classmates. In a study that controlled a broader array of background characteristics and pooled blacks with whites, middle-SES Chicago teenagers also reported committing more serious crimes in the early 1970s if they lived in poor neighborhoods. But contrary to what most people assume about the effects of concentrated poverty, poor Chicago teenagers reported committing fewer serious crimes if they lived in poor neighborhoods.

### Teenage Sexual Behavior

Among unmarried 16- to 18-year-old girls living with their families in 1970, those living in very poor neighborhoods were considerably more likely to have had a child than those living in more affluent neighborhoods. This was true even with parental SES controlled and it was true for both blacks and whites. Black teenagers who lived in very poor Chicago neighborhoods in 1979 were also more likely to have become pregnant than those who lived in more affluent neighborhoods, and this remained true with parental

SES controlled. The effect of poor neighborhoods on pregnancy appeared to derive both from the fact that girls from poor neighborhoods initiated intercourse younger and from the fact that they were less likely to use contraception. With mother's education controlled, blacks in classrooms that were more than four-fifths black also reported having initiated sexual intercourse earlier than blacks in classrooms that were less than four-fifths black.

## Labor Market Success

Growing up in an urban neighborhood that is either predominantly black or has a high rate of welfare dependency reduces men's chances of finding well-paid jobs in adulthood. A neighborhood's median income does not appear to affect young people's economic prospects independent of its racial mix or welfare recipiency rate.

Blacks who attend racially mixed schools are more likely to work in white-collar occupations than blacks who attend all-black schools. We found no evidence that a school's racial mix or mean SES affected its students' economic success independent of their own family background.

## Empirical Generalizations

Social scientists need to be very cautious about estimates of neighborhood or school effects that control only one or two family background characteristics. As a rule, the more aspects of family background we control, the smaller neighborhood and school effects look. Initially, for example, we thought that attending a low-SES high school substantially reduced twelfth graders' chances of attending college. Today, using more elaborate background measures, we are reasonably certain that the effect is trivial. The same pattern may hold for other outcomes.

The literature we reviewed does not, therefore, warrant any strong generalizations about neighborhood effects. Based on what we now know, however, we offer two tentative hypotheses:

- When neighbors set social standards for one another or create institutions that serve an entire neighborhood, affluent neighbors are likely to be an advantage.
- When neighbors compete with one another for a scarce resource, such as social standing, high school grades, or teenage jobs, affluent neighbors are likely to be a disadvantage.

Because the balance between these two kinds of influence varies from one outcome to another, there is no general rule dictating that affluent neighbors will always be an advantage or a disadvantage. Nor is there any general rule about how large the advantage or disadvantage will be relative to other determinants of children's life chances.

Our best guess is that better data would support the following empirical generalizations:

- Advantaged classmates encourage both rich and poor children to learn more in elementary school, finish high school, and delay sexual intercourse.
- Advantaged classmates lower both rich and poor students' grades.
- Advantaged classmates have no effect on high school seniors' chances of attending college.
- Advantaged neighbors discourage teenagers from having children out of wedlock, encourage teenagers to finish high school, and increase teenagers' future earnings.
- Advantaged neighbors discourage crime among affluent teenagers but encourage it among poor teenagers, at least if they are also black.

The evidence we reviewed does not allow us to draw even tentative conclusions about whether the poor gain more from residential or school desegregation than the rich lose. There is some reason to think that blacks may gain more from school desegregation than whites lose, but the evidence on this point would not convince a skeptic.

### Methodological Implications

If social scientists want to make research on neighborhoods useful to public officials and legislators, they need to alter their analytic methods in at least three ways:

- Future research should pay more attention to the most politically salient and easily understood differences between neighborhoods and schools, such as their poverty rate and racial composition. The effects of a school or neighborhood's poverty rate and racial mix should be estimated with no other neighborhood characteristics controlled.[56]
- Future research should report whether the effects of racial composition and poverty rates are linear. If the effects are roughly linear, as social scientists tend to assume, moving the poor to more

---

[56]Reporting reduced-form results of the kind we described above does not rule out estimating multivariate models that look at the effects of many different neighborhood characteristics simultaneously. In most cases, however, the number of neighborhoods is too small and neighborhood characteristics are too highly correlated with one another to separate the effects of specific advantages or disadvantages with much confidence.

affluent neighborhoods will redistribute the cost of having poor neighbors from the poor to the more affluent, but it will not reduce the costs to society as a whole. Such a change is unlikely to win broad political support.

• Future research should investigate whether poor families are more sensitive than affluent families to neighborhood and school characteristics. If poor families gain more from living in a richer neighborhood than affluent families lose from living in a poorer neighborhood, reducing economic segregation can yield significant benefits to society as a whole. If affluent families lose more than poor families gain, reducing economic segregation will have significant overall costs. The same logic applies to race.

## Implications for the Organization of Research

Everyone believes that both residential segregation and school segregation have important social consequences. Home buyers believe it, which is why they are willing to pay more to live in a good neighborhood. Judges believe it, which is why they turn cities upside down in order to desegregate their schools. Even committees of the National Research Council believe it, which is why they become concerned when the Census Bureau releases data suggesting that more people were living in very poor neighborhoods in 1980 than in 1970.

Given the central role that everyone assigns to residential and school segregation, we were surprised by how little effort social scientists had made to measure the effect on individual behavior of either neighborhood or school composition. The subject is, of course, quite difficult to study. On reflection, however, we found this explanation for its neglect unconvincing. All social science problems are difficult, almost by definition. The easy questions were answered long ago. Compared with most of the problems that currently concern social scientists, estimating neighborhood and school effects is not especially difficult.

The reason we don't know more is not that the questions are so hard to answer but that we have not invested much time or money in looking for answers. Efforts to estimate the effect of a high school's socioeconomic composition on graduating seniors' educational plans and subsequent attainment are the exception that proves this rule. Sociologists invested a lot of time and money in this problem, and the eventual convergence of their findings was remarkable. This is a case in which sociologists can truly claim to have learned something nobody knew to begin with, namely that a high school's socioeconomic mix has very little net effect on whether graduating seniors plan to attend college, actually attend college, or graduate from college. Sociologists have also developed quite plausible explanations of why this is so.

One obvious reason why social scientists have learned less about the other consequences of having low-SES classmates is that they have collected less data on those outcomes. Every follow-up of high school seniors asks about their educational attainment. Many follow-ups also ask about labor market experiences, but few studies follow graduates long enough to get meaningful estimates of how much they are likely to earn when they grow up. Few follow-ups ask about sexual behavior or criminal activity. None tests high school graduates to see how much they remember of what they studied in school. In principle, it should be easier to follow elementary school students through secondary school to see whether their elementary school's social composition has long-term effects on their cognitive development, but no one has done this either.

We know less about neighborhood effects than about school effects because collecting data on neighborhoods is more expensive than collecting data on schools. Only the Census Bureau has enough money to collect data on the socioeconomic composition of large representative samples of neighborhoods, and it has released only one data tape that includes both individual records (cleansed of identifying information) and data on the individual's neighbors. The only way to link individual characteristics and neighborhood characteristics, therefore, is to conduct private surveys of individuals and then add census data on the neighborhoods in which respondents live.

Because data have been so scarce, there has never been an "invisible college" of social scientists grappling with the problems of estimating neighborhood effects, encouraging one another to use the best available analytic methods, criticizing questionable results before they reach print, or replicating important results after they are in print. Without such an invisible college, no field of inquiry makes much progress.

If funding agencies wanted to encourage research on problems of this kind, the first step would be to make money available for collecting appropriate data. But while data collection is a necessary first step, it will not suffice. Funding agencies must also create more incentives for talented scholars to analyze the data in ways that are useful to policy analysts. At the moment, scholars cannot expect many rewards for doing such work.

Like all scholars, economists, sociologists, and social psychologists talk mainly to one another. As a result, economists are interested in problems that interest other economists, sociologists are interested in questions that interest other sociologists, and social psychologists are interested in problems that interest other social psychologists. Furthermore, these scholars' careers depend mainly on their success in finding answers to questions that interest other members of their discipline. To worry about questions that only interest public officials and policy analysts is quite risky.

If legislators and public officials want first-rate work on policy questions, they will have to ensure that people who work on such issues can survive in universities. At present, their survival is problematic. A handful of public policy schools reward their faculty for doing such work, but they are too few in number to provide a clear career line for young scholars.

Despite widespread cynicism about the value of social science, we believe that research on neighborhood and school effects could tell us a lot if it were properly organized. This would mean a number of major changes:

- Funding agencies would have to make a long-term commitment (e.g., 10 years) to research in this area. Social science research, like most other research, involves a lot of false starts. Funding agencies must expect this and must be willing to wait for better answers. When slow progress is politically or institutionally unacceptable, as it often is, investing in social science research is a mistake.
- Funding agencies must make money available for collecting new data on a regular basis.
- Funding agencies must find ways to create a group of technically competent scholars with a long-term commitment to understanding neighborhood and school effects. This means they cannot rely entirely on contract research firms to do their work. They must also involve university-based social scientists. To attract good university-based social scientists, funding agencies must give them enough time to do what they and their colleagues regard as professionally respectable work.
- Funding agencies also need more social scientists on their own staffs. Funding agencies without such staff members seldom specify in appropriate empirical terms the policy-related question they want answered. Nor do they usually negotiate acceptable compromises between their agency's policy agenda and the disciplinary agenda of university-based scholars. Nor are they likely to make realistic judgments about how long it will take to answer a question correctly—though even social scientists are almost always overly optimistic on this score.

None of the above conditions is currently met. Those who fund applied social science research seldom stay interested in any question for more than a few years. Little money is available for data collection. Partly as a result, few scholars have shown sustained interest in the field over the past generation. Thus, while much *could* be learned, there is little prospect that much *will* be learned unless we alter the way we organize our efforts.

Public concern about geographically concentrated poverty and homelessness is currently high. As a result, the federal government may spend substantial sums for low-income housing during the 1990s. The way we make these expenditures could either increase or decrease the current level of housing segregation. If the government tries to "save" existing public housing projects, extreme concentrations of poverty will persist. If the government builds scattered-site housing or provides housing vouchers, residential segregation might decline, but less housing might also be built.

At the moment, we have no way of knowing how changes in residential segregation would affect either adults or children. Nor is there any way we can answer such questions in the next year or two. This means that social science cannot provide reliable evidence to inform near-term changes in government policy. But it does not follow that there is no point in doing research on such questions. If we begin now, we might have some fairly reliable findings by the turn of the century. If we procrastinate, we will be as ignorant a generation hence as we are now.

## ACKNOWLEDGMENTS

We are indebted to Georg Matt for his assistance in reviewing studies of schools' effects on college plans and academic achievement, to Karl Alexander, Thomas Cook, Robert Crain, Roberto Fernandez, Adam Gamoran, Bennett Harrison, John Meyer, and Michael Wiseman for helpful comments on earlier drafts, and to Anthony Bryk, James Davis, Frank Furstenberg, Stephen Gottfredson, Dennis Hogan, and Philip Morgan for checking our summaries of their work. Needless to say, any errors that remain are our own. The Center for Urban Affairs and Policy Research at Northwestern University provided financial assistance.

## REFERENCES

Abrahamse, Allan F., Peter Morrison, and Linda J. Waite
1988    Beyond stereotypes: Who becomes a teenage mother? Santa Monica, Calif.: Rand Corporation.
Alexander, Karl L., and Bruce K. Eckland
1975    Contextual effects in the high school attainment process. *American Sociological Review* 40:402-416.
Altonji, Joseph G.
1988    The Effects of Family Background and School Characteristics on Education and Labor Market Outcomes. Department of Economics, Northwestern University. Evanston, Ill.

Alwin, Duane F.
    1976        Assessing school effects: Some identities. *Sociology of Education* 49:294-303.
Alwin, Duane F., and Luther B. Otto
    1977        High school context effects on aspirations. *Sociology of Education* 50:259-273.
Armor, David J.
    1984        The evidence on desegregation and black achievement. Pp. 43-67 in *School Desegregation and Black Achievement*. Washington, D.C.: The National Institute of Education.
Asch, Solomon E.
    1951        Effects of group pressure upon the modification and distortion of judgment. In *Groups, Leadership and Men*, Harold Guetzkow, ed. Pittsburgh: Carnegie Press.
Bott, Elizabeth
    1957        *Family and Social Network*. London: Tavistock.
Broman, Sarah H., Paul L. Nichols, and Wallace A. Kennedy
    1975        *Preschool IQ: Prenatal and Early Developmental Correlates*. Hillsdale, N.J.: Lawrence Erlbaum.
Bryk, Anthony S., and Mary Erina Driscoll
    1988        The High School as Community: Contextual Influences and Consequences for Students and Teachers. National Center on Effective Secondary Schools, University of Wisconsin, Madison.
Bryk, Anthony S., and Stephen W. Raudenbush
    1987        Application of hierarchical linear models to assessing change. *Psychological Bulletin* 101:147-158.
    1988        Toward a more appropriate conceptualization of research on school effects: A three-level hierarchical linear model. *American Journal of Education* 97:65-108.
Bryk, Anthony, and Yeow Meng Thum
    1988        The Effects of High School Organization on Dropping Out: An Exploratory Investigation. Department of Education, University of Chicago, Chicago, Ill.
Bureau of Justice Statistics
    1987        *Sourcebook of Criminal Justice Statistics—1986*. Washington, D.C.: U.S. Government Printing Office.
Coleman, James S., E. Q. Campbell, C. J. Hobson, J. McPartland, A. M. Mood, F. D. Weinfeld, and R. L. York
    1966        *Equality of Educational Opportunity*. Washington D.C.: U.S. Government Printing Office.
Cook, Thomas D
    1984        What have black children gained academically from school integration? Examination of the meta-analytic evidence. Pp. 7-42 in *School Desegregation and Black Achievement*. Washington, D.C.: The National Institute of Education.
Corcoran, Mary, Roger Gordon, Deborah Laren, and Gary Solon
    1987        Intergenerational Transmission of Education, Income and Earnings. Political Science Department, University of Michigan.
    1989        Effects of Family and Community Background on Men's Economic Status. Working Paper 2896, National Bureau of Economic Research, Cambridge, Mass.
Crain, Robert
    1970        School integration and occupational achievement of Negroes. *American Journal of Sociology* 75:593-606.

1971     School integration and the academic achievement of Negroes. *Sociology of Education* 44:1-26.
Crain, Robert, and Rita Mahard
1978     School racial composition and black college attendence and achievement test performance. *Sociology of Education* 51:81-101.
1983     The effect of research methodology on desegregation-achievement studies: A meta-analysis. *American Journal of Sociology* 88:839-854.
Crain, Robert, and Jack Strauss
1985     School Desegregation and Black Occupational Attainments: Results From a Long-Term Experiment. Center for Social Organization of Schools, Johns Hopkins University.
Crane, Jonathan
forth-    The pattern of neighborhood effects on social problems. *American Journal*
coming   *of Sociology*.
Datcher, Linda
1982     Effects of community and family background on achievement. *The Review of Economics and Statistics* 64:32-41.
Davis, James A.
1966     The campus as a frog pond: An application of the theory of relative deprivation to career decisions of college men. *American Journal of Sociology* 72:17-31.
Furstenburg, Frank F., Jr., S. Philip Morgan, Kristin A. Moore, and James Peterson
1987     Race differences in the timing of adolescent intercourse. *American Sociological Review* 52:511-518.
Gamoran, Adam
1987     The stratification of high school learning opportunities. *Sociology of Education* 60:135-155.
Gottfredson, Denise C., Rich J. McNeil, and Gary D. Gottfredson
1987     Community Influences on Individual Delinquency. Paper presented at the Annual Meeting of the American Society of Criminology, November.
Gottfredson, Stephen D., and Ralph B. Taylor
1986     Person-environment interactions in the prediction of recidivism. Pp. 133-155 in *The Social Ecology of Crime.* James M. Byrne and Robert J. Sampson, eds. New York: Springer-Verlag.
1987     Community contexts and criminal offenders. In *Communities and Crime Reduction*, T. Hope and M. Show, eds. London: Her Majesty's Stationery Office.
Hauser, Robert M.
1969     Schools and the stratification process. *American Journal of Sociology* 74:587-611.
1971     *Socioeconomic Background and Educational Performance.* Washington, D.C.: American Sociological Association.
Hauser, Robert M., William H. Sewell, and Duane F. Alwin
1976     High school effects on achievement. In *Schooling and Achievement in American Society*, William H. Sewell, Robert M. Hauser, and David L. Featherman, eds. New York: Academic Press.
Hindelang, Michael J., Travis Hirschi, and Joseph G. Wells
1981     *Measuring Delinquency.* Beverly Hills, Calif.: Sage.
Hogan, Dennis P., and Evelyn M. Kitagawa
1985     The impact of social status, family structure, and neighborhood on the fertility of black adolescents. *American Journal of Sociology* 9:825-855.

Hogan, Dennis, Nan Marie Astone, and Evelyn Kitagawa
    1985    Social and environmental factors influencing contraceptive use among black adolescents. *Family Planning Perspectives* 17:165-169.
Hotchkiss, Lawrence
    1984    Effects of Schooling on Cognitive, Attitudinal, and Behavioral Outcomes. Technical Report. The National Center for Research on Vocational Education, The Ohio State University.
Jencks, Christopher
    1969    A reappraisal of the most controversial educational document of our time. *The New York Times Magazine*, August 10:12-13 and 33-44.
    1972a    The Coleman report and the conventional wisdom. Pp. 69-115 in *On Equality of Educational Opportunity*, Frederick Mosteller and Daniel Patrick Moynihan, eds. New York: Random House.
    1972b    The quality of the data collected by the Equality of Opportunity Survey. Pp. 437-512 in *On Equality of Educational Opportunity*, Frederick Mosteller and Daniel Patrick Moynihan, eds. New York: Random House.
    forth-    Is the underclass growing? In Christopher Jencks and Paul Peterson, eds.,
    coming    *The Urban Underclass*. Washington, D.C.: Brookings Institution.
Jencks, Christopher, and Marsha Brown
    1975a    The effects of desegregation on student achievement: Some new evidence from the Equality of Educational Opportunity Survey. *Sociology of Education* 48:126-140.
    1975b    The effects of high schools on their students. *Harvard Educational Review* 45:273-324.
Jencks, Christopher, Marshall Smith, Henry Acland, Mary Jo Bane, David Cohen, Herbert Gintis, Barbara Heyns, and Stephen Michelson
    1972    *Inequality*. New York: Basic Books.
Jencks, Christopher, Susan Bartlett, Mary Corcoran, James Crouse, David Eaglesfield, Gregory Jackson, Kent McClelland, Peter Mueser, Michael Olneck, Joseph Schwartz, Sherry Ward, and Jill Williams
    1979    *Who Gets Ahead?* New York: Basic Books.
Johnstone, John W. C.
    1978    Social class, social areas and delinquency. *Sociology and Social Research* 63:49-72.
Krol, Ronald A.
    1980    A meta analysis of the effects of desegregation on academic achievement. *The Urban Review* 12:211-224.
Mare, Robert
    1980    Social background and school continuation decisions. *Journal of the American Statistical Association* 75:295-305.
Massey, Douglas S., and Nancy A. Denton
    1987    Trends in residential segregation of blacks, Hispanics, and Asians: 1970-1980. *American Sociological Review* 52:802-825.
Massey, Douglas S., and Mitchell L. Eggers
    1990    The ecology of inequality: Minorities and the concentration of poverty 1970-1980. *American Journal of Sociology* 95:1153-1188.
Mayer, Susan E.
    forth-    How much does a high school's racial and economic mix affect graduation
    coming    rates and teenage fertility rates? In Christopher Jencks and Paul Peterson, eds., *The Urban Underclass*. Washington, D.C.: Brookings Institution.

McDill, Edward L., and Leo C. Rigsby
    1973    *Structure and Process in Secondary Schools: The Academic Impact of Educational Climates.* Baltimore: Johns Hopkins University Press.

Meyer, John W.
    1970    High school effects on college intentions. *American Journal of Sociology* 76:59-70.

Michael, John A.
    1961    High school climates and plans for entering college. *Public Opinion Quarterly* 25:585-595.

Mosteller, Frederick, and Daniel Patrick Moynihan, eds.
    1972    *On Equality of Educational Opportunity.* New York: Random House.

Myers, David E.
    1985    The relationship between school poverty concentration and students' reading and math achievement and learning. Pp. D-17 to D-60 in Mary Kennedy, Richard Jung, and Martin Orland, eds., *Poverty, Achievement and the Distribution of Compensatory Education Services.* Office of Educational Research and Improvement. Washington, D.C.: U.S. Department of Education.

Nelson, Joel I.
    1972    High school context and college plans: The impact of social structure on aspirations. *American Sociological Review* 37:143-148.

Reiss, Albert J., Jr., and Albert Lewis Rhodes
    1961    The distribution of juvenile delinquency in the social class structure. *American Sociological Review* 26:720-732.

Rosenbaum, James E., Leonard S. Rubinowitz, and Marilynn J. Kulieke
    1986    Low-Income Black Children in White Suburban Schools. Center for Urban Affairs and Policy Research, Northwestern University. Evanston, Ill.

St. John, Nancy H.
    1975    *School Desegregation Outcomes for Children.* New York: John Wiley & Sons.

Sewell, William H., and J. Michael Armer
    1966    Neighborhood context and college plans. *American Sociological Review* 31:159-168.

Sewell, William H., Robert M. Hauser, and Wendy C. Wolf
    1980    Sex, schooling, and occupational status. *American Journal of Sociology* 86:551-583.

Simcha-Fagan, Ora, and Joseph E. Schwartz
    1986    Neighborhood and delinquency: An assessment of contextual effects. *Criminology* 24:667-703.

Smith, Douglas A.
    1986    The neighborhood context of police behavior. Pp. 313-341 in *Communities and Crime.* Albert J. Reiss, Jr., and Michael Tonry, eds. Chicago: University of Chicago Press.

Sum, Andrew
    1986    Childbearing Behavior of Unmarried Women (20-24) in the United States and Their Relationship With AFQT Test Scores: Findings of the 1979-1981 NLS Interviews. Working paper, Center for Labor Market Studies, Northeastern University, Boston.

Summers, Anita A., and Barbara L. Wolfe
    1977    Do schools make a difference? *The American Economic Review* 67(September): 639-652.

Thornton, Clarence H., and Bruce K. Eckland
    1980    High school contextual effects for black and white students: A research
            note. *Sociology of Education* 53:247-252.
Turner, Ralph A.
    1964    *The Social Context of Ambition.* San Francisco: Chandler.
Wilson, Alan B.
    1959    Residential segregation of social classes and aspirations of high school boys.
            *American Sociological Review* 24:836-845.
Wilson, William Julius
    1987    *The Truly Disadvantaged.* Chicago: The University of Chicago Press.

# 5
# Residential Segregation, Job Proximity, and Black Job Opportunities

CHRISTOPHER JENCKS AND SUSAN E. MAYER

In 1968 John Kain published a seminal paper in which he argued that the high level of joblessness among urban blacks was partly attributable to the fact that a growing fraction of urban jobs—especially blue-collar manufacturing jobs—had moved to the suburbs while exclusionary housing practices had kept blacks penned up in central cities. Kain argued that the resulting "spatial mismatch" reduced both employers' willingness to hire black workers and black workers' ability to find jobs that were in principle open to them.

In assessing these arguments it is important to draw a sharp distinction between Kain's demand-side and supply-side stories. On the demand side, Kain argued that suburbanization of jobs was likely to reduce employers' willingness to hire black workers because many suburban firms feared that bringing black workers into an all-white suburb would offend white residents. Yet Kain also noted the possibility that residential segregation might benefit blacks, since employers in all-black areas might be more willing to hire blacks than employers in the mixed areas that would come into existence if cities were not segregated.

Kain's demand-side analysis of the way residential segregation and the suburbanization of blue-collar employment affected demand for black workers rested on social considerations, many of which appear to have changed since 1968. Perhaps for this reason, subsequent research has seldom tried to test the validity of Kain's demand-side argument. Yet for those interested in explaining aggregate black employment or earnings, this part of his argument is probably more important than his supply-side argument.

On the supply side, Kain argued that even when suburban employers were willing to hire blacks, the fact that blacks lived farther than whites from suburban jobs meant that blacks were less likely to hear about suburban job vacancies before they were filled. In addition, he argued that even when blacks could get suburban jobs, the fact that they had to spend more time and money than whites on commuting was likely to result in lower rates of labor force participation among blacks, who would more often conclude that working was not worth the bother.

Unlike Kain's demand-side argument, his analysis of the way distance cut the supply of black workers available to suburban firms was based largely on geographic considerations that have not changed in any fundamental way since 1968. Most blacks still live in the central city, and there are probably even fewer good blue-collar jobs available in the central city today than in the late 1960s. Central-city jobs are increasingly likely to require high levels of education (Kasarda, 1989), and while the educational gap between young black and young white workers has narrowed dramatically, there are still substantial disparities in academic skill.[1] As a result, many scholars, political leaders, and journalists still view the spatial mismatch hypothesis as a plausible explanation of rising black joblessness.[2]

This chapter reviews the currently available evidence regarding Kain's major hypotheses. The first section looks at Kain's demand-side arguments, reviewing both the theoretical reasons for thinking that residential segregation might reduce demand for black workers and the empirical evidence for this hypothesis. The second section turns to Kain's supply-side arguments, discussing the effects of living far from major centers of employment on workers' job prospects. The third section reviews evidence on the closely related question of whether black workers who live in the suburbs find better jobs than those who live in the central city. The fourth section compares the earnings of central-city blacks who commute to the suburbs to the earnings of similar blacks who work in the central-city ghetto. The closing section discusses the implications of the findings and pressing research needs.

We do not take up the question of whether a neighborhood's mean socioeconomic status (SES) affects adult black workers' economic prospects. Wilson (1987) and others have suggested that living in an urban ghetto where few adults have steady jobs may sap an individual's motivation to work. In addition, Wilson and others have suggested that living in a neighborhood where nobody has a good job makes it harder to find such a

---

[1] The proportion of 25- to 29-year-old nonwhites without a high school diploma fell from 41.6 percent in 1970 to 15.7 percent in 1986. Among whites, the proportion declined from 22.2 to 13.5 percent. The National Assessment of Educational Progress shows that the disparity in test performance between black and white 17-year-olds who were enrolled in school also narrowed after 1970, though not as much as the disparity in years of school completed (National Center for Education Statistics, 1988, Tables 8 and 81-87.)

[2] Wilson (1987) and Kasarda (1989) both endorse variants of this hypothesis.

job even if you try. These hypotheses strike us as plausible, but we have not been able to find any empirical studies that assess their validity for adults.

The absence of such research reflects the complexity of the problem. An individual's employment status and earnings can correlate with the mean SES of his or her neighborhood for two different reasons. Living in a high-SES neighborhood can increase your chances of finding a good job, but finding a good job can also enable you to move to a high-SES neighborhood. As a result, individuals in low-SES neighborhoods would be less likely to hold steady, well-paid jobs even if their place of residence had no effect whatever on their job prospects. We would need longitudinal data to estimate the contribution of selective migration to the correlation between earnings and community characteristics. No such data were available when we did this review, so there was no way to estimate the effect of a neighborhood's mean SES on adults' job opportunities.[3]

## RESIDENTIAL SEGREGATION AND DEMAND FOR BLACK WORKERS

### Theoretical Issues

Kain argued that a firm's attitude toward hiring black workers was likely to vary with the racial mix of the neighborhood in which it was located. Following economic convention, we refer to such variations in firms' attitudes toward hiring blacks as variations in the demand for black labor. Noneconomists should bear in mind that this usage refers to more than whether firms prefer a black or white worker for a given job. A firm's demand for black labor is highest when it prefers black workers to equally competent white workers, somewhat lower when it is neutral between equally competent blacks and whites, still lower when it prefers whites to equally competent blacks, and lowest of all when it refuses to hire blacks at all.

A firm can express its demand for black or white workers in several ways. Firms that prefer white to black workers must set wages high enough to attract white workers, and they must then devise plausible criteria for hiring white rather than black applicants. To minimize the cost of preferring whites, these firms are also likely to locate where white workers are relatively cheap and black workers are relatively scarce. Firms that prefer white workers therefore tend to locate either in white rural areas or on the fringes of major metropolitan areas. Firms with a weaker preference

---

[3]Because of increased interest in neighborhood effects, the Panel Study of Income Dynamics has been adding data to its files on the characteristics of the census tracts in which respondents lived.

for white workers are more likely to locate in the central city, where a large pool of cheap black labor is readily available.

Kain did not discuss the effect of firms' racial preferences on their location decisions. Instead, he assumed that location decisions were exogenous and discussed their effect on a firm's demand for black workers. He argued that since local whites might resent the firm's bringing black workers into their all-white neighborhood, firms in such neighborhoods would try to avoid hiring blacks.

Kain was mainly concerned with black workers' access to manufacturing jobs. The argument that manufacturing firms in white areas would avoid hiring blacks to avoid local resentment does not strike us as very plausible. Blue-collar workers who commute to large suburban manufacturing plants typically drive to the plant's parking lot, go to their job, put in their time, go back to the parking lot, and drive home. They are unlikely to have much contact with the community in which they work, especially if they are black and the community is entirely white. Local resentment is therefore likely to be minimal. Furthermore, suburban whites who *do* resent the fact that a local plant hires blacks have few effective mechanisms for expressing their displeasure unless they resort to violence, which is rare. (Whites who work in a plant have many effective ways of expressing racial resentment, but they can do this no matter where the plant is located.)

Kain's argument seems more plausible when applied to the service sector than when applied to manufacturing, and it seems especially plausible when applied to small firms that deal directly with the public. It is easy to imagine suburban restaurants, grocery stores, gas stations, dry cleaners, and repair services refusing to hire blacks because they think their customers prefer dealing with whites and will take their trade elsewhere if the firm does not cater to their prejudices.

Kain did not discuss the likely behavior of firms in racially mixed areas. His arguments imply, however, that manufacturing firms in mixed areas would be indifferent between equally competent black and white workers, since they would not be worried about bringing blacks into mixed areas. The picture is more complicated for retail firms. If both blacks and whites preferred doing business with retail firms that hired people of their own race, and if blacks and whites who lived in mixed neighborhoods had roughly equal incomes, retail firms in mixed areas would presumably try to hire a mix of employees similar to the mix of local residents. If whites were quite averse to firms that hired blacks while blacks were not so averse to firms that hired only whites, or if whites had far more money than blacks, most retail firms in mixed areas might end up discriminating against blacks.

Finally, Kain noted that firms in all-black areas might hire more blacks than an average firm. This could occur for two reasons. First, ghetto firms would hire disproportionate numbers of blacks if white workers were un-willing to work in the ghetto or demanded "combat pay" for working there.[4] Second, retail firms in the ghetto would hire disproportionate numbers of blacks if black customers preferred dealing with blacks.

If these general hypotheses are correct, the persistence of all-black neighborhoods can either increase or decrease aggregate demand for black workers. The net effect of a residential ghetto on demand for black workers will depend on whether the increase in demand within the ghetto offsets the decline elsewhere. The balance between the gains in black employment within the ghetto and the losses elsewhere should depend on two factors: the absolute number of jobs inside and outside the ghetto, and the relative strength of ghetto firms' preference for blacks compared to nonghetto firms' preference for whites.

All the factors that influence the costs and benefits of residential segregation are likely to have changed over the past 30 years. Thus even if we were to accept Kain's claim that residential segregation reduced aggregate demand for black workers in Chicago and Detroit in the 1950s, we could not assume segregation had the same effect today. The effects of residential segregation are also likely to vary from one part of the country to another. Finding that residential segregation lowers demand for black workers in Chicago and Detroit may not, therefore, imply that it has the same effect in California. Finally, residential segregation is likely to have different effects on different ethnic groups. Thus even if we found that Chinese immigrants did better when they moved to highly segregated cities, the same might not hold for Mexican immigrants, much less for blacks.

### Empirical Evidence

Kain's analysis of Chicago and Detroit employment patterns in the 1950s convinced him that blacks would have gotten a larger share of all jobs if there were no ghetto, but this was not because his model implied that residential desegregation would increase demand for black workers. Kain's model implied that residential desegregation would have no effect whatever on overall demand for black workers. Residential desegregation increased black employment only because it brought black workers closer to most jobs and thereby increased the supply of black workers available to fill these jobs at any given wage.

---

[4] A downward shift in the local supply of white workers does not necessarily lead to an upward shift in local demand for black workers. When the local supply of white workers available at a given price falls, firms may move elsewhere rather than hiring more blacks. We return to this point below.

Kain used the proportion of nonwhites in a neighborhood ($R$) as a proxy for demand and used the number of miles from a neighborhood to the edge of a city's major ghetto ($d^m$) as a proxy for supply. He assumed that both these measures had linear effects on blacks' share of neighborhood employment. Using these two measures to predict nonwhites' share of total employment ($W$) in a Chicago neighborhood in 1956, Kain's best estimate was that:

$$W = 9.28 + .456R - .409d^m \tag{1}$$

Since this model assumes that the effects of $R$ and $D^m$ are linear, it implies that the fraction of all Chicago-area jobs held by blacks ($\overline{W}$) depends entirely on the areawide means of $R$ and $d^m$. The dispersion of $R$ (an indicator of the level of segregation) is irrelevant. Segregation will, of course, increase demand for black workers in black neighborhoods and lower demand in white neighborhoods, but the two changes will exactly offset one another, leaving aggregate demand unchanged. Since residential desegregation does not alter the total number of blacks or whites, at least in the short run, it does not change the overall mean of $R$. Using Kain's assumptions, therefore, residential segregation only affects blacks' share of total employment indirectly, that is, by affecting their average proximity to jobs ($\bar{d}^m$).

While Kain implicitly assumed that desegregation would leave overall demand for black workers unchanged, he did not try to test this assumption. In order to do so we need to ask whether, when all else is equal, demand for black workers in neighborhoods whose racial mix mirrors that of the metropolitan area as a whole is higher or lower than demand in the metropolitan area as a whole. So far as we can discover, only one study has investigated this issue.

Offner and Saks (1971) reanalyzed Kain's Chicago data and found that blacks fared quite badly in racially mixed areas. Employers in all-black neighborhoods hired a lot of blacks. Employers in all-white areas hired very few blacks. Employers in racially mixed areas acted like employers in all-white areas, hiring very few blacks. As a result, blacks' share of employment was lower in racially mixed neighborhoods than in the Chicago area as a whole.

Offner and Saks's statistical results cannot tell us *why* employers in mixed neighborhoods hired so few blacks, but several possible explanations come to mind. If white Chicago residents were reluctant to trade with firms that hired blacks in the 1950s, while Chicago blacks were willing to trade with firms that hired only whites, blacks would not have gotten many retail jobs in racially mixed areas. And if white workers were willing to work in racially mixed areas for the same wages as in all-white areas in the 1950s, firms in racially mixed areas would have had no more incentive to hire blacks than firms in all-white areas.

These conjectures all assume that a firm's employment practices depend on the racial mix of its neighborhood. In the racially mixed Chicago neighborhoods with which we are familiar, however, residential mix is a by-product of local employment patterns, as well as the other way round. The areas around the University of Chicago and Michael Reese Hospital, for example, were located in the path of black residential growth. Ordinarily, these areas would have become entirely black. They remained racially mixed because firms employing white professionals remained in the area, and many of these white workers wanted to live near their workplace.

Whatever the explanation, Offner and Saks's results show that if residential desegregation had led all Chicago firms to act like those in racially mixed neighborhoods, job opportunities for blacks would have contracted, not expanded. Luring blacks and whites to the same neighborhoods would have reduced blacks' chances of getting jobs in what had once been ghetto firms without opening up an equivalent number of new jobs in firms outside the old ghetto.

In the long run, of course, residential desegregation might have reduced white prejudice against blacks, increasing demand for black workers. One way to test the validity of this hypothesis is to ask whether blacks do better economically in relatively desegregated cities. The evidence on this point, while hardly conclusive, suggests that residential segregation has very little effect on blacks' economic success.

Masters (1974) studied the ratio of nonwhite to white earnings in 65 large Standard Metropolitan Statistical Areas (SMSAs) in 1959. Contrary to what we would expect if residential segregation reduced demand for nonwhite workers, the ratio of nonwhite to white incomes was slightly higher in highly segregated SMSAs. This relationship was not reliably different from zero, but the fact remains that Masters's findings offer no support for the contention that desegregation increases demand for black workers.[5] Masters (1975) replicated this result using 1969 data from 77 SMSAs with large black populations. Unfortunately, Masters's 1969 results changed when he excluded SMSAs with substantial amounts of agricultural employment. Once he dropped these SMSAs, there was some evidence that both black men's chances of having a job and their relative earnings were

---

[5] Kain (1974) argues that Masters's results are inconclusive, since they do not take account of city-to-city differences in the degree to which jobs are suburbanized, the relative tightness of urban and suburban labor markets, or the distance from the black ghetto to centers of employment. But Kain offers neither theoretical arguments nor empirical evidence that including these omitted variables would make the coefficients of Masters's segregation measures negative instead of positive.

more favorable in less segregated SMSAs.[6] Thus we cannot say with any confidence whether residential segregation raised or lowered demand for black workers in the 1960s. Nor can we rule out the possibility that the level of residential segregation depended on the relative earnings of blacks and whites rather than the other way round. All we can say with confidence is that the relationship between residential segregation and relative earnings is weak.

In any event, the effects of residential segregation on a firm's demand for black workers are likely to change over time. Kain's data described Chicago in the 1950s, when employers were under no legal or social pressure to hire blacks and when hiring blacks for nonmenial jobs often caused firms a lot of trouble. Masters's data describe the world of 1959 and 1969, before affirmative action programs had much impact. Much has changed since then, both outside and inside the ghetto.

Outside the ghetto, white customers appear to have become more confortable seeing blacks in nontraditional roles. Political and social pressures have led many managers, especially in large firms, to open up new kinds of jobs to blacks and to make more aggressive recruiting efforts. All these efforts have, however, focused largely on blacks who act more or less like whites. At the same time, some black workers have become more assertive in their dealings with whites, increasing employers' fears that blacks will cause "trouble." The net effect of these trends on demand for black workers is not obvious.[7]

---

[6] Masters presents bivariate results for 77 SMSAs and multivariate results for 65 of these SMSAs. The 12 excluded SMSAs had high levels of agricultural employment in their more remote suburbs and low black-white income ratios. Almost all coefficients change sign in his multivariate model, so trimming the sample makes a big difference. Unfortunately, he presents no bivariate results for the trimmed sample, and his multivariate results include four separate measures of residential segregation, along with two control variables designed to measure job dispersion and accessibility. With these controls, the Taeubers' measure of residential segregation raised blacks' income relative to whites ($t = 2.4$) but lowered blacks' relative likelihood of having a job ($t = .6$).

The multivariate model is hard to interpret, however, because Masters's measure of central-city blacks' access to suburban jobs ($A$) is $(J_{Bc}/J_{Bt})/(J_{NBc}/J_{NBt})$, where $J_B$ is the number of jobs held by blacks in a given area, $J_{NB}$ is the number of jobs held by nonblacks, the subscript $c$ denotes jobs in the central city, and the subscript $t$ denotes all jobs in the SMSA. Unfortunately, this ratio measures not only the relative accessibility of suburban jobs to blacks and whites but the relative willingness of suburban employers to hire blacks rather than whites ("demand"). Kain's argument implies that $A$ is at least partly endogenous and should not be controlled when estimating the effects of residential segregation. The use of four different segregation measures, which may well be quite collinear, also makes Masters's results hard to interpret. Bivariate statistics for the trimmed sample would have made his findings more instructive.

[7] Kirschenman and Neckerman (forthcoming) describe a survey of Chicago employers that shows very high levels of prejudice against unskilled black males, but they do not relate these attitudes to the actual numbers of blacks hired in a given firm.

Predicting changes in demand for black workers inside the ghetto is as hard as predicting changes outside the ghetto. Black ghetto residents may have grown less willing to patronize firms that hire only whites, but we know of no evidence on this point. The wage premium that whites demand for working in the ghetto has probably risen since 1969, because crime has increased even more in the ghetto than elsewhere,[8] but again, we know of no hard evidence on this point.

If whites do, in fact, demand higher premiums for working in the ghetto, this is likely to have had two contradictory effects on job opportunities for blacks. On the one hand, we would expect firms that remained in the ghetto to have substituted cheap black workers for more expensive white workers. On the other hand, we would expect firms that wanted to retain significant numbers of whites to have left the ghetto. Taken together, these trends would lead to an increase in the fraction of ghetto jobs going to blacks, combined with a decrease in the fraction of all jobs located in ghetto areas.[9] Again, the net effect on the number of jobs available to blacks in the ghetto is not obvious.

The only data we have found that speak to this issue come from Leonard's (1987) study of Chicago and Los Angeles firms' payrolls in 1974 and 1980.[10] Leonard's data do not, of course, measure changes in firms' demand for black workers. Rather, they measure changes in the actual level of black employment inside and outside the ghetto. Such changes depend on the supply of black and white workers available to different sorts of firms as well as on firms' demand for such workers.

Leonard's data suggest that blacks' share of blue-collar jobs in the ghetto increased slightly in both Chicago and Los Angeles between 1974 and 1980, which is what we would expect if whites were less willing to work in the ghetto. Blacks' share of blue-collar jobs outside the ghetto rose in

---

[8] The *percentage* increase in crime since the mid-1960s has been greater among whites than among blacks, but the *absolute* increase has been greater among blacks than among whites. From the viewpoint of the potential victim, it is the absolute increase that matters, so the wage premium required to lure people to all-black areas is likely to have risen.

[9] Most ghettos occupy a larger fraction of the metropolitan area in which they are located today than they did in 1960. As a result, the fraction of all jobs located in the ghetto has often grown, even when the number of jobs per square block has fallen. For analytic purposes, however, the crucial issue is not the fraction of all jobs located in the ghetto but the ratio of this fraction to the fraction of all persons living in the ghetto. The argument in the text reflects conventional wisdom in assuming that this ratio has fallen, but we have not seen any hard data supporting that view.

[10] Leonard's sample covers 1,911 Chicago firms and 2,389 Los Angeles firms surveyed by the Office of Federal Contract Compliance in both 1974 and 1980. Since the sample excludes firms that came into existence or went out of existence between 1974 and 1980, it is not fully representative of all firms surveyed in either year. Nor are firms surveyed by the OFCC fully representative of all firms.

Los Angeles but fell in Chicago. As a result, the jobs held by black male Chicagoans were more likely to be in the ghetto in 1980 than in 1974, even though ghetto firms accounted for a smaller fraction of all Chicago-area jobs. In Los Angeles, in contrast, the jobs held by black men were less likely to be in the ghetto in 1980 than in 1974, even though ghetto firms were growing faster than those in mixed areas.

The difference between Chicago and Los Angeles may well reflect differences in the two cities' racial climates, which in turn affect firms' location decisions. The main conclusion we draw from Leonard's findings is that generalizing from a single city to the nation as a whole would be very dangerous.

Taking all the evidence together, the effect of residential segregation on firms' overall demand for black workers remains almost as uncertain as it was 20 years ago. If we rely on Masters's findings for 1959 and 1969, the safest conclusion would be that at that time residential segregation had no consistent effect on firms' interest in hiring blacks. It is important to emphasize, however, that Masters' findings reflect the combined effects of supply and demand, and that they describe employment patterns 20 to 30 years ago, not today. It is also important to emphasize that we know nothing whatever about how residential segregation along *economic* lines affects demand for black workers.

## EFFECTS OF JOB PROXIMITY ON LABOR SUPPLY

Kain showed that as a neighborhood's distance from the central-city ghetto increased the proportion of neighborhood jobs held by nonwhites declined. This was true even with the neighborhood's own racial mix controlled (see equation 1, above), and it was true in Detroit as well as in Chicago. Leonard (1987) found the same pattern for Chicago and Los Angeles in 1974 and 1980.

Kain argued that distance from the central-city ghetto affected the racial mix of a neighborhood's labor force by affecting the supply of black workers available to firms in different neighborhoods. Distance affected labor supply in two ways. First, it increased the effort prospective workers had to make in order to learn about jobs before they were filled. Second, distance raised workers' commuting costs, making remote jobs less attractive.

The argument that information and commuting costs encourage prospective workers to choose jobs near where they live is not controversial. The controversial part of Kain's supply-side argument was his suggestion that workers who could not find jobs near home were likely to stop looking and withdraw from the labor force. If this were true, the high rate of joblessness among urban blacks could be reduced either by discouraging the movement of jobs from the central city to remote suburbs or by encouraging black residential movement from the central city to the suburbs. To test this part of Kain's argument, we need to investigate two questions:

1.  Do blacks fare better economically when they live in neighborhoods that are near a lot of blue-collar jobs?

2.  Do blacks fare better when they live in metropolitan areas where blue-collar jobs are still mainly located in the central city rather than in the suburbs?

We take up these questions in turn.

### Neighborhood Comparisons

One way to estimate the effect of job proximity on black employment is to measure how far different neighborhoods are from blue-collar jobs and then ask whether blacks who live in neighborhoods with a lot of nearby blue-collar jobs have unusually high rates of employment. In the 1950s, for example, Chicago blacks were concentrated in two areas: the West Side, which was a major center of manufacturing and warehousing, and the South Side, which had relatively few jobs of this kind. One way of testing Kain's arguments about the importance of job proximity would have been to ask whether blacks on the West Side were more likely to have jobs than blacks on the South Side. This strategy runs an obvious risk, since employment influences residential choices as well as the other way round. If Chicago's West Side firms had hired blacks in large numbers, many blacks who worked for these firms would presumably have moved to the West Side, even if they had lived on the South Side when they got their jobs. If West Side firms had paid blacks better or offered them steadier employment than other Chicago firms, as Kain's argument implied they should, West Side blacks would have had higher rates of employment and higher wages than other Chicago blacks. This would not have proved that living on the West Side helped blacks get good jobs. It would only have proved that blacks, like everyone else, prefer a short trip to work.

If we set aside this methodological hazard for the moment, it is still important to ask whether a neighborhood's proximity to various kinds of jobs is positively correlated with the fraction of adult residents who hold jobs or negatively correlated with its unemployment rate. Two studies have correlated job proximity with employment among adult males. Hutchinson (1974) used a Pittsburgh traffic survey to construct an index of the number of jobs located at various distances from each respondent's home. He measured the distance between homes and jobs by estimating the time required to reach the job by public transportation. His index of job proximity had a modest positive effect on the probability that white males would be employed in 1967, but it had a negative (though statistically unreliable) effect on the probability that black males would be employed.[11] Leonard (1986) also found that the ratio of nearby jobs to neighborhood population had a negative (but statistically unreliable) effect on Los Angeles men's chances of being employed in 1980.

The negligible correlation between job proximity and male employment rates in Pittsburgh and Los Angeles is puzzling, since we would expect workers with steady jobs to settle near their workplace. The weak correlation suggests that neighborhoods located near major centers of employment may have undesirable social or aesthetic attributes that discourage workers in nearby firms from living there. The weak correlation may also reflect the fact that most commuters use automobiles in both Los Angeles and Pittsburgh, making distance less important than it is in some other places.

We would expect job proximity to have a stronger effect on female employment than on male employment, since women earn less and are more likely than men to work part-time, making long journeys to work less worthwhile. Leonard (1986) did find that the ratio of nearby jobs to neighborhood residents had a positive effect on women's employment rates in Los Angeles in 1980, but the effect was not reliably greater than zero. No one else has investigated this issue.

Job proximity does seem to exert a small but statistically reliable influence on teenage employment rates. Ellwood (1986) used both the ratio of neighborhood jobs to neighborhood residents and the mean commuting time of adult blue-collar workers living in a neighborhood to estimate the proximity of different Chicago neighborhoods to jobs. Both measures showed that males between the ages of 16 and 21 who were no longer in school were more likely to be working in 1970 if they lived in neighborhoods with a lot of nearby jobs. Leonard (1986) also found that the ratio of nearby jobs to population had a significant positive effect on Los Angeles teenagers' chances of being employed in 1980. Ihlanfeldt and Sjoquist (1990) found the same pattern in Philadelphia, Chicago, and Los Angeles in 1980.

The finding that job proximity is more important for teenagers than for adults is consistent with economic theory. Many teenagers work part-time and few earn much money. As a result, teenagers are less likely than

---

[11] Hutchinson actually had two separate measures of distance. One (AC2) measured travel time by public transportation. The other (AC5) measured travel time by automobile and had a value of zero for individuals who did not own automobiles. The coefficient of AC2 is small but significant for whites. It is even smaller, insignificant, and wrong-signed for blacks. Since Hutchinson's equations do not include a dummy variable for having an automobile, AC5 is largely a proxy for automobile ownership. Its coefficient is highly significant. This finding tells us only that having a job increases the likelihood of owning an automobile. Whether automotive commuting time affects an automobile owner's chances of having a job remains unclear.

adults to own cars. We would expect job proximity to be more important to workers who walk or take public transportation to work than to those who can drive.

While all the available evidence suggests that living in a neighborhood with a lot of nearby jobs increases a teenager's chances of working, there is less agreement about the size of these effects. Both Ellwood and Leonard found very small effects in their studies of Chicago and Los Angeles. Using somewhat better measures of job proximity, Ihlanfeldt and Sjoquist found relatively large effects in Philadelphia, Chicago, and Los Angeles. They divided the Philadelphia SMSA into 26 areas, calculated the average travel time of low-wage workers in each area, and used this average as a measure of low-wage jobs' accessibility from that area. A 3.7 minute (1 standard deviation) increase in mean travel time reduced the percentage of 16- to 24-year-old blacks with jobs by 4 to 6 points, depending on their exact age and whether they were in school. The results for young blacks in Chicago and Los Angeles, while less precise, were roughly similar to those in Philadelphia. The effect of job proximity on employment rates among whites was roughly the same as for blacks in Philadelphia, but job proximity did not vary much for whites in Los Angeles, and it did not have much effect in Chicago.

Ihlanfeldt and Sjoquist also found that, at least in Philadelphia, blacks lived much further from low-wage jobs than whites did. Young Philadelphia blacks lived in areas where low-wage workers spent an average of 26 minutes getting to work, whereas young whites lived in areas where low-wage workers spent only 18.5 minutes getting to work. Controlling for job proximity reduced the racial gap in employment by roughly a third, both among 16- to 19-year-olds who had left school and among 20- to 24-year-olds who were still living with their parents. (For young people no longer living with their parents, we cannot tell whether residential choices are a cause or an effect of job location.) Ihlanfeldt and Sjoquist do not tell us whether Chicago or Los Angeles blacks lived in areas with unusually long travel times for low-wage workers, so we cannot tell how much of the racial disparity in youth employment for these cities was due to the fact that young blacks lived in the wrong places. Based on Ihlanfeldt and Sjoquist's work, however, we can say that location is a major factor in the high rate of joblessness among young Philadelphia blacks.

### City-to-City Comparisons

A second way of estimating the effect of distance on employment opportunities is to compare cities with highly dispersed employment patterns to cities with more concentrated patterns. Mooney (1969) used aggregate data on the 25 metropolitan areas with the largest nonwhite populations to estimate the impact of firms' moving to the suburbs on nonwhite male employment in 1960. His best estimate was that

$$R = .63 - 2.86U + .19D + .24A$$
$$(.05) \quad (.56) \quad (.06) \quad (.06)$$

(2)

where,

    $R$   is the probability that a nonwhite male living in the poorest central-city census tracts held a job in March 1960.

    $U$   is the unemployment rate for the SMSA as a whole in 1960.

    $D$   is the fraction of all jobs in manufacturing, wholesale trade, retail trade, and selected services located in the central city. (This is supposed to be a measure of job dispersal.)

    $A$   is the probability that an employed nonwhite living in the central city will work in the suburbs. (This is supposed to be a measure of the suburban ring's accessibility to central-city nonwhites.)

The numbers in parentheses are the standard errors of the coefficients.

The overall tightness of the local labor market was clearly the most important determinant of black men's employment rates. A 1-point increase in an SMSA's overall unemployment rate led to a 2.86-point reduction in the employment rate among black men living in central-city poverty areas. But black men also did worse in cities where manufacturing, trade, and services were more suburbanized. A 10-point increase in the proportion of such jobs located in the suburbs led to a 1.9 point decline in employment among black ghetto residents.

Farley (1987) conducted an analogous study using 1980 census data on all metropolitan areas of 50,000 or more. After controlling an SMSA's overall racial mix and a measure of black-white educational inequality in the SMSA, the ratio of black to white unemployment was lower in SMSAs where manufacturing, trade, and service jobs were mainly located in the central city.[12]

In explaining Mooney and Farley's findings it is important to bear in mind that they did not find that the *absolute* level of black employment was higher in cities where manufacturing, trade, and services were concentrated in the central city. They only found that the black-white *gap* was smaller in these cities.[13] The black-white difference could be larger in cities with

---

[12] Farley also found that the ratio of black to white unemployment was lower when a high proportion of blacks lived in the suburbs rather than in the central city. Whether this indicates that unemployment falls when blacks move to the suburbs or that blacks move to the suburbs when they have steady jobs is unclear.

[13] Mooney uses the absolute black employment rate as his dependent variable, but since he controls the overall unemployment rate, the estimated effect of suburbanized employment is conceptually (though not statistically) equivalent to its effect on the black-white disparity.

decentralized employment patterns either because whites do better in such cities or because blacks do worse.

Ihlanfeldt and Sjoquist (1989) avoid this ambiguity by looking at the effect of job decentralization on the earnings of both blacks and whites who either worked or said they wanted to work in 1978. Their sample came from the Panel Study of Income Dynamics and included only men and women who had not attended college and lived in the central city of an SMSA. Their measure of earnings was total earnings in 1978, less commuting costs. Their primary measure of job decentralization was the percentage of all low-skill jobs in the SMSA located outside the central city of the SMSA in 1980. All their estimates controlled respondents' age, education, job tenure, marital status, and physical health, as well as the SMSA's overall unemployment rate, racial mix, and rate of population growth between 1970 and 1980.

Among black central-city males without higher education, a 16 point (one standard deviation) decline in the percentage of low-skill jobs located in the central city was associated with a $929 (10 percent) decline in 1978 earnings. Among white central-city men without higher education, the decline was $849 (6 percent). Job decentralization had a small (and statistically unreliable) negative effect on white women's earnings, no effect on black women's earnings, and no effect on college-educated workers' earnings.

Ihlanfeldt and Sjoquist did not investigate whether job decentralization lowered central-city men's net earnings by lowering their wages, lowering their hours, or raising their commuting costs. This is a serious limitation. When firms move to the suburbs, housing values in the central city often fall. This may lead unskilled workers who find suburban jobs to live in the central city, since they may save enough on housing to offset their extra commuting costs. Because they include commuting costs while excluding housing costs, Ihlanfeldt and Sjoquist probably overestimate the adverse effect of job decentralization on central-city residents' economic welfare.

Furthermore, we cannot draw strong conclusions about the impact of job decentralization on either black or white workers' economic welfare unless we know how it affects the welfare of those who live in the suburbs as well as those who live in the central city. Ihlanfeldt and Sjoquist did not investigate this issue.

### Reconciling Neighborhood Studies With SMSA Studies

Comparisons of metropolitan areas imply that job proximity affects black men's employment prospects, while Hutchinson and Leonard's comparisons of different neighborhoods in the same city suggest that job proximity makes little difference for adults. We can think of at least three explanations for these apparently contradictory findings.

First, Mooney and Farley's city-to-city comparisons may be picking up the effect of job proximity on teenagers. This explanation strikes us as unlikely, however, since teenage employment is not a large fraction of total employment.

Second, Hutchinson and Leonard's findings may be peculiar to Pittsburgh and Los Angeles. Job proximity may be more important in cities where public transportation plays a large role in commuting.

Third, the correlation between geographically centralized employment and the black/white employment ratio in Mooney and Farley's city-to-city comparisons may be attributable to the fact that both firms' location decisions and blacks' job prospects depend on other unmeasured characteristics of the SMSA, such as the level of interracial conflict and prejudice. Firms in SMSAs with a lot of racial conflict may be especially likely to move to the suburbs, and firms in these SMSAs may also be especially reluctant to hire blacks. If this explanation is correct, we should dismiss Mooney and Farley's findings as spurious and put our faith in Hutchinson and Leonard's findings. We would need some direct evidence before accepting this explanation, however.


## CAN BLACKS EARN MORE IN THE SUBURBS?

The spatial mismatch hypothesis assumes that blacks are less likely than whites to have steady, well-paid jobs because they live farther from the kinds of firms that might offer them such jobs. This hypothesis depends on two empirical assumptions: that distance affects a worker's chances of finding a job and that there are, in fact, better jobs available to blacks in distant areas (Kasarda, 1989). One way to test the latter assumption is to ask whether blacks in the central city who commute to the suburbs earn more than those who work in the ghetto (or in the central business district). Danziger and Weinstein (1976) studied Cleveland, Detroit, and St. Louis men between the ages of 21 and 64 who lived in central-city neighborhoods with high poverty rates in 1970. (Here and throughout we use the term "ghetto" to describe these poor, black central-city neighborhoods.) They found that ghetto blacks in all three cities were about as likely to work in the suburbs as in the ghetto.[14] This finding does not suggest that information

---

[14] Since Danziger and Weinstein do not include individuals who worked in the central city but outside the poverty areas where they lived, their findings do not imply that half of all ghetto blacks worked in the suburbs. Hughes and Madden (forthcoming) report that among black male household heads who worked full-time, year-round, in 1980 in the Cleveland SMSA, 49 percent worked in the suburbs. The rates were 42 percent in Detroit and 31 percent in Philadelphia.

costs posed a very serious problem for blacks seeking jobs in the suburbs, although the percentage of blacks working in the suburbs would presumably have been even higher if information costs had been lower.

Blacks who worked in the suburbs earned 11 percent more than those who worked in the ghetto. The main reason blacks earned more in the suburbs was that they worked in better-paid occupations and industries than ghetto workers. Danziger and Weinstein treated a worker's occupation and industry as fixed personal characteristics, so they concluded that commuting to the suburbs was of little economic value to blacks. But a worker's occupation and industry are not, in fact, fixed. About 9 percent of all workers changed occupations every year during the 1970s (Byrne, 1975), and industry changes are likely to be at least as frequent. Furthermore, changing occupation or industry is one common way of getting a better job. It therefore seems reasonable to suppose that blacks commute to the suburbs partly because commuting allows them to get jobs in well-paid occupations and industries. Controlling occupation and industry when estimating the payoff to commuting is therefore likely to underestimate the benefits of commuting.

Danziger and Weinstein did not find much educational difference between blacks who worked in the suburbs and blacks who worked in the ghetto. Their findings are therefore consistent with the hypothesis that blacks who worked in the ghetto could have earned almost 11 percent more than they did if they had had jobs in the suburbs.

Most researchers agree that distance plays a minor role in determining white-collar workers' job opportunities. The spatial mismatch hypothesis should therefore apply primarily to blacks without higher education. Danziger and Weinstein did not investigate whether blacks without higher education gained more than college-educated blacks by commuting to the suburbs, but Straszheim (1980) did. Using data collected in the San Francisco Bay area in 1965, Straszheim found that blacks who had not attended college earned about 10 percent more if they worked in the San Francisco or Oakland suburbs than if they worked in San Francisco or Oakland itself. This pattern was reversed among blacks who had attended college.

The Danziger-Weinstein and Straszheim results for 1965-1970 are, in our judgment, consistent with the spatial mismatch hypothesis. But they are also consistent with a more traditional view, namely that suburban jobs pay more than ghetto jobs because they impose higher commuting costs on most workers.

---

These percentages would be lower for blacks who lived in central cities and still lower for blacks living in central-city poverty areas.

According to Danziger and Weinstein, commuting to a suburb length-ened the average ghetto resident's working day by about 26 minutes. Assuming an 8-hour day, and further assuming that workers are indifferent between spending their time commuting and spending it working, a 26-minute increase in commuting time is equivalent to a 5 percent reduction in hourly wages. Danziger and Weinstein estimated that the extra out-of-pocket expenses associated with suburban jobs reduced black suburban workers' effective wages by an additional 2 to 4 percent. Thus while black suburban workers earned 11 percent more than ghetto workers, their net wages were only 2 to 4 percent higher than those of ghetto workers.

Since blacks who worked in the suburbs were a trifle better educated than those who worked in the ghetto, we would have expected the suburban workers to earn a trifle more. Danziger and Weinstein's findings therefore suggest to us that in 1970 the suburban wage premium was just sufficient to cover ghetto residents' commuting costs. This finding is reassuring. If ghetto residents could have realized substantially higher net earnings by commuting to the suburbs, we would have had to ask why so many of them chose to work in the ghetto. At least in 1970, however, the answer is clear: Blacks could not appreciably increase their net earnings by commuting to the suburbs.

Ihlanfeldt (1988) used census data to examine wage differentials between various parts of the Atlanta SMSA in 1980. He found significant location differentials for whites but not for blacks. Black service workers made more in one county north of Atlanta (Clayton), but so did white service workers. This seems to reflect a general shortage of service workers in Clayton County.

Hughes and Madden (forthcoming) also use 1980 census data to investigate wages in different parts of the Cleveland, Detroit, and Philadelphia SMSAs. Unfortunately for our purposes they do not report average wages in central cities and in the suburbs. Instead, they divide SMSAs into 13 to 27 work zones. These work zones include each SMSA's central business district, the rest of the central city, and 11 to 25 suburban areas. Hughes and Madden identify the work zone in each SMSA where male household heads who worked full-time, year-round earned the most, after adjusting for their age, education, occupation, industry, and commuting costs. They then estimate the gain in net earnings, after adjusting for changes in commuting costs, if all workers were paid at the same rate as those in the best-paid area.

These calculations imply that if all black men had worked in the best-paid part of their SMSA in 1980 they would have earned 38 to 48 percent more than they actually did. Hughes and Madden are rightly skeptical about these estimates. If blacks could have increased their net earnings by 38 to 48 percent by, say, working in a remote suburb rather than the central business district, many would surely have done so. Since they didn't, we must ask why.

The most obvious answer is that blacks who worked in poorly paid areas could not get the jobs that were available in the best-paid areas. Hughes and Madden try to deal with this possibility by controlling workers' age, education, occupation, and industry.[15] But because they are estimating wage differentials for small areas using small samples, their results are likely to be quite sensitive to the presence of a few high-wage firms in one of these areas. Firms that pay substantially more than the areawide average are usually quite choosy about whom they hire. Such firms also tend to set high performance standards and fire workers who do not meet them. As a result, there are likely to be large unmeasured differences between the workers in these firms and apparently similar workers in firms with lower pay scales.

Our suspicion that intrametropolitan wage gradients reflect unmeasured differences in worker characteristics is supported by the fact that Hughes and Madden's method also implies that whites could have increased their net earnings by 30 to 36 percent if they had worked in different parts of these SMSAs in 1980. Since there were no obvious constraints on where whites worked, this finding suggests that Hughes and Madden's wage equations probably omit important worker characteristics.[16]

All else equal, Hughes and Madden found that blacks earned more when they worked near the periphery of the Cleveland and Philadelphia SMSAs rather than near the center, but the difference was substantively trivial and statistically unreliable. Blacks earned significantly less when they worked near the periphery of the Detroit SMSA than when they worked near the center. These results make it hard to argue that central-city blacks work in low-wage areas because they are poorly informed about high-wage jobs in more remote areas.

Hughes and Madden's findings are also at odds with those of Danziger and Weinstein, which implied that blacks earned more near the periphery of the Cleveland, Detroit, and St. Louis SMSAs than near the center. The most plausible explanation is that Hughes and Madden studied all blacks

---

[15]For reasons already discussed, controlling a worker's occupation and industry could yield downwardly biased estimates of the benefits of changing job location. In practice, however, Hughes and Madden's estimates are almost certainly biased upward.

[16]Since the estimated gap between observed and optimal wages is larger for blacks than for whites, Hughes and Madden assume that blacks could increase their earnings more than whites by working in different places. The gap between average and optimal wages is, however, also likely to be a function of sample size, since there is more random variation in area-specific wages using small samples than using large ones. The larger gap among blacks could, therefore, be due to the fact that there are fewer of them—or to the fact that unmeasured differences between workers in different areas are larger among blacks than among whites.

in these SMSAs, whereas Danziger and Weinstein studied only ghetto residents. Ghetto blacks will only take suburban jobs if these jobs pay more than they think they can get in the ghetto, since they will want compensation for their extra commuting costs. Conversely, suburban blacks will only take central-city jobs if those jobs pay more than the jobs they think they could get near home, since they too will want to cover their extra commuting costs. Thus even if suburban and ghetto jobs offer the same average wage for a worker with specified characteristics, workers will only commute long distances if they are offered a job that pays more than this average for some reason. In such a world, samples of commuters will always show that commuting "pays." But it will not follow that average wages are higher in one place than the other.[17]

Taken together, the available data offer little support for the notion that blacks could get better jobs if they worked in the suburbs rather than in central cities. Neither Danziger and Weinstein's work nor Hughes and Madden's suggests that either improvements in public transportation between central cities and the suburbs or other devices for making suburban jobs more accessible to central-city blacks would have much effect on black workers' potential earnings. The modest role of commuting costs in both studies also suggests that if suburban firms wanted to hire more blacks, they could attract them relatively easily.

## HOW DO BLACKS FARE WHEN THEY LIVE IN THE SUBURBS?

At bottom, the spatial mismatch hypothesis is rooted in the observation that exclusionary housing practices have kept blacks from moving to the suburbs, where their job prospects might be better than they are in the central city. If blacks who live in the suburbs do no better than those in the central city, we have to conclude, with David Ellwood (1986), that the problem is "race, not space."

Much popular thinking about these issues is rooted in the easy assumption that there are no blacks in the suburbs of major American cities. Yet some blacks have always lived in the suburbs, and their numbers have grown steadily over the past generation. In metropolitan areas of 1 million or more inhabitants, which are the central focus of spatial mismatch theories and which we will hereafter call "large SMSAs," 19 percent of working-age blacks lived outside the central city in 1967. By 1986 the proportion had risen to 27 percent (Bureau of the Census, 1969: Table 1; 1988: Table 31).

---

[17] An alternative explanation of the difference between the Hughes-Madden and Danziger-Weinstein studies is that the suburban wage advantage disappeared in Cleveland and turned negative in Detroit between 1970 and 1980. This explanation strikes us as highly unlikely.

These suburban blacks mostly live in places like Yonkers, Waukegan, and East Palo Alto, not in places like Scarsdale, Winnetka, and Mill Valley. Furthermore, most suburban blacks live next to other blacks, not whites (Massey and Denton, 1988). When we estimate the economic impact of living in the suburbs, therefore, we are mainly estimating the impact of location, not the impact of racial or economic desegregation. If residential location exerts a significant influence on black workers' job opportunities, and if the best jobs open to blacks are now located in the suburbs, blacks who live in the suburbs should experience less unemployment and should earn more money than blacks who live in central cities.

Simply contrasting the unemployment rate or earnings of workers who live in suburbs to analogous statistics for workers who live in central cities cannot, of course, yield definitive estimates of how much residential location influences economic success, because people's earnings affect where they live as well as the other way round. In 1983, for example, the median value of owner-occupied homes was 25 percent higher in suburbs than in central cities, and median monthly rent averaged 19 percent higher in suburbs than in central cities. For blacks, the price differences were even larger: 28 percent for owner-occupied homes and 30 percent for rent.[18]

Price differences between central-city and suburban housing ensure that migration between central cities and suburbs would be somewhat selective even if residential choices had no effect whatever on job opportunities. Family heads with steady, well-paid jobs can afford to live in the suburbs. Family heads who do not have (or cannot keep) such jobs are likely to have trouble finding housing they can afford in the suburbs. Living in the suburbs may also have other important drawbacks for household heads who do not work regularly. The suburbs are farther from friends and relatives who can help out when you are out of money, farther from the welfare and unemployment offices, and provide fewer opportunities for making money illegally. As a result, those who do not work regularly are likely to gravitate to the central city.

Nor are migration patterns between central cities and suburbs likely to depend exclusively on employment status or income. One major reason why parents move to the suburbs is that they think suburban schools are better than inner-city schools. Highly educated parents tend to be even more concerned about the quality of their children's schooling than poorly educated parents with similar incomes. As a result, we would expect that even among families with the same incomes, highly educated parents would

---

[18]These estimates are from the Annual Housing Survey (Bureau of the Census, 1983), renamed the American Housing Survey thereafter. The 1985 survey used the 1980 census as its sampling frame, as well as a new questionnaire. The pre-1983 and post-1983 surveys evidently do not yield comparable estimates of many housing characteristics, and the Census Bureau had not published data from the 1985 or 1987 surveys when we were writing this paper.

be more likely to end up in the suburbs while the less educated would be more likely to end up in the central city.

Estimating the determinants of selective migration requires longitudinal data. Such data exist, but so far as we have been able to discover, no one has used them to analyze black migration between central cities and suburbs.[19] This means that even if we find a relationship between living in the suburbs and economic success we cannot tell how much of the relationship is due to selective migration and how much, if any, is due to the fact that suburbanites have better access to certain kinds of jobs. But if we find *no* difference between those who live in the suburbs and those who live in the central city, it is hard to argue that living in a suburb improves job opportunities.

In 1968, when Kain first proposed the spatial mismatch hypothesis, suburban blacks seem to have been no better off than their central-city counterparts. Harrison (1972, 1974) used data from the Census Bureau's Survey of Economic Opportunity (SEO) to compare men who lived in the central cities and the suburbs of the nation's 12 largest metropolitan areas in 1966. When he compared whites with the same number of years of schooling, he found that central-city men were better off than suburban men, which is what we would expect if there were a lot of selective migration. When he compared nonwhites with the same amount of schooling, however, he found that suburban nonwhites were as likely to be unemployed and earned almost exactly the same amount as central-city nonwhites.

Bell (1974) conducted a similar study of black wives using the SEO. When he controlled a wife's personal characteristics, the size of her family, and her family's income from sources other than her earnings, he found that black wives were slightly *more* likely to have a job if they lived in central cities. Central-city wives who worked also earned slightly more than their suburban counterparts.[20]

These findings suggest that living in a suburb was of little economic value to blacks in the mid-1960s and that migration between central cities

_____

[19]The Panel Study of Income Dynamics (PSID) conducted by the Survey Research Center at the University of Michigan and the National Longitudinal Surveys conducted by the Department of Labor provide annual data on both the residential location and employment status of individuals.

[20]Both Harrison and Bell divided their central-city samples into two groups based on the average income in the neighborhood. As one would expect, central-city men who lived in poor neighborhoods earned less than those who lived in better neighborhoods. In order to focus on the effects of location, we averaged the estimates for central-city poverty and nonpoverty areas and contrasted the resulting means with the suburban means for individuals at the same educational level. Our urban-suburban comparisons for males are only approximate, because Harrison does not report means for either group. He does report regression coefficients, but he does not report either intercepts or insignificant coefficients. As a result, we had to estimate the mean urban-suburban difference from his graphs.

and suburbs was not closely tied to income. The situation may have changed since then, however. Blue-collar employment has continued to leave central cities (Kasarda, 1989). Many manufacturing jobs are now located in relatively remote suburbs accessible only by automobile. Central-city blacks may therefore have more trouble getting reliable information about suburban job openings today than they did in 1966. Commuting to suburban jobs may also consume a larger fraction of a central-city resident's earnings, making such jobs less economically attractive and making migration to the suburbs more attractive.

Every year since 1968 the Census Bureau's Current Population Survey (CPS) has reported the proportion of adults in the central cities and the suburbs who worked full-time throughout the previous year. For our purposes the estimates for large SMSAs are especially relevant, since physical access to remote suburbs is more of a problem in these SMSAs. Table 5-1 shows that in 1967-1971 black men who lived in the central cities of large SMSAs were about as likely to work regularly as blacks who lived in the suburbs surrounding these cities.[21] This is consistent with Harrison's findings. After 1971, however, the percentage of black men with regular jobs fell sharply in the central city while holding steady in the suburbs. Table 5-1 suggests, in other words, that while Kain may have been wrong about the benefits of suburban residence when he published his paper in 1968, he may be right today.

Kasarda (1989) has used CPS data tapes to make analogous calculations for men between the ages of 16 and 64 who were no longer in school, were not in the armed forces, and had not finished high school. In 1969, joblessness among such men averaged 18.8 percent in central cities and 16.3 percent in the suburbs, suggesting that black suburbanites with limited education were not much better off than their central-city counterparts.[22] This finding is consistent with both Harrison's work and Table 5-1. Joblessness among black dropouts rose steadily after 1969 in both central cities

---

[21] The sampling error of the urban-suburban difference for any one year is quite large. In 1967, for example, the CPS estimated that there were 2.1 million black men over the age of 14 in the central cities of SMSAs with 1 million or more inhabitants and 530,000 black men in the suburbs of these SMSAs. The 1967 CPS sampled roughly 0.73 percent of all U.S. households, so it should have sampled about 1,500 blacks in the central cities and 390 in the suburbs of these SMSAs. Since roughly half of all black men in these SMSAs worked full-time, year-round, in 1967, the sampling error of the difference between central cities and suburbs was roughly $[.5^2/1,500 + .5^2/390]^5 = 0.028$. To minimize such random noise, we averaged the results over five-year periods. The sampling error of the mean difference for a five-year interval is roughly 0.013. These sampling errors would be lower if we included blacks in metropolitan areas of less than 1 million, but such areas provide a weaker test of the spatial mismatch model.

[22] We use the term "jobless" to subsume all males who were not working. The term therefore includes both those who were looking for work (the officially "unemployed") and those who were not.

TABLE 5-1  Employment and Earnings of Black Males Aged 14 and Over in SMSAs of 1
Million or More, by Location and Year

|  | Percent Working Full-Time, Year-Round | | | Suburban Earnings as Percent of Central City[a] |
| --- | --- | --- | --- | --- |
|  | Central City | Suburbs | Suburban Advantage | |
| 1967-1971 | 48.8 | 49.3 | .5 | 111.6 |
| 1972-1976 | 41.0 | 46.3 | 5.3 | 110.3 |
| 1977-1981 | 38.9 | 47.4 | 8.5 | 109.1 |
| 1982-1986[b] | 38.6 | 47.7 | 9.1 | 112.8 |

[a]For full-time, year-round workers.
[b]Data not published for 1984.

SOURCE:  Bureau of the Census, Current Population Reports, Series P-60, "Money Income of
Households, Families, and Persons in the United States," annual.

and suburbs, but it rose much faster in central cities than in suburbs. By
1987, 49.5 percent of all black dropouts in central cities were jobless in a
typical month, compared to "only" 33.4 percent in the suburbs.

Kasarda focused on black men who had not finished high school
because the spatial mismatch hypothesis suggests that residential location should be especially important for such men. Black men who have
attended college are likely to work in white-collar jobs, often in the government. These jobs are still concentrated in central cities. If college-
educated suburban blacks also enjoy an economic advantage over their
central-city counterparts, therefore, we would be inclined to attribute the
suburban-urban difference to selective migration rather than to differential
job opportunities.

Table 5-2 shows urban-suburban differences in the mean number of
weeks worked in 1959, 1969, and 1979 by black men with different amounts
of schooling. There is no clear difference between central cities and suburbs
in either 1959 or 1969. This is consistent with Table 5-1 as well as with
both Harrison and Kasarda's findings for the 1960s. By 1979, black men
worked more weeks if they lived in the suburbs than if they lived in central
cities, although the difference among poorly educated blacks was smaller
than the difference Kasarda reported for that period.

The big "news" in Table 5-2 is that suburban residence did as much for
college-educated blacks as for those who had not finished high school. The
apparent benefits of living in a suburb could, of course, reflect selective
migration among college-educated blacks and differential job opportunities
among those with less education. But the most parsimonious explanation
of Table 5-2 is that movement between central cities and suburbs became
more selective at all educational levels during the 1970s.

TABLE 5-2 Weeks Worked by Black Males Living in Metropolitan Areas Aged 18 to 59 Who Were Not in School or in Institutions, by Location, Education, and Year

| | 1959 | | 1969 | | 1979 | |
|---|---|---|---|---|---|---|
| Years of School | Central City | Outside Central City | Central City | Outside Central City | Central City | Outside Central City |
| 0-8 | 39.4 | 40.2 | 39.1 | 41.2 | 30.9 | 31.0 |
| (N) | (903) | (228) | (612) | (174) | (322) | (104) |
| 9-11 | 38.9 | 40.6 | 39.3 | 39.1 | 31.6 | 36.2** |
| (N) | (495) | (80) | (676) | (148) | (611) | (198) |
| 12 | 42.1 | 41.5 | 41.9 | 43.1 | 35.1 | 39.4** |
| (N) | (376) | (51) | (706) | (178) | (878) | (391) |
| 13+ | 45.6 | 41.0 | 43.1 | 45.0 | 40.8 | 43.6* |
| (N) | (159) | (31) | (284) | (84) | (549) | (256) |
| All | 40.2 | 40.5 | 40.5 | 41.8 | 34.9 | 39.0** |
| (N) | (1,993) | (390) | (2,278) | (584) | (2,410) | (949) |

*Urban-suburban differences significant at the 0.05 level.
**Urban-suburban differences significant at the 0.001 level.

NOTE: Estimates exclude roughly one-fourth of all urban blacks who lived in SMSAs for which the Census Bureau does not provide an urban-suburban identifier because of confidentiality requirements.

SOURCE: Census Bureau 1/1,000 Public Use sample.

A second way to test the spatial mismatch hypothesis is to look at black men's earnings when they live in suburbs rather than central cities. If black men have access to better jobs when they live in the suburbs, they should not only work more regularly but earn more when they work. Column 4 of Table 5-1 shows that in large SMSAs black suburban males with steady jobs earned 12 percent more than their central-city counterparts in 1967–1971, 11 percent more in 1972–1976, 9 percent more in 1977–1981, and 13 percent more in 1982–1986.[23] These figures are consistent with the claim that job opportunities are better for suburban men, but they could also be due to selective migration.

Harrison's findings suggest that, at least in the 1960s, the earnings differential between central-city and suburban blacks should disappear once we control educational attainment. To see if this was the case, we calculated weekly earnings by educational level for central-city and suburban blacks

---

[23]The sampling error of the suburban/urban wage ratio for blacks in large metropolitan areas in a given year is about seven percentage points. Averaging over five years reduces the sampling error to about two points. The results in Table 5-1 are thus consistent with the null hypothesis that the underlying ratio did not change from 1967 to 1986.

using 1/1,000 census samples for 1960, 1970, and 1980. Table 5-3 summarizes the results. Like Harrison, we find no significant difference in weekly earnings between central-city and suburban blacks in either 1959 or 1969 once we control education.[24] By 1979, however, black males who had not attended college were earning appreciably more if they lived in suburbs rather than central cities. Table 5-3 is thus consistent with the view that by 1979 unskilled and semiskilled blacks could find better jobs if they lived in suburbs than if they lived in central cities. But it is also consistent with the view that highly paid blacks became more inclined to move to the suburbs after 1970.

Price and Mills (1985) tell a similar story using data from the May 1978 Current Population Survey. They estimated the effect of suburban residence on the earnings of 25- to 59-year-old full-time, year-round workers. With both education and occupation controlled, black males earned 6 percent more if they lived in suburbs rather than central cities, while white males earned 8 percent more.[25] Vrooman and Greenfield (1980) also estimated the effect of suburban residence on black men and women's earnings in the early 1970s, but their sample is so small and unrepresentative that we cannot put much weight on their findings.[26]

---

[24]Table 5-3 shows no difference in weekly earnings between central-city and suburban blacks in either 1959 or 1969, even when we do *not* control education. Table 5-1, in contrast, suggests that regularly employed suburban blacks earned about 10 percent more than central-city blacks in large SMSAs in 1969. We do not know whether the inconsistencies between the two tables are due to differences in geographic coverage, differences in age coverage, or the inclusion of men who did not work full-time, year-round, in Table 5-3.

[25]The small size of Price and Mills's black sample raises troubling questions about its representativeness. They took their data from the May 1978 CPS. At that time the CPS sampled roughly 0.7 percent of all households. The Bureau of the Census (1980) indicates that 2.3 million black men between the ages of 25 and 54 worked full-time, year-round in 1978, so the May CPS should have included at least 1,600 such men. Yet after excluding men who provided less than half their family's total income, Price and Mills ended up with a sample of only 500 such men. Dropping men whose earnings constituted less than half their family's total income could hardly have eliminated 70 percent of all black men who worked full-time, year-round. Something else must be going on here, but we cannot say what. Because the sample is small, the sampling error of the 6.0 percent difference between urban and suburban blacks is 3.6 percent. The 95 percent confidence interval for the difference therefore ranges from a 13.2 percent advantage for suburbanites to a 1.2 percent advantage for central-city residents.

[26]Vrooman and Greenfield used a sample surveyed by the Opinion Research Corporation that included 293 blacks. Almost two-fifths of the black sample lived in suburban areas, which is considerably higher than we would expect on the basis of CPS data. Suburban black males earned 74 percent more than inner-city black males, while suburban black females earned 55 percent more than inner-city black females. No census or CPS survey reports urban-suburban differences of this magnitude. We therefore suspect that the Opinion Research Corporation's sampling frame was unrepresentative for some reason. Assessing Vrooman and Greenfield's results is also complicated by their obscure presentation and by arithmetic errors discussed in Reid (1984).

Almost all these comparisons between central-city and suburban blacks support two broad empirical conclusions:

1.  In the 1960s, central-city blacks did no better economically than comparable suburban blacks.
2.  Since 1970 the economic gap between central-city and suburban blacks has grown appreciably.[27]

These facts are compatible with two very different hypotheses:

1.  The spatial mismatch between black job opportunities and black housing options that Kain described in 1968, while exaggerated at that time, has become quite important since then.
2.  Because social conditions in black central-city neighborhoods deteriorated dramatically between 1965 and 1975, black migration between central cities and suburbs became far more selective than it had previously been.

We cannot choose between these two explanations without new data on selective migration.

Comparing the studies of blacks who *live* in the suburbs with the studies of blacks who *work* in the suburbs, discussed in the previous section, also raises an important puzzle. Both Straszheim and Danziger and Weinstein found that black ghetto residents earned slightly more if they worked in the suburbs rather than the central city in 1965–1970. Yet Bell, Harrison, and our Table 5-3 all indicate that blacks who lived in the suburbs in 1965–1970 earned no more than blacks with the same amount of schooling who lived in central cities. The difference between the two kinds of studies may be due to the fact that they cover different cities or different kinds of workers. But the difference may also mean that living in the suburbs is not strongly associated with working in the suburbs.

This same paradox arises in opposite form in 1980. Most of the evidence we have examined suggests that by 1980 blacks who lived in suburbs earned more per week than blacks with the same amount of education who lived in central cities. Yet Hughes and Madden found that, with all else equal, Cleveland, Detroit, and Philadelphia blacks who worked regularly in 1980 earned no more when they worked far from the center of their SMSA than when they worked near its center. Once again, we need simple descriptive data showing where blacks who live in different parts of an SMSA work, and how much they earn, in order to reconcile these superficially contradictory findings.

If we were to find that blacks could earn more by living in the suburbs, we would also have to ask why so many of them continue to live in central

---

[27]The main apparent exception to this generalization is the data on earnings among full-time, year-round, nonwhite male workers in large metropolitan areas, shown in Table 5-1.

TABLE 5-3 Weekly Earnings (in current dollars) of Blacks in Metropolitan Areas Aged 18 to 59 Who were Not in School or Institutions, and Who Worked in 1959, 1969, or 1979, by Sex, Education, and Location

| Years of School | 1959 | | | 1969 | | | 1979 | | |
|---|---|---|---|---|---|---|---|---|---|
| | Central City | Outside Central City | Ratio | Central City | Outside Central City | Ratio | Central City | Outside Central City | Ratio |
| **Males** | | | | | | | | | |
| 0-8 | 80 | 76 | 0.956 | 129 | 111 | 0.854 | 280 | 325 | 1.162 |
| (N) | (814) | (218) | | (522) | (155) | | (221) | (73) | |
| 9-11 | 80 | 83 | 1.042 | 134 | 139 | 1.037 | 265 | 328 | 1.238 |
| (N) | (444) | (75) | | (589) | (129) | | (491) | (169) | |
| 12 | 83 | 75 | 0.898 | 144 | 143 | 0.993 | 280 | 316 | 1.127 |
| (N) | (354) | (48) | | (645) | (163) | | (704) | (352) | |
| 13+ | 106 | 123 | 1.161 | 186 | 203 | 1.090 | 366 | 368 | 1.004 |
| (N) | (156) | (30) | | (264) | (80) | | (500) | (238) | |
| All | 83 | 81 | 0.981 | 143 | 142 | 0.991 | 299 | 334 | 1.118 |
| (N) | (1,768) | (371) | | (2,020) | (527) | (1,916) | | (832) | |

| | | | | | | | | | |
|---|---|---|---|---|---|---|---|---|---|
| Females | | | | | | | | | |
| 0-8 | 44 | 35 | 0.796 | 76 | 69 | 0.904 | 190 | 164 | 0.862 |
| (N) | (498) | (125) | | (329) | (105) | | (139) | (55) | |
| 9-11 | 47 | 46 | 0.974 | 92 | 84 | 0.914 | 182 | 193 | 1.090 |
| (N) | (400) | (61) | | (515) | (118) | (384) | | (126) | |
| 12 | 57 | 46 | 0.804 | 111 | 96 | 0.861 | 205 | 204 | 0.997 |
| (N) | (322) | (53) | | (730) | (170) | | (858) | (341) | |
| 13+ | 75 | 84 | 1.119 | 139 | 149 | 1.074 | 280 | 278 | 0.994 |
| (N) | (177) | (27) | | (310) | (80) | (580) | | (273) | |
| All | 52 | 45 | 0.861 | 105 | 96 | 0.919 | 221 | 226 | 1.020 |
| (N) | (1,397) | (226) | | (1,884) | (473) | | (1,961) | (795) | |

NOTE: Weekly earnings were estimated by dividing annual earnings by weeks worked. All earnings are in current dollars. The estimates exclude roughly one-fourth of all urban blacks who lived in SMSAs for which the Census Bureau does not provide an urban-suburban identifier because of confidentiality requirements.

SOURCE: Census Bureau 1/1,000 Public Use sample.

cities. The conventional answer is that blacks cannot buy housing in all-white suburbs, or that they do not feel comfortable in such suburbs. Racial discrimination is certainly a real problem, both in the housing market and in the social lives of black suburbanites. But for our purposes the question is not why so few blacks live in white suburbs but why so few live in *black* suburbs and black neighborhoods of racially mixed suburbs. If job opportunities are better for blacks who live in black suburbs, blacks should keep moving to these suburbs until local demand for black workers is saturated and the suburban wage advantage disappears.

Whites have, of course, resisted the growth of black suburban neighborhoods. But they have also resisted the growth of black urban neighborhoods. Our question is therefore comparative: Has white resistance to black residential growth been more effective in the suburbs than in the central cities and, if so, why? The easiest way to answer this question is to investigate whether the supply of black suburban housing has kept pace with demand. If it has not, the price differential between housing in black central-city and black suburban neighborhoods should be greater than the price differential between comparable housing units in white central-city and suburban neighborhoods. The price of housing in black suburbs should also have increased faster over the past 20 years than the price of comparable housing in black central-city neighborhoods.

We have not reviewed the literature on housing prices, but our informal inquiries uncovered no work on trends in the relative price of housing in urban versus suburban black neighborhoods.[28] Unless the price of black suburban housing has risen faster than the price of comparable housing in other areas, it is hard to argue that discrimination has discouraged blacks from moving to black suburban areas—although one can certainly argue that discrimination has discouraged blacks from moving to *white* areas. If discrimination has not discouraged black movement to the suburbs, the basic premise of the spatial mismatch hypothesis needs to be reexamined.

---

[28] Using a 1/1,000 sample of census records, we found that among whites gross rent (i.e., rent plus heat and utilities) in the suburbs exceeded gross rent in the central city by 9 percent in 1960, 10 percent in 1970, and 11 percent in 1980. Among blacks, gross rent averaged 20 percent less in the suburbs than in the central city in 1960, 4 percent more in 1970, and 21 percent more in 1980. If the figures for blacks covered the same housing units in all three years, they would provide strong support for the hypothesis that demand for suburban housing rose faster than supply during this period. In fact, however, the housing stock rented by blacks in 1980 was much larger and of much higher quality than that rented by blacks in 1960. Much of the apparent increase in relative prices may, therefore, reflect improvement in housing quality rather than increased demand for suburban locations. A convincing analysis of this issue would have to compare price trends in specific black, white, and mixed neighborhoods throughout this period. A study of land values in black and white areas would also be instructive.

## WHERE DO WE GO FROM HERE?

We began with four questions:

- How does residential segregation affect demand for black workers?
- How does proximity to work affect the supply of black workers available for employment?
- Can black central-city residents earn more by commuting to the suburbs?
- Can black central-city residents earn more if they live in the suburbs?

Our tentative answers to these questions are as follows.

### Demand for Black Workers

Residential segregation is likely to reduce demand for black workers in white areas and increase demand for black workers in black areas. Whether the net result is to increase or decrease aggregate demand for black workers depends on a number of factors: how strongly whites dislike working in black areas, how strongly blacks dislike working in white areas, whether black customers prefer trading with firms that discriminate in favor of black workers, whether white customers prefer trading with firms that discriminate in favor of white workers, whether firms that mainly hire blacks are more or less productive than firms that mainly hire whites, and hence whether firms prefer hiring relatively cheap labor in the ghetto or more expensive labor in white areas. All these factors are likely to change over time. They also vary from place to place. As a result, we cannot predict the economic consequences of residential segregation by using deductive logic.

When we turn from theory to evidence, we find that the level of residential segregation in a metropolitan area had very little effect on income differences between black and white men in either 1959 or 1969. No one has investigated changes since 1969. Nor has anyone studied the effect of residential segregation on the earnings of black women or black teenagers. Based on what we now know, it is hard to draw any strong conclusions about how residential segregation currently affects demand for black workers. All we can say is that it did not appear to have much impact in 1959 or 1969.

### Job Proximity and Labor Supply

The supply of black workers available to a firm at any given wage rate clearly diminishes as distance from black residential areas increases. But it does not follow that moving black workers closer to major centers of employment would increase the number of blacks taking jobs at any given wage rate.

Comparisons among Pittsburgh and Los Angeles neighborhoods suggest that job proximity has little impact on black men's chances of holding a job. Distance does have an effect on black *teenagers'* chances of working in Philadelphia, Los Angeles, and Chicago, however, and in the best currently available study distance explains 30 to 50 percent of the racial gap in teenage employment rates.

While job proximity does not appear very important for adults in Pittsburgh or Los Angeles, blacks do seem to have done better economically in both 1960 and 1980 when they lived in SMSAs where manufacturing, trade, and service jobs were concentrated in the central city rather than in the suburbs.

### Suburban Versus Central-City Wages

In 1965–1970, ghetto blacks who worked in the suburbs of Cleveland, Detroit, St. Louis, and San Francisco earned about 10 percent more than those who worked in the ghetto. This wage premium was roughly sufficient to cover the extra cost of commuting to the suburbs. In 1980, however, Hughes and Madden found that the overall wage level for *all* black workers was no higher near the periphery of the Cleveland and Philadelphia SMSAs than near the center, and it was slightly lower near the periphery of the Detroit SMSA. The most likely explanation of this apparent contradiction is that for blacks suburban wages were roughly equal to central-city wages in both 1970 and 1980, but that inner-city black workers only commute to the suburbs if they happen to find a job that pays more than they think they could earn nearer home.

### Blacks Who Live in the Suburbs

We found no evidence that suburban blacks fared better than comparable central-city blacks in 1966-1970, when Kain first advanced the spatial isolation hypothesis. Since 1970, however, joblessness has risen faster among central-city blacks than among suburban blacks. We do not know whether this was because of selective migration or because demand for black workers fell more in central cities than in the suburbs.

### Policy Implications

Taken together, these findings tell a very mixed story. They provide no direct support for the hypothesis that residential segregation affects the aggregate level of demand for black workers. They provide some support for the idea that job proximity increases the supply of black workers, but the support is so mixed that no prudent policy analyst should rely on it. Those who argue that moving blacks to the suburbs would improve their job prospects, or that improving public transportation to the suburbs would reduce unemployment in the central-city ghetto, must recognize that there is as much evidence against such claims as for them.

## Future Research

Because of its intuitive appeal, the spatial mismatch hypothesis is unlikely to go away, no matter what the evidence shows. When the evidence is mixed, as it is now, those who find the theory appealing will continue to defend it, and policymakers who find it appealing will continue to listen. Under these circumstances we ought to make a serious effort to improve the quality of the available evidence. Four steps seem especially pressing.

First, since theory suggests that the effects of living in the central-city ghetto are likely to have changed over time, since the available descriptive statistics also point to such changes, and since much of the most widely cited evidence in this debate is now more than 20 years old, we need to use the census, the CPS, and the PSID to assemble time series comparing:

- blacks who live in suburbs to blacks who live in central cities;
- blacks who work in suburbs to blacks who work in central cities;
- blacks who live in very large cities, where the spatial mismatch hypothesis seems likely to have its strongest effect, to blacks who live in smaller cities, where travel time to suburban jobs is likely to be modest;
- blacks who live in cities where most blue-collar jobs are far from the central-city ghetto to blacks who live in cities where most blue-collar jobs are close to the central-city ghetto; and
- blacks who live in highly segregated SMSAs to blacks who live in less segregated SMSAs.

All these tabulations should be broken down by sex, educational level, and age. Having descriptive material of this kind readily available in a Census Bureau publication would do more than almost any piece of primary research to raise the level of both public understanding and scholarly argument about these issues.

Second, we need more fine-grained descriptions of specific cities, including maps that show where workers with specified characteristics earn the most and the least, which neighborhoods have major centers of blue-collar employment, and which neighborhoods have the highest and lowest rates of labor force participation. This is a field where a picture is worth considerably more than a thousand words.

Third, we need to look more carefully at the effects of changes over time in cities' residential and employment patterns. Cross-sectional comparisons among SMSAs can sometimes be instructive, but they have severe limitations. If any one city pursues policies that benefit blacks, its reward will be to attract new black migrants, whose presence will drive up black unemployment and drive down black wages. This means that no city can expect to keep demand for black labor much tighter than the national average for a protracted period (e.g., more than 20 years). It follows that if we want to estimate the effects of *national* policies aimed at keeping manufacturing near the central-city ghetto or at helping central-city blacks move to the suburbs, city-to-city comparisons may lead us badly astray, seriously underestimating the benefits of the policies in question. In order to do better, we need dynamic models that take account of intercity as well as intracity migration.

Fourth, and perhaps most important, we need to investigate the determinants of residential movements between central cities and suburbs. We then need to estimate the contribution of selective migration to employment and earning differences between central-city and suburban blacks. Social scientists' collective failure to take account of selective migration is probably the single most important reason why we have learned so little about this subject in the two decades since Kain first advanced the spatial mismatch hypothesis.

## ACKNOWLEDGMENTS

We are indebted to Bennett Harrison, Harry Holzer, Jonathan Leonard, and Michael Wiseman for comments on earlier drafts of this chapter. The Center for Urban Affairs and Policy Research at Northwestern University provided financial assistance.

## REFERENCES

Bell, Duran, Jr.
　　1974　　Residential location, economic performance, and public employment. Pp. 55-75 in *Patterns of Racial Discrimination*, Vol. 1, George M. Von Furstenberg, Bennett Harrison, and Ann R. Horowitz, eds. Lexington, Mass.: Lexington Books.
Bureau of the Census
　　1969　　Income in 1967 of Persons in the United States. *Current Population Reports*, Series P-60, No. 60. Washington, D.C.: U.S. Department of Commerce.
　　1980　　Money Income of Families and Persons in the United States: 1978. *Current Population Reports*, Series P-60, No. 123. Washington, D.C.: U.S. Department of Commerce.
　　1983　　Financial Characteristics of the Housing Inventory for the United States and Regions: 1983. Annual Housing Survey: 1983, Part C. *Current Housing Reports*, Series H-150-83. Washington, D.C.: U.S. Department of Commerce.

1988 Money Income of Families and Persons in the United States: 1986. *Current Population Reports*, Series P-60, No. 159. Washington, D.C.: U.S. Department of Commerce.

Byrne, James J.
1975 Occupational mobility of workers. *Special Labor Force Report, No. 176.* Washington, D.C.: Bureau of Labor Statistics.

Danziger, Sheldon, and Michael Weinstein
1976 Employment location and wage rates of poverty-area residents. *Journal of Urban Economics* 3:127-145.

Ellwood, David T.
1986 The spatial mismatch hypothesis: Are there teen-age jobs missing in the ghetto? Pp. 147-190 in *The Black Youth Employment Crisis*, Richard B. Freeman and Harry J. Holzer, eds. Chicago: University of Chicago Press.

Farley, John E.
1987 Disproportionate black and Hispanic unemployment in US metropolitan areas. *American Journal of Economics and Sociology* 46:129-150.

Harrison, Bennett
1972 The intrametropolitan distribution of minority economic welfare. *Journal of Regional Science* 12:23-43.
1974 Discrimination in space: Suburbanization and black unemployment in cities. Pp. 21-53 in *Patterns of Racial Discrimination*, Vol. 1, George M. Von Furstenberg, Bennett Harrison, and Ann R. Horowitz, eds. Lexington, Mass.: Lexington Books.

Hughes, Mark Alan
1987 Moving up and moving out: Confusing ends and means about ghetto dispersal. *Urban Studies* 24:503-517.

Hughes, Mark Alan, and Janice Fanning Madden
Forth- Residential segregation and the economic status of black workers: New
coming evidence for an old debate. *Journal of Urban Economics.*

Hutchinson, Peter M.
1974 The effects of accessibility and segregation on the employment of the urban poor. Pp. 77-96 in *Patterns of Racial Discrimination*, Vol. 1, George M. Von Furstenberg, Bennett Harrison, and Ann R. Horowitz, eds. Lexington, Mass.: Lexington Books.

Ihlanfeldt, Keith R.
1988 Intra-metropolitan variation in earnings and labor market discrimination: An economic analysis of the Atlanta labor market. *Southern Economic Journal* 55:123-140.

Ihlanfeldt, Keith R., and David L. Sjoquist
1989 The impact of job decentralization on the economic welfare of central city blacks. *Journal of Urban Economics* 26:110-130.
1990 Job accessibility and racial differences in youth employment rates. *American Economic Review* 80:267-276.

Kain, John F.
1968 Housing segregation, Negro employment, and metropolitan decentralization. *The Quarterly Journal of Economics* 82:175-197.
1974 Reply to Stanley Masters' comment on "Housing Segregation, Negro Employment, and Metropolitan Decentralization." *Quarterly Journal of Economics* 88:511-519.

Kasarda, John
   1989        Urban industrial transition and the underclass. *The Annals of the American
               Academy of Political and Social Science* 501:26-47.
Kirschenman, Joleen, and Kathryn Neckerman
   Forth-      We'd love to hire them, but . . . : The meaning of race for employers.
   coming      In Christopher Jencks and Paul Peterson, eds. *The Urban Underclass*.
               Washington, D.C.: Brookings Institution.
Leonard, Jonathan S.
   1986        Space, Time, and Unemployment: Los Angeles 1980. Unpublished paper,
               School of Business Administration, University of California, Berkeley.
   1987        The interaction of residential segregation and employment discrimination.
               *Journal of Urban Economics* 21:323-346.
Massey, Douglas S., and Nancy A. Denton
   1988        Suburbanization and segregation in U.S. metropolitan statistical areas. *Amer-
               ican Journal of Sociology* 94(3):592-626.
Massey, Douglas S., and Mitchell L. Eggers
   1989        The ecology of inequality:  Minorities and the concentration of poverty
               1970-1980. National Opinion Research Center, University of Chicago.
Masters, Stanley H.
   1974        A note on John Kain's "Housing Segregation, Negro Employment, and
               Metropolitan Decentralization." *Quarterly Journal of Economics* 88:505-519.
   1975        *Black-White Income Differentials: Empirical Studies and Policy Implications*.
               New York: Academic Press.
Mooney, Joseph D.
   1969        Housing segregation, Negro employment, and metropolitan decentralization:
               An alternative perspective. *Quarterly Journal of Economics* 83:299-311.
National Center for Educational Statistics
   1988        *Digest of Educational Statistics*. Washington, D.C.: U.S. Government Printing
               Office.
Offner, Paul, and Daniel H. Saks
   1971        A note on John Kain's "Housing Segregation, Negro Employment, and
               Metropolitan Decentralization." *The Quarterly Journal of Economics* 191:147-
               160.
Price, R., and E. S. Mills
   1985        Race and residence in earnings determination. *Journal of Urban Economics*
               17:1-18.
Reid, Clifford
   1984        Are blacks making it in the suburbs? *Journal of Urban Economics* 16:357-359.
Straszheim, Mahlon R.
   1980        Discrimination and the spatial characteristics of the urban labor market for
               black workers. *Journal of Urban Economics* 7:119-140.
Vrooman, John, and Stuart Greenfield
   1980        Are blacks making it in the suburbs? Some new evidence on intrametropoli-
               tan spatial segmentation. *Journal of Urban Economics* 7:155-167.
Wilson, William Julius
   1987        *The Truly Disadvantaged*. Chicago: University of Chicago Press.

# 6
# Ghetto Poverty and Federal Policies and Programs

MICHAEL G.H. MCGEARY

Other chapters in this report have reviewed what is known about the geographic and socioeconomic dimensions of concentrated urban poverty in the United States and its effects on children and adults. This chapter reviews the evidence concerning several additional questions that must be addressed in a policy analysis of concentrated urban poverty: What effects, if any, have federal policies and programs had on the concentration of poverty in central-city ghettos of the United States? What role could they have in reducing concentration or alleviating its negative effects?

The United States does not have a true urban policy in the sense of a set of comprehensive federal policies and programs that explicitly try to influence the size, location, or internal spatial structure of urban settlements as such (Mills, 1987). As a result, private market forces play the predominant role in shaping urban areas. Some policies and programs, however, such as those for urban mass transportation, are explicitly intended to increase the mobility of poor people, and many other, nonurban policies have indirect or unintended spatial effects (Barro, 1978; Glickman, 1980; Mills, 1987; Tolley et al., 1979; Vaughan, 1977a, b; Vaughan and Vogel, 1979).

Mills (1987) reviewed the evidence and found that federal policies have probably had an insignificant impact on the overall level of urbanization in the United States, compared with the effects of the private market. Mills concluded, however, that in the aggregate, federal policies and programs have influenced the shape or pattern of urbanization by reinforcing and extending private market forces that encourage the suburbanization of employment growth and of better-off residents of metropolitan areas (p. 568). Another review concluded that federal policies have favored the development of new and growing regions over older, settled regions and thereby caused older cities in the Northeast and Midwest to experience higher unemployment and poverty rates than they otherwise would have (Glickman and Wilson, 1986:22-25).

To the extent that they actually have accelerated or increased the suburbanization of employment and population within urban areas, and given the income and racial barriers facing poor people who try to move out of a central city, federal policies and programs have tended to reinforce the growing concentration of the poor and minorities in central cities relative to what would have occurred in their absence. Policies and laws against segregation have enabled many better-off minorities to move out of the inner city (Jaynes and Williams, 1989:Ch.4). Well-designed education and training programs could increase the earnings of low-skilled residents of poverty areas, enabling them to move out also. Such programs, however, are limited in size. Few are targeted enough to reach many residents of high-poverty neighborhoods.

## FEDERAL POLICIES AND PROGRAMS THAT PROMOTE OR FAIL TO PREVENT INCOME SEGREGATION

The research on federal housing policies and programs, policies against housing discrimination, and transportation, economic development, and welfare programs is reviewed in this section for evidence of effects on the geographic concentration of poverty. Federal policies and programs have tended to promote concentration indirectly, for example, by encouraging the suburbanization of the better-off while having little or no direct effect in the opposite direction (e.g., through increasing low-income housing in the suburbs or commuting of the poor across city lines).

### Housing

Because housing links all households to a specific location, federal housing policies and programs could have a direct effect on the clustering of low-income households in particular areas of central cities. The deductibility of mortgage interest from federal taxes, for example, has promoted the suburbanization of higher income homeowners by making more expensive housing in the suburbs relatively cheaper for them (Mills, 1987:564-565), which in turn gives further impetus to the concentration of the poor in central cities. Historically, the low-rent public housing program has contributed directly to the concentration of poverty by locating high-rise projects in poorer and minority sections of central cities and, later, by lowering income ceilings. In addition, the early practices of the Federal Housing Administration, which adopted the racially discriminatory practices of private real estate and mortgage lending institutions, helped to create predominantly white suburbs and increase the concentration of minorities in older, less expensive housing in central cities (Lief and Goering, 1987:228-231; Orfield, 1974).

### Tax Treatment of Housing

The federal tax code and many state tax codes have permitted homeowners to deduct mortgage interest from their income before determining their tax liability. Because the federal tax schedule is progressive, housing-related deductions are worth more to high-income owners than low-income owners. Although suburbanization has occurred in the metropolitan areas of other advanced industrialized countries, it has proceeded further in the United States, led by high-income households (Mills, 1987:563). Making housing relatively less costly for high-income than for low-income owners adds to the incentives for high-income homeowners to live in suburbs in which they can consume expensive housing where land is cheaper, receive expensive local government services, and at the same time, use zoning and other land-use controls to avoid subsidizing low-income taxpayers. To the extent that federal tax policies have increased the suburbanization of high-income households relative to poor households, they have reinforced the concentration of the poor in central cities.

### Federal Housing Subsidy Programs

The 1.3 million units in low-rent public housing projects account for a third of all publicly subsidized housing units, and most of them—72 percent—are located in central cities (Rasmussen, 1980:261). These projects probably account for many of the census tracts that had poverty rates of 60 percent or more in 1980, and, to the extent that public housing residents are less mobile than other residents of high-poverty tracts, contributed to the large increase in concentrated poverty between 1970 and 1980. For example, 59 percent of the households in the census tract containing the Cabrini-Green high-rise public housing project in Chicago had lived in the same housing unit between 1975 and 1980, compared with 40 percent in the surrounding poverty tracts without high-rise public housing.

In addition, a series of federal policy changes beginning with the Brooke amendment of 1969 lowered income limits for households in public housing. This enabled people with very low incomes to afford public housing and increased the supply of housing for such households. It also populated family projects with predominantly low-income rather than mixed-income residents.

The 1.3 million units built by more recent supply-side federal housing programs (e.g., Section 236, Section 202, and Section 8 New Construction and Rehabilitation) are less concentrated in central cities. Nevertheless, more than half these units are in central cities, but because they tend to be in smaller projects and more scattered, they are less concentrated within central cities.

Special attempts were made to locate Section 8 New Construction in the suburbs. An evaluation using 1979 data found that, while 88 percent of the residents of central-city projects had come from the central city, 40 percent of the residents of projects built in the inner suburbs had come from the central city, which resulted in a net shift of 10 percent of households in the program from the central cities to the suburbs. Participating black households moved to census tracts in which the minority share of the population was 19 percentage points less, on average. Black families, however, benefited much less than single and elderly blacks. They decreased the minority percentage of their census tracts by only 7 points on average, from 37 to 30 percent. A strong correlation remained between minority concentration in the Section 8 New Construction projects and minority concentration in the census tracts in which the projects were located (Newburger, 1987:Table 11, using data from Wallace et al., 1981).

In recent years, federal low-income housing policy has shifted to demand-side, or voucher-type, rent supplement programs, largely because of the high per-unit cost of supply-side programs but also in the hope that providing assistance directly to low-income families would encourage mobility and reduce income and racial segregation. These programs will be more important in the future, because new construction of low-income housing with federal funds has almost ceased. The number of commitments for new supply-side rental subsidies was less than 18,000 in 1986, down from more than 180,000 a year in the late 1970s (Newburger, 1987:Table 8b).

The effects of demand-side programs on mobility have been limited, however. For example, analyses of the effects of the federally funded Housing Assistance Supply Experiment on mobility and desegregation by income and race found that about 40 percent of the renters participating in the program in St. Joseph County, Indiana, moved in an 18-month period, but that was less than the 54 percent that researchers estimated would have moved without the program (Lowry, 1983:212-218). Nearly two-thirds of the 3,600 moves were within the same group of neighborhoods and averaged less than a mile. The rest of the moves were between neighborhoods that differed in degree of segregation, but the net shift toward majority or 95 percent white neighborhoods was just 98 renters. Those moves did not noticeably affect the racial or income composition of any of the neighborhood populations, even in the group of neighborhoods in which more than one-fifth of all households were enrolled and even though 12 percent of all the renters in the county received housing allowances.

The Housing Assistance Supply Experiment, also supported by the

Department of Housing and Urban Development, randomly assigned participants in Phoenix and Pittsburgh to treatment and control groups, which allows a direct comparison of the effects of housing allowances on mobility and desegregation by income and race. The control groups exhibited high mobility rates; 35 percent moved in Pittsburgh and 53 percent moved in Phoenix over two years. The provision of housing allowances increased mobility another 5 percentage points in Pittsburgh and 10 percentage points in Phoenix (Rossi, 1981:168, using data from MacMillan, 1978:57). Although participants, on average, moved into neighborhoods that had fewer poor and minorities and better amenities, including transportation, they were no more likely to do so than control households (Rossi, 1981:170).

In the Section 8 Existing Housing program, an early evaluation found that half the black households that moved went to areas with lower percentages of black residents and 29 percent went to areas with higher percentages (Drury et al., 1978:74). In the absence of controls, however, the possibility cannot be ruled out that low-income movers without Section 8 housing certificates were just as likely to go to less segregated areas as the control group members were in the housing-allowance experiment.

Historically, federal housing supply programs for low-income households have contributed to concentrated poverty in central cities because they were more likely to be located in neighborhoods that were already poor, although recent programs have tended to be more dispersed within central cities and within most metropolitan areas. Supply-side subsidies go with the unit rather than the tenant, and the number of units is small compared with the number of eligible households. There is some evidence that tenants of subsidized housing are less likely to move, probably because they would lose a significant benefit. There is little evidence that voucher-type, demand-side programs by themselves enable recipients to move to neighborhoods less segregated by income or race (compared with the poor in private housing). Mobility rates are probably higher than in subsidized projects, however.

### Residential Desegregation

Title VIII of the Civil Rights Act of 1968 prohibited racial and other discrimination in the sale or rental of most housing. In 1968 the Supreme Court decided in the *Jones v. Mayer* case (392 U.S. 409) that the Thirteenth Amendment of the Constitution banned racial discrimination in all housing. These laws, along with favorable changes in the racial attitudes of whites (Schuman et al., 1985:Table 3.3; Taylor et al., 1978) and higher economic status among some minorities (R. Farley, 1984), enabled many minorities to move in the 1970s to higher income tracts, which were more likely to be suburban. This outward movement of minorities lowered the high levels of residential segregation by only a little, however, because suburbanizing minorities tended to move to neighborhoods that were already minority or were becoming minority. And minority suburbanization resulted in increased income segregation within minority groups, with the poorer among them remaining in central cities.

Between 1970 and 1975 there was a net out-migration of 243,000 blacks from central cities; between 1975 and 1980 it was 439,000. There was net in-migration of blacks to the suburbs of 381,000 between 1970 and 1975 and of 556,000 between 1975 and 1980 (Bureau of the Census, 1981:Table F). Most of the increase in the number of black suburbanites resulted from migration from central cities (Spain and Long, 1981). As a result, the black proportion of the suburban population increased from 4.8 to 6.1 percent (Long and DeAre, 1981:Table 1). Only 20 percent of the black population lived in the suburbs in 1980, however, compared with 42 percent of the nonblack population.

According to the index of dissimilarity, which measures how evenly a minority group is distributed over census tracts within a metropolitan area on a scale from 0 to 100, spatial segregation of blacks from whites decreased. In a sample of the 50 largest MSAs (metropolitan statistical areas) plus 10 MSAs with large Hispanic populations, the index went from 79.2 in 1970 to 69.4 in 1980, a drop of 12.4 percent (Massey and Denton, 1987:Table 3). In the 161 MSAs that had populations that were at least 4 percent black, the index went from 74 to 68, a drop of 8 percent (Wilger, 1987:6). The index went down in all regions and in all metropolitan areas whether grouped by size, rate of population growth, size of minority population, or rate of minority in-migration (R. Farley and Wilger, 1987:Table C; Massey and Denton, 1987:Table 4). The absolute level of black-white segregation remained very high, however. Nearly 70 percent of blacks would have had to move to achieve complete integration in 1980 in the 60 cities studied by Massey and Denton.

The indices for black-white dissimilarity were especially high in the five northeastern and midwestern metropolitan areas whose central cities experienced large increases in concentrated poverty during the 1970s. On average (unweighted for size), the index went from 84.4 to 83.4. In Chicago it fell from 91.9 to 87.8, in Philadelphia from 79.5 to 78.8, and in Detroit from 88.4 to 86.7. In New York it increased from 81.0 to 82.0, and in Newark it increased from 81.4 to 81.6.

Another dimension of residential segregation is exposure, or the likelihood that minorities will encounter a white resident or another minority resident in their home census tract. Despite the higher proportion of minorities in metropolitan areas in 1980 compared with 1970, exposure indices increased slightly. The average probability of blacks interacting with non-Hispanic whites, for example, increased from .333 in 1970 to .376 in 1980 in the 60 large metropolitan areas studied by Massey and Denton (1987:Table 1). Isolation, or the probability of contact with other blacks, fell from .553 to .491.

In MSAs with high and fast-growing levels of concentrated poverty in their central cities, the isolation of blacks was especially high, even in 1980. In the Chicago MSA, for example, the level of black isolation was .828 (it was .855 in 1970). The probability of contact with whites was .125, a bare improvement over 1970, when it was .118 (Massey and Denton, 1987:14). Although the level of isolation was lower in the New York, Detroit, Philadelphia, and Newark MSAs than in Chicago in 1980, it had actually increased (the unweighted average for the four metropolitan areas was .675 in 1970, .697 in 1980), and the probability of interaction with whites had fallen (from .245 to .211) (calculated from Massey and Denton, 1987:Table 1).

Black suburbanization also did not have much impact on the level of residential segregation in the suburbs (Wilger, 1987:15). Segregation of blacks from whites across suburbs was nearly as great in 1980 as in 1970 (Logan and Schneider, 1984:Table 1). Apparently, blacks were moving to suburban neighborhoods that were either already black or in the midst of racial transition (see J. Farley, 1982, and Lake, 1981, for studies of this process in St. Louis and New Jersey, respectively).

The timing of the suburban movement of blacks indicates that federal fair housing laws were a factor (McKinney and Schnare, 1986:16-17; Wilger, 1987:18-19). Black incomes grew rapidly in the 1960s, from 55 percent of white incomes, on average, to 64 percent, but segregation levels increased overall and in neighborhoods at each income level; the proportion of blacks living in lower income census tracts fell only from 85 percent to 80 percent (McKinney and Schnare, 1986:Tables 4, 5, 6). In the 1970s the ratio of median black income to median white income fell from 61 percent to 58 percent, yet the movement of blacks out of lower income census tracts and central cities increased greatly.

The proportion of housing built in an MSA after 1969 might also contribute to lower levels of residential segregation. Most new housing is built in large tracts by a single owner, which makes it easier to enforce fair housing laws. New tracts are also less likely to be racially labeled and may not deter prospective white buyers fearful of racial transition or black buyers reluctant to be the first blacks in an all-white neighborhood (Wilger, 1987:13). Indeed, the greater the proportion of housing built after 1969 in an MSA, the greater the decrease in the index of dissimilarity between 1970 and 1980. Where the proportion of new housing was 30 percent or more in 1980, the index fell more than 11 percent in the 1970s. If the proportion of new housing was less than 15 percent, the index fell only 1 percent. If new housing amounted to between 15 and 30 percent of the stock, the index fell between 5 and 8 percent (Wilger, 1987:Table 3).

Although the level of residential segregation did not decrease much despite black suburbanization, the income disparities between suburban blacks and central-city blacks increased sharply in the 1970s. Average household income for central-city blacks fell from 92 percent of that of suburban blacks in 1970 to 78 percent in 1980 (among whites it went from 84 to 81 percent) (Manson and Schnare, 1985:Table II-9). This trend occurred at a time when inequality of income distribution among blacks was increasing (Jaynes and Williams, 1989:275). It is consistent with the finding that increases in the concentration of poverty between 1970 and 1980 were caused in large part by out-migration of better-off minorities as well as whites.

Federal civil rights laws and policies helped many better-off minorities move to the suburbs. Only a few moved to predominantly white suburbs, however. Segregation levels remained high in metropolitan areas, especially for blacks. At the same time, the movement of working- and middle-class blacks out of ghetto areas into higher income neighborhoods in central cities and the suburbs, especially in the Midwest and the Northeast, increased income segregation among blacks. One result was the further concentration of poor blacks and other minorities in central-city poverty neighborhoods. Reducing the income segregation of minorities presumably would require policies and programs that increase the supply of affordable housing as well as overcome racial discrimination in higher income neighborhoods in the central cities and suburbs.

## Transportation

In 1980 federal assistance accounted for a major portion of government spending on urban transportation: 40 percent of capital expenditures on urban highways, 80 percent of capital assistance for urban mass transit, and 30 percent of mass transit operating subsidies (Gomez-Ibanez, 1985:183). Annual federal capital expenditures (in 1984 dollars) on highways, which were $11 billion in 1980, had peaked in 1965 at $16 billion and had declined steadily during the 1970s as the interstate highway system was completed (Congressional Budget Office, 1985:Fig. 7). But half of the 1,200 uncompleted miles in the interstate system are in urban areas (Congressional Budget Office, 1985:14-15). Federal capital and operating expenditures for mass transit grew rapidly from small beginnings in 1964, increasing 40 percent annually in the 1970s to more than $2.8 billion in 1980 (Congressional Budget Office, 1985:42). Operating subsidies began in 1974, and new subway systems were built in Atlanta, Baltimore, Miami, San Francisco, Washington, D.C., and begun in Los Angeles and San Jose.

### Highways

Federal assistance in the construction of highways has helped to reduce the cost of commuting by automobile (Vaughan and Vogel, 1979:94-95). Although the main purpose of the interstate highway system is to improve the intercity transportation system, the urban segments of the system are used most by suburbanites to travel to work in central cities and in the suburbs (Mills, 1987:563). Beltways and radial freeways (and radial transit systems) provide much higher travel-to-work cost savings to suburban households than to central-city households. This enables the growing number of white-collar jobs that require relatively high levels of education and skills to locate in central business districts without a commensurate increase in the number of nonpoor households in the central city (Small, 1985:212-213).

Although urban highway users as a group more than pay for the capital and operating expenses of those highways through fuel taxes, rush-hour commuters to the densely settled central cities of larger metropolitan areas probably pay less than the full costs because downtown highway segments are very expensive to build and maintain and their external social costs are high (Gomez-Ibancz, 1985:199). This encourages excessive highway use and permits workers to live farther from their place of employment than if they paid the full user charge (Mills, 1987:563; Vaughan and Vogel, 1979:94-95). Although the net impact of federal highway programs on the spatial extent of suburbanization has been large, the impact on the proportion of the population living in suburbs may have been much less. However, it may have promoted the suburbanization of high-income households, for whom lower transportation costs facilitate paying more for housing.

### Mass Transit

The federal government became involved in the support of urban mass transportation to help cities maintain their financially failing mass transit systems and discourage the use of private automobiles (Hilton, 1974:3). Mass transit has also been expected to increase the mobility of the poor (as well as the elderly and the handicapped) and to improve land use by promoting more concentrated urban development (Gomez-Ibanez, 1985:206).

Despite the large increases in federal mass transit operating subsidies beginning in the 1970s, increases in ridership gains have been modest, and the impact on automobile use has been negligible. At the same time, federal operating subsidies have helped the poor only marginally by lowering transit fares. Since 1975 only 24 percent of additional government subsidy dollars have gone to reduce fares; the rest supported low-ridership service expansions to new suburban markets or went to higher factor prices (e.g., higher wage rates and fuel costs) and to compensate for lower productivity within the industry (Cervero, 1985; Pickrell, 1986). The frequency of bus service in many central cities was cut back (Pickrell, 1983). In addition, most of the federal capital subsidies have gone to aid subways and commuter rail projects rather than bus systems, which are used most by the poor (Pucher, 1981:Table 3).

Only 23 percent of federal operating assistance went to low-income users in 1983; most long-distance, peak-hour commuters were individuals from upper income groups who used the more costly subway and commuter rail services. Only 8 percent of commuter rail users were poor, for example. Accordingly, travelers from low-income households received a federal subsidy of 12 cents per transit trip compared with 20 cents a transit trip for persons from households with incomes of $50,000 or more (Charles River Associates, 1986, quoted in Urban Mass Transportation Administration, 1987:29). Moreover, new and extended subway systems appear to have the same impact as radial freeways, although to a lesser extent (Gomez-Ibanez, 1985:209). They stimulate high-rise office development and, therefore, employment in the downtown area, while favoring the suburbanization of higher income households (Small, 1985:213).

In 1980 only 6.4 percent of all workers nationwide used public transit (down from 9 percent in 1970), but transit use was much higher in the Northeast, where more than 14 percent of workers used it (Fulton, 1983). More than 45 percent of the workers in the New York MSA relied on public transit in 1980, and they accounted for 28 percent of all workers using transit in the United States. Workers in the Chicago area had the next highest reliance on public transit—18 percent. Only 10 other MSAs had more than 10 percent of their workers using public transit, most of them in the Northeast or the Midwest.

Fewer workers rode mass transit in 1980 than in 1970, however. The net loss nationally of metropolitan workers using transit was 487,000, but metropolitan areas in the Northeast lost 596,000 and in the Midwest 211,000. Public transit in the New York MSA alone lost 355,000 workers (17 percent). In the Chicago MSA, public transit lost 82,000 (13 percent), in Philadelphia 108,000 (28 percent), and in Detroit 61,000 workers (49 percent).

Another study of public transit ridership in 1970 and 1980 in the 25 largest urbanized areas found that there was a substantial gain in the number of workers using mass transit to commute from suburban homes to central-city jobs, but it was more than offset by the loss of central-city

TABLE 6-1  Number of Workers Using Public Transit in the 25 Largest Urbanized Areas, by Origin and Destination, 1970 and 1980

| Type of Trip | 1970 (000) | 1980 (000) | Difference | Percentage Change |
|---|---|---|---|---|
| Central-city home to central-city job | 3,230.2 | 2,727.0 | −503.2 | −15.6 |
| Suburban home to central-city job | 686.5 | 1,014.0 | +327.5 | +47.7 |
| Central-city home to suburban job | 343.0 | 192.6 | −150.4 | −43.8 |
| Suburban home to suburban job | 503.8 | 357.4 | −146.4 | −29.1 |

NOTES:  Public transit includes bus/streetcar, subway/elevated rail, commuter railroad, and taxi.  Workers are all persons aged 16 years or older living in the 25 largest urbanized areas who use mass transit to get to work.  "Urbanized areas" include the central city and only that part of the surrounding suburban area with at least 1,000 persons per square mile.  MSA boundaries include entire counties and thus can include rural areas.  This criterion excludes the thinly settled outer fringes of metropolitan areas.  It should be noted that work-related trips account for less than half of all trips on public transit.

SOURCE:  Calculated from Joint Center for Political Studies (1985), Tables M-70 and M-80.

workers using mass transit (Joint Center for Political Studies, 1985). There were also losses in the number of "reverse commuters," those using public transit to get from central-city residences to suburban jobs, and in the number of workers using public transit to commute within the suburbs (Table 6-1).

The precise impact of these changes in transit use patterns on central-city poor people is unknown. The reduced number of work trips within central cities and between central cities and suburbs may be accounted for by workers who moved from the central cities to the suburbs during the 1970s, but the resulting cutback in bus schedules in the central cities would have reduced the mobility of those left in the central cities. This may have been a factor in the reduction in earnings among families remaining in high-poverty tracts.

According to the Federal Highway Administration's 1977-1978 Nationwide Personal Transportation Study, households with low incomes (less than $6,000 a year) constituted 12 percent of travelers using all forms of transit but 25 percent of the users of public transit (Pucher et al., 1981). Poor people also accounted for 27 percent of all taxi trips, more than higher income groups. However, they relied on transit for less than 7 percent of all trips (8.3 percent of all work trips) and on taxis for 0.5 percent of all trips. Poor people were much more likely to travel by car (66 percent of all trips) or by foot (23 percent).

Noting the low use of public transit by the poor, the high cost of subsidizing low fares for all regardless of income, and the limits of public transit systems in providing transportation for central-city workers to suburban job locations, analysts of federal transportation policies have recommended the use of user subsidies, in conjunction with paratransit alternatives, to meet the needs of poor, elderly, and handicapped people (Altshuler, 1979; Congressional Budget Office, 1979; Kirby, 1981; Kirby et al., 1975; Meyer and Gomez-Ibanez, 1981). User subsidies permit designated groups of individuals to buy rides from a provider at reduced fares by using a voucher, token, or scrip that the provider can redeem at full-fare value from the subsidizing agency. Paratransit modes include taxis, car and van pools, and dial-a-ride services.

During the late 1970s, the Urban Mass Transportation Administration funded a number of demonstrations and case study evaluations of user subsidies, usually shared-ride taxi services for elderly and handicapped people. Evaluations of these federal demonstrations and case studies of local initiatives showed that such programs were feasible, reached the most transit-dependent and reduced their travel costs, and were more flexible than fixed-route transit (Spear, 1982). These programs, however, were not true experiments and, in the absence of control groups, it is impossible to know what the real effects were. None of the demonstrations took place in a large urban area, and only one included poor people (Santa Fe). There was also an indication that, although the unit costs of subsidizing a dial-a-ride or shared taxi trip may be lower, the increase in demand from those previously unable to afford or use conventional fixed-route transit can result in large total program costs (Echols, 1985:85-87). Costs can be controlled by limiting per-trip subsidies or the number of trips or by restricting eligibility, but such limitations reduce the effectiveness of the program or create inequities.

In summary, the federally financed freeway system has enabled those able to afford an automobile to live at a distance from their jobs in the suburbs and provided incentives to the very poor to stay in central cities, where low-cost public transit, primarily buses and taxis, is more available. Federal subsidization of fixed-rail transit, justified in part as a means of helping the poor, has probably had the primary effect of enabling well-educated, highly skilled suburbanites to reach white-collar service jobs that are concentrating in central cities. Radial transit systems, whether subways or highways, are not well suited for reverse commuting from the central city to low-skilled employment in the suburbs. Meanwhile, federal operating subsidies have tended to go to expanding suburban bus service, while bus service within central cities has been reduced.

## Economic Development[1]

Historically, federal infrastructure programs (e.g., highways; sewage and water treatment facilities) and tax policies (e.g., investment tax credits that favor construction of new plant and facilities over rehabilitation; tax exemption of industrial development bonds) have reinforced private market forces that have promoted the suburbanization of jobs and higher income people (Vaughan and Vogel, 1979). At the same time, economic development programs aimed at revitalizing central business districts and blighted neighborhoods have not had much of a countervailing impact (Mills, 1987:565-566).

Cost-effective public actions to foster economic activity in particular locations are difficult to develop and implement, and public intervention in the economic decisions of firms has uncertain effects and tends to be costly. Federal strategies usually focus on providing preferential tax treatment for firms that locate in specified places or hire workers with particular characteristics. Policies toward urban enterprise zones, for example, try to encourage businesses to locate in depressed areas and to hire unemployed or underemployed workers by providing tax subsidies to the employing organization. A voluminous literature on the economics of firm location, however, finds nearly universally that taxes are too small a component of firm costs or even of firm profits to have much impact on location decisions (Leonard, 1986:Ch. 5). Other variables—labor costs, site acquisition costs, transportation costs—tend to exhibit substantially more variation across sites than tax variables can (Advisory Commission on Intergovernmental Relations, 1981; Carlton, 1983; Kieschnick, 1981; Schmenner, 1982). Tax relief has relatively little capacity to compensate for higher labor costs, higher construction or site acquisition costs, higher transport costs, or higher energy costs.

Firms that can be influenced to locate in or near areas of concentrated poverty will tend to bring jobs that cannot break the cycle of concentrated poverty. Any firm whose location decisions are sensitive to modest differences in tax benefits is one that faces intense competition. Such firms tend to be unreliable because they can easily be influenced to change locations again in response to foreign wage reductions, fluctuations in foreign exchange rates, and a host of other factors beyond the control of their host communities. Also, the jobs they can offer a community are often in low-skill and low-paying manufacturing activities that offer little training or prospect for advancement or growth and little in the way of benefits. Full-time, year-round employment in many of these jobs will not get a poor family above the poverty line.

---

[1] This section is based on material prepared by Herman B. Leonard.

Even if firms can be induced to locate in areas of concentrated poverty, they may not hire the most disadvantaged residents. Even in areas of concentrated poverty, many of the residents are not below the poverty line. Many are employed, some in skilled occupations. Creating new opportunities for appropriate employment closer to where they live may result in shifts in their employment location rather than an increase in employment among those not currently employed.

The jobs that are needed—moderate-skill, light manufacturing in growing firms with reasonably assured future prospects—are the hardest to identify and nurture. High-skill jobs are beyond the reach of most who live in areas of concentrated poverty; those who have such skills in occupations for which firms have open slots have, for the most part, found their way into good jobs and out of concentrated poverty. There are moderate-skill jobs (custom light manufacturing jobs, like printing, rebuilding car parts, and assembling scaffolding) that can be mastered relatively quickly but that require some skill, provide some training, and that can pay reasonably high wages. Firms doing that kind of work, however, tend to be small, hard to identify, and difficult to assess. They have a high rate of business failure. Trying to specify programs whose subsidies could be targeted on that subset of these firms that can be expected to be successful and to provide long-term, stable employment would almost surely result in subsidies flowing to many firms that will come to depend on public support for their competitive edge and their continued existence, or alternatively, the subsidies may go to support activities that would have taken place anyway. Such substitution effects have been found in federal economic development programs (Congressional Budget Office, 1983:47).

In short, the prospects for using public intervention to create economic development in areas of concentrated poverty as a means of increasing the employment of the very poor are not promising, although the strategy may work in certain situations.

### Welfare

Income maintenance transfers, which are mostly federally financed (including Aid to Families With Dependent Children [AFDC], Supplemental Security Income [SSI], food stamps, local general assistance, energy assistance, refugee assistance, and earned-income tax credits) have been a growing component of income in the United States. Income transfers increased from .92 percent of total personal income in 1969 to 1.28 percent of total personal income in 1984 (Garnick, 1988:Tables 12, 14). In the same period, in the central counties of MSAs, which contain the central cities, income maintenance transfers increased from 1.09 percent to 1.54 percent of personal income.

Between 1970 and 1980 in the 50 largest central cities, the number of families with public assistance income who were living in high-poverty areas increased from 129,568 to 309,117. More important, the proportion of families with public assistance income who were living in high-poverty areas increased from 30.2 percent to 42.5 percent, and the proportion of families with earnings income fell from 74.4 percent to 62.6 percent, which indicates a greater reliance on welfare during the time period among families living in high-poverty areas (calculated from Bureau of the Census, 1973, 1985).

Welfare benefits for similar recipients differ from state to state, even though welfare programs are funded mostly with federal dollars, because federal welfare policies permit a high degree of local discretion in setting payment levels and eligibility requirements. In 1985, for example, the maximum AFDC benefit that a family of four could receive in California was $698 a month, nearly five times the maximum benefit the same family could receive in Mississippi. The addition of food stamps reduces the interstate variation by about half, because food stamp benefit levels are nationally uniform, but the combined benefits for a family of four in California are still double those in Mississippi (P. Peterson and Rom, 1988:27).

The influence of these interstate differences in benefit levels on the migration patterns of the poor has been a much-studied subject. Using a variety of data sets, variables, and statistical techniques, most early studies did not find a significant effect of high benefit levels on in-migration to states or metropolitan areas (for a review of the leading studies, see P. Peterson and Rom, 1987:22-27). The few that did find migration effects had methodological shortcomings. Researchers also discovered that black interstate migrants to big cities, including migrants from the South, were less likely to be poor or on welfare than blacks born in the states in which the cities were located (Long, 1974, using 1970 census data). Several studies of New York found that most recipients who had migrated to New York City had not applied for welfare until several years after arrival (DeFerranti et al., 1974; Ostow and Dutka, 1975).

Studies of decisions to migrate have found that the primary determinants of migration patterns are differences in employment opportunities and wage rates, although other factors, such as local spending and taxing policies, weather conditions, pollution levels, and differences in other amenities, are also significant. Differences in unemployment and wage rates, however, were larger factors in explaining in-migration than out-migration. In-migration, for example, is stimulated by low unemployment rates, but out-migration is insensitive to locally high unemployment rates (see review of research in Vaughan and Vogel, 1979:28-31), even though the unemployed move more than any other group (Bureau of the Census, 1981:3).

In 1969 the Supreme Court ruled in *Shapiro v. Thompson* (394 U.S. 618) that states could not impose duration-of-residence requirements (typically one year) on applicants for AFDC and that new state residents are, therefore, immediately eligible for AFDC (assuming they meet the other eligibility requirements). Recent studies that have focused on trends since the Supreme Court decision have found that differential welfare benefits have statistically significant migration effects (Blank, 1988; Gramlich and Laren, 1984; P. Peterson and Rom, 1987). The interstate differences in benefits for recipients in similar circumstances can be quite large, even taking into account differential wage and tax rates (Blank, 1985). The migration effect, while significant, is small but could result in substantial cumulative effects over time. Few AFDC beneficiaries move to another state over a five-year period, for example, but when they do move they are much more likely to go to a state with higher AFDC benefits (Gramlich and Laren, 1984:505-506). The studies also found, however, that policymakers in high-benefit states reduce benefit levels in the face of in-migration by the poor (Gramlich and Laren, 1984; P. Peterson and Rom, 1987).

Assuming that differences in state welfare benefits have a significant long-term effect on the distribution of poor people, they could have increased the concentration of the poor in central cities if those moving in order to take advantage of higher benefits had a propensity to settle in central cities. There are some published data providing evidence that this occurs. According to a Census Bureau report on geographic mobility in the United States, for example, 9.1 percent of the 3.3 million households on welfare in 1979 had moved to a central city from somewhere else between 1975 and 1980 (a few from other central cities), compared with 4.1 percent of the nonwelfare households (calculated from Bureau of the Census, 1981:Table 35). (And, as discussed below, welfare households already living in central cities were much less likely to move out than nonwelfare households.) Unfortunately, the published data do not permit a similar comparison of poor and nonpoor households or of where households that were poor in 1975 ended up in 1980 in comparison with nonpoor households. The published data also do not show the flows of public assistance recipients in and out of high-poverty tracts within central cities.

The main factors in the growth of concentrated poverty during the 1970s were (1) out-migration of the nonpoor at a higher rate than the poor from tracts that were or became high-poverty tracts and (2) increasing poverty among existing residents of those tracts. It is, however, impossible to tell from the net migration data in the published reports on high-poverty areas how much the in-migration of poor people from outside the central city was replacing some of the poor people who left concentrated poverty tracts, thereby keeping concentration levels higher than they would have been and contributing to the higher proportion of welfare recipients in high-poverty areas in 1980 than in 1970.

The final possibility is that differences in welfare benefits and the availability of other programs benefiting poor people in central-city poverty areas slowed their out-migration from high-poverty areas. One of the early studies of welfare effects on migration, for example, found that receipt of public assistance reduced the tendency of poor families to leave a central city and that the low rate of out-migration contributed to the growing concentration of welfare recipients within central cities (Long and Heltman, 1976, cited in Vaughan and Vogel, 1979:32). A recent analysis of data from the Census Bureau's Survey of Income and Program Participation (Clark, 1988) found that welfare recipients, especially AFDC recipients, are significantly less likely to move to another state. That study controlled for characteristics common to welfare recipients that also act to inhibit out-migration (racial minority status, having young children, less education, receiving public housing assistance, and not being in the labor force). It also controlled for characteristics that tend to increase mobility (youth and female-headed family structure).

Census data on geographic mobility between 1975 and 1980 show that 65 percent of the households receiving public assistance in 1979 had moved, compared with only 51 percent of nonwelfare households. The central-city households receiving public assistance, however, were much more likely to move within the same central city (47 percent compared with 23 percent of nonwelfare households) and much less likely to move out of the metropolitan area. After five years, 82 percent of the public-assistance households remained in the same city, 5 percent moved to the central city of another MSA, and 13 percent moved outside the central city to a suburb or nonmetropolitan area. Among households not receiving public assistance in 1979, the comparable figures were 72 percent, 5 percent, and 24 percent (calculated from Bureau of the Census, 1981:Table 35).

Finally, a number of federally subsidized programs and services for poor people are relatively more available in central cities. The historical legacy of low-income, high-rise public housing and its role in concentrating poverty in poor, minority neighborhoods of central cities, and the tendency of recipients of housing allowances or vouchers to make only short moves to areas similar in racial composition and income, have already been discussed. Bus and taxi services, which are disproportionately used by poor people, are also most available in central cities. Other social and health services subsidized with federal funds are disproportionately located in central cities. During the 1970s most of the federal funding for community health centers went to centers in central cities, and about half the federal funding for maternal and child health (MCH) services was earmarked for special projects in urban areas for maternity and infant care and for child and youth services (replaced after 1981 by MCH block grants) (G. Peterson et al., 1986:Ch. 5). Many community mental health centers are also located in central cities, as are many community action agencies that administer community service and low-income energy assistance programs (G. Peterson et al., 1986:Ch. 3, 4). State and local general assistance and medical assistance programs also vary in some states and tend to be both more available and more generous in central cities (Burke, 1987:63-66).

Services and programs for poor people are usually located in central-city poverty areas because that is where the people who need them are. But a number of studies using data from the 1960s found that high expenditures for local public services were associated with higher in-migration and lower out-migration, especially among poor and minority households. Wealthy white households tended to leave or avoid high-expenditure localities, apparently because of the high tax rates usually associated with high public expenditures (Cebula, 1974, 1979; Greenwood and Sweetland, 1972; Pack, 1973).

In summary, whether or not the greater availability of welfare, social, health, and other services for poor people in central cities relative to suburbs or rural areas played a role in attracting poor in-migrants during the 1970s, it may have played an inadvertent role in slowing the out-migration of the poor (see Kasarda, 1985, 1988). This effect, if it existed at all, was probably very small, not least because most programs reached small proportions of those in poverty. Some of the services, such as education and training and other human-capital investment programs, which are reviewed in the next section, may have enabled more people to escape dependence and migrate out than the number of people that such programs may have "anchored" in central cities.

## FEDERAL PROGRAMS THAT COULD REDUCE POVERTY CONCENTRATION

Some federal programs that are or could be targeted at central-city poverty areas have the potential of increasing the long-range ability of poor people to increase their incomes and move into nonpoverty areas. Such programs include education and employment training programs.

### Education

Family income has a positive association with the academic achievement of children and their subsequent earnings (Sewell and Hauser, 1975). A recent study of the effects of parental characteristics on the educational achievement of children and their economic success when they grow up (using longitudinal data from the Panel Study of Income Dynamics conducted by the University of Michigan's Survey Research Center—PSID) confirms the positive but modest effect of family income on achievement and income. In addition, a spell of family poverty has an independent and strong negative impact on the achievement, earnings, and income of sons (Corcoran et al., 1987:Table 4). The same study, as well as an earlier one using PSID data (Datcher, 1982), also found that neighborhood characteristics, such as high unemployment rates, high welfare participation rates, and high proportion of female-headed families, as measured at the zip code level, have a negative effect on educational attainment and income (Chapter 4 in this volume discusses these studies).

Given that the poor and minorities are concentrated in central cities, that public schools are locally controlled by each community in a metropolitan area, and that federal policies do not require the transportation of poor students to nonpoor schools across community boundaries, it is not surprising that central-city schools have a disproportionate share of poor students. The federal government funds two major education programs aimed at counteracting the educational disadvantage of poor children and of low-achievers in poor schools: Head Start and Chapter 1 of the Education Consolidation and Improvement Act (formerly Title 1 of the Elementary and Secondary Education Act of 1965).

Head Start, which began with the Economic Opportunity Act of 1964, is a preschool program that provides year-round, comprehensive education and other child development services (medical, dental, nutritional, social) to children from poor families or families that would qualify for AFDC if they did not have child care assistance. The program costs about $1.2 billion a year in federal funds and serves about 460,000 three- to five-year-olds a year (but only a fifth of them are in full-day programs) (U.S. Congress, 1985:341). Although more than 90 percent of the participants are below the poverty line, the program reaches just 20 percent of all poor preschool children in a given year. The program is operated by local school systems and nonprofit sponsors; it is not aimed at cities per se, and an unknown percentage of the funding goes to programs located in central cities.

A number of research studies have found that preschool programs for disadvantaged children, some of them Head Start programs, can have immediate effects on cognitive test scores compared with control groups, but these effects disappear after several years. They also can achieve longer term gains on other indicators of school success (the Head Start studies are synthesized in Aitken et al., 1985; studies of other preschool programs in Lazar and Darlington, 1978; Lazar et al., 1982). Head Start children are, for example, less likely to be placed in special education programs or to repeat a grade. A follow-up study of one of the best-known non-Head Start experiments, the Perry Preschool Project, found that poor children in the project had higher employment rates and lower rates of criminal behavior when they were 19 years old than individuals in the control group (but the sample sizes were very small) (Barrueta-Clement et al., 1984).

The Chapter 1 education program serves almost 5 million children in elementary and secondary schools, at a cost of $4.3 billion in 1988. Chapter 1 is intended to support special compensatory services for low-achieving students in schools with high concentrations of poor children. The focus of the program is consistent with research evidence that there is a strong association between family poverty and average achievement in a school and only a weak association with individual student achievement (Kennedy et al., 1986a:3-4, citing a review of studies of the relationship between socioeconomic status and academic achievement by White, 1982). Chapter 1 funds are distributed in proportion to the number of poor children in a school district. The district, in turn, provides special services to children, poor or nonpoor, of low educational achievement in schools with above-average concentrations of poverty. The services provided are primarily basic skills instruction in reading and mathematics for elementary school students (Birman et al., 1987:Ch. 3).

Schools with as few as 10 low-income students are eligible for Chapter 1 services, and more than 90 percent of the school districts in the United States participate. Nevertheless, because funding is proportional to the number of poor students in a school district, the poorest quartile of districts contains 45 percent of the students receiving Chapter 1 services. Central-city districts, which have 26 percent of all students, have 37 percent of the Chapter 1 students. Still, 13 percent of schools with more than half their students in poverty offer no Chapter 1 services, and some schools with Chapter 1 services have very few poor students (Birman et al., 1987:Ch. 2).

In a single year, about 11 percent of school-aged children are served by Chapter 1, but, with a 40 percent turnover rate annually, an estimated 25 percent of all public school students receive services at some point (Kennedy et al., 1986b:7). There are no recent data on the proportion of Chapter 1 recipients who are poor.

Academic achievement, at least as measured by standardized tests, dropped substantially from the mid-1960s until the mid-to-late 1970s (Congressional Budget Office, 1986:Ch. 3). In the subsequent upturn in test scores, minority students, students in schools with a high proportion of minorities, and students in disadvantaged urban areas made greater relative gains than other students (Congressional Budget Office, 1986:Ch. 4). Some researchers have attributed the gains to federal funding because the pattern of increases in achievement scores paralleled patterns of increased federal financial support (LaPointe, 1984; Riddle, 1984). Only one evaluation, using data from 1976-1979, followed a set of students over time, including comparable students who did not receive Chapter 1 services (there are no evaluations of the program's impact using a randomly selected control group). The study found that Chapter 1 students, especially in the early grades, gained relative to comparable students, but not enough to bring them close to the achievement levels of advantaged students. A more recent cross-sectional study without a comparison group found more substantial gains relative to advantaged students, but again the gains were not enough to bring Chapter 1 students close to the level of the average student (both studies are reanalyzed and their methodological shortcomings discussed in Kennedy et al., 1986b:Ch. 3). A careful evaluation of the research evidence by the Congressional Budget Office (1987:94-98) concluded that Chapter 1 services could have contributed only a small amount to the upturn in test scores of minorities and of students in the early grades.

In summary, federally subsidized education programs aimed at poor students and poor schools can improve the educational achievement and attainment and, therefore, the future employment and income prospects of poor children, including those in poor neighborhoods. Any impact on the concentration of poverty would be long term, however, and the magnitude of that impact would depend on how large and well targeted the programs were on poor families in areas of concentrated poverty and on how well designed and well delivered the programs were. As already noted, Head Start reaches about 20 percent of poor children aged three to five years; Chapter 1 reaches about 25 percent of all school-aged children at some point. The proportion of Chapter 1 students that are poor is unknown, but it is known that some schools with concentrations of poor children do not participate and that nonpoor children participate in other schools. The formulas for distributing program funds do not try to target the funding geographically but spread the program widely. The variation among individual Head Start and Chapter 1 projects in their effects is considerable, and their average impact would be increased appreciably if less effective programs performed as well as more effective programs (Kennedy et al., 1986a:Ch. 5).

## Training

Federal involvement in employment and training programs began in the Great Depression. The federal-state Employment Service has long existed to address the short-term, or frictional, unemployment of those temporarily between jobs. Many other federal employment and training programs were created to reduce cyclical unemployment caused by downturns in the business cycle. The most pertinent programs for residents of concentrated poverty areas, however, are those intended to reduce the long-term, or structural, unemployment of low-skilled workers (Bassi and Ashenfelter, 1986).

Despite the long history of federal involvement in training programs, few programs have been subjected to experimental analysis using randomly assigned control groups. Some of those that have, however, demonstrate significant positive and cost-effective results, including the National Supported Work Demonstration, the state welfare-to-work experiments inspired by the supported work experiment, and the Job Corps.

The National Supported Work Demonstration ran from 1975 through 1979 in 15 sites. It subsidized highly structured and closely supervised work experiences that gradually became more demanding until they approximated regular private employment. The program had the most positive impact on the long-term employment and earnings of enrollees from two target groups, long-term AFDC recipients and former drug addicts (there was no postprogram impact on the two other target groups, former offenders or young school dropouts). The AFDC recipients averaged about nine months in the program. Eighteen months later, 42 percent of the enrollees were employed, compared with 35 percent of the control group members. Enrollees worked 62 hours a month on average, compared with 46 hours among control group members, and they averaged $248 a month in earnings, about $81 more than the control group average (Hollister et al., 1984:Table 4.6). Similar results were obtained by the former drug users (Hollister et al., 1984:Table 5.5).

The Supported Work Demonstration was also cost-effective for the AFDC recipients and former drug users. In the long run, the costs of the program were far outweighed by the higher income and reduced dependence on welfare payments of the AFDC recipients and by the higher income and reduced criminal activity of the former drug users (Hollister et al., 1984:Table 8.6).

The Manpower Demonstration Research Corporation, which was created to run and evaluate the Supported Work Demonstration, has subsequently conducted experimental evaluations of a number of state-level programs aimed at increasing the employment of AFDC recipients. Those programs, which rely on relatively inexpensive interventions (e.g., job clubs), have proven in most cases to have a significant and cost-effective impact, although the impact is typically modest (Gueron, 1987).

The Job Corps, which was established in 1964, is a residential program for school dropouts between ages 14 and 21 that provides them with basic education, vocational skills, and health care for an average of 30 months per participant. About 90 percent of the enrollees are from poor or welfare-dependent households, more than 75 percent are minorities, and 30 percent are female (Betsey et al., 1985:110-116, describe the program and assess evaluations of it). An evaluation in 1982 by Mathematica Policy Research found that participants in the Job Corps did better than comparison group members along several dimensions that can be attributed to the program

(Mallar et al., 1982). After three and a half years, for example, Job Corps enrollees were employed an average of 26 weeks a year, compared with 23 weeks among nonparticipants; they earned an average of $2,592 (1977 dollars), compared with $2,025 among nonparticipants; and they had less income from welfare or unemployment. Moreover, they experienced better health and were arrested less often for serious crimes. After an initial six-month period after completing the program, when enrollees did worse than the comparison group members, these outcomes emerged and persisted during the rest of the four-year follow-up (Betsey et al., 1985:112, summarizing Mallar et al., 1982).

Like educational programs, carefully designed and targeted training programs have the potential of increasing the career earnings of low-skilled, disadvantaged residents of concentrated poverty areas and enabling them to move to nonpoor neighborhoods. The most successful of the programs (Job Corps, Supported Work), however, are very expensive and pay for themselves only in the long run. The state welfare demonstration programs are cheaper, but their impact is much more modest.

## CONCLUSION

Historically, federal policies and programs have had five main if unintentional effects on the spatial distribution of poverty. First, federal programs have favored the suburbanization of higher income people relative to lower income people, thereby reinforcing the concentration of poor people, many of them minorities, in central cities. Second, federal actions have encouraged the development of new areas in the South and the West relative to the older, developed metropolitan areas in the Midwest and the Northeast. The economies of the latter regions have declined in relative and, in some cases, absolute terms; as a result, poverty has increased in the central cities of those regions and it has become even more difficult for poor people there to escape poverty through work. Third, some federal programs, such as high-rise public housing projects, have had the direct effect of concentrating poverty, especially after changes in the income eligibility rules drastically reduced the average income levels in public housing after 1969. Fourth, after 1968, fair housing laws helped nonpoor minorities to leave ghetto areas, which contributed to the dramatic increase in concentrated poverty among central-city minorities during the 1970s. Fifth, some federal policies intended to increase the mobility of poor families, such as housing vouchers and mass transit subsidies, have not had the expected effect of reducing residential or income segregation. Other programs, such as AFDC, may have the unintended effect of discouraging mobility. There is evidence, however, that programs that improve the education and training skills of the poor can increase the career earnings of low-skilled residents of high-poverty areas and thus enable them to move to nonpoor neighborhoods, although these programs are limited in size and are not well targeted geographically to high-poverty ghettos.

## REFERENCES

Advisory Commission on Intergovernmental Relations
    1981    *Regional Growth: Interstate Tax Competition*. Report No. A-76. Washington,
            D.C.: Advisory Commission on Intergovernmental Relations.
Aitken, Sherrie S., Ruth Hubell McKey, Larry Condelli, Harriet Ganson, Barbara J. Barrett,
Catherine McConkey, and Margaret C. Plantz
    1985    *The Impact of Head Start on Children, Families and Communities: Final
            Report of the Head Start Evaluation, Synthesis and Utilization Project*. Report
            prepared by CSR, Inc., for the Head Start Bureau. Washington, D.C.: U.S.
            Department of Health and Human Services.
Altshuler, Alan A., with James P. Womack and John R. Pucher
    1979    *The Urban Transportation System: Politics and Policy Innovation*. Cambridge,
            Mass.: MIT Press.
Barro, Stephen M.
    1978    *The Urban Impacts of Federal Policies. Vol. 3, Fiscal Conditions*. Report No.
            R-2114-KF/HEW. Santa Monica, Calif.: Rand Corporation.
Barrueta-Clement, John R., Lawrence H. Schweinhart, W. Steven Barnett, Ann S. Epstein,
and David P. Weikart
    1984    *Changed Lives: The Effects of the Perry Preschool Program on Youths Through
            Age 19*. Ypsilanti, Mich.: High/Scope Press.
Bassi, Laurie J., and Orley Ashenfelter
    1986    The effect of direct job creation and training programs on low-skilled
            workers. Pp. 133-151 in *Fighting Poverty: What Works and What Doesn't*,
            Sheldon H. Danziger and Daniel H. Weinberg, eds. Cambridge, Mass.:
            Harvard University Press.
Betsey, Charles L., Robinson G. Hollister, Jr., and Mary R. Papageorgiou, eds.
    1985    *Youth Employment and Training Programs: The YEDPA Years*. Committee
            on Youth Employment Programs, National Research Council. Washington,
            D.C.: National Academy Press.
Birman, Beatrice F., Martin E. Orland, Richard K. Jung, Ronald J. Anson, Gilbert N.
Garcia, Mary T. Moore, Janie E. Funkhouser, Donna Ruane Morrison, Brenda J. Turnbull,
and Elizabeth R. Reisner
    1987    *The Current Operation of the Chapter 1 Program*. Washington, D.C.: U.S.
            Department of Education.
Blank, Rebecca M.
    1985    The impact of state economic differentials on household welfare and labor
            force behavior. *Journal of Public Economics* 28(Fall):25-58.
    1988    The effect of welfare and wage levels on the location decisions of female-
            headed households. *Journal of Urban Economics* 24:186-211.
Bureau of the Census
    1973    *Low-Income Areas in Large Cities*. 1970 Census of Population, Subject
            Report PC(2)-9B. Washington, D.C.: U.S. Department of Commerce.
    1981    *Geographical Mobility: March 1975 to March 1980*. Current Population
            Reports, Series P-20, No. 368. Washington, D.C.: U.S. Department of
            Commerce.

1985    *Poverty Areas in Large Cities.* 1980 Census of Population, Subject Report PC80-2-8D. Washington, D.C.: U.S. Department of Commerce.

Burke, Vee
1987    *Cash and Noncash Benefits for Persons with Limited Incomes: Eligibility Rules, Recipient and Expenditure Data, FY 1984-86.* Report No. 87-759 EPW. Washington, D.C.: Congressional Research Service.

Carlton, Dennis
1983    The location and employment choices of new firms. *Review of Economics and Statistics* 65(August):440-449.

Cebula, Richard J.
1974    Local government policies and migration: An analysis for SMSAs in the United States, 1965-1970. *Public Choice* 19(Fall):85-93.
1979    *The Determinants of Human Migration.* Lexington, Mass.: Lexington Books.

Cervero, Robert
1985    The anatomy of transit operating deficits. *Urban Law and Policy* 6(January): 477-497.

Charles River Associates
1986    Allocation of Federal Transit Operating Subsidies to Riders by Income Group. Draft research report submitted to the Urban Mass Transportation Administration.

Clark, Rebecca
1988    Outmigration Among Welfare Recipients. Paper presented at conference on Individuals and Families in Transition: Understanding Change through Longitudinal Data, sponsored by the Social Science Research Council, Annapolis, Md., March 16-18.

Congressional Budget Office
1979    *Urban Transportation for Handicapped Persons: Alternative Federal Approaches.* Washington, D.C.: U.S. Government Printing Office.
1983    *The Federal Government in a Federal System: Current Intergovernmental Programs and Options for Change.* Washington, D.C.: U.S. Government Printing Office.
1985    *The Federal Budget for Public Works Infrastructure.* Washington, D.C.: U.S. Government Printing Office.
1986    *Trends in Educational Achievement.* Washington, D.C.: U.S. Government Printing Office.
1987    *Educational Achievement: Explanations and Implications of Recent Trends.* Washington, D.C.: U.S. Government Printing Office.

Corcoran, Mary, Roger H. Gordon, Deborah Laren, and Gary Solon
1987    Intergenerational Transmission of Education, Income, and Earnings. Institute of Policy Studies, University of Michigan.

Datcher, Linda
1982    Effects of community and family background on achievement. *The Review of Economics and Statistics* 64(February):32-41.

DeFerranti, David M., et al.
1974    *The Welfare and Nonwelfare Poor in New York City.* Report No. R-1381-NYC. New York: New York City-Rand Institute.

Drury, M., O. Lee, M. Springer, and L. Yap
1978    *Nationwide Evaluation of the Existing Housing Program.* Washington, D.C.: U.S. Department of Housing and Urban Development.

Echols, James C.
    1985      Use of private companies to provide public transportation services in
              Tidewater Virginia. Pp. 79-100 in *Urban Transit: The Private Challenge to
              Public Transportation*, Charles A. Lave, ed. San Francisco: Pacific Institute
              for Public Policy Research.
Farley, John E.
    1982      Metropolitan housing segregation in 1980: The St. Louis case. *Urban Affairs
              Quarterly* 18(March):347-359.
Farley, Reynolds
    1984      *Blacks and Whites:  Narrowing the Gap?*  Cambridge, Mass.:  Harvard
              University Press.
Farley, Reynolds, and Robert J. Wilger
    1987      Recent Changes in the Residential Segregation of Blacks From Whites:
              An Analysis of 203 Metropolises. Background report prepared for the
              Committee on the Status of Black Americans, National Research Council,
              Washington, D.C.
Fulton, Philip N.
    1983      Public transportation: Solving the commuting problem? Pp. 1-9 in *Trans-
              portation Research Record 928*. National Research Council. Washington,
              D.C.: Transportation Research Board.
Garnick, Daniel H.
    1988      Local area economic growth patterns: A comparison of the 1980s and
              previous decades. Pp. 199-254 in *Urban Change and Poverty*, Michael G. H.
              McGeary and Laurence E. Lynn, Jr., eds. Committee on National Urban
              Policy, National Research Council. Washington, D.C.: National Academy
              Press.
Glickman, Norman J., ed.
    1980      *The Urban Impacts of Federal Policies*. Baltimore: Johns Hopkins University
              Press.
Glickman, Norman J., and Robert H. Wilson
    1986      National contexts for urban economic development. Pp. 15-36 in *Local
              Economies in Transition: Policy Realities and Development Potentials*, Edward
              M. Bergman, ed. Chapel Hill: University of North Carolina Press.
Gomez-Ibanez, Jose A.
    1985      The federal role in urban transportation. Pp. 183-223 in *American Domestic
              Priorities: An Economic Appraisal*. John M. Quigley and Daniel L. Rubinfeld,
              eds. Berkeley: University of California Press.
Gramlich, Edward M., and Deborah S. Laren
    1984      Migration and income redistribution responsibilities. *Journal of Human
              Resources* 19(October):489-511.
Greenwood, Michael J., and D. Sweetland
    1972      The determinants of migration between standard metropolitan statistical
              areas. *Demography* 9(November):665-692.
Gueron, Judith M.
    1987      *Reforming Welfare With Work*. Occasional Paper 2, Ford Foundation Project
              on Social Welfare and the American Future. New York: Ford Foundation.
Hilton, George W.
    1974      *Federal Transit Subsidies: The Urban Mass Transportation Assistance Program*.
              Washington, D.C.: American Enterprise Institute.

Hollister, Robinson G., Peter Kemper, and Rebecca A. Maynard, eds.
  1984     *The National Supported Work Demonstration.* Madison: University of Wis-
           consin Press.
Jaynes, Gerald D., and Robin M. Williams, Jr., eds.
  1989     *A Common Destiny: Blacks and American Society.* Committee on the
           Status of Black Americans, National Research Council. Washington, D.C.:
           National Academy Press.
Joint Center for Political Studies
  1985     Demographic Change and Worktrip Travel Trends. Vol. II, Statistical tables.
           Report prepared for the Urban Mass Transportation Administration under
           cooperative agreement DC-09-7009. Joint Center for Political Studies,
           Washington, D.C.
Kasarda, John D.
  1985     Urban change and minority opportunities. Pp. 33-67 in *The New Urban
           Reality.* Paul E. Peterson, ed. Washington, D.C.: Brookings Institution.
  1988     Jobs, migration, and emerging urban mismatches. Pp. 148-198 in *Urban
           Change and Poverty,* Michael G. H. McGeary and Laurence E. Lynn, Jr.,
           eds. Committee on National Urban Policy, National Research Council.
           Washington, D.C.: National Academy Press.
Kennedy, Mary M., Richard K. Jung, and Martin E. Orland
  1986a    *Poverty, Achievement and the Distribution of Compensatory Education Services.*
           Washington, D.C.: U.S. Department of Education.
Kennedy, Mary M., Beatrice F. Birman, and Randy E. Demaline
  1986b    *The Effectiveness of Chapter 1 Services.* Washington, D.C.: U.S. Department
           of Education.
Kieschnick, Michael
  1981     *Taxes and Growth: Business Incentives and Economic Development.* Wash-
           ington, D.C.: Council of State Planning Agencies.
Kirby, Ronald F.
  1981     Targeting money effectively: User-side transportation subsidies. *Journal of
           Contemporary Studies* 4(Winter):45-52.
Kirby, Ronald F., Kiran U. Bhatt, Michael A. Kemp, Robert G. McGillivray, and Martin
Wohl
  1975     *Para-Transit: Neglected Options for Urban Mobility.* Washington, D.C.: Urban
           Institute.
Lake, Robert W.
  1981     *The New Suburbanites: Race and Housing in the Suburbs.* Rutgers University.
           New Brunswick, N.J.: Center for Urban Policy Research.
LaPointe, Archie E.
  1984     The good news about American education. *Phi Delta Kappan* 65(June):663-
           668.
Lazar, Irving, and Richard B. Darlington
  1978     *Lasting Effects After Preschool.* Report of the Consortium for Longitudinal
           Studies. Washington, D.C.: U.S. Department of Health, Education, and
           Welfare.
Lazar, Irving, Richard Darlington, Harry Murray, Jacquiline Royce, and Ann Snipper
  1982     Lasting effects of early education. *Monograph of the Society for Research
           in Child Development,* Vol. 47, Nos. 2-3, Serial No. 195. Washington, D.C.
           Society for Research in Child Development.

Leonard, Herman B.
    1986    Checks Unbalanced: The Quiet Side of Public Spending. New York: Basic
            Books.
Lief, Beth J., and Susan Goering
    1987    The implementation of the federal mandate for fair housing. Pp. 227-267
            in Divided Neighborhoods: Changing Patterns of Racial Segregation. Gary A.
            Tobin, ed. Vol. 32, Urban Affairs Annual Reviews. Newbury Park, Calif.:
            Sage Publications.
Logan, John R., and Mark Schneider
    1984    Racial segregation and racial change in American suburbs, 1970-1980.
            American Journal of Sociology 89:874-888.
Long, Larry H.
    1974    Poverty status and receipt of welfare among migrants and nonmigrants in
            large cities. American Sociological Review 39(February):46-56.
Long, Larry H., and Diane DeAre
    1981    The suburbanization of blacks. American Demographics 3 (September):17-21.
Long, Larry H., and Lynne R. Heltman
    1976    Do Welfare Payments Reduce Migration Potential? Paper presented at
            the Annual Meeting of the American Sociological Association, New York,
            August.
Lowry, Ira S., ed.
    1983    Experimenting with Housing Allowances: The Final Report of the Housing
            Assistance Supply Experiment. Cambridge, Mass.: Oelgeschlager, Gunn &
            Hain.
MacMillan, Jean
    1978    Mobility in the Housing Allowance Demand Experiment. Draft report. Abt
            Associates, Cambridge, Mass.
Mallar, C., S. Kerachsky, C. Thornton, and D. Long
    1982    Evaluation of the Impact of the Job Corps Program, Third Follow-up
            Report. Mathematica Policy Research, Princeton, N.J.
Manson, Donald M., and Ann B. Schnare
    1985    Change in the City-Suburb Income Gap, 1970-1980. Project Report. Wash-
            ington, D.C.: Urban Institute.
Massey, Douglas S., and Nancy A. Denton
    1987    Trends in residential segregation of blacks, Hispanics, and Asians: 1970-1980.
            American Sociological Review 52(Dec):802-825.
McKinney, Scott, and Ann B. Schnare
    1986    Trends in Residential Segregation by Race: 1960-1980. Project Report.
            Washington, D.C.: Urban Institute.
Meyer, John R., and Jose A. Gomez-Ibanez
    1981    Autos, Transit, and Cities. Cambridge, Mass.: Harvard University Press.
Mills, Edwin S.
    1987    Non-urban policies as urban policies. Urban Studies 24(December):561-569.
Newburger, Harriet B.
    1987    The Impact of Federal Housing Programs on Black Americans. Background
            report prepared for the Committee on the Status of Black Americans,
            National Research Council, Washington, D.C.
Orfield, Gary
    1974    Federal policy, local power and metropolitan segregation. Political Science
            Quarterly 89(Winter):777-785.

Ostow, Miriam, and Anna B. Dutka
    1975    *Work and Welfare in New York City*. Baltimore: Johns Hopkins University
            Press.
Pack, Janet Rothenberg
    1973    Determinants of migration to central cities. *Journal of Regional Science*
            13(August):249-260.
Peterson, George E., Randall R. Bovbjerg, Barbara A. Davis, Walter G. Davis, Eugene C.
Durman, and Theresa A. Gullo
    1986    *The Reagan Block Grants: What Have We Learned?* Washington, D.C.:
            Urban Institute.
Peterson, Paul E., and Mark C. Rom
    1987    Federalism and Welfare Reform: The Determinants of Interstate Differences
            in Poverty Rates and Benefit Levels. Paper presented at the Annual Meeting
            of the American Political Science Association, Chicago, September 3-6,
    1988    The case for a national welfare standard. *Brookings Review* 6(Winter):24-32.
Pickrell, Don H.
    1983    The Causes of Rising Transit Operating Deficits. Report MA-11-0037. John
            F. Kennedy School of Government, Harvard University, Cambridge, Mass.
    1986    Federal operating assistance for urban mass transit: Assessing a decade
            of experience. Pp. 1-10 in *Transportation Research Board 1078*. National
            Research Council. Washington, D.C.: Tranportation Research Board.
Pucher, John
    1981    Equity in transit finance: Distribution of transit subsidy benefits and costs
            among income classes. *Journal of the American Planning Association* 47:387-
            407.
Pucher, John, Chris Hendrickson, and Sue McNeil
    1981    Socioeconomic characteristics of transit riders: Some recent evidence. *Traffic
            Quarterly* 35(July):461-483.
Rasmussen, David W.
    1980    The urban impacts of the Section 8 Existing Housing assistance program.
            Pp. 243-263 in *The Urban Impacts of Federal Policies*, Norman J. Glickman,
            ed. Baltimore: Johns Hopkins University Press.
Riddle, W.
    1984    *Achievement Score Trends and Federal Involvement in Elementary and Sec-
            ondary Education: An Exploration of Their Relationships*. Report No. 84-627
            EPW. Washington, D.C.: Congressional Research Service.
Rossi, Peter H.
    1981    Residential mobility. Pp. 147-172 in *Do Housing Allowances Work?* Katharine
            L. Bradbury and Anthony Downs, eds. Washington, D.C.: Brookings Insti-
            tution.
Sewell, William H., and Robert M. Hauser
    1975    *Education, Occupation and Earnings*. New York: Academic Press.
Small, Kenneth A.
    1985    Transportation and urban change. Pp. 197-223 in *The New Urban Reality*,
            Paul E. Peterson, ed. Washington, D.C.: Brookings Institution.
Schmenner, Roger W.
    1982    *Making Business Location Decisions*. Englewood Cliffs, N.J.: Prentice-Hall.
Schuman, Howard, Charlotte Steeh, and Lawrence Bobo
    1985    *Racial Attitudes in America: Trends and Interpretations*. Cambridge, Mass.:
            Harvard University Press.

Spain, Daphne, and Larry H. Long
    1981      *Black Movers to the Suburbs: Are They Moving to Predominantly White
              Suburbs?* Special Demographic Analysis. Washington, D.C.: Bureau of the
              Census.
Spear, Bruce D.
    1982      User-side subsidies: Delivering special-needs transportation through private
              providers. Pp. 13-18 in *Transportation Research Record 850.* National
              Research Council. Washington, D.C.: Transportation Research Board.
Taylor, D. Garth, Paul B. Sheatsley, and Andrew M. Greeley
    1978      Attitudes toward racial integration. *Scientific American* 238(June):42-49.
Tolley, George, Philip E. Graves, and John L. Gardner
    1979      *Urban Growth Policy in a Market Economy.* New York: Academic Press.
Urban Mass Transportation Administration
    1987      *The Status of the Nation's Local Mass Transportation: Performance and Con-
              ditions.* Report to Congress by the Secretary of Transportation. Washington,
              D.C.: U.S. Department of Transportation.
U.S. Congress
    1985      *Children in Poverty.* Prepared for the Committee on Ways and Means by
              the Congressional Research Service and the Congressional Budget Office.
              Ways and Means Committee Print 99-8. 99th Cong., 1st sess. Washington,
              D.C.: U.S. Government Printing Office.
Vaughan, Roger J.
    1977a     *The Urban Impacts of Federal Policies.* Vol. 1, *Overview.* Report No.
              R-2206-KF/HEW. Santa Monica, Calif.: Rand Corporation.
    1977b     *The Urban Impacts of Federal Policies.* Vol. 2, *Economic Development.*
              Report No. R-2028-KF/RC. Santa Monica, Calif.: Rand Corporation.
Vaughan, Roger J., and Mary E. Vogel
    1979      *The Urban Impacts of Federal Policies.* Vol. 4, *Population and Residen-
              tial Location.* Report No. R-2205-KF/HEW. Santa Monica, Calif.: Rand
              Corporation.
Wallace, James, Jr., S. Bloom, William L. Holshouser, S. Mansfield, and Daniel H. Weinberg
    1981      *Participation and Benefits in the Urban Section 8 Program: New Construction
              and Existing Housing.* Cambridge, Mass.: Abt Associates.
White, K.R.
    1982      The relationship between socioeconomic status and academic achievement.
              *Psychological Bulletin* 91(May):461-481.
Wilger, Robert J.
    1987      Black-White Residential Segregation in 1980: Have the Civil Rights Laws
              Made a Difference? Unpublished paper, Population Studies Center, Uni-
              versity of Michigan.

# 7
# Conclusions

In this chapter we present our findings and conclusions concerning the causes, trends, and effects of ghetto poverty and review possible effects of federal policies and programs on it. We also offer some suggestions for improving our knowledge about ghetto poverty, especially about the effects of federal policies and programs.

In formulating these findings, conclusions, and policy options, the committee chose to draw broadly on available knowledge. We began by reading widely in the literature and incorporating relevant findings; citations to the literature in the sections below reflect our effort to be comprehensive. We then focused on specific issues by asking leading scholars and researchers to draft the central chapters in this volume; their work constitutes an important contribution to the ongoing policy debate, focusing as it does on some of the most critical issues. Extensive discussions in our committee deliberations, synthesizing the knowledge thus gained, resulted in the conclusions that follow.

## FINDINGS

As we have shown in this volume, several factors have caused variations among cities in ghetto poverty: changes in poverty and unemployment rates, differential in- and out-migration of poor and nonpoor people, and changes in racial and family composition. (Again, the term *ghetto* refers to any neighborhood with an overall poverty rate of 40 percent or more; the level of ghetto poverty is the proportion of poor people living in ghettos).

First, there is a strong positive bivariate relationship between poverty rates in standard metropolitan statistical areas (SMSAs) and levels of ghetto poverty in both 1970 and 1980. A similar relationship existed between

253

increasing SMSA poverty rates and increases in ghetto poverty between 1970 and 1980.

Second, in-migration of poor people into existing ghettos did not play the major role generally ascribed to it in increasing ghetto poverty. Out-migration of nonpoor people was especially evident in particular cities, especially Chicago and, to a lesser extent, New York. But in general (see Chapter 2), the process of ghetto formation, expansion, and contraction is complicated, reflecting the combined effects of population dispersion, changes in overall poverty levels, and racial segregation.

Third, poor blacks are much more concentrated within inner cities than nonblacks (see Chapter 2). Average real family income in persistently poor neighborhoods was also depressed by growth in the number of female-headed families (see Chapter 3). For example, the number of female-headed households in ghettos increased 84 percent between 1970 and 1980 in the 50 largest cities and 309 percent in the four cities with the biggest increases in concentration during the time period (calculated from Bureau of the Census, 1973, 1985). Thus, growth in the poor black population and in the numbers of female-headed families could have contributed to some of the increases in concentration.

Multivariate analysis of ghettos, holding boundaries constant between 1970 and 1980, shows that the economic fortunes of residents in persistently poor neighborhoods improved when the economies of the metropolitan areas encompassing them improved in terms of growth in family income or a decrease in unemployment rates (see Chapter 3). They did not, however, benefit as much as the rest of the metropolitan area. For example, although a 10 percent increase in real household income at the SMSA level was associated with a 4 percent gain in a typical persistently poor neighborhood, a 5 percent metropolitan-wide gain was accompanied by a 2 percent loss in the poverty neighborhood. In general, an increase of 1 percentage point in the unemployment rate for the metropolitan area raised the poverty neighborhood's unemployment rate on about a one-for-one basis and had little effect on labor force participation rates.

### The Changing Structure of Urban Economies

The long-term structural shift in urban economies from manufacturing to service industries has concurrently decentralized low-wage service jobs to the suburbs and increased the education and skill requirements for the types of white-collar service jobs that are expanding most rapidly in many large cities. Although it seems plausible that the growing spatial separation between the inner-city location of low-income, mostly minority workers with low education and skill levels and the suburban location of entry-level jobs would cause higher unemployment in central cities, previous research has not confirmed a causal connection (see Chapter 4) of the studies of the spatial mismatch hypothesis uses data later than 1970. This is because, holding individual characteristics constant, blacks are equally unlikely to be employed no matter where they live in the metropolitan area.

During the 1970s, the suburbs' share of jobs continued to grow, especially in metropolitan areas in which ghetto poverty was increasing the fastest. That trend suggests that the increasing distance from employment opportunities may have been one cause for lower employment rates in ghetto areas. Despite the suburbanization of jobs, however, the regression analysis detailed in Chapter 3 of the changes in unemployment between 1970 and 1980 in ghettos does not find an association with changes in the central-city share of jobs in metropolitan areas. There was a significant but small association of 1970-1980 changes in ghetto unemployment with changes in the labor force participation of ghetto residents; it would have taken a decline of 17 percentage points in central-city job share for labor force participation in the poverty neighborhoods to decline by 2 percentage points.

This analysis does not address the argument made by Kasarda (1988) that there is a skills rather than a spatial mismatch between inner-city workers and jobs in sectors that are growing in central cities and metropolitan areas. However, the regression analyses of changes in unemployment and labor force participation in ghetto neighborhoods show that, in addition to demand factors such as the metropolitan-area unemployment rate, a number of neighborhood population characteristics were significant. These characteristics included age, race, and, depending on the sample of cities, education and household composition (see Chapter 3).

## Effects of Ghetto Poverty

This study explored the extent and location of ghetto poverty as well as the question of whether poor people living in ghettos are worse off than poor people living elsewhere. The results of our analyses do not necessarily indicate that living in areas of concentrated poverty make poor people worse off than they would be otherwise, but neither do they suggest that living under such conditions does not matter at all.

The large differences in social and economic conditions between ghetto neighborhoods and others are not necessarily caused by the effects on residents of living in extremely poor areas. Neighborhoods with concentrations of poor people differ in their racial composition and numbers of poor residents from nonpoor neighborhoods, and their characteristics may simply result from the large numbers of poor minorities that have massed in them rather than from any negative effects of living in those neighborhoods.

One way to examine the question of concentration effects is to compare the rates of certain social and economic behaviors of poor people living in ghettos with those of poor people living in areas with less severe poverty—i.e., lower average levels (Bane and Jargowsky, 1988). Such a comparison shows differences of moderate to substantial size: 30 percent of poor adults—virtually all of whom were minorities—age 16 and older living in ghettos were unemployed, compared with 23 percent of the poor blacks and 16 percent of the poor Hispanics in census tracts with less severe poverty; 61 percent of poor families in ghettos received public assistance, compared with 39 percent of the poor blacks and Hispanics in tracts with less severe poverty; 77 percent of poor children in ghettos lived in female-headed families, compared with 71 percent of poor black children and 47 percent of Hispanic poor children in tracts with less severe poverty. These differences, however, may result from unmeasured differences between poor people in ghettos and those in areas with less severe poverty. For example, poor people in ghettos may be poorer (i.e., further below the poverty line); or in areas with less severe poverty more poor people may be working; or the availability of relatively affordable apartments in high-rise public housing projects, coupled with discrimination against large, poor, and minority families elsewhere, may account for the higher proportions of poor female-headed families among poor people in ghettos.

## Contextual Effects

It is difficult to know if living in a ghetto causes higher rates of social and economic problems because, first, people who move into them may differ systematically from people who move into other kinds of neighborhoods or, second, people who stay may differ from those who leave. As detailed in Chapter 4, it is necessary to disentangle the effects of living in extremely poor neighborhoods from the effects of exogenous factors that influence people's behavior wherever they live.

There is a small body of research on the contextual effects of living in a mostly poor or minority neighborhood that appropriately tries to control the exogenous characteristics of families and individuals. These studies, reviewed in Chapter 4, have found some significant contextual effects of neighborhood poverty and racial characteristics; however, the more exogenous effects were statistically controlled, the smaller the magnitude of the neighborhood effects. The effects also vary by type of behavior and time period. For example, although a neighborhood's distance from or proximity to employment opportunities did not affect the current employment chances of residents, a study of the effects of one's neighbors' race and income on one's earnings 10 years later found significant differences. A study of the effects of classmates' race and family income (Furstenberg et al., 1987) found that having poor classmates significantly increased the odds that a 15- or 16-year-old had sexual intercourse (67 compared with 40 percent). Another study of age of first intercourse and first pregnancy in a Chicago sample of unmarried black teenagers (Hogan and Kitagawa, 1985) looked at the effect of living in one census tract rather than another. After controlling for a number of exogenous individual characteristics, the study found that living in a low-quality rather than a middle-quality neighborhood increased the odds by a third of becoming pregnant in a given month, and living on the West Side of Chicago (which was heavily and irreversibly damaged in the riots of the 1960s) raised the odds another two-fifths.

Some studies found countervailing negative effects of being poor in a nonpoor neighborhood. For example, a study of serious crime by teenagers in Chicago (Johnstone, 1978) found that poor teenagers living in high-income neighborhoods were *more* likely to commit crimes than their poor counterparts in middle- or low-income neighborhoods, presumably because of the relative deprivation and racial hostility they experience or because they were more tempted by the greater opportunities for gain. Other studies reviewed in Chapter 4 show that the family income of students or the racial composition of a high school has little effect on the educational aspirations and subsequent educational attainment of seniors, because the positive effects on the aspirations of poor seniors in wealthy schools are cancelled out by their lower grades and class standings.

Relatively little is known about neighborhood effects on some kinds of behavior—such as teenage crime, teenage sexual behavior, and the achievement of minority high school students—even when the socioeconomic or racial composition of a neighborhood or school appear from the limited existing research to be important. Almost nothing is known about other important potential neighborhood effects—such as the effect of socioeconomic mix on the cognitive growth of children before high school or on high school graduation rates, or on the development of job-related skills and attitudes toward working.

## The Existence of an Urban Underclass

Although definitions of an urban underclass vary, the term is usually applied to a set of people who suffer from more than just a lack of income. Their problems are purportedly persistent rather than temporary, usually including lack of participation in the labor force, reliance on public assistance or the underground economy, broken homes, and children born to unmarried mothers. These same problems, it is said, are likely to be experienced by their children through some process of intergenerational transmission. Members of the underclass live near one another in inner-city neighborhoods and are isolated from mainstream society. Some analyses attribute these problems to personal shortcomings of underclass members that make them "behaviorally dependent" and therefore unable to hold a job or stay in school, stay married, or stay off welfare. Others stress the lack of opportunities facing a group with less education and fewer skills during a decade of slow economic growth (Wilson, 1987). In either case, as discussed in Chapter 2, determining the existence and extent of an urban underclass in ghettos involves sorting out the relationships among ghetto poverty, persistent and intergenerational poverty, and underclass behaviors.

Data adequate to determine the existence of an urban underclass do not exist; decennial census data cannot settle the issue. Although high levels of welfare receipt, low levels of labor force attachment, and other characteristics of ghettos are consistent with the underclass hypothesis, decennial census data on poverty concentration are cross-sectional rather than longitudinal and are reported at the tract, not individual, level. It is therefore impossible to use them to prove that there are individual-level linkages among social pathologies and the concentration or persistence of poverty. The Survey of Income and Program Participation (SIPP), a relatively new longitudinal survey conducted by the Bureau of the Census, does not have a sample large enough to compare ghetto residents with other metropolitan-area residents, although it may be possible to compare all central-city residents with suburban and nonmetropolitan populations. If plans to add census-tract information to the University of Michigan's Panel Survey of Income Dynamics (PSID) are carried out, it will be easier to investigate the question of an urban underclass.

Longitudinal analyses of PSID data have found that most persistently poor people live outside the large cities of the Midwest and the Northeast (Corcoran et al., 1985; Duncan, 1984). In the period 1969–1978, for example, only 2.2 percent of the U.S. population was persistently poor (i.e., living in families below the poverty line for eight years or more). Only 21 percent of persistently poor people lived in a county with a city of 500,000 population or more; one-third lived in a county with no town of 10,000 or more; more than two-thirds lived in the South.

Although most persistently poor people live outside large cities or in the South, large urban areas probably have more than their share (Adams et al., 1988). Between 1974 and 1983, 5.2 percent of the population of the core counties of large metropolitan areas lived in persistently poor families.[1] Although this persistent poverty was disproportionately concentrated among blacks, especially households headed by black women, persistently poor

---

[1] Although the 5.2 percent of the population of core counties of large metropolitan areas that is persistently poor is relatively larger than the 2.2 percent that is persistently poor nationally, the two figures are based on surveys taken in different time periods and thus are not strictly comparable.

blacks were no more likely to live in areas with 40 percent or more poverty than other poor blacks or even nonpoor blacks. (Persistently poor whites were more likely to live in such high-poverty areas, but they accounted for few of the persistently poor in urban areas.)

There were some favorable demographic changes in highly urban areas in the 1970s: the negative effect of the increase in female-headed families was more than offset by the positive effects of the decrease in the numbers of large families and of families headed by persons with less than a high school education. Nevertheless, poverty became more persistent after 1975: the proportion of urban residents that escaped poverty each year, which had increased from about 32 percent in 1970 to 37 percent in 1975, dropped to 23 percent in 1982 (poverty was defined as having family income below 125 percent of the federal poverty line; Adams et al., 1988). This occurred largely because the typical urban poor person was further below the poverty line in 1982 than in 1970: the fraction of urban poor with incomes less than three-quarters of the poverty line increased from 50 to 63 percent.

University of Michigan researchers and others have used longitudinal data from the PSID and the National Longitudinal Survey (NLS) to investigate the attitudinal and behavioral dimensions of poverty and welfare. Most of these studies have found little evidence that attitudes cause poverty or welfare dependence (Hill et al., 1985; O'Neill et al., 1984), although studies using the NLS have tended to find that some attitudinal measures toward work did have a significant relationship to subsequent success in the labor market, and vice versa (Andrisani and Parnes, 1983). Rather, economic changes (getting or losing a job, marriage, or divorce) make people feel more or less motivated, efficacious, optimistic about the future, etc. (Corcoran et al., 1985). Even NLS analyses find that attitudinal measures are strongly shaped by major labor market events. However, due to small sample sizes, these studies could not distinguish between poor people and welfare recipients living in areas with 40 percent or more poverty and those living elsewhere. It is therefore impossible to know if there are significant differences in attitudes or behavior between the two groups.

Similarly, studies of how the children of families who were poor or on welfare fared as adults have found that most do not go on welfare themselves, although they are still somewhat more likely than others to become welfare recipients (Duncan et al., 1988; Hill et al., 1985). For example, one study of a PSID sample of women looked at their welfare status in two three-year periods: when they were 13 to 15 years old and again when they were 21 to 23 years old. Nearly two-thirds of the women raised in families dependent on welfare for all three years when they were young teenagers did not receive any welfare themselves during the three years when they were young adults; only 20 percent received welfare during all of both three-year periods. However, only 3 percent of the daughters of nonwelfare families received assistance during all three years of young adulthood (Duncan et al., 1988). These differences may arise from unmeasured but systematic differences between individuals with welfare backgrounds who end up on welfare and those who do not. For example, their parents might be less educated, they might live in poorer neighborhoods, or they might go to lower-quality schools. Studies of the intergenerational transmission of poverty that attempt to control for these differences have had conflicting results (Duncan et al., 1988)

## CONCLUSIONS

On the basis of the findings summarized above, the committee reached four major conclusions. First, *recent trends in ghetto poverty are best understood for policy purposes as symptoms of broader economic and social changes.* For example, as we have seen, cross-tabular analysis of characteristics associated with different degrees of change in the concentration of poverty in different cities indicates that cities with rapid growth in concentration also experienced increases in the poverty rate, while cities with slow or negative growth in concentration simultaneously experienced reductions in poverty; this association was observed even in cities with very high levels of concentration. The multivariate analysis in Chapter 3 confirms that favorable economic trends in the metropolitan economy—that is, reductions in poverty rates—had a positive impact on the economic fortunes of households in ghettos. Accordingly, the committee believes that developments in the national economy are consequential in determining the extent of ghetto poverty, a conclusion that has implications for demand-side macroeconomic policies.

Second, *many ghetto residents would fare poorly in any job market.* The analyses in Chapter 3 indicate that the characteristics of the population were a factor in increasing poverty and unemployment in ghettos. In addition to lacking education, skills, and work experience, many household heads living in ghettos are women with young children who need extensive support services, especially day care. The committee concludes that some ghetto residents would not be able to take full advantage of tight labor markets; this conclusion implies that education and training and other supply-side policies may be important in reducing ghetto poverty and unemployment.

Third, the committee has documented some negative effects of living in ghettos. While some members conclude that there are special problems associated with living in such areas, others, citing the absence of convincing empirical data, are less sure. In any event, currently available data are insufficient to support a stronger finding at this time. Other factors affecting ghetto residents, such as racial discrimination and inadequate education and skills, are better understood at present. Nevertheless, *the committee believes that current antipoverty programs and policies meet with special problems in ghettos.* The fact that the concentration of poor people living in these areas is higher than it is elsewhere may affect delivery of antipoverty program benefits. For example, existing programs may be overwhelmed by the greater number of poor people trying to obtain benefits. More broadly, resources intended to combat poverty may not be as concentrated as the poverty itself in ghettos. The committee thus concludes that the delivery and therefore the effectiveness of current antipoverty programs can be significantly undercut by ghetto poverty. The committee believes that discriminatory barriers preventing mobility to better neighborhoods should be deliberately undermined by federal policies and programs.

Fourth, *additional research on the causes and effects of ghetto poverty is essential to increasing the government's ability to design and administer policies and programs that are more effective with respect to alleviating poverty and its consequences.*

In the next sections we discuss policy options that are based on these conclusions.

### Macroeconomic Policies

Ghetto poverty, like other types of poverty, could be reduced by national demand-side policies that stimulate gains in economic productivity and sustained economic growth. During the first two decades after World War II, productivity rates and economic growth rose more rapidly and more steadily than at any other time in the twentieth century (Levy, 1987). As a result, poverty rates in the United States were cut nearly in half (Gottschalk and Danziger, 1984). Since the early 1970s, economic productivity and growth rates have averaged between 1 and 2 percent, gains in family income have been small, and the hourly earnings of employees have actually declined. Affected by the ups and downs of the business cycle, the poverty rate has fluctuated around an average rate that has not changed significantly since the early 1970s.

The poverty rate, which is sensitive to the unemployment rate, was higher from 1973 until just recently than it was from World War II to 1973. The period after 1973 was one of slow economic growth and a sharp increase in the rate of new labor market entrants—the postwar baby boom cohort, women, and immigrants. In a persistently slack economy, those with the fewest marketable skills, least education, minority status, and who live in areas with outmoded industrial structures are the least likely to be employed (Reischauer, 1987). Sawhill (1986) estimates that reducing the unemployment rate from 6 to 5.5 percent would reduce the number of poor people by about 2.5 million. At least some of these would be poor people living in ghettos, although the benefits of macroeconomic growth probably would not apply proportionately to central cities and suburbs (see Chapter 3).

There are limits to the extent to which demand-side policies will reduce poverty. Even if overall economic conditions improve, demographic changes among the population in poverty, especially the growth of families headed by single women, who are least helped by economic growth, will keep poverty rates somewhat higher than they would have been even with economic growth (0.1 percentage points a year, according to a simulation by Gottschalk and Danziger, 1984). The macroeconomic approach is also limited by the effects of structural economic change affecting labor markets—the location of jobs and the levels of education and skill requirements. So, although a strong economy may be an essential component of any effective antipoverty strategy, it is not sufficient.

## Human Capital Investment

In many cases, ghetto residents are unprepared to take full advantage of opportunities presented by economic growth. Additional resources and supports should be devoted to helping this group become productive workers, whom employers will hire at wages high enough to make economic self-sufficiency possible.

Evidence of the importance of such a strategy is provided by looking again at the characteristics of ghetto residents. Whether or not residence in a high-poverty area in itself contributes to disadvantage, these areas contain disproportionate numbers of people who are detached from the labor force and poorly prepared to enter it. They have few positive role models. As Chapter 2 documents, relatively few of the adults living in ghettos are employed. Although the median years of schooling in these areas improved during the 1970s, it was barely 10 years in 1980 (see Chapter 3). In cities with high rates of Hispanic immigration, substantial proportions of ghetto residents have only limited proficiency in English. The typical nonworking adult in these areas is not an experienced, skilled, and literate laborer or craftworker who lost a well-paying manufacturing job when the plant moved south. Many are young single mothers or high school dropouts who have worked intermittently, if at all (Chapter 2). At least some of the adult males may have records of crime or participation in the underground economy. Many are likely to have difficulty obtaining and keeping adequately paid employment, even in a tight labor market.

These characteristics suggest that policies aimed at enhancing the employability and productivity of ghetto residents would effectively complement policies focused on employment opportunities. Such policies need not be specially developed for, or targeted on, ghetto residents; they can instead grow out of broader-based efforts to develop the human capital of poor and disadvantaged people. Such policies include:

- Investments in education, including preschool education, compensatory basic skills education for disadvantaged elementary and secondary students, dropout prevention programs, and programs for youth that facilitate the transition from school to work;
- Investments in health, especially teenage pregnancy prevention, prenatal care, nutrition, childhood immunization and other preventive health programs, and prevention and treatment of substance abuse;
- Employment and training programs for adults, including job search, job matching, job seeking and employability skills training, specific skills training, work experience, and supported work.

Careful analyses and evaluations of such programs indicate that at least some of them—Head Start, WIC, Job Corps, and Supported Work, for example—are demonstrably effective and deliver benefits that exceed their costs. (See, for Head Start, Aitken et al., 1985; for Chapter 1, Kennedy et al., 1986; for teenage pregnancy prevention, Hayes, 1987; for the Job Corps, Supported Work, Betsey et al., 1985; for Supported Work, Manpower Demonstration Research Corporation, 1980, Hollister et al., 1984; for state work-welfare experiments, Gueron, 1987.) Some programs, for example many of the work-welfare demonstrations conducted by the states, seem to be most effective with the most disadvantaged clients (Gueron, 1987). Programs like these, which are apparently effective in improving the health, skill levels, employability, and productivity of disadvantaged children and adults, are obvious candidates for adoption by governments interested in attacking urban poverty. They are logical and perhaps necessary complements to policies directed at overall employment and economic growth.

These programs should be undertaken with caution, however, for two reasons. First, they will not work miracles. Although carefully evaluated programs have been shown to be effective, the benefits are modest. Careful evaluations of effective work-welfare programs show earnings advantages of only a few hundred dollars and declines in welfare dependence of only a few percentage points for program participants compared with controls (Gueron, 1987). Evaluations of even the most effective preschool programs show modest improvements in achievement and school attendance that translate into small earnings gains among adults (Barrueta-Clement et al., 1984). Even the most effective of the programs that have been tested—and a great many variants have been tried—will at best achieve small but steady improvements in economic self-sufficiency, not dramatic reductions in poverty or welfare receipt.

Second, effective programs often cost more money than elected officials have been prepared to raise. The evaluations suggest that net benefits of the effective programs are positive over the long run. But not all programs that are tried will be effective, even if the best current models are adopted. Even the effective programs cost money in the short term; they cannot be financed by current-year welfare savings. Governments intending to dent the problem must be prepared to invest current resources in the hope of long-term payoffs. Investments in education, health, and employment and training programs are an important part of a policy that addresses poverty, including ghetto poverty.

### Increasing Mobility

Some findings reported in this study—that being poor in a ghetto may have a negative effect, and that some federal policies have had an indirect effect of concentrating the poor and minorities in central cities—suggest that the spatial implications of government policies, especially the effects of government programs on poverty concentrations, must be considered carefully. For example, poor people living in ghettos may be less likely to benefit from federal antipoverty programs, because these programs may not be designed to deal with such a high proportion of poor people in a given area. Similarly, poor people who live in ghettos may be farther away from services and jobs than they would be if they lived in other neighborhoods and may be less able to benefit from them.

Therefore, federal policies and programs should seek to eliminate barriers to residential mobility through full enforcement of fair housing, equal access, and other antidiscrimination laws and regulations, enabling people to leave ghettos if they choose, for example through programs of housing vouchers and fair-share housing construction throughout metropolitan areas.

A strategy to enhance the mobility of ghetto residents cannot, however, solve the problem of ghetto poverty by itself. It depends on where the poor people who move end up. First, simply hastening the emptying out of ghettos through residential mobility would not in itself have much impact on the fortunes of the people who had lived there. They would continue to have problems no matter where they lived, because they typically face the liabilities of low levels of education, skills, and work experience; poor health and disabilities; teenage and single parenthood; and racial discrimination. They would still have problems with access to affordable health care, day care, and transportation.

Second, those left behind, even temporarily, face serious transition problems. In the 1970s, despite relatively high rates of residential mobility from ghettos, resulting in substantially fewer ghetto residents, social and economic conditions among those remaining deteriorated badly. Public services also probably deteriorated and crime may have increased, although there are no data on these points.

Third, increased mobility may have the unintended effect of spreading ghetto poverty to adjacent areas. Most of the growth in concentrated poverty between 1970 and 1980 occurred through the addition of new ghetto neighborhoods in a few cities, and most of those were contiguous to the ghettos that existed in 1970. These poor people tend to move short distances to areas similar to those they left. Many migrating from ghettos probably ended up in nearby locations, which helped to turn them into ghettos, too (also some previously nonpoor residents probably became poor during the 1970s).

Because of these problems with and limits to enhanced mobility as a strategy for reducing ghetto poverty, the committee stresses the importance of macroeconomic policies and human capital investment in reducing ghetto poverty. Mobility means little unless it leads to a higher-quality social environment and to improved economic opportunity. This could be accomplished either by enabling poor ghetto residents to move beyond contiguous neighborhoods to stable, higher-income areas, or by stabilizing contiguous neighborhoods by consciously encouraging the building of working-class and mixed-income housing that could absorb out-migrants from ghettos and otherwise attempting to keep them from turning into new ghettos, or both. The specific policy mix would vary, because conditions such as patterns of land use and composition of the building stock vary by city.

Factors that prevent many poor and minority Americans from relocating to areas of job growth and opportunity include, in addition to poverty itself: overt and illegal housing discrimination that denies poor people the choice to purchase or rent units in areas near employment opportunities; restrictive zoning, such as minimum lot size requirements that effectively limit new housing to those with moderately high incomes; racial steering, in which real estate agents avail only certain housing choices to low-income groups; and fiscal zoning, in which communities zone land predominantly for high tax-yielding land uses, such as commercial-office development, at the expense of underzoning for housing. Most poor people living in ghettos are black or Hispanic, and many heads of household are female. The latest evidence on residential discrimination indicates that it declined very little in the 1970s and hardly at all in the large cities experiencing the greatest concentrations of poverty (see Chapter 6). It even increased in some (Massey and Denton, 1987; Farley and Wilger, 1987). At a minimum, federal policies should be pursued that vigorously enforce antidiscrimination laws and uphold the constitutional right of citizens to move as they choose.

In pursuing a policy of enhancing mobility, policy makers need not decide that poor people should be actively removed from ghetto neighborhoods; policy makers need agree only that the actions of the government should not make leaving more difficult or more costly than staying. This means that government policies and programs to help low-income and poverty households should not encourage concentration but should permit geographic mobility.

Geographically targeted support programs for the poor must be evaluated very carefully, so that they do not have the unintended, yet perverse, effect of keeping them isolated from job opportunities elsewhere. To the extent that the availability of social welfare support systems—e.g., welfare centers, family counseling offices, health clinics, and missions—anchor the poor in areas of economic decline and inhibit them from entering society's mainstream, federal programs should be as locationally neutral as possible. At the least, they should not introduce incentives to remain in areas characterized by persistent poverty (Kasarda, 1988, 1985).

There is evidence, for example, that high-rise public housing built under previous housing policies had the effect of concentrating poverty in certain areas. Higher welfare benefit levels in states in declining regions may have had the unintended effect of discouraging migration to areas with growing economies but lower welfare benefits. Other policies, such as government-supported fixed-rail mass transportation, which were supposed to increase the mobility of the poor, have not had the intended effect (see Chapter 6).

In principle, housing programs should provide benefits that are portable, either through supply-oriented programs diffused throughout the metropolitan areas or, more directly, through demand-oriented programs, or both. User-side transportation subsidies for poor people, if they are to be enacted, should facilitate movement to sites where jobs are profitably located, be they inner-city poverty areas or suburban areas. Job-subsidy and training programs should be used to direct business activity to sites where the activity will be most efficient and profitable.

All urban poverty initiatives do not necessarily have to be spatially neutral. Other urban dilemmas, such as traffic congestion or spot pollution, call for initiatives that encourage spatial redistribution, such as the coordination of job growth and housing growth in a particular district. The problem of ghetto poverty, however, is one area in which place-oriented policies provide few, if any, additional benefits for the poor, and that could potentially have the unfortunate effect of inhibiting their mobility.

## RESEARCH DIRECTIONS

The committee was not able to study the effects of federal programs on poverty concentration in great detail, and there are knowledge gaps in the literature even in issues that were carefully examined. The knowledge base for policy making needs to be improved.

First, the Bureau of the Census should continue to produce statistics on urban poverty concentration from the decennial censuses, as it did for the 1970 and 1980 censuses (Bureau of the Census, 1973, 1985), to enable researchers to track trends in ghetto poverty over a longer period of time. For 1990, the bureau should publish tables of data on residents of 40-percent poverty areas for an expanded set of variables, by poverty status, race, and ethnic origin. These additional variables should include information on family structure; income and income sources (including public assistance); education; labor force status, type, condition; and cost-of-housing characteristics. The 1970 and 1980 data on the same set of variables should be made available to researchers on public-use tapes.

In addition, the Bureau of the Census should provide data on neighborhood characteristics in public-use tapes for various surveys, including, for example, the Current Population Survey, the American Housing Survey, and the Survey of Income and Program Participation. This was done for the 1970 decennial survey, but, due to problems with the way the neighborhoods were defined, little use was made of the data. The current interest in the persistently poor and the possible development of an underclass will ensure their use at this time.

Second, federal agencies with an interest in concentrated poverty and dependence (e.g., research programs in the departments of Health and Human Services, Housing and Urban Development, Labor, and Education) should sponsor methodologically sound studies of neighborhood or contextual effects on the social and economic behavior of residents of poor neighborhoods. These studies should include neighborhoods with extreme characteristics (to detect nonlinear effects) and should examine important outcome variables that are now understudied (e.g., cognitive development of children in elementary school).

To facilitate research on neighborhood effects (and on other effects on poverty and dependence), federal research programs should subsidize the addition of spatial variables (i.e., inner-city versus suburban versus nonmetropolitan location) and contextual variables (i.e., census tract characteristics) to longitudinal panel surveys (e.g., the Panel Study of Income Dynamics, the National Longitudinal Survey).

Finally, the departments of Housing and Urban Development, Transportation, Commerce, Treasury, Labor, Education, and Health and Human Services should evaluate the locational impacts of their policies and programs on poverty—including housing, transportation, education and training, health, economic development, and public assistance programs.

## REFERENCES

Adams, Terry K., Greg J. Duncan, and Willard L. Rodgers
    1988    Persistent Urban Poverty: Prevalence, Correlates and Trends. Unpublished paper prepared for Rockefeller Foundation conference, "The Kerner Report: Twenty Years Later."
Aitken, Sherrie S., Ruth Hubell McKey, Larry Condelli, Harriet Ganson, Barbara J. Barrett, Catherine McConkey, and Margaret C. Plantz
    1985    *The Impact of Head Start on Children, Families and Communities: Final Report of the Head Start Evaluation, Synthesis and Utilization Project.* Report prepared by CSR, Inc., for the Head Start Bureau. Washington, D.C.: U.S. Department of Health and Human Services.
Andrisani, Paul J., and Herbert S. Parnes
    1983    Commitment to the work ethic and success in the labor market: a review of research findings. In Jack Barbash, ed., *The Work Ethic—A Critical Analysis.* Madison, Wis.: Industrial Relations Research Association.
Bane, Mary Jo, and Paul A. Jargowsky
    1988    Urban Poverty Areas: Basic Questions Concerning Prevalence, Growth and Dynamics. Center for Health and Human Resources Policy Discussion Paper Series, John F. Kennedy School of Government, Harvard University.
Barrueta-Clement, John R., Lawrence H. Schweinhart, W. Steven Barnett, Ann S. Epstein, and David P. Weikart
    1984    *Changed Lives: The Effects of the Perry Preschool Program on Youths Through Age 19.* Ypsilanti, Mich.: High/Scope Press.
Betsey, Charles L., Robinson G. Hollister, Jr., and Mary R. Papageorgiou, eds.
    1985    *Youth Employment and Training Programs: The YEDPA Years.* Commitee on Youth Employment Programs, National Research Council. Washington, D.C.: National Academy Press.
Bureau of the Census
    1973    *Low-Income Areas in Large Cities.* 1970 Census of Population, Subject Report PC(2)-9B. Washington, D.C.: U.S. Department of Commerce.
    1985    *Poverty Areas in Large Cities.* 1980 Census of Population, Subject Report PC80-2-8D. Washington, D.C.: U.S. Department of Commerce.
Corcoran, Mary, Greg J. Duncan, Gerald Gurin, and Patricia Gurin
    1985    Myth and reality: the causes and persistence of poverty. *Journal of Policy Analysis and Management* 4(Summer):516-536.
Duncan, Greg J.
    1984    *Years of Poverty, Years of Plenty: The Changing Economic Fortunes of American Workers and Families.* Ann Arbor: Institute for Social Research, University of Michigan.
Duncan, Greg J., Martha S. Hill, and Saul D. Hoffman
    1988    Welfare dependence within and across generations. *Science* 239(January 29):467-471.
Farley, Reynolds, and Robert J. Wilger
    1987    Recent Changes in the Residential Segregation of Blacks from Whites: An Analysis of 203 Metropolises. Unpublished background report prepared for the Committee on the Status of Black Americans, National Research Council, Washington, D.C.

Furstenberg, Frank, F., Jr., S. Philip Morgan, Kristin A. Moore, and James Peterson
  1987    Race differences in the timing of adolescent intercourse. *American Socio-logical Review* 52:511-518.
Gottschalk, Peter, and Sheldon Danziger
  1984    Macroeconomic conditions, income transfers, and the trends in poverty. Pp. 185-215 in D. Lee Bawden, ed., *The Social Contract Revisited: Aims and Outcomes of President Reagan's Social Welfare Policy.* Washington, D.C.: Urban Institute Press.
Gueron, Judith M.
  1987    *Reforming Welfare with Work.* Occasional Paper 2, Ford Foundation Project on Social Welfare and the American Future. New York: Ford Foundation.
Hayes, Cheryl D., ed.
  1987    *Risking the Future: Adolescent Sexuality, Pregnancy, and Childbearing.* Vol. 1. Panel on Adolescent Pregnancy and Childbearing. Washington, D.C.: National Academy Press.
Hill, Martha S., Sue Augustyniak, Greg J. Duncan, Gerald Gurin, Patricia Gurin, Jeffrey K. Liker, James N. Morgan, and Michael Ponza
  1985    Motivation and Economic Mobility. Research Report Series. Survey Research Center, Institute for Social Research, University of Michigan.
Hogan, Dennis P., and Evelyn M. Kitagawa
  1985    The impact of social status, family structure, and neighborhood on the fertility of black adolescents. *American Journal of Sociology* 9:825-855.
Hollister, Robinson G., Peter Kemper, and Rebecca A. Maynard, eds.
  1984    *The National Supported Work Demonstration.* Madison: University of Wisconsin Press.
Johnstone, John W.C.
  1978    Social class, social areas and delinquency. *Sociology and Social Research* 63:49-72.
Kasarda, John D.
  1985    Urban change and minority opportunities. Pp. 33-67 in Paul E. Peterson, ed., *The New Urban Reality.* Washington, D.C.: Brookings Institution.
  1988    Jobs, migration, and emerging urban mismatches. Pp. 148-198 in Michael G.H. McGeary and Laurence E. Lynn, Jr., eds., *Urban Change and Poverty.* Committee on National Urban Policy. Washington, D.C.: National Academy Press.
Kennedy, Mary M., Beatrice F. Birman, and Randy E. Demaline
  1986    *The Effectiveness of Chapter 1 Services.* Washington, D.C.: U.S. Department of Education.
Levy, Frank
  1987    *Dollars and Dreams: The Changing American Income Distribution.* New York: Russell Sage Foundation.
Manpower Demonstration Research Corporation
  1980    *Summary and Findings of the National Supported Work Demonstration.* Cambridge, Mass.: Ballinger.
Massey, Douglas S., and Nancy A. Denton
  1987    Trends in residential segregation of blacks, Hispanics, and Asians: 1970-1980. *American Sociological Review* 52(Dec.):802-825.
O'Neill, June A., Douglas A. Wolf, Laurie J. Bassi, and Michael T. Hannan
  1984    An Analysis of Time on Welfare. Project report prepared for the U.S. Department of Health and Human Services. Urban Institute, Washington, D.C.

Reischauer, Robert D.
    1987        America's Underclass: Four Unanswered Questions. Paper prepared for
                The City Club, Portland, Oregon, January 30.
Sawhill, Isabel
    1986        *Anti-Poverty Strategies for the 1980s.* An Urban Institute Research Report.
                December. Washington, D.C.: Urban Institute.
Wilson, William Julius
    1987        *The Truly Disadvantaged: The Inner City, the Underclass, and Public Policy.*
                Chicago: University of Chicago Press.

# Index

271